2 PETER

This commentary on the second epistle of Peter offers a fresh examination of a key New Testament text. Relying on newly available research, A. Chadwick Thornhill brings a multipronged approach to his study through his use of a range of methods including narrative theology and historical, social, cultural, literary, rhetorical, discourse, and linguistic analysis. Thornhill challenges existing paradigms pertaining to the composition of 2 Peter, asks new questions regarding authorship and genre, and revisits the identification of the text as a pseudonymous testament, as it has most recently been understood. His study enables new insights into the letter's message as it would have been understood in its ancient context. Written in an accessible style, Thornhill's commentary concludes by offering reflections on 2 Peter's contributions to the theology of the New Testament and its relevance for the late modern world.

A. Chadwick Thornhill is Professor of Biblical and Theological studies at the John W. Rawlings School of Divinity at Liberty University.

NEW CAMBRIDGE BIBLE COMMENTARY

GENERAL EDITOR: Ben Witherington III

HEBREW BIBLE/OLD TESTAMENT EDITOR: Bill T. Arnold

EDITORIAL BOARD
Bill T. Arnold, *Asbury Theological Seminary*
James D. G. Dunn, *University of Durham*
Michael V. Fox, *University of Wisconsin-Madison*
Robert P. Gordon, *University of Cambridge*
Judith M. Gundry, *Yale University*

The New Cambridge Bible Commentary (NCBC) aims to elucidate the Hebrew and Christian Scriptures for a wide range of intellectually curious individuals. While building on the work and reputation of the Cambridge Bible Commentary popular in the 1960s and 1970s, the NCBC takes advantage of many of the rewards provided by scholarly research over the last four decades. Volumes utilize recent gains in rhetorical criticism, social scientific study of the Scriptures, narrative criticism, and other developing disciplines to exploit the growing advances in biblical studies. Accessible jargon-free commentary, an annotated "Suggested Readings" list, and the entire *New Revised Standard Version, Updated Editon* (NRSVue) text under discussion are the hallmarks of all volumes in the series.

PUBLISHED VOLUMES IN THE SERIES
Isaiah 40–66, Katie Heffelfinger
1–2 Samuel, Marvin A. Sweeney
The Letters of John, Duane F. Watson
The Pastoral Epistles, Scot McKnight
The Book of Lamentations, Joshua Berman
Hosea, Joel, and Amos, Graham Hamborg
1 Peter, Ruth Anne Reese
Ephesians, David A. deSilva
Philippians, Michael F. Bird and Nijay K. Gupta
Acts, Craig S. Keener
The Gospel of Luke, Amy-Jill Levine and Ben Witherington III
Galatians, Craig S. Keener
Mark, Darrell Bock
Psalms, Walter Brueggemann and William H. Bellinger, Jr.
Matthew, Craig A. Evans
Genesis, Bill T. Arnold
The Gospel of John, Jerome H. Neyrey
Exodus, Carol Meyers
1–2 Corinthians, Craig S. Keener
James and Jude, William F. Brosend II
Judges and Ruth, Victor H. Matthews
Revelation, Ben Witherington III

2 Peter

A. Chadwick Thornhill
Liberty University

Shaftesbury Road, Cambridge CB2 8EA, United Kingdom

One Liberty Plaza, 20th Floor, New York, NY 10006, USA

477 Williamstown Road, Port Melbourne, VIC 3207, Australia

314–321, 3rd Floor, Plot 3, Splendor Forum, Jasola District Centre, New Delhi – 110025, India

103 Penang Road, #05–06/07, Visioncrest Commercial, Singapore 238467

Cambridge University Press is part of Cambridge University Press & Assessment, a department of the University of Cambridge.

We share the University's mission to contribute to society through the pursuit of education, learning and research at the highest international levels of excellence.

www.cambridge.org
Information on this title: www.cambridge.org/9781009280938

DOI: 10.1017/9781009280884

© A. Chadwick Thornhill 2026

This publication is in copyright. Subject to statutory exception and to the provisions of relevant collective licensing agreements, no reproduction of any part may take place without the written permission of Cambridge University Press & Assessment.

When citing this work, please include a reference to the DOI 10.1017/9781009280884

First published 2026

A catalogue record for this publication is available from the British Library

A Cataloging-in-Publication data record for this book is available from the Library of Congress

ISBN 978-1-009-28093-8 Hardback
ISBN 978-1-009-28092-1 Paperback

Cambridge University Press & Assessment has no responsibility for the persistence or accuracy of URLs for external or third-party internet websites referred to in this publication and does not guarantee that any content on such websites is, or will remain, accurate or appropriate.

For EU product safety concerns, contact us at Calle de José Abascal, 56, 1°, 28003 Madrid, Spain, or email eugpsr@cambridge.org

Contents

Acknowledgments	page ix
Ancient Sources	xi
List of Abbreviations	xv

INTRODUCTION	1
Reading Scripture as Ancient Texts	2
Authorship and Date	8
Audience and Setting	34
Social Dynamics	38
2 Peter as Story	41
2 Peter as Christian Scripture	43
Suggested Readings	54

COMMENTARY	55
2 Peter 1:1–2: Greeting	56
2 Peter 1:3–12: Life with God	63
2 Peter 1:13–21: Prophetic Testimony	89
2 Peter 2:1–11 The Description of the False Teachers	108
2 Peter 2:12–22: The Fate of the False Teachers	133
2 Peter 3:1–13: The Day of the Lord	156
2 Peter 3:14–18: Closing Remarks	193

A THEOLOGY OF 2 PETER	207
God the Father and Jesus Christ	207
Revelation, Prophecy, and Inspiration	211
Judgment and Salvation	213
Theosis	216

Appendix A A Structural Diagram of 2 Peter (Phrases and Clauses)	219
Appendix B Hapaxes in 2 Peter	231
Appendix C Common Vocabulary between 1 and 2 Peter, Including Cognate Terms	241
Bibliography	245
Ancient Sources Index	257
Index	275

Acknowledgments

I am very grateful to Dr. Ben Witherington for the invitation to contribute to this series. I'd like to thank my wife and family for both their interest and support in this project. I am grateful to the participants at the Ellis Foundation for Biblical Research conference on the "The Pastoral Implications for Pseudepigraphy and Anonymity in the New Testament," who gave helpful feedback on some of the early formulation of the ideas for this project, as well as my graduate and doctoral students whose conversations and presentations in our 2 Peter and Jude exegetical courses were very valuable.

Several students and colleagues offered helpful feedback on various drafts of this commentary. In particular, Noah Fate-Cloud, Dr. Mark Allen, and Dr. Dottie Rhoads offered helpful remarks on the introductory material. A special thank-you is needed for Dr. Matt Bovard who offered extensive and constructive feedback on the introduction as well. I am grateful for the prayers and interest of many who have encouraged me along the way through the production of this work. Having taught advanced New Testament exegetical courses for over a decade now, I am very grateful for the opportunity to contribute to the discipline and to the life of the Church in this small way.

Ancient Sources

APOLLODORUS

Bibl.　　　*Bibliotheca*

ARISTOTLE

Eth. nic.　　*Nicomachean Ethics*
Pol.　　　　*Politics*

CICERO

Disc.　　　*Discourses*
Inv.　　　　*De Inventione* (On Invention)
Nat. d.　　 *De Natura Deorum* (On the Nature of the Gods)
Tusc.　　　*Tusculanae Disputationes* (Tuscula Disputations)

CLEMENT OF ALEXANDRIA

Paed.　　　*Paedagogus* (The Instructor)

DIO CHRYSOSTOM

Or.　　　　　*Orationes* (Discourses)
Diog. Laert.　Diogenes Laertius

EPICTETUS

Diatr.　　　*Diatribai* (Discourses)
Diss.　　　 *Dissertationes* (Discourses)

EUSEBIUS

Eccl. His   *Ecclesiastical History*

HERACLITUS

All.   *Allegoriae Homericae* (Homeric Problems)

HESIOD

Theo.   *Theogonia* (Birth of the Gods)

IRENAEUS

AH   *Against Heresies*

ISOCRATES

Demon.   *To Demonicus*

JEROME

De Vir.   *De Viris Illustribus* (On Illustrious Men)

JOSEPHUS

Ag. Ap.   *Against Apion*
Ant.   *The Antiquities of the Jews*

LECRETIUS

DNT   *De Rerum Natura* (On the Nature of the Universe)

LUCIAN

Pisc.   *Piscator* (Fisherman)

MAXIMUS OF TYRE

Or.   *Orations*

Origen

Comm. Jo	*Commentary on the Gospel According to John*
Hom. Num	*Homilies on Numbers*

Philo

Abr.	*De Abrahamo* (On the Life of Abraham)
Aet.	*De Aeternitate Mundi* (On the Eternality of the World)
Agr.	*De Agricultura* (On Agriculture)
Conf.	*De Confusione Linguarum* (On the Confusion of Tongues)
Congr.	*De Congressu Eruditionis Gratia* (On Mating for the Sake of Learning)
Decal.	*De Decalogo* (On the Decalogue)
Her.	*Quis rerum divinarum heres sit* (Who is the Heir of Divine Things?)
Leg. Alleg	*Legum Allegoriae* (Allegorical Interpretation)
Migr.	*De Migratione Abrahami* (On the Migration of Abraham)
Mos.	*De vita Moses* (On the Life of Moses)
Opif.	*De Opificio Mundi* (On the Creation of the World)
QG	*Quaestiones et solitiones in Genesin* (Questions and Answers on Genesis)
Sacr.	*De Sacrificiis Abelis et Caini* (On the Sacrifices of Cain and Abel)
Spec.	*De Specialibus Legibus* (On Special Laws)
Virt.	*De Virtutibus* (On the Virtues)

Plato

Exsecr.	*De Exsecrationibus* (On Curses)
Resp.	*Respublica* (Republic)
Tim.	*Timaeus*

Plutarch

Is. Os.	*De Iside et Osiride* (Isis and Osiris)
Mor.	*Moralia* (Morals)

Pseudo-Aristotle

Virt. Vit.   *De virtute et vitio* (On Virtue and Vice)

Pseudo-Diogenes

Ep.   *Epistulae* (Letters)

Seneca the Younger

Brev. Vit.   *De Brevitate Vitae* (On the Shortness of Life)

Virgil

Aen.   *Aenid*

Abbreviations

ABC	*Anchor Bible Commentary*
BAGL	*Biblical and Ancient Greek Linguistics*
BibSac	*Bibliotheca Sacra*
BBR	*Bulletin of Biblical Research*
BECNT	Baker Exegetical Commentary on the New Testament
BNTC	Black's New Testament Commentaries
BTCB	Brazos Theological Commentary on the Bible
CBR	*Currents of Biblical Research*
CBQ	*Catholic Biblical Quarterly*
CSC	Christian Standard Commentary
EQ	*Evangelical Quarterly*
ICC	International Critical Commentary
JBL	*Journal of Biblical Literature*
JBTM	*Journal for Baptist Theology & Ministry*
JETS	*Journal of the Evangelical Theological Society*
JSNT	*Journal for the Study of the New Testament*
NA	Nestle-Aland
PCNT	ΠΑΙΔΕΙΑ Commentaries on the New Testament
RTR	*Reformed Theological Review*
SBL	Society of Biblical Literature
SBT	Studies in Biblical Theology
SWJT	*Southwestern Journal of Theology*
TB	*Tyndale Bulletin*
THNTC	Two Horizons New Testament Commentary
TNTC	Tyndale New Testament Commentary

TOTC	Tyndale Old Testament Commentary
WBC	Word Biblical Commentary
WBT	Word Biblical Themes
WUNT	Wissenschaftliche Untersuchungen zum Neuen Testament

Introduction

While Christians may believe that all Scripture is useful (cf. 2 Tim. 3:16), not all Scripture is equally used. With the major theological influences of texts like Matthew, Romans, John, or Hebrews, 2 Peter may seem an insignificant addition to the New Testament corpus. Furthermore, the epistle of 2 Peter has the most checkered past of any work in the New Testament.[1] Belonging to the "catholic epistles,"[2] which themselves are often neglected, 2 Peter was a letter heavily disputed in regard to its authenticity and canonical status. Its debated status in the early church led to it being one of the last documents agreed upon in the New Testament canon. As Kelly summarizes, "no NT document had a longer or tougher struggle to win acceptance than 2 Peter."[3] The Reformers shared misgivings as well over the nature of the letter's authorship. Calvin was aware of the stylistic differences that distinguished it from 1 Peter, though he concluded on theological grounds that its inclusion in the canon merited recognition of Peter as its author.[4]

These historical questions no doubt continue to cast a shadow upon 2 Peter today. The *Revised Common Lectionary* contains only two inclusions of 2 Peter in its readings, one as a reading for the Transfiguration (2 Peter 1:16–21) and another during Advent (2 Peter 3:8–15a).[5] At roughly

---

[1] As Peter Davids describes, it has become the "ugly stepchild" of the New Testament (Peter H. Davids, *The Letters of 2 Peter and Jude* [Grand Rapids: Eerdmans, 2006], 121).
[2] This grouping includes Hebrews, James, 1–2 Peter, 1–3 John, and Jude.
[3] J. N. D. Kelly, *The Epistles of Peter and of Jude*, Black's New Testament Commentaries (London: Adam and Charles Black, 1969), 224.
[4] John Calvin, *Commentaries on the Catholic Epistles* (Edinburgh: The Calvin Translation Society, 1855), 363.
[5] Pheme Perkins, *First and Second Peter, James, and Jude*. Interpretation: A Bible Commentary for Teaching and Preaching (Louisville: Westminster John Knox Press, 1995), 2.

1,100 words,[6] this letter offers a brief but forceful contribution to the collection of the New Testament. In all the questions of its origins and authenticity in the early church, what was never in question was its consistency with apostolic teaching. It is perhaps that reason above all others that 2 Peter was and should continue to be embraced by Christians despite the historical questions that surround it.

The letter contains two primary points of focus, both functioning as rebuttals to the influence of certain false teachers within the community. First, the letter maintains the importance of the Second Coming, or παρουσία, of Christ, and the judgment that he will bring at his return. Here, again, we stand in the tradition of the apostolic faith. The Apostles' Creed, for example, affirms that Christ will come again from heaven "to judge the living and the dead," an event described or referenced widely across the New Testament (Matt. 24:30–51; 25:1–13, 31–46; Mark 13:20–37; Luke 12:35–59; 17:20–37; 21:5–38; Acts 1:10–11; 1 Cor. 15:35–58; Phil. 3:20; Col. 3:4; 1 Thess. 1:9–10; 4:16–17; 5:2–4; 2 Thess. 1:7–10; 2:1–8; 1 Tim. 6:14–15; 2 Tim. 4:1; Titus 2:13; Heb. 9:28; Jas. 5:7–8; 1 Pet. 1:7; 5:4; 1 John 2:28; 3:2; Rev. 1:7; 3:11; 16:15; 22:7–20). Second, the letter emphasizes the theme of moral holiness, which it relates closely to the παρουσία. Followers of Jesus are to live life in transformative union with God, growing in conformity to his character until the day of Christ's return and the consummation of their salvation. Though its contents are brief, its history is checkered, and its tone may be even off-putting to a modern audience, there is indeed still great wisdom contained with this oft-neglected letter.

READING SCRIPTURE AS ANCIENT TEXTS

As late-modern readers of the New Testament, it is inescapable that our own preconceptions, presuppositions, and frameworks influence how we interpret New Testament texts. While our own interests and agendas need not completely be set aside as we interact with the scriptural texts, a first point of consideration ought to be the historical context and function of these texts in their original settings. To some extent we must speculate over what exactly these situations were, and this is certainly the case with 2 Peter, a letter whose historical situation is murky at best. To undertake a historical

---

[6] Only 2 Thessalonians, Titus, Philemon, 2 John, 3 John, and Jude are shorter.

orientation to the text, we must immerse ourselves into the ancient world, and its values, beliefs, customs, and social arrangements. These features of the ancient world offer commonalities to our own situations and in other ways offer stark contrasts. Knowing the difference requires the reader to be attuned both to the settings of the ancient world, particularly as it relates to Greco-Roman and Jewish contexts, as well as to their own world. It is these "two horizons"[7] to which we as readers must attend.

The New Testament is a product of the literary conventions and methods of the ancient world.[8] What we find in its pages, though in some respects unique, quite often feels "at home" with the literary styles and rhetorical forms of the Greco-Roman world and Second Temple Judaism. When we compare what we know from the New Testament itself of its composition, distribution, and strategies of persuasion, we find significant overlap with the common practices of literary production from the ancient world.[9]

Second Peter, as a "catholic epistle," fits the mold of an "ancient letter," though not all the components usually found in such documents can be found within its contents.[10] Since the author identifies its form as a letter (3:1), and its introduction and conclusion follow other epistolary conventions, such an identification is uncontroversial. Many documents in the ancient world, however, evidence a "blending" of genres. It has become customary among scholars to also categorize 2 Peter under the genre of ancient Jewish testament, an identification that, perhaps most notably, Richard Bauckham makes in his influential commentary.[11]

---

[7] Anthony C. Thiselton, *The Two Horizons: New Testament Hermeneutics and Philosophical Description with Special Reference to Heidegger, Bultmann, Gadamer, and Wittgenstein* (Grand Rapids: Eerdmans, 1980).

[8] For a study of ancient Jewish letter writing, see Lutz Doering, *Ancient Jewish Letters and the Beginnings of Christian Epistolography* (Tübingen: Mohr Siebeck, 2012).

[9] See, for example, E. Randolph Richards, *Paul and First-Century Letter Writing: Secretaries, Composition and Collection* (Downers Grove: IVP Academic, 2004); Jeffrey A. D. Weima, *Paul the Ancient Letter Writer: An Introduction to Epistolary Analysis* (Grand Rapids: Baker Academic, 2016).

[10] See, for example, Jerome Neyrey, *2 Peter, Jude*, Anchor Bible Commentary (New Haven: Yale University Press, 2004), 246.

[11] Richard J. Bauckham, *Jude–2 Peter*, WBC (Nashville: Word, 1983), 131. The genesis of the view appears to originate with Johannes Muck, "Discours d'Adieu dans le Nouveau Testament et dans la Literature Biblique," in *Aux Sources de la Tradition Chrétienne Mélanges Offerts a M. Maurice Goguel a l'Occasion de Son Soixante-Dixième Anniversaire* (Neuchâtel: Delachaux & Niestlé, 1950), 155–70.

The identification of 2 Peter as a testament has proved a more controversial claim.[12] The testament was an ancient literary form in Second Temple Judaism, written under the name of a long-deceased figure, in which their final words are recounted, typically along with a deathbed scene. According to Bauckham, testaments typically contained both ethical admonitions and revelations of the future.[13] He cites 2 Peter 1:12–15 as evidence that "would leave no contemporary reader in doubt that 2 Peter belonged to the genre of 'testament.'"[14] Within more recent scholarship, however, such certainty about the testamentary nature of 2 Peter has been questioned. Formal Jewish testamentary literature (e.g., *Testament of the Twelve Patriarchs*,[15] *Testament of Moses*, and *Testament of Job*) contains a narrative framework in which the main character offers a deathbed speech preceding the event of their death and recounting significant aspects of their life.[16] As Bauckham notes, this is usually accompanied by some form of ethical instruction or apocalyptic vision forming the content of the author's last words.[17] While 2 Peter does contain some features found in testamentary literature (particularly its ethical and apocalyptic elements, as well as its reference to Peter being near the end of his life), it does not contain the narrative framework present in other testaments, nor a description of Peter's death or a deathbed scenario. To complicate matters further for Bauckham's categorization, no other examples of a testament in epistolary form currently exist.[18]

---

[12] Bauckham's thesis has been quite influential in New Testament scholarship. Scholars who follow his designation include N. T. Wright and Michael Bird, *The New Testament in Its World: An Introduction to the History, Literature, and Theology of the First Christians* (Grand Rapids: Zondervan, 2019), 765; and David deSilva, *An Introduction to the New Testament: Contexts, Methods, and Ministry Formation* (Downers Grove: IVP Academic, 2004), among many others. Such a designation is often taken for granted in present NT scholarship.

[13] Bauckham, *Jude–2 Peter*, 131. Bauckham cites genre parallels as *T. Mos.*; *T. 12 Patr.*; *T. Job*; *1 Enoch* 91–104; Tob. 14:3–11; 4 Ezra 14:28–36; *2 Apoc. Bar.* 57–86; *Jub.* 21–22; 35–36:18; *Bib. Ant.* 19:1–5; 24:1–5; 28:3–4, 5–10; 33; *Adam and Eve* 25–29; Josephus, *Ant.* 4.309–19.

[14] Bauckham, *Jude–2 Peter*, 132.

[15] This text is included though its origin is debated as to whether its composition was from Jewish or Christian circles.

[16] Robert A. Kugler, "Testaments," in *The Eerdman's Dictionary of Early Judaism*, ed. John J. Collins and Daniel C. Harlow (Grand Rapids: Eerdmans, 2010), 1295; David A. deSilva, "Testament of Moses," in *Dictionary of New Testament Background*, ed. Craig A. Evans and Stanley E. Porter (Downers Grove: InterVarsity Press, 2000), 1195.

[17] deSilva, "Testament of Moses," 1195.

[18] For a recent analysis of these issues, see Mark D. Mathews, "The Genre of 2 Peter: A Comparison with Jewish and Early Christian Testaments," *BBR* 21.1 (2011): 51–64.

Bauckham suggests that 2 Peter, as a testament, would have been a sort of "transparent fiction," meaning it would be widely known that as a testament, Peter was not the actual author of the document, similar to other pseudonymous ancient Jewish works.[19] In their essay, Richards and Boyle argue that the testamentary genre was actually not understood in the ancient world as "obviously pseudonymous" as Bauckham has suggested. In examining the reception of testaments by other ancient authors, Richards and Boyle conclude, "In these texts, there is no hint that their authors or audiences knew the testaments were pseudepigraphic. Rather, the ancient authors appeared to cite the testamentary material as authentic, reliable, even authoritative tradition."[20] If this is the case, accepting testaments as a "transparent fiction" seems a difficult possibility as it relates to 2 Peter's authorship and genre. Since it is likewise known that ancient authors were at times suspicious of texts known to be pseudonymous, substantial evidence to the contrary would need to be offered to establish Bauckham's claim in light of Richards' and Boyle's challenge.

In interacting with the genesis of the testamentary thesis from Munck, Mark Mathews argues that whereas testaments and "farewell speeches" are sometimes conflated, Munck's work maintained a distinction between the two and identified 2 Peter as a form of farewell speech.[21] Mathews notes

---

Bauckham cites 2 *Apoc. Bar.* 78–86 as an example of an epistolary testament (Bauckham, *Jude–2 Peter*, 133). The parallels, however, are not exact. The *Epistle of Baruch* is a letter embedded within a narrative, though the Syriac form of the letter appears to have circulated apart from the narrative. While the letter does contain testamentary features (Lutz Doering, *Ancient Jewish Letters and the Beginnings of Christian Epistolography* [Tübingen: Mohr Siebeck, 2012], 252), it lacks the characteristics of a formal testament mentioned above. Further, concerning 2 Peter, as Mathews states, the text being written so close to the death of the individual in question would be an anomaly for the genre as well (Mathews, "The Genre of 2 Peter," 63).

[19] For a critique of pseudepigraphic testaments being transparent fictions, see E. Randolph Richards and Kevin J. Boyle, "Did the Ancients Know the Testaments Were Pseudepigraphic? Implications for 2 Peter," *BBR* 30.3 (2020): 403–23. On the broader question, see Terry L. Wilder, "Revisiting Pseudonymity, the New Testament, and the Noble Lie," *JBTM* 19.2 (2022): 367–80. Meier suggests that the author of 2 Peter did not even try to emulate Peter in his authoring of this text (John P. Meier, "Forming the Canon on the Edge of the Canon: 2 Peter 3:8–18," *Mid-Stream* 38 (1999): 65–70). Wright and Bird largely follow Bauckham's assessment, Wright and Bird, *The New Testament in Its World*, 765. See also I. Howard Marshall, *New Testament Theology: Many Witnesses, One Gospel* (Downers Grove: IVP Academic, 2004), 670.

[20] Richards and Boyle, "Did the Ancients Know the Testaments Were Pseudepigraphic?," 422.

[21] Mathews, "The Genre of 2 Peter," 54.

Bo Reicke developed the argument further to suggest that, since testaments grew out of the farewell speech, 2 Peter could be associated with the genre of testament, though Reicke also downplayed its epistolary features.²²

Formal Jewish testaments, of which scholars of Judaism typically identify only three texts (*Testament of Moses*, *Testament of Job*, and *Testament of the Twelve Patriarchs*) contain the following literary features: (1) a narrative framework with an introduction to the testator and a conclusion that narrates their death and (2) the presence of parenesis, eschatological or apocalyptic material, or both.²³ Based on these criteria, only the three aforementioned texts may be classified as Jewish testaments. While 2 Peter alludes to its author being near the end of their life and contains both parenesis and eschatological/apocalyptic material, it lacks the features of the narrative framework found in our other testaments. Davids, in comparison, notes five common features of Jewish testaments, with some obvious overlap: (1) they are embedded in narrative or historical frameworks; (2) they provide a final charge from the hero to their children or followers; (3) they contain prophecies about the futures of the individuals addressed; (4) there is a deathbed scene and final blessing; (5) they are typically written centuries or millennia after the death of their figure of focus.²⁴ By his criteria, 2 Peter matches almost none of the required criteria of a Jewish testament. Davids also summarizes the characteristics of farewell speeches, which he states contain five major features: (1) prediction of death, (2) prediction of future crises, (3) exhortation to virtue, (4) blessing or commission, and (5) reference to the legacy of the dying person.²⁵ Here again, while 2 Peter shares certain features of this form (particularly 1–4, though number 4 is common of epistles in general), it does not fit the mold entirely. Mathews concludes his study in stating:

> While 2 Peter does include some basic elements of the tradition of the farewell speech, it lacks significant features that are evident in most testaments, that is, deathbed scene, ancient figure from Israel's past, death, burial, response. More importantly, it lacks the most consistent element, the third-person narrative framework.²⁶

---

[22] Mathews, "The Genre of 2 Peter," 55.
[23] Kugler, "Testaments," 1295. For further discussion, see Mathews, "The Genre of 2 Peter," 51–64.
[24] Davids, *The Letters of 2 Peter and Jude*, 146.
[25] Davids, *The Letters of 2 Peter and Jude*, 191–92.
[26] Mathews, "The Genre of 2 Peter," 63–64.

On the basis of this evidence, we ought to say that some elements of the literary genres/forms of the testament or farewell speech have been integrated into 2 Peter, but 2 Peter, quite simply, should be classified as an ancient letter rather than both a letter and testament.[27]

While discussion of authorship will follow below, the lack of conformity to the genre of a testament undercuts part of Bauckham's argument of 2 Peter's origins. He states: "The evidence which really rules out composition *during Peter's lifetime* is that of literary genre and that of date. Either of these might be fatal for any degree of Petrine authorship. Together they must be regarded as entirely conclusive against Petrine authorship."[28] If we remove the label of "testament" from 2 Peter, which the above evidence indicates we should, Bauckham's argument of reading 2 Peter as a "transparent fiction" misunderstands the nature of the letter. The date of the letter, however, is another matter entirely, which will be addressed shortly below.

Second Peter adopts the general framework and expectation that ancient letters carried, though the application of the standard features of letters could be broad. Ancient letters in the Greco-Roman world could take the form of personal correspondence, business discussions and transactions, official legal or governmental correspondence, or religious treaties, prayers, and curses.[29] Letters were often viewed as personal correspondences, representing the presence of a person in their physical absence. Demetrius understood them to imitate a conversation (*On Style*, 223–27).

---

[27] According to Bauckham, Most ancient pseudepigraphal letters can be classified as either imaginative literature ... or historiography (Richard Bauckham, "Pseudo-Apostolic Letters," *JBL* 107.3 [1988]: 475). In these cases, Bauckham argues, the author "does not want his fictional letter to perform for him and his readers the function which an authentic real letter would perform" (Bauckham, "Pseudo-Apostolic Letters," 477). Should the author want to address a contemporary audience in a way that would impact their behavior and beliefs, Bauckham suggests their apparent options were to address the ancient ancestors of the audience, to depict the historical situation in a way analogous to the contemporary one, or to author their letter as a testament or farewell speech (Bauckham, "Pseudo-Apostolic Letters," 477. As noted previously, the examples of Jewish pseudepigraphal letters that Bauckham suggests as parallels to his classification of 2 Peter as a testamentary-letter are both insufficient parallels (they typically occur as a part of larger texts) and are not of the same epistolary nature as 2 Peter. See, again, the critique in Mathews, "The Genre of 2 Peter," 51–64. The evidence for an established genre of "testamentary letter" appears much thinner than Bauckham concludes.

[28] Bauckham, *Jude–2 Peter*, 159.

[29] See John White, "The Greek Documentary Letter Tradition Third Century BCE to Third Century CE," *Semeia* 22 (1981): 89–106.

Seneca couched a successful letter as giving the air of a conversation had sitting in the company of another (*Epistulae Morales ad Lucilium*, 75.1). White defines the form as "a written message ... sent because the corresponding parties are separated spatially ... [for] keeping oral conversation in motion ... either to disclose/seek information or needing to request/command something of the recipient."[30] Letters thus had inherent rhetorical intent, depending on the goals the author wanted to achieve.

While distinct forms of letters can be categorized (personal, official, or business, for example), these could also be mixed for various purposes.[31] Writing on Paul's letters, Judd notes that these documents are personal in tone and yet contain a mixture of personal and religious/philosophical remarks. He anticipates his letters will be read publicly in various Christian communities, making them not entirely private documents, and integrates a blend of the personal and religious functions of ancient letters.[32] Second Peter likewise contains some mix of personal elements, though with limited details and combined with focused religious content, directed particularly toward the situation of its recipients. Second Peter's classification as a letter is most appropriate. As a letter, however, understanding the particular situation and social dynamics of the author-audience relationship has historically proved difficult due to the questions that surround its historical locatedness.

AUTHORSHIP AND DATE

Second Peter opens with an apparently straightforward identification of its author: "Simeon Peter, a slave and apostle of Jesus Christ" (Συμεὼν Πέτρος δοῦλος καὶ ἀπόστολος Ἰησοῦ Χριστοῦ). On appearances, this seems a clear designation of the letter as originating with Simon Peter, the passionate disciple of Jesus and major apostolic leader in the early church. Simon and his brother Andrew were the first disciples Jesus called at the outset of his

---

[30] White, "The Greek Documentary Letter Tradition," 91.
[31] Judd has recently challenged that genres themselves are never static entities but have relatively stable structures that authors use to convey meaning but can be modified for various purposes (Andrew Judd, *Modern Genre Theory: An Introduction for Biblical Studies* [HarperCollins, 2024], 3–82).
[32] Judd, *Modern Genre Theory*, 227–28.

public ministry (cf. Matt. 4:18–19; Mark 1:16).[33] Peter is named first in Mark's list of the twelve (cf. 3:13–18), followed by James and John, who together are portrayed as the central circle of Jesus' disciples in the Gospels. Peter and his brother were fishermen by trade before they embarked with Jesus on his itinerant ministry. Peter, perhaps most famous for his public denial of Jesus (Matt. 26:69–75; Mark 14:66–72; Luke 22:54–62; John 18:15–18, 25–27) and his forceful personality, eventually takes on a central leadership role in the early church, as evidenced throughout the book of Acts.

A majority of scholars, many evangelicals included, however, see 2 Peter as a work of pseudepigraphy.[34] Writing in the 1960s, J. N. D. Kelly surmised, "Scarcely anyone nowadays doubts that 2 Peter is pseudonymous,"[35] and the opinion has only become more entrenched since. The reasons for this are both internal to the text and external to it and will be dealt with in detail below. To summarize briefly, 2 Peter's use of Jude, flamboyant Hellenistic style and vocabulary, allusion to ideas present in "second generation Christianity," references to a collection of Paul's letters, debated canonical inclusion in the history of the church, dissimilarity to 1 Peter, and lack of discussion of issues present in early Christianity (such as the place of the law for Christian obedience) all seem to stack up against the authenticity of the letter.[36]

---

[33] John portrays Andrew first coming to Jesus and then bringing along his brother; cf. John 1:40–42.

[34] In his recent essay, Travis Williams states the following: "The overwhelming majority of modern interpreters reject the authenticity of 2 Peter, with the style being one of many contributing factors (e.g., Schrage 1993c: 126–27; Fuchs and Reymond 1988: 30–32; Schelkle 1988: 179–81; Knoch 1990: 215–18; Frankemölle 1990: 80–82; Paulsen 1992: 89–91, 93–95; Neyrey 1993: 118–20, 134–35; Vögtle 1994: 122–27; Craddock 1995: 92; Danker 1995: 84; Knight 1995: 22–23; Perkins 1995: 160–61; Horrell 1998: 136; Richard 2000: 308–9; Kraftchick 2002: 75–76; Harrington 2003: 236; Skaggs 2004: 86–88; McKnight 2003: 1504; Hartin 2006: 48–49; Wilson 2010a: 269–70; Donelson 2010: 208–9; Aichele 2012: 4–9; Callan 2012: 137–39; Frey 2018: 213–20; Ostmeyer 2021: 107–8)" (Travis B. Williams, "The Amanuensis Hypothesis in New Testament Scholarship: Its Origin, Evidential Basis, and Application," *CBR* 22.1 [2023]: 42).

[35] Kelly, *The Epistles of Peter and of Jude*, 235.

[36] Gilmour summarizes ten key issues involved in the debate, adding to our list the wider tradition of pseudo-Petrine writings and the regard for apostolic authority, which can fall under the "second generation Christianity" category above (Michael J. Gilmour, "Reflections on the Authorship of 2 Peter," *EQ* 73.4 (2001): 291–309). See also Werner George Kümmel, *Introduction to the New Testament*, rev. ed. (Nashville: Abingdon Press, 1975), 430–34 and the detailed discussion in Donald Guthrie, *New Testament Introduction*, 4th ed. (Downers Grove: IVP Academic, 1990), 805–42.

The evidence presented, particularly related to the internal evidence noted, is, at times, overdetermined.[37] By "overdetermined," I refer to attributing more meaning or significance to a passage than the text itself warrants.[38] Other matters of evidence are weightier in terms of favoring post-Petrine authorship. While a majority of scholars accept the pseudonymous origins of the letter and view the evidence against authenticity as too overwhelming to make a reasonable case for Petrine authorship, some scholars argue for its authenticity. Major defenders of the authenticity of the letter include Gene Green,[39] Michael Green,[40] Kruger,[41] and Schreiner.[42]

A number of difficulties exist in assessing the data. Apart from the details in the Gospels and Acts, we know very little about the life of Peter. The New Testament does not record information on his family, upbringing, education,[43] or general biography beyond events surrounding his role as a disciple of Jesus and his role in the early church as recorded in Acts 1–12. Some traditions preserved in the early church exist, but even here, evidence is limited.[44] We also do not possess a sufficient corpus of Petrine writings with which to compare what we find in 2 Peter. We have 1 Peter, which itself is at times disputed, and Peter's brief words in the Gospels and speeches in Acts, all of which come with their own historical

---

[37] I first came across this term in Doug Campbell's *The Deliverance of God: An Apocalyptic Rereading of Justification in Paul* (Grand Rapids: Eerdmans, 2009).
[38] One example here would be reading the language of "the fathers" in 2 Pet. 3:4 to the church fathers, which neither the context nor language used supports.
[39] Green, *Jude and 2 Peter*, 139–50.
[40] Green, *2 Peter and Jude*, 19–47.
[41] Michael A. Kruger, "The Authenticity of 2 Peter," *JETS* 42 (1999): 645–71.
[42] Thomas R. Schreiner, *1 & 2 Peter and Jude*, CSC (Nashville: Holman, 2020), 200–217.
[43] Though see Acts 4:13.
[44] Jerome, for example, records: "Simon Peter the son of John, from the village of Bethsaida in the province of Galilee, brother of Andrew the apostle, and himself chief of the apostles, after having been bishop of the church of Antioch and having preached to the Dispersion – the believers in circumcision, in Pontus, Galatia, Cappadocia, Asia and Bithynia – pushed on to Rome in the second year of Claudius to overthrow Simon Magus, and held the sacerdotal chair there for twenty-five years until the last, that is the fourteenth, year of Nero. At his hands he received the crown of martyrdom being nailed to the cross with his head towards the ground and his feet raised on high, asserting that he was unworthy to be crucified in the same manner as his Lord." Jerome, *De vir.*, 3.1, trans. Ernest Cushing Richardson, in *Nicene and Post-Nicene Fathers*, Second Series, vol. 3, ed. Philip Schaff and Henry Wace. (Buffalo: Christian Literature, 1892), www.newadvent.org/fathers/2708.htm.

Authorship and Date

questions and difficulties. Our limited knowledge necessarily restricts the force of many of the objections related to the authenticity of the letter. The broad range of objections to authorship will each be addressed in what follows.

Hellenistic and Asiatic Style

One of 2 Peter's claims to fame is that it contains a higher proportion of *hapax legomena* than any other New Testament book: fifty-three words that occur only in this letter in the New Testament.[45] Of these fifty-three words, thirty-two do not occur in the LXX either (though two occur in other versions of the Greek OT), fifteen occur in other Jewish sources (*Sib. Or.*, *Ep. Arist.*, Philo, and Josephus), seventeen in the Apostolic Fathers, and one in the Gnostic text *Apoc. Pet.* Three of 2 Peter's *hapax* do not occur anywhere else in extant literature.[46] The language of 2 Peter is often ornate and unusual in comparison to the rest of the New Testament and often sourced from within Hellenistic literature.[47]

Beyond the unusual words in the letter, the style of the letter also contains elements less common in other New Testament texts. It likely reflects differences related to Greek rhetorical orations and adopts an Asiatic or embellished style over and against the more common and traditional Attic style. Attic style delivered its persuasion through logical argumentation in an ordered and concise fashion. While most of the New Testament adopts the Attic style, 2 Peter opts for the Asiatic style. The Greek rhetor Cicero saw the Attic style as more suited to arguments of *logos* or *ethos*, while the Asiatic style was best suited for *pathos*.[48] Cicero's own works preferred Asiatic style, as he thought *pathos* the most effective form of persuasion, though he admitted Attic, Asiatic, and the "middle style" (Rhodian), which combined Attic and Asiatic features, all had their uses.[49] Skilled rhetors could adopt different styles to suit their purposes

---

[45] Bauckham, *Jude–2 Peter*, 135.
[46] ἀκατάπαστος in 2:14, which may be a misspelling of ἀκατάπαυστος in 3:3; and παραφρονία in 2:16; Bauckham, *Jude–2 Peter*, 136. See Appendix B: Hapaxes in 2 Peter.
[47] See Bauckham, *Jude–2 Peter*, 134–36.
[48] Peter Auksi, *Christian Plain Style: The Evolution of a Spiritual Ideal* (Montreal; Kingston: McGill-Queen's University Press, 1995), 54–56.
[49] As he comments, "the plain style for proof, the middle style for pleasure, the vigorous style for persuasion" (Cicero, *Orator*, in *Cicero: Brutus, Orator*, Loeb Classical Library,

and audiences and need not be bound to one, though there were fierce defenders of each approach.

What typified Asianism is complex. As Witherington explains:

> In fact there seem to have been two kinds of Asianism. Cicero (Brutus 325) says that one kind of Asian style is epigrammatic and brilliant (called smooth, sententious, and euphonious) with a focus on utterances that are neat and charming. This was generally the less substantive form of Asiatic rhetoric. The other form of Asiatic rhetoric was noted for a torrent of speech full of ornamentation, redundancy, and fine language. This style was called swift and impetuous. Cicero says that the latter was especially prevalent in his day.[50]

It is this second, more intense form of Asiatic rhetoric that is found in 2 Peter.[51] As Kelly describes it in relation to 2 Peter, it contains "violent alternations of mood, and its Greek, more Hellenistic in flavour, tends to be tortuous, ungainly and at times pretentiously elaborate in the 'Asiatic' manner."[52] Vasaly, more positively, notes that Asiatic style "aimed at artistic expression and often privileging sound and general impression over precision of meaning."[53] Thurén agrees, adding the Asiatic style of 2 Peter is especially concerned with *ethos* and *pathos*, seeking to move the audience more than to change their minds.[54] Witherington agrees, noting the style of the letter contains "lengthy and sometimes convoluted sentences, grandiloquent phrases and vocabulary, amplification and

---

342, ed. Jeffrey Henderson [Cambridge, MA: Harvard University Press, 1962], 357). Cicero also came to argue that the Asiatic style was more suited for youth than for the aged (Karen Cokayne, *Experiencing Old Age in Ancient Rome* [Abingdon: Taylor & Francis, 2013], 30). Different regions and orators could favor certain styles while being adept at others as well. As Ramsay notes, for instance, "In Tarsus the Greek qualities and powers were used and guided by a society which was on the whole, more Asiatic in character" (Sir William Mitchell Ramsay, *The Cities of St. Paul: Their Influence on His Life and Thought* [New York: A. C. Armstrong, 1908], 89).

[50] Ben Witherington III, *The Letters to Philemon, the Colossians, and the Ephesians: A Socio-Rhetorical Commentary on the Captivity Epistles* (Grand Rapids: Eerdmans, 2007), 4.

[51] For an assessment of 2 Peter's style based on Greco-Roman rhetorical handbooks, see Terrence Callan, "The Style of the Second Letter of Peter," *Biblica* 84 (2003): 202–24.

[52] Kelly, *The Epistles of Peter and of Jude*, 228.

[53] Ann Vasaly, "Cicero's Early Speeches," in *Brill's Companion to Cicero*, ed. James M. May (Leiden: Brill, 2002), 86.

[54] Lauri Thurén, "Style Never Goes Out of Fashion: 2 Peter Re-Evaluated," in *Rhetoric, Scripture and Theology: Essays from the 1994 Pretoria Conference*, ed. S. E. Porter and T. H. Olbricht (Sheffield: Sheffield Academic Press, 1996), 343.

redundancy – all to make the honorable look more glorious and the dishonorable look more despicable."⁵⁵

Many scholars think that these Hellenistic features of the letter cast doubt upon the authenticity of 2 Peter, since it is unlikely Peter was trained rhetorically and especially unlikely that he would have compositional familiarity with Asiatic style (see Acts 4:13). From what we know of ancient literary production, however, it is possible none of the traditionally named authors of the New Testament would have physically written their publications. Rather, it is most likely they employed a secretary or amanuensis who had received scribal training to perform such work. Paul frequently notes or alludes to this in his own writings (Rom. 16:22; 1 Cor. 16:21; Gal. 6:11; Col. 4:18; Philem. 19), and given his formal training likely exceeded many of the other designated authors of the NT, it is safe to assume they would have employed secretaries as well. Authorship in the ancient world was often more complex than modern readers recognize.

In his work on the subject, Richards describes how different models of authorship existed in the ancient world in relation to writing practices. A secretary could certainly take a dictated letter or work but might also take notes and edit them into a composition or even compose the letter for the author as a surrogate.⁵⁶ While the "author" would then, under normal circumstances, proofread the composition before giving their approval for distribution, secretaries at times would have maintained more intentional and individual influence on the composition of the letter.⁵⁷ The secretary may even insert material that did not originate with the author, though typically with the author's approval, if it supported the author's argument.⁵⁸ Given such variations in writing practices, with inevitable differences in resulting style (particularly if an author employed different secretaries at times), stylistic considerations for authenticity ought to be given far less weight than they often are.

---

55 Ben Witherington III, *Letters for Hellenized Christians*, vol. II (Downers Grove: IVP Academic, 2007), 298–99; See also Witherington, *The Letters to Philemon, the Colossians, and the Ephesians*, 67.
56 Richards, *Paul and First-Century Letter Writing*, 64–80. Richards notes that it was less common for a scribe to compose a letter without the author's approval of the draft, and this was often done in cases when the author did not care much about the letter's content or its effect on the recipient (summarized in Richards, *Paul and First-Century Letter Writing*, 92).
57 Richards, *Paul and First-Century Letter Writing*, 64–65, 77–79.
58 Richards, *Paul and First-Century Letter Writing*, 109–21.

As an example, Witherington has argued, convincingly in my mind, that the stylistic differences in Ephesians and Colossians, which notably vary from Paul's other writings and often lead scholars to conclude they are pseudonymous, can be explained as the work of Paul's scribe adapting his address to the conventions of the region. Ephesians in particular, he argues, contains "so many of these stylistic features and techniques ... that it is hard to understand why Ephesians has not more readily been recognized as an exercise in an Asiatic style of rhetoric."[59] Since rhetors were expected to adapt to what would be most affective to their audience, the fact that a stylistic adaption may occur, whether through the skill of the named author or their literary collaborators, should not be grounds for rejecting the authenticity of a work. Stylistic considerations are therefore a subjective and indecisive measure of authenticity.

The range of options of ancient compositions noted by Richards could explain some of the Hellenistic imagery found in this text (e.g., ταρταρώσας in 2 Pet. 2:4). For 2 Peter, the style could be explained through several options. It could be the work of Peter himself directly writing, which is the most unlikely option based on what we know of his education. These differences could also be the work of a secretary or perhaps the influence of a combination of collaborators. Even if the same secretary as 1 Peter was employed, they could have adapted the style to a differing situation or context. It is also possible that 2 Peter may be written by a close associate of Peter near or after his death. Some, of course, also favor seeing the letter as a work of forgery, though if the author knows 1 Peter (cf. 2 Pet. 3:1), he seems to do his best to make this letter look like a work of a completely different sort. In any of these cases, the style of the document cannot ultimately be a deciding factor, since there are too many variables and a plausible variety of options of explanation from a historical perspective.

Dissimilarity to 1 Peter

Related to the Hellenistic style of the letter is the question of the relation of 1 Peter to 2 Peter.[60] Certainly, if both works are authentic, one would expect a high degree of compatibility, particularly in their theological

---

[59] Witherington, *The Letters to Philemon, the Colossians, and the Ephesians*, 5–6.
[60] For a discussion, see Kelly, *The Epistles of Peter and of Jude*, 235; Perkins, *First and Second Peter, James, and Jude*, 159.

expressions. Here we again find diverse opinions. Frey, for example, states, "The author makes no attempt at congruency with 1 Pet – not only in terms of form and language, but also in substance."[61] Similarly, Bauckham suggests, "Second Peter in fact provides no evidence that its author was influenced by or made any use of 1 Peter when writing 2 Peter."[62] While both letters promote a vision of Christian holiness, some dissonance arises with the focus of 1 Peter on suffering and 2 Peter on the return of Christ.

A comparison of these two texts is constrained by several limitations. First, we do not possess a sufficient Petrine corpus to determine what may be seen as typical in Peter's personal style and theological thought.[63] First Peter is itself a contested text, so even making a comparison for the sake of authenticity may be unhelpful.[64] Furthermore, Richards warns that comparisons of style and statistical presentations of word usage can fail to recognize several known dimensions of ancient letter writing, including: (1) the use of preformed material, (2) the contributions of a co-author, (3) the influence of the secretary, and, again, (4) the limited size of a writing sample.[65]

That there are stylistic differences between 1 and 2 Peter is undoubted. The general syntactical structures of sentences and word choice are frequently different. Jobes has argued that 1 Peter contains a significant number of "Semitic interferences," indicating perhaps that its author knew Greek as a secondary language. This would mean that though the Greek is difficult, it is not necessarily artfully stylized.[66] Second Peter, on the other hand, is commonly argued to be thoroughly Asiatic in its style, an influence of Hellenistic rhetorical approaches, in clear contrast with the style of 1 Peter.

First Peter, however, also contains a number of features of Asiatic style, though less obviously so than 2 Peter. As Achtemeier has noted, there are repeated uses of comparison (1:7, 13; 2:2, 16, 25; 3:4–5; 5:8), words with similar sounds (1:4, 19; 3:18), an accumulation of synonyms (1:8, 10; 2:25; 3:4), the use

---

[61] Jörg Frey, *The Letter of Jude and the Second Letter of Peter: A Theological Commentary* (Waco: Baylor University Press, 2018), 369.
[62] Bauckham, *Jude–2 Peter*, 286.
[63] See Green, *Jude and 2 Peter*, 145.
[64] For an overview of authorship issues with 1 Peter, see Karen H. Jobes, *1 Peter*, BECNT (Grand Rapids: Baker Academic, 2005), 5–18.
[65] Richards, *Paul and First-Century Letter Writing*, 143–44.
[66] Jobes, *1 Peter*, 325–38.

of anaphora with parallel phrases (4:11), frequent use of parallelism (1:14–15, 18–21, 23; 2:14, 16, 22–23; 3:18; 4:6, 11; 5:2–3), and long, elaborate sentences (e.g., 1:17–21), which are customary of Asiatic style.[67] First Peter seems to fall more to the "middle style" of Greek rhetoric, and so its Asianisms are a bit less forceful and obvious as 2 Peter, though still present.

Further, a lexical comparison of the two letters shows their vocabulary is not as distinct as sometimes assumed. There are 545 unique lemmas (lexical forms) in 1 Peter and 397 in 2 Peter. When compared, the two letters share 155 common lemmas (39 percent of lemmas), and when expanded to include cognate terms (such as including ἁμαρτωλός or πιστεύω/πιστός with the shared terms ἁμαρτάνω/ἁμαρτία or πίστις), the number expands to 283 cognate terms (roughly 70 percent of lemmas) in 2 Peter that are also found in 1 Peter. This means roughly 70 percent of the unique words found in 2 Peter are found in 1 Peter with either the same lemma (39 percent), or a cognate term of that lemma (71 percent). Rather than 1 and 2 Peter having no linguistic similarities, there does exist a broad common vocabulary between the two letters.[68] First Peter also has a significant number of *hapaxes* (61), with roughly half of these words occurring also in the LXX.[69] Boobyer, summarizing Mayor's work, notes the following parallels:

Coincidences in language in spite of prevailing differences (2 Pet. 1:2 and 1 Pet 1:2; 2 Pet. 3:14 and 1 Pet. 1:19 are examples from a longer list); the prominence of the second-advent theme in both; the mention of Noah and seven others saved from the flood (2 Pet. 2:5, cf. 3:5 ff. and 1 Pet. 3:19 ff.); the μακροθυμία of God related in 2 Pet. 3:15 to the coming conflagration and in 1 Pet. 3:20 to the flood; and the accounts in 2 Pet. 1:16–21 and 1 Pet. 1:10–12 (cf. 2 Pet. 3:1f.) of prophecy as a divinely inspired foretelling of Gospel events now announced by apostles.[70]

---

[67] Paul Achtemeier, *1 Peter*, Hermeneia (Minneapolis: Fortress Press, 1996), 3–4. While Achtemeier has made these linguistic observations, Witherington and Myers make the specific connection to Asiatic style (Ben Witherington III and Jason A. Myers, *New Testament Rhetoric*, 2nd ed. [Eugene: Cascade Books, 2022], 214).

[68] Some of the common vocabulary shared are terms common across all Greek literature, while others may show a closer relationship. See Appendix C: Common Vocabulary between 1 and 2 Peter, including Cognate Terms.

[69] Witherington and Myers, *New Testament Rhetoric*, 212.

[70] G. H. Boobyer, "The Indebtedness of 2 Peter to 1 Peter," in *New Testament Essays: Studies in Memory of T. W. Manson*, ed. A. J. B. Higgins (Manchester: University of Manchester Press, 1959), 35

Where does this comparison leave the conversation concerning authorship? It has been argued from both directions that the differences in argumentation and style are indications that 2 Peter is clearly from a pseudepigrapher and, in contrast, that the lack of conformity to the style of 1 Peter indicates a pseudepigrapher was not behind the work, since they would be expected to mimic its style in order to make the forgery convincing. The absence of themes from 1 Peter in 2 Peter has also been used to argue against its authenticity; though from the other direction, Gilmour suggests that "it is reasonable to assume that the author of the second letter would not want to repeat material already found in the first."[71] Similar to the discussion of style above, we are left with an inconclusive argument for authorship related to the relation between these two letters. Given the insufficient parallels, the variations that could occur due to the work of a secretary, and the possible regional stylistic differences that could have influenced the letter, the relationship between 1 and 2 Peter is ultimately inconclusive to the question of origin. Though clear stylistic differences are present, the conclusion that the letters have no stylistic or linguistic overlap is overstated based upon the evidence, though this also does not provide a clear case for authenticity.

Recasting of Jude

A major set of questions for the authenticity of 2 Peter is its use of other sources, and one prominent issue here is the author's apparent recasting of the epistle of Jude.[72] It is clear in comparing these two letters that a likely literary relationship exists between them. Scholars have suggested various possibilities for the nature of this relationship. As Neyrey summarizes:

The very close similarity between Jude and 2 Peter has led scholars to take one or another of the following four options. (1) Jude depends on 2 Peter, which position was found in the early church and was held by Luther and even modern scholars (e.g., Bigg, *The Epistles of St. Peter and St. Jude*, 216–23). (2) 2 Peter depends on Jude, which represents the viewpoint of most modern commentators

---

[71] Michael J. Gilmour, *The Significance of Parallels Between 2 Peter and Other Early Christian Literature*, Academia Biblica 10 (Atlanta; Leiden: SBL; Brill, 2002), 95.

[72] For a recent discussion of the differences between the situations of 2 Peter and Jude, see Herbert W. Bateman IV, "'Memories' about the Old Testament in Jewish and Christian Tradition Inform 2 Peter and Jude, Part 1," *JETS* 67.1 (2024): 103–12.

(e.g., J. Chaine, *Les Epîtres catholiques* [Paris: Gabalda, 1939], 18-24; K. Schelkle, *Die Petrusbriefe, Der Judasbrief* [Freiburg: Herder, 1961], 138-39). (3) Both depend on a common source (e.g., B. Reicke, *The Epistles of James, Peter and Jude* [Garden City, NY: Doubleday, 1964], 189-90; C. Spicq, *Les Epîtres de Saint Pierre* [Paris: Gabalda, 1966], 197). (4) Both were written by the same author (e.g., J. A. T. Robinson, *Redating the New Testament* [London: SCM, 1976], 192-95).[73]

The position that would square most easily with the letter's authenticity would obviously be Jude's use of 2 Peter, since it is far more difficult to explain why a "pillar" in the early church (cf. Gal. 2:9) would feel the need to rely on the words of an obscure brother of Jesus for the composition of his letter.[74] The substance of the data, however, seems to point in the opposite direction, toward the view of the dependence of 2 Peter upon Jude. The major portions of these texts in question are Jude 4-18 and 2 Peter 2:1-18; 3:1-3, and even a cursory glance will demonstrate the clear overlap between them. Where the texts differ, one often finds the references in Jude being made "more elaborate and verbose"[75] in 2 Peter, which seems to indicate 2 Peter adapts Jude's content to its own unique style.

Watson conducted a thorough comparative analysis in his important study.[76] He argues that since the portions in Jude that overlap in 2 Peter are a part of Jude's *narratio* (v. 4) and *peroratio* (vv. 17-18), while the portions in 2 Peter which overlap with Jude are only found in the *probatio* (2:1-10a; 3:1-3) and *digressio* (2:10b-18), it is more likely that 2 Peter integrated Jude's material rather than the other way around.[77] In other words, Jude's material is essential to Jude's letter, while the overlapping material in 2 Peter is supplemental. While not all of the evidence points in the direction of 2 Peter using Jude, the majority of comparisons do. Watson summarizes,

---

[73] Neyrey, *2 Peter, Jude*, 121.
[74] See Gene L. Green, *Jude and 2 Peter*, BECNT (Grand Rapids: Baker Academic, 2008), 144.
[75] Kelly, *The Epistles of Peter and of Jude*, 226.
[76] See also Frey, *The Letter of Jude and the Second Letter of Peter*, 182-92.
[77] The *narratio* was the portion of the text which narrated the events in question or explained the nature of the argument to come. The *peroratio* is the conclusion of the speech which summarizes the central message. The *probatio* provided the central argument and proofs of the persuasion. The *digressio* offered a departure from the main subject to give additional context or argument. Duane Frederick Watson, *Invention, Arrangement, and Style: Rhetorical Criticism of Jude and 2 Peter*, SBL Dissertation Series, 104 (Atlanta: Scholars Press, 1988), 170. See also Gilmour, *The Significance of Parallels*.

"Sometimes the priority of neither can be argued, and occasionally the priority of 2 Peter is indicated. Most often, however, the priority of Jude is indicated on the grounds of invention, arrangement, and style."[78]

This leaves the question, of course, as to whether the apostle would have used a letter like Jude to compose his own work. While it is a possibility, it seems less likely for the apostle Peter to incorporate the words of Jude as it seems to provide no advantage for his authorial purposes. On the other hand, considering that Peter likely used an amanuensis or secretary to compose the letter if authentic, it is possible that a degree of freedom could have been given to his secretary in the composition of the letter, and the secretary chose to integrate the material. Relevant here would be the dating of Jude itself, which some scholars[79] place as early as the 50s or 60s and others place later in the first century or even into the second.[80] While not a singular determinative factor in considering the authenticity of the letter, the relationship with Jude does raise questions concerning 2 Peter's authenticity.

Account of the Transfiguration and Other Gospel Parallels

Another issue of relevance for 2 Peter's use of sources concerns its reference to the events of the Transfiguration recorded in the Gospels in 2 Pet. 1:16–18. There 2 Peter states:

For we did not make known to you the power and presence of our Lord Jesus Christ by following cleverly created myths but by becoming eyewitnesses of that man's majesty. For when he received honor and glory from God a voice such as this was brought to him by the Majestic Glory, "This is my son, my beloved, this is one with whom I take delight," and we heard this voice brought from heaven when we were with him on the holy mountain.

The summary of this event does not precisely match the language or details of any of the canonical accounts, though it most closely resembles the account in Matthew's Gospel. Bauckham, given the lack of precise verbal

---

[78] Watson, *Invention, Arrangement, and Style*, 187. Gilmour's conclusion is similar: "The case of 2 Peter's dependence on Jude remains more convincing than the reverse" (Gilmour, *The Significance of Parallels*, 90). Thurén observes that the changes made by 2 Peter are frequently stylistic in nature (Thurén, "Style Never Goes Out of Fashion," 338).

[79] E.g., Green, *Jude and 2 Peter*, 17–18; Davids, *The Letters of 2 Peter and Jude*, 14–23.

[80] E.g., Bauckham, *Jude-2 Peter*, 13–14; Frey, *The Letter of Jude and the Second Letter of Peter*, 31–32.

parallels, argued 2 Peter's account "was not dependent on the synoptic Gospels but on independent tradition, which could perhaps be his [the testament author's] own knowledge of Peter's preaching."[81] If 2 Peter were utilizing Matthew's account, this would certainly put the text out of the date range of authenticity to be attached to the historical Peter, with Matthew generally dated to the 70–80s,[82] and traditions placing Peter's death in the early 60s. Frey has argued that 2 Peter is informed by the Synoptic tradition but by way of the *Apocalypse of Peter*, which would result in 2 Peter being a mid- to late second century work, though the evidence offered is, in my opinion, unconvincing.[83]

Other potential Gospel parallels have also been noted, including Peter's reference to his coming death (2 Pet. 1:14; cf. John 21:18), the claim of the state of the false teachers becoming "worse than the first" (2 Pet. 2:20; cf. Matt. 12:45), the day of the Lord coming as a thief (2 Pet. 3:10; cf. Matt. 24:43), God delivering the righteous from temptation (2 Pet. 2:9; Matt. 6:13), and the timing of the parousia (2 Pet. 3:4; cf. Mark 9:1). Most of these parallels are weaker in terms of linguistic similarities than the Matthew account and can also likely be explained as sharing common traditions about Jesus' teachings, which were certainly circulating in the church as early as the mid-first century.[84]

The lack of precise verbal parallels means no definitive line of influence can be draw from the Gospels to 2 Peter, and thus cannot be definitive in determining its authorship or date. Gregory the Great actually saw the inclusion of the account of the Transfiguration as a validation that the apostle himself was responsible for the letter.[85] Most modern scholars read these Gospel recollections as indications of the work of a later author, but the absence of clear textual connections makes the argument indeterminate in the conversation on authorship. If oral sources are factored into consideration, as Bauckham has suggested, the Gospel parallels become less relevant for the question of the date and authenticity of the letter.

---

[81] Bauckham, *Jude–2 Peter*, 210.
[82] Bernier, however, places it after 45 and before c. 60 (Jonathan Bernier, *Rethinking the Dates of the New Testament: The Evidence for Early Composition* [Grand Rapids: Baker, 2022]).
[83] See discussion in textual notes below on 2 Pet. 1:17.
[84] See Michael F. Bird, *The Gospel of the Lord: How the Early Church Wrote the Story of Jesus* (Grand Rapids: Eerdmans, 2014).
[85] Gregory the Great, *Sermons on Ezekiel*, 2.6.11.

Reference to Paul's Letters

A final major issue of Peter's source material concerns 2 Peter's mention of a collection of Paul's letters. In 2 Peter 3:15–16, the author writes:

> Just as also our beloved brother Paul wrote to you, in accordance with the wisdom which was given to him, as he does also in all his letters, speaking in them about these things, in which some things are hard to understand, which the ignorant and unstable will distort to their own ruin, as they do with the rest of the Scriptures.

Paul began his letter writing ministry as early as the late 40s, and certainly by the early 50s, with Galatians often being acknowledged first (c. AD 48–49), and the Thessalonian letter(s) following shortly after. Paul's letter writing, at least in terms of "authentic writings," would have ended c. AD 64–67 when he was executed, though the details of his death is a matter of some debate.[86] Assuming Peter and Paul's deaths were approximate to one another, the likelihood of a formalized, completed collection of Paul's letters during the lifetime of Peter seems doubtful.[87]

The text itself does not necessarily require that a formalized, completed collection is in mind. The phrase "in all his letters" (ἐν πάσαις ἐπιστολαῖς) requires only knowledge of a number of letters (i.e., at least three), not necessarily a formally completed collection. It is reasonable to consider the question if the historical Peter would have known that Paul had written letters of substance to many of his churches. In my estimation, it would be far more likely that the historical Peter would be aware of Paul's letter writing than that he would not. For Peter to demonstrate knowledge of written letters of Paul during his lifetime should be uncontroversial, as they were not only contemporaries but directly acquainted with one another (cf. Gal. 2:6–10). Indeed, since their paths at times overlapped, and they likely heard news of one another through the network of churches to which they ministered, one can imagine Peter himself even seeing some of Paul's letters in his ministry travels. Though Paul details a conflict between Peter and himself at Antioch in Galatians (2:11–14), he indicates in later letters that he has respect for Peter as an apostle (1 Cor. 1:12; 3:22; 9:5; 15:5) and does not show any lingering animosity toward him. The idea of a

---

[86] For a recent examination, see Sean McDowell, *The Fate of the Apostles: Examining the Martyrdom Accounts of the Closest Followers of Jesus* (New York: Routledge, 2015).
[87] Perkins, *First and Second Peter, James, and Jude*, 160.

perpetual conflict between the two is often more the result of scholarly imagination than established historical reality.

Peter's familiarity with Paul's writings could be explained by the circulation of these letters being intended by Paul himself. Based on Col. 4:16, one might recognize, as Laird does, that "an exchange of letters was encouraged during the first century."[88] Further, given ancient literary conventions, it is possible that an initial collection of Paul's letters was developed early, with discussions perhaps even beginning during Paul's lifetime.[89] An author in the ancient world may have been involved in the collection and preservation of their own writings, not necessarily leaving it to others to determine this entirely after their death. Paul indeed could have given direction to his associates on what to do with his writings after his passing. In his study, Laird concludes, "the evidence ... indicates that the personal involvement of Paul's associates best accounts for the early formation and circulation of the various editions" of Paul's writings.[90] It is possible both that an early core of Pauline writings was known during Paul's lifetime, that Paul's letters began circulating during his lifetime, and that through some combination of the circulation of these letters and the oral transmission of Pauline teachings, Peter himself had awareness of significant elements of Paul's teachings and letter writing ministry.

Neyrey has documented a considerable list of parallels between the vocabulary of Paul's letters and 2 Peter.[91] Such overlap may be evidence that 2 Peter is familiar with Paul's thought at the literary level, though some

---

[88] Benjamin P. Laird, *The Pauline Corpus in Early Christianity: Its Formation, Publication, and Circulation* (Peabody: Hendrickson Academic, 2022), 122.

[89] See Laird, *The Pauline Corpus in Early Christianity*, 17–39.

[90] Laird, *The Pauline Corpus in Early Christianity*, 317.

[91] Acknowledgment (*epignōsis*, 1:2) – Rom 1:28; faith, steadfastness, love (1:5–7) – 1 Thess 1:3; 5:8; kinship affection (*philadelphias*, 1:7) – Rom 12:10; 1 Thess 4:9; entry into the kingdom (*eisodos*, 1:11) – although Paul speaks of an *eisodos* (1 Thess 1:9; 2:1), it is his own entry, not that of Christ; nevertheless, it is an unusual term; the kingdom (*basileian*, 1:11) of the Lord – 1 Cor 6:9; fruitless (*akarpous*, 1:8) – 1 Cor 14:14; in this bodily tent (*skēnōmati*, 1:13, 14) – 2 Cor 5:1–4; the coming (*parousian*, 1:16) of the Lord Jesus – 1 Thess 4:15; the Master who bought them (*agorasanta*, 2:1) – 1 Cor 6:20; 7:23; stored up for fire (*tethēsaurismenoi*, 3:7) – Rom 2:5; reckon "delay" as forbearance (*makrothymei*, 3:9) – Rom 2:4; the day of the Lord will come like a thief (3:10) –1 Thess 5:2; strive to be found by him (*heurethēnai*, 3:14) – 1 Cor 4:2; spotless and unblemished (*aspiloi kai amōmētoi*) – Phil 2:15; fall away from your constancy (*stērigmou*, 3:17) – 1 Thess 3:13; according to the wisdom given him (3:16) – 1 Cor 3:10; 15:10 (Neyrey, *2 Peter, Jude*, 133).

of the language here is common across the New Testament and likely speaks more to a common vocabulary among early Christian teachers, likely originating from the oral transmission of the teachings of Jesus (e.g., kingdom, fruit, tent, coming, thief, etc.) than from necessary literary dependence. Though these parallels and references to Paul's letters raise important questions, they do not require a late date for the letter.

Second-Generation Christianity

Another challenge often posed against the authenticity of 2 Peter is the apparent presence of matters of theological concern more at home in second-century Christianity than the first. The position originates, to some extent, with Ernst Käsemann's oft-cited essay on "Primitive Christian Eschatology."[92] Several key portions of the letter (particularly 1:12-21; 3:1-10, 14-16), are thought to be clear products of "early Catholicism" or, as Käsemann terms it, "primitive Christianity."[93] In this paradigm, the document is primarily concerned with enforcing a firm sense of apostolic authority, eliminating tensions concerning the delay of the parousia, and addressing Gnostic criticisms of apostolic teachings, evidencing a mid-second-century situation.[94] Käsemann suggests, "The whole community is embarrassed and disturbed by the fact of the delay of the Parousia."[95] The letter is read, therefore, as a text that seeks to enforce tradition, defeat heretics, and, according to Käsemann, make "faith into a mere assent to the dogmas of orthodoxy."[96]

Kelly summarized the argument in this way:

> He [the author] lived at a time when the first Christian generation had passed away (iii.4), and when a collection of Paul's letters had been compiled (iii.15f.) ... his concern for the orthodox interpretation of scripture (i.20f.; iii.15f.) and for the apostolic tradition (e.g., ii.21; iii.2) smacks of emergent "Catholicism" rather than of first-generation Christianity.[97]

---

[92] Ernst Käsemann, "An Apologia for Primitive Christian Eschatology," in *Essays on New Testament Themes*, trans. W. J. Montague, SBT 41 (London: SCM, 1964), 169-95.
[93] Käsemann, "An Apologia for Primitive Christian Eschatology," 169.
[94] Käsemann, "An Apologia for Primitive Christian Eschatology," 169-72.
[95] Käsemann, "An Apologia for Primitive Christian Eschatology," 170.
[96] Käsemann, "An Apologia for Primitive Christian Eschatology," 195.
[97] Kelly, *The Epistles of Peter and of Jude*, 235.

While my interpretation of these texts will be presented in the commentary below, the conclusions drawn by Käsemann and others who see evidence of second-century Christianity in this text is, in my evaluation, an overdetermination of what the text says. To offer a brief rebuttal, while apostolic authority is important to this letter, it is not as obvious a feature as many interpreters contend, having virtually no presence in the second chapter of the letter, and occurring in only three or four units of the letter in chapters 1 and 3. Biographical details of Peter are, contrary to the frequent comment otherwise, not generally maximized to reinforce the letter's authority. In fact, such details are quite scant, only mentioning his coming death and his presence at the Transfiguration. Nothing else of Peter or his authority and experiences is described, and it is certainly not maximized. One might compare, for example, Paul's appeal to establish his authority in his letters to the Corinthians, which are generally not disputed to their authenticity and appeal more firmly to apostolic authority. Furthermore, the suggestion that the "fathers" who have died in 3:4 are clearly the apostles is a further overdetermination of the text. That phrase is, first, not at home within the writings of second-century Christianity and, second, does not contextually make sense (see commentary on 3:4). Finally, the question of the "delay of the *parousia*" is also not at home within the theological discussion of second-century Christian writings. Bauckham asserts, "The 'problem' of the delay of the parousia is not discussed anywhere in the Christian literature of the second century. This is, in my view, a good argument for dating 2 Peter in the late first century, no earlier and no later."[98] The thesis that the theological argumentation of the letter favors the mid- to late second century comes up lacking in consideration of the evidence.

Canonical Inclusion

Perhaps the most difficult challenge for the authenticity of 2 Peter is its reception in the early church.[99] While evidence for its existence in the late

---

[98] Richard J. Bauckham, "2 Peter and the Apocalypse of Peter Revisited: A Response to Jörg Frey," in *2 Peter and the Apocalypse of Peter: Towards a New Perspective*, ed. Jörg Frey, Matthijs Dulk, and Jan van der Watt (Leiden: Brill, 2019), 274.

[99] For an overview of the issues, see Kelly, *The Epistles of Peter and of Jude*, 235.

Authorship and Date

second century establishes the possibility of its authenticity,[100] the mixed nature of the evidence raises significant questions as well. This letter holds the unenviable title of the most disputed work to find its way into the canon. While debates persist on how early knowledge of 2 Peter is found in the writings of the church fathers, it is unavoidable that the work was noted as questioned by most of the authors in the church who discussed these matters.[101] Two layers of evidence merit consideration for both the authenticity and date of 2 Peter as it relates to its canonical inclusion: (1) possible early quotations or allusions to the work and (2) direct discussions of its authenticity with the writings of the early church.

Picirilli has examined the existence of possible allusions to 2 Peter in the apostolic fathers. While not all of his examples have been equally convincing to most scholars, some of the more evident allusions create the possibility that Clement (c. AD 35–99) did indeed know the work.[102] First Clem. 11:1–2 and 2 Pet. 2:6–10 both share a similar application of the Lot story and contain some overlapping vocabulary, as well as some terms that occur elsewhere in 2 Peter but are uncommon in the NT (e.g., δεσπότης). Similar parallels exist between 1 Clem. 23:3, 2 Clem. 11:2, and 2 Pet. 3:4's expression concerning "our fathers,"[103] and further parallels exist at the word/phrase level. Laird observes that "2 Pet 2:5 is the sole reference in the New Testament to the preaching of Noah,"[104] which is paralleled in 1 Clem. 7:6 and 9:4.[105] Both 2 Peter and 1 Clement describe the divine "magnificent glory" (1 Clem. 9:2: τῇ μεγαλοπρέπει δόξῃ αὐτοῦ; 2 Pet. 1:17: ὑπὸ τῆς μεγαλοπρέπους δόξης) and contain other phrases in common such as "way of truth" (τῇ ὁδῷ τῆς ἀληθείας, cf. 1 Clem. 35:5; 2 Pet. 2:2:) and "prophetic word" (ὁ προφητικὸς λόγος, cf. 2 Clem. 11:2; 2 Pet. 1:19, which also appears three times in Justin's *Dialogue with Trypho*). Justin also bears

---

[100] Davids cites its presence in 𝔓72 and an early Coptic NT as supporting evidence (Davids, *The Letters of Peter and Jude*, 121).
[101] For a detailed review of the evidence, see Charles Bigg, *A Critical and Exegetical Commentary on the Epistles of St. Peter and St. Jude*, ICC (Edinburgh: T&T Clark, 1910), 199–215.
[102] Robert E. Picirilli, "Allusions to 2 Peter in the Apostolic Fathers," *Journal for the Study of the New Testament* 33 (1988): 57–83. Since the authorship of 2 Clement is debated and often considered in authentic, its allusions may therefore be a few decades later, sometime early in the second century AD.
[103] See Bauckham, *Jude–2 Peter*, 284.
[104] Laird, *The Pauline Corpus in Early Christianity*, 118.
[105] Laird, *The Pauline Corpus in Early Christianity*, 118.

some resemblance to 2 Pet. 2:1 in his *Dialogue* 82.1, where he comments on the presence of false prophets and false teachers in a similar to fashion to 2 Peter, which appears to be a combination of terms occurring only in those two texts in Christian literature.[106]

Kruger argues that Irenaeus also knew the text of 2 Peter:

We read in Irenaeus: ἡ γαρ ημέρα κυρίου ως χίλια ετη; and in 2 Peter 3:8: ὅτι μία ἡμερα παρά κυρίῳ ως χίλια ετη – hardly a coincidence. Of course, as some have observed, Irenaeus could have simply been quoting Psalm 90:4. However, this Psalm reads: οτι χίλια ετη ἐν οφθαλμοῖς σου ως ἡ ἡμερα ἡ εχθές, ἥτις διῆλθε. Irenaeus's quotation varies widely from the LXX, as does 2 Peter's, but they are virtually identical with each other. It is highly unlikely that they both would independently diverge from the LXX in the exact same manner, thus inclining us to think Irenaeus was quoting directly from 2 Peter.[107]

The allusions above do not provide indisputable evidence that the apostolic fathers knew the work, but they do create the possibility that this was the case.

Related to the use of 2 Peter in the church fathers is the overlap between 2 Peter and the *Apocalypse of Peter*, which Frey argues was more widely accepted than 2 Peter until the end of the second century.[108] The work of Richard Bauckham argued that the relationship between 2 Peter and the *Apocalypse of Peter* was built on the priority of 2 Peter,[109] though this has been questioned in recent scholarship by Gilmour,[110] Grünstäudl,[111] and Frey[112] and is discussed further in the commentary notes on 2 Pet. 1:17.

Concerning the writings of the church fathers, little direct discussion exists of the document until the third and fourth centuries. Origen (c. 185–253) offers some of the earliest written testimony on the status of 2 Peter in the church. In his *Commentary on John*, he acknowledges the

---

[106] See Bauckham, *Jude–2 Peter*, 237.
[107] Kruger, "The Authenticity of 2 Peter," 653.
[108] Jörg Frey, "Second Peter in New Perspective," in *2 Peter and the Apocalypse of Peter: Towards a New Perspective*, ed. Jörg Frey, Matthijs Dulk, and Jan van der Watt (Leiden: Brill, 2019), 17.
[109] Richard J. Bauckham, "The Apocalypse of Peter: A Jewish Christian Apocalypse from the Time of Bar Kokhba," *Apocrypha* 5 (1994), 7–111.
[110] Gilmour, *The Significance of Parallels*.
[111] Wolfgang Grünstäudl, *Petrus Alexandrinus: Studien zum historischen und theologischen Ort des Zweiten Petrusbriefes*, WUNT 2.315 (Tübingen: Mohr Siebeck, 2013).
[112] Frey, *The Letter of Jude and the Second Letter of Peter*.

first epistle of Peter was recognized as genuine, but the authenticity of a second letter was doubtful and disputed.[113] In his *Homilies on Numbers*, however, he refers to a quotation from 2 Peter 2:16 as Scripture.[114] Didymus of Alexandria (313–98) accepted 2 Peter as authentic but stated in his commentary, "It should not be ignored, therefore, that the present letter is forged, and although it is published, it is not included in the canon."[115]

Eusebius (c. 260–339) gives our fullest discussion of the status of 2 Peter in the church. In his *Ecclesiastical History*, he writes that while the first letter of Peter is acknowledged as genuine and is freely used, his second letter was not yet considered canonical, though it was profitable and had been used alongside of the rest of the Scriptures.[116] This is in contrast to the apocryphal works of Peter (*Acts of Peter*, *Gospel of Peter*, *Preaching of Peter*, and *Apocalypse of Peter*), which Eusebius understood as universally rejected in the church.[117] Eusebius notes that 2 Peter was "recognized by many" but had not yet achieved universal confidence.[118] Eusebius was cognizant of the emerging "canon consciousness" in the church and reported that those writings that were known to be falsely ascribed were rejected by the church.[119] Second Peter had not yet garnered full acceptance but was not rejected as a known *pseudepigraphon* at that time.[120]

Jerome (c. 345–420) noted the style, character, structure, and words of 2 Peter differ significantly from 1 Peter and suggested a different scribe may have been involved in its production,[121] though he noted that many consider this second letter to not be authentic.[122] Jerome, like Eusebius,

---

[113] "And Peter, on whom the Church of Christ is built, against which the gates of hell shall not prevail, left only one epistle of acknowledged genuineness. Suppose we allow that he left a second; for this is doubtful." (Origen, *Comm. Jo.* 5.3).

[114] Origen, *Hom. Num.* 13.8.1, though this is in Rufinus' Latin translation of the homily and may not reflect Origen's original words. The Greek text of this work has not been preserved.

[115] Cf. Bigg, *The Epistles of St. Peter and St. Jude*, 200.

[116] Eusebius, *Eccl. His.*, 3.1–4.

[117] Eusebius, *Eccl. His.*, 3.1–4.

[118] Eusebius, *Eccl. His.*, 3.25.2–3. In book 6, Eusebius expresses doubt of 2 Peter's authenticity, though it seems he is recounting Origen's opinion (6.25.8).

[119] Eusebius, *Eccl. His.*, 6.12.3–4.

[120] Athanasius reports in his Letter 39 (AD 367) that there is one letter of Peter to be acknowledged as canonical though he gives no discussion concerning the nature of the second letter.

[121] Jerome, *Letters*, 120.11.

[122] Jerome, *De vir.*, 3.1.

considered 2 Peter useful while rejecting the apocryphal works of Peter (*Acts of Peter, Gospel of Peter, Apocalypse of Peter, Preaching of Peter,* and *Martyrdom of Peter*).[123] Davids also suggests that two other early church fathers, "Clement of Alexandria and Cyprian apparently knew it, although they do not mention it by name."[124] By the close of the fourth century,[125] the Council of Carthage (397) affirmed the New Testament canon found in most Christian Bibles today, including twenty-seven books and "two epistles of the apostle Peter."[126]

The evidence from the early church presents us with a mixed bag. While none of the orthodox fathers fully rejected the work as pseudepigraphal, and its use in the church may extend as far back as the late first or early second century, most authors who discuss it note its disputed nature, while also finding it as instructive for the churches. It was not rejected as "spurious" as the other works circulating in Peter's name were at that time. It seems 2 Peter won acceptance into the canon primarily on the grounds of its widespread use and theological consistency with the apostolic message.[127] It is here that its claim to apostolic origin differs from the other works written in Peter's name, which often depart from the teachings in the New Testament, frequently in the development of or compatibility with Gnostic beliefs.

Summary of Authorship and Date

The data surveyed above leaves us wanting of a firm conclusion. In my opinion, scholars should abandon identifying 2 Peter as a testament, along with the notion that such works were "transparent fictions," because it does not fit the characteristics described above. This, subsequently, should not be determinative in the analysis of its authorship and date. Second Peter is a public letter that contains some features of testaments and/or farewell

---

[123] Jerome, *De vir.*, 3.1.
[124] Davids, *The Letters of 2 Peter and Jude*, 121.
[125] Green cites additional acceptance of 2 Peter among Athanasius, Cyril of Jerusalem, and Gregory of Nazianzus (Green, *Jude and 2 Peter*, 143).
[126] "Third Council of Carthage," trans. B. F. Westcott, *A General Survey of the History of the Canon of the New Testament*, 5th ed. (Edinburgh, 1881), pp. 440, 541–42. For further summary, see Bigg, *The Epistles of St. Peter and St. Jude*, 211.
[127] See M. Eugene Boring, *An Introduction to the New Testament: History, Literature, Theology* (Louisville: Westminster John Knox Press, 2012), 459.

speeches but is not a letter-testament or a testament by nature of the definitions of those writings. The data surveyed above concerning the major challenges to its authenticity may be summarized as follows:

Challenge to Authenticity	Implication for Authorship
Hellenistic Style	Indeterminate
Dissimilarity to 1 Peter	Indeterminate
Recasting of Jude	Suspicious, but not decisive
Account of the Transfiguration	Indeterminate
Reference to a Pauline collection	Indeterminate
Evidence of second-generation Christianity	Indeterminate
Canonical Inclusion	Legitimate Difficulty

While other pieces of evidence, such as its style, relationship to Jude and 1 Peter, account of the transfiguration, reference to Paul's letters, and evidence of second-generation Christian thought, are relevant to the discussion of authorship, none of them are ultimately decisive, and each has other plausible explanations that could fit the scenario of Petrine origination or pseudonymity. The chief difficulty that 2 Peter faces in terms of its authenticity is its hesitant reception in the church. Here the evidence suggests the possibility that 2 Peter was known and accepted as early as the second century, but doubts lingered into the third and early fourth centuries until the text was ultimately accepted, seemingly on the grounds of its theological consistency with other New Testament writings rather than an erasure of doubts about its literary origins.

Concerning the question of its authorship and date, Davids details three options: (1) if one accepts the tradition that Peter was martyred during the reign of Nero and accepts Peter as author, it must be written by AD 68; (2) if one rejects the Petrine martyrdom tradition, it could be written by Peter as late as AD 80; (3) if it was written after Peter's death by a pseudepigrapher, the likely latest date is AD 110–40.[128] This third option may be split into two further options: (3a) 2 Peter may be written by an associate of Peter after his death, or (3b) 2 Peter may be written by an unassociated pseudepigrapher after his death. Which option is to be preferred is difficult,

---

[128] Davids, *The Letters of 2 Peter and Jude*, 130–31. Bernier's assessment is similar: "2 Peter was written no earlier than 60 and no later than 69 if it is Petrine, and no earlier than 60 and no later than 125 if pseudo-Petrine" (Bernier, *Rethinking the Dates of the New Testament*, 241).

and the possibility of pseudonymity requires some understanding of the practice of pseudonymity in the ancient world.

Authorship, Amanuenses, and Pseudonymity

While some scholars have suggested pseudonymity (falsely attributing a work to someone else) as a practice was essentially deceptive, the evidence in antiquity suggests a broader set of motivations were likely at work. Wilder summarizes: "Three views currently seem to dominate the issue [of] ... pseudepigrapha in the NT: (1) they were not written to deceive their readers regarding their authorship, but nonetheless their readers were deceived; (2) they were not written to deceive their readers, and they did not in fact do so; and (3) they were written to deceive their readers and they were successful in doing so."[129] Metzger documented that the reasons for pseudonymity in the ancient world were varied, including financial gain, malicious intent, love and respect, modesty, dramatic use, deceit, error, and convenience.[130] According to Baum, a work of pseudonymity might not be considered deceptive simply on the grounds of its attribution but rather more so on the basis of its content.[131] Soon's conclusions are similar, suggesting "conceptions of forgery are ethically malleable depending on one's position and situatedness in relation to the creation, circulation, and use of a pseudepigraphon."[132] Wilder also makes a similar case, suggesting, "Might not a disciple whose teacher had trusted him as a reliable exponent of his thought publish an account of his teacher's thought after the latter's death and attribute it to his teacher without raising the concerns which applied in other cases of pseudepigraphy?"[133] In light of this, he notes,

---

[129] Terry L. Wilder, *Pseudonymity, the New Testament, and Deception: An Inquiry into Intention and Reception* (Lanham: University Press of America, 2004), 5.

[130] Bruce M. Metzger, "Literary Forgeries and Canonical Pseudepigrapha," *JBL* 92 (1972): 5–12. Baum notes, for example, "In the first quarter of the fourth century CE, the Neoplatonic philosopher Iamblichus of Chalcis mentioned books that circulated under the name of Pythagoras but had been composed by his disciples on the basis of his lectures" (Armin D. Baum, "Content and Form: Authorship Attribution and Pseudonymity in Ancient Speeches, Letters, Lectures, and Translations – A Rejoinder to Bart Ehrman," *JBL* 136.2 [2017]: 388).

[131] Baum, "Content and Form," 402.

[132] Isaac T. Soon, "Before Deception: The Amoral Nature of Ancient Christian Forgery," *Early Christianity* 14.4 (2023): 432.

[133] Wilder, *Pseudonymity, the New Testament, and Deception*, 61–62.

"some precedent can be found for non-deceptive pseudonymous letters, if they exist in the NT."[134] Returning to Metzger's examination, he concluded "that literary forgeries were many kinds, from the amusing hoax to the most barefaced and impudent imposture, and that the moral judgment to be passed on each must vary accordingly. Indeed, in many cases such a judgment can be only tentative."[135] With such examinations in mind, the evidence indicates that pseudonymous works could be composed for a variety of reasons, and deception need not necessarily factor into the equation depending on the nature of the work.

The prospect of pseudonymity creates obvious sorts of implications for the New Testament canon. Meade notes that on two ends of the spectrum some would deny the possibility of canonicity and pseudonymity being maintained at the same times on the grounds of a commitment to the inerrancy of the text, while others would defend pseudonymity as evidence against the inerrancy of the text.[136] Mediating positions would understand that the two can be reconciled or coexist in some sense. Meade himself argues that the authority of the biblical text is derived primarily from the understanding that the words of the text are a living word from God, which is autonomous, unified, and coherent and also adaptable to new meanings in new contexts as the plan of God unfolds.[137] As it relates to 2 Peter's authorship, he finds the emphasis to be on "an assertion of authoritative tradition, not literary origins."[138] Meade's work illustrates that a simple logical and historical correlation between pseudonymity and falsehood or textual error does not exist. The early church, however, did operate with such a correlative perspective. In surveying opinions on pseudonymity in the early Church, Wilder recognizes, "Christians did not regard the fictive use of another person's name with indifference."[139] The fathers certainly demonstrated concern as to whether or not a text was falsely attributed. From a historical perspective, however, more options were possible than "authentic" and "forged."

---

[134] Wilder, *Pseudonymity, the New Testament, and Deception*, 111.
[135] Metzger, "Literary Forgeries and Canonical Pseudepigrapha," 19.
[136] Meade, *Pseudonymity and Canon*, 3.
[137] Meade, *Pseudonymity and Canon*, 108.
[138] Meade, *Pseudonymity and Canon*, 190.
[139] Wilder, *Pseudonymity, the New Testament, and Deception*, 147. As Meade recognizes, the emphasis of the discussion in the early church tended to lay upon continuity with the apostolic message (Meade, *Pseudonymity and Canon*, 208).

As it relates specifically to 2 Peter, it seems here that the theoretical possibilities are broader than simply Peter or "pseudonymous forgery." It is possible that an associate of Peter could be writing in Peter's name, after Peter's death, with knowledge of Peter's testimony and teaching. While this can neither be proven nor disproven, it does provide the possibility of a pseudepigraphal writing existing with apostolic authority and with benign intent. While Meade suggests that the author of 2 Peter's "only acquaintance with Peter is literary,"[140] this seems more speculative than the evidence requires, especially on the grounds of the literary connections between 1 and 2 Peter. Witherington similarly argues that pseudonymity was not simply an exercise in deceptive creativity but rather that authors had "ways of preserving sources and traditions from the past and applying them in later situations, with the editors neither claiming authorship nor trying to deceive anyone about the sort or identity of their sources."[141] He concludes concerning 2 Peter, "it is likely that this document was drawn up after Peter's (and Paul's) death, by someone in the Petrine circle."[142] The effect of Meier's suggestion is similar, offering that "the author takes upon himself the mantle, the heritage, the authority of the leading apostle to bolster the truth of the gospel against some errors threatening the church of his day. In effect, the author is claiming: This is what Peter, who saw Jesus' transfiguration in glory during the public ministry, would say to those who deny that all believers will see Jesus' coming in glory on the last day."[143]

It is possible to imagine a scenario where the historical Peter, aging and near death, seeks to address an important issue in a church community or communities. Peter, in all likelihood, was not scribally educated, and thus likely would have employed a secretary to compose this letter. The secretary, understanding the regional preferences of the audience (Asiatic), and with some authorized liberty, constructs the letter, integrating existing material from another text (Jude), which addresses a similar problem, integrates the teachings of Peter, and constructs a compelling argument to address the audience. Peter perhaps gives input after the initial draft is

---

[140] Meade, *Pseudonymity and Canon*, 196.
[141] Witherington, *Letters for Hellenized Christians*, 270.
[142] Witherington, *Letters for Hellenized Christians*, 271.
[143] Meier, "Forming the Canon on the Edge of the Canon," 67.

composed and approves the text before it is sent out. The "voice" of the letter, due to the secretary's own influence, is unique but presents the content of Peter's thoughts in the words and style of the secretary.

It is also possible to imagine other scenarios, such as an associate of Peter employing a secretary, being authorized or believing themself authorized to do so, and directing Peter's teachings at an audience sometime after Peter's death. This scenario would better account for the reception of the letter. Indeed, the use of Jude and other sources in 2 Peter, Hellenistic style, references to Paul's letters, and dissimilarity to 1 Peter may all be accounted for with the variations present in ancient scribal practices and the possibility that the letter was an authorized composition but completed after Peter's death. I find it least likely that the letter is a work of a pseudepigrapher who had no personal knowledge of Peter or his teaching due primarily to the fact that the letter offers a consistent presentation of apostolic teachings, though with some unique emphases of its own. Unlike many known pseudonymous writings in the names of apostles, 2 Peter does not advance any novel teachings or contain significant embellishments that capitalize on the identity of the author.[144]

The evidence, as illustrated above, is complex, so certainty on the matter from a historical perspective seems to me unachievable.[145] Gilmour here agrees, stating, "Did Peter write 2 Peter? In the end it must be admitted that, on *purely* historical grounds, we don't know – not that he couldn't have, not that he must have. The arguments for and against have been repeated time and again but the fact remains that there is simply not enough evidence to achieve a consensus."[146] As a colleague of mine has been known to say, "I could be more certain, but I would be less honest." From a personal perspective, and as a confessing Christian, I trust the ancient church in its evaluation and likewise affirm what I believe the early fathers believed: that 2 Peter is a faithful witness to the apostolic gospel and preserves apostolic teachings concerning the ministry, instruction, and authority of Jesus Christ. Though doubts on its historical origins may linger, because of its consistency with the apostolic witness, we may

---

[144] See Schreiner, *1 & 2 Peter and Jude*, 304–5.
[145] See Davids, *The Letters of 2 Peter and Jude*, 149.
[146] Gilmour, "Reflections on the Authorship of 2 Peter," 308.

proclaim with confidence that 2 Peter ought to be taught and preached in our churches as a true "word from the Lord."

AUDIENCE AND SETTING

Just as the details of origination with 2 Peter are cloudy, so too are the details of its audience and setting. The letter says little of the location or social situation of its recipients. Second Pet. 3:1 states that this letter is the "second letter" that the author writes to this audience, and though other alternatives have been suggested, most scholars hold this would mean some kind of overlap with the audience of 1 Peter.[147]

If the audience of 2 Peter overlaps in some way with 1 Peter, the destinations could include the provinces of Bithynia and Pontus, Galatia, Cappadocia, or Asia, which roughly correspond to the modern-day country of Turkey. Notable among the list is the province of Asia, which was the main region home to the Asiatic style in which 2 Peter is written. This style is comparable to that of Ephesians and Colossians, which reside in the province of Asia as well. While Davids, for example, suggests that "we would never have imagined that 2 Peter was written to the northwest quadrant of Asia Minor unless we had 1 Peter,"[148] the Asiatic style of the letter could point readers in this direction on its own. Though Asiatic style was not restricted to Asia Minor, it did originate and was most popular there, hence its naming convention.[149]

Just as historical questions surround the identity of the audience, so too with its opponents. Several theories have been proposed concerning the nature of the false teachers 2 Peter opposes. An older view, though unpopular among modern commentators since Neyrey, was that the opponents were Gnostics. M. Green, for example, sees a type of "proto-Gnosticism" evident in the letter's attention to γνῶσις (cf. 1:2–3, 5–6, 8; 2:20; 3:18),

---

[147] If the letter is a true pseudepigraphon, this may be fictionalized. So Bauckham writes, "Not only does the 'I' in a pseudepigraphal letter not refer to the real author, but 'you' does not refer to the real readers. The readers of a pseudepigraphal letter cannot read it as though they were being directly addressed either by the supposed author or by the real author (except in the special cases to be noted later); they must read as a letter written to other people, in the past" (Bauckham, "Pseudo-Apostolic Letters," 475).

[148] Davids, *The Letters of 2 Peter and Jude*, 259.

[149] Kelly suggests the possibility of an Asia Minor destination as well, though not firmly (Kelly, *The Epistles of Peter and of Jude*, 353).

Provinces of the Roman Empire
Molly Whittaker, Jews & Christians: Graeco-Roman Views (Cambridge: Cambridge University Press, 1984), xiii–xiv

arrogance toward the "unenlightened," interest in angels, denial of the apocalyptic, and licentiousness, though the letter lacks attention to the dualism typical of the movement.[150] Callan supports the view as well, though he acknowledges the challenges against it.[151] Following Wand and Smith,[152] Callan suggests the false teachers may have been Gnostic followers of Basilides, which would account for their "ethical libertinism" and lack of concern for the "salvation of the material world."[153]

---

[150] Michael Green, *2 Peter & Jude*, TNTC (Downers Grove: IVP Academic, 1987), 39–43.
[151] Terrence Callan, "The Second Letter of Peter, Josephus and Gnosticism," in *2 Peter and the Apocalypse of Peter: Towards a New Perspective*, ed. Jörg Frey, Matthijs Dulk, and Jan van der Watt (Leiden: Brill, 2019), 128–44.
[152] J. W. C. Wand, *The General Epistles of St. Peter and St. Jude* (London: Methuen, 1934), 142; Terence V. Smith, *Petrine Controversies in Early Christian: Attitudes Toward Peter in Christian Writings of the First Two Centuries*, WUNT 2.15 (Tübingen: Mohr Siebeck, 1985), 92–93.
[153] Callan, "The Second Letter of Peter, Josephus and Gnosticism," 140.

Neyrey has instead argued that Epicurean teaching was at the heart of the problem, a view which has won much approval in the scholarship on 2 Peter. As Neyrey describes,

> The ancient world knows Epicureans as those who deny the traditional doctrine of a provident Deity ("they pelt providence," Plutarch: *De Sera* 548C). Indeed, in literature ranging from Cicero's *Nat. Deor.*, Philo's *De Providentia*, and Seneca's *De Providentia* to Lactantius' *De Ira* and Origen's *Contra Celsum*, Epicureans were known in terms of their denial of divine judgment."[154]

Further, they denied "that a rational being providentially created the world and so can predict future events (Plutarch, *Defectu* 434D; *Pythiae* 414E; 418E; *Non Posse* 1100D-E; *Adv. Colotem* 1116E)."[155] At the center of Epicurius' thought was that life should be free from trouble and distress.[156] A provident deity who accounts for the rights and wrongs of humans and will bring divine judgment would not be consistent with such an ideology. Neyrey argues such a belief became widespread, to the extent that Josephus even categorizes the Sadducees as holding such similar doctrines.[157]

Neyrey notes four elements in the Epicurean argument against divine providence, which can also be found in certain Jewish polemics against theodicy: (1) the world was made by chance, (2) providence destroys moral freedom, (3) unfulfilled prophecy demonstrates the falsity of divine foreknowledge, and (4) the absence of justice on the wicked demonstrates God does not punish or reward.[158] Neyrey suggests 2 Peter's opponents were "either Epicureans, who rejected traditional theodicy, or 'scoffers' ... who espoused a similar deviant theology."[159]

David Burge has recently argued for reading 2 Peter as a letter opposing the "Second Sophistic," a descriptor emerging from Philostratus in his

---

[154] Neyrey, *2 Peter, Jude*, 122.
[155] Neyrey, *2 Peter, Jude*, 127; see also Jerome H. Neyrey, "The Form and Background of the Polemic in 2 Peter," *JBL* 99.3 (1980): 407–31.
[156] Diog. Laert. 10.128–32
[157] Neyrey, *2 Peter, Jude*, 124; cf. *B.J.* 2.164–65; see *Ant.* 13.173; 18.16–17; see also Davids, *The Letters of 2 Peter and Jude*, 134.
[158] Neyrey, "The Form and Background of the Polemic in 2 Peter," 409.
[159] Neyrey, *2 Peter, Jude*, 122. Largely following Neyrey, Witherington suggests, "The opponents of our author are (1) moral relativists; (2) those who reject early Christian eschatology, and especially the notion of the second coming; (3) those who seem to assume a steady-state universe, one that will certainly not end in final judgment or conflagration" (Witherington, *Letters for Hellenized Christians*, 278).

Vitae Sophistarum.¹⁶⁰ Building from the work of Bowersock¹⁶¹ and Winter,¹⁶² Burge argues the sophists, known for their rhetorical skills, ability to deceive and profit from such deceptions, use of mockery, and embrace of freedom over virtue, make for a more plausible connection with Peter's opponents.¹⁶³ Philo even complained of the sophists that "they are powerful at speaking, but are powerless (ἀδύνατος) to do what is best."¹⁶⁴ Burge points particularly to 2 Pet. 1:16 and the "sophistic myths" (σεσοφισμένοις μύθοις; his translation), which Peter denies reflect the apostolic testimony,¹⁶⁵ as well as to the criticisms of Philo against the sophists that they mocked the idea of a cosmic judgment or destruction.¹⁶⁶

Gene Green has argued instead for understanding the opponents in 2 Peter as evidencing philosophical eclecticism rather than a single philosophical movement in the ancient world. As Green describes,

> There were those who could be tagged "seed-pickers" (Acts 17:18), who snatched up philosophical scraps and joined them together in alliance. In fact, the Eclectic movement that flourished from the second century BC through the first century AD was known for this very practice (Diogenes Laertius, *Lives* 2.12; *OCD* 502).¹⁶⁷

Green, like Burge, recognizes the possible influences from both Epicureans and sophists, the latter particularly based on the overlapping evidence from Philo, but concludes instead that, due to their presence within the Christian community and incompatibility with any singular system, we should view them as having "an eclectic admixture of beliefs, not all of which can be melded into a harmonious whole."¹⁶⁸

The broader overlaps of the teaching of Peter's opponents and the diverse philosophical systems that seem to feed into them (primarily Epicureanism, Stoicism, and sophistry), make Green's suggestion appealing. We find the false teachers in 2 Peter not as outsiders who are

---

¹⁶⁰ David K. Burge, "A Sub-Christian Epistle? Appreciating 2 Peter as an Anti-Sophistic Polemic," *JSNT* 44.2 (2021): 310–32.
¹⁶¹ G. W. Bowersock, *Greek Sophists in the Roman Empire* (Oxford: Clarendon Press, 1969).
¹⁶² Bruce W. Winter, "Is Paul among the Sophists?," *RTR* 53.1 (1994): 28–38; *Philo and Paul among the Sophists* (Grand Rapids: Eerdmans, 2002).
¹⁶³ Burge, "A Sub-Christian Epistle?," 314–18.
¹⁶⁴ Philo, *Cong.*, 57.
¹⁶⁵ Burge, "A Sub-Christian Epistle?," 320–22.
¹⁶⁶ Burge, "A Sub-Christian Epistle?," 322–23, cf. Philo, *Opif.*, 158; *Aet.* 20–24.
¹⁶⁷ Green, *Jude and 2 Peter*, 157.
¹⁶⁸ Green, *Jude and 2 Peter*, 328.

teaching against the apostolic tradition, but insiders who had been seen as part of the Christian community. They have come to deny not only the return of Jesus and his future judgment (cf. 3:8–13), along with Christian ethical teachings (cf. 2:10–19), and even their own redemption (2:1). The false teachers are former believers who were viewed as converts and appear to have even been present at the observance of the Eucharist (cf. 2:13) but have now strayed from the path of the kingdom (cf. 2:2–22) and are now attempting to take others along with them (cf. 2:18–19). This, in part, separates them from the opponents in Jude, who are painted as outsiders. Furthermore, unlike Jude, a central concern of 2 Peter is the denial of the false teachers of the παρουσία.[169] As Watson notes, Peter "considers their doctrine and deeds equivalent to a denial of Christianity, a return to the bondage to sin (2:2, 15, 19–22), and a guarantee of destruction (2:1, 3, 4–10a, 12; 3:7; cf. 2:17)."[170] This may explain the strong agitation that comes across in the tone of the letter, since these false teachers should "know better" and formerly confessed the things which they now deny. These details are clearer in the letter, while its background and setting still lack a consensus due to the limited nature of the internal evidence.

SOCIAL DYNAMICS

Given that the ancient world was much different than our own, a further area of needed reflection to properly contextualize 2 Peter are the different social dynamics that existed in the first-century Greco-Roman world. Neyrey, for example, denotes five major areas of social concern that are relevant to the author and audience of 2 Peter: (1) honor and shame, (2) patron-client relations, (3) purity and pollution, (4) the physical body, and (5) group-oriented society,[171] each of which bears some importance for interpreting the text. We might add here the function of "religion" in the ancient world along with the tensions that existed between Jews and Gentiles as topics of relevance to 2 Peter.

The culture of the first-century Mediterranean world existed within the framework of honor-shame. The first-century world was stratified, with

---

[169] Green, 2 Peter & Jude, 43.
[170] Watson, Invention, Arrangement, and Style, 82.
[171] See Neyrey, 2 Peter, Jude, 2–20.

cultural elites and nobles wielding significant cultural power and laborers, outcasts, and slaves, who constituted the majority of the population, filling out the bottom of the social hierarchy. The early Christian movement, though appearing to be significantly composed of the lower echelons of the social stratum, also contained wealthy merchants and even some figures of political significance (as Paul's letters to the Romans and Corinthians indicate). Honor functioned as "the public affirmation of a person's value by his or her peers," while shame constituted "the loss of honour due one's social position or through actions that cause one to lose face."[172] Rhetorical exchanges often became contests of honor and shame, and honor and shame also deeply connected to the collective nature of the first century world.[173]

The ancient Mediterranean world was as a group-focused or collectivist culture in contrast to the kind of individualism that dominates in the late-modern Western world. This is perhaps most clearly illustrated in the way in which kinship served as a central focal point of life for those in the first century. A kind of stratification can again be noticed here, where the *paterfamilias* would typically serve a "ruling" function in the household, with children and slaves serving ancillary positions in the home. Marriage in the ancient world often functioned for the benefit of the family rather than for personal happiness, though if both could be achieved that may be seen as ideal. For a group-oriented society, one's personal desires were necessarily subordinated to the goal of the larger group, and those who acted otherwise would be a source of shame in the community.[174]

Related further was the patron-client system, which connected both to the dynamics of honor-shame and the collectivist nature of culture. Here a patron would provide "various forms of assistance, benefaction, or protection" and the client "was expected to express gratitude and to behave in certain supportive ways toward the patron."[175] The client thus benefited from the generosity, be it social, financial, or some combination thereof, while the patron would expect their reputation to be enhanced by the public praises of their clients. A major concern of the collectivism of the

---

[172] Wright and Bird, *The New Testament in Its World*, 114.
[173] See Neyrey, *2 Peter, Jude*, 3–7.
[174] See Neyrey, *2 Peter, Jude*, 18.
[175] Donald A. Hagner, *The New Testament: A Historical and Theological Introduction* (Grand Rapids: Baker Academic, 2012), 49.

ancient world was also to determine group boundaries, which served to demarcate certain social boundaries for everyday life.[176]

Purity and pollution also serve as important categories of social interaction in the first century. In a Jewish context, this may be seen in the purity practices associated with cleanness/uncleanness in relation to sacred space but could extend also to things like washing and meals. While uncleanness would not necessarily constitute "sin," one could also speak of a kind of moral purity that differed from ritual purification. Cultic ritual frequently took on a place of prominence in the practice of "religion" in the ancient world.[177] Religious rituals were thus strongly embodied matters, and the care of the physical body, both in relation to cultic and moral purity, was a matter of significant importance.[178]

We might also point out the broader dynamics between the Jewish and Greco-Roman worlds that existed. The Hellenization of the ancient world is widely discussed and generally taken for granted. While at times the Jewish and Greco-Roman worlds are discussed as if they are two worlds with firm boundaries, the realities are that Hellenism influenced Jewish culture, even in Judea, if nothing else at the level of language and communication. While urban areas would have fostered more thorough and dynamic contexts for culture influence, there existed nonetheless a "continuum from more to less Hellenistic encroachment."[179] As a result, a diversity of perspectives existed within Judaism, and differing postures toward cultural influence were taken. Scholars thus often speak now of the "Judaisms" of the ancient world, reflecting the reality that a diversity of perspectives existed within the Jewish world on various matters of belief and practice. Even in noting merely the Hellenistic style and the presence of Jewish apocalypticism in the letter, 2 Peter very clearly illustrates the collision that can be seen between these two worlds in the first century.

---

[176] Paul J. Achtemeier, Joel B. Green, and Marianne Meye Thompson, *Introducing the New Testament: Its Literature and Theology* (Grand Rapids: Eerdmans, 2001), 49. See also Neyrey, *2 Peter, Jude*, 7–10.

[177] Bird and Wright suggest five major contrasts of ancient and modern religion: "1. Concern with the present life rather than with an afterlife .... 2) Focus on cultic ritual rather than on doctrinal beliefs .... 3) No secularism with a separation of religion and state .... 4) Pluralism but not necessarily tolerance" (Wright and Bird, *The New Testament in Its World*, 153–58).

[178] See Neyrey, *2 Peter, Jude*, 10–17.

[179] Achtemeier et al., *Introducing the New Testament*, 25.

We will attend to these various dimensions of the social and cultural realities of the first-century Mediterranean world as they relate to the argument of the overall letter of 2 Peter.

2 PETER AS STORY

An additional area of interpretive insight that has emerged in recent decades is that of narrative interpretation. While 2 Peter is not a narrative text but a letter, we might still consider the "storied" elements of such a work. As Wright has argued, a significant dimension of understanding the question of "worldview" is the "element of story."[180] Concerning 2 Peter specifically, Miller suggests, "This document portrays a symbolic narrative world and attempts to persuade its auditors to locate themselves within it."[181] While "narrative theology" and "narrative interpretation" have various methods through which they are approached,[182] we can situate the story of 2 Peter in several different ways. First, one might read 2 Peter with various connections to a "metanarrative," which examines major moments of significance in the canonical story. In general, stories are structured to examine a central conflict that builds to a point of climax and then falls toward a resolution (e.g., Creation, Fall [conflict], Covenants, Christ and the Kingdom [climax], New Creation [resolution]).[183] Given that 2 Peter falls within this metanarrative, we can read it as existing between the climax and resolution of the Christian story (or what has often been called the "now" and "not yet"). Wall suggests "four pivotal events" in 1 and 2 Peter, which he labels as follows: promise of restoration, arrival of Jesus who fulfills the promise, the church as recipients of God's salvation, the

---

[180] N. T. Wright, *The New Testament and the People of God*, Christian Origins and the Question of God, vol. 1 (Minneapolis: Fortress Press, 1992), 32.

[181] James C. Miller, "The Sociological Category of 'Collective Identity' and Its Implications for Understanding Second Peter," in *Reading Second Peter with New Eyes: Methodological Reassessments of the Letter of Second Peter*, ed. Robert L. Webb and Duane F. Watson (London: Bloomsbury, 2010), 148.

[182] For a brief overview, see Craig G. Bartholomew and Michael W. Goheen, "Story and Biblical Theology," in *Out of Egypt: Biblical Theology and Biblical Interpretation*, ed. Craig Bartholomew, Mary Healy, Karl Moller, and Robin Parry (Grand Rapids: Zondervan, 2004), 146.

[183] See also Joel B. Green, "Narrating the Gospel in 1 and 2 Peter," *Interpretation* 60.3 (2006): 262–77.

church as witness to final consummation.[184] Each of these appears in the letter of 2 Peter, though its emphasis is upon the church's experience of salvation and the coming return and judgment of Christ, which ushers in the final consummation. There is thus both a sense of urgency and anticipation that the narrative features of 2 Peter create.

Davids, also examining the "big picture" of the narrative of 2 Peter, suggests, "There are two competing narratives informing 2 Peter. The first is the implied narrative of the Roman Empire ... [which] is challenged and replaced by an alternative implied narrative."[185] As Davids describes, the kingdom of God, which Christ rules as Sovereign, replaces in this implied narrative the Roman empire, with Caesar as Sovereign. While anti-imperial rhetoric is not prominent in the text, in its context, 2 Peter contrasts the ways of the eternal kingdom with the corruptions of the world/empire, which are represented chiefly in the latter's absence of divine virtue and manifest in a variety of ungodly behaviors.

Another means of examining narrative in 2 Peter would be to examine the unique story which it tells for itself. Here Miller observes:

From 2 Peter itself, we can describe the immediate cause and purpose of the letter as follows. Peter wrote to counter the effects of a group he labels "false teachers" (ψευδοδιδάσκαλοι; 2.1), describes as "scoffers" (ἐμπαῖκται; 3.3), and compares with "false prophets" (ψευδοπροφῆται; 2.1). These teachers apparently understood themselves, and were understood by Peter's auditors, as followers of Christ, though Peter saw them as having turned from the faith (2.20–22). Peter's instructions indicate these people were an ongoing influence among the Christian group(s) to whom the letter was addressed. He entertained some level of concern that the false teachers might lead his hearers astray. He therefore urged them, "Guard yourselves lest you be led astray by these lawless people and lose your own stability" (3.17). These persons' teachings provoked an impassioned response from Peter at two points. First, they denied any final judgment (3.3–9). Second, and consequently, they advocated a libertine approach to moral issues (2.2, 10–19).[186]

---

[184] Robert W. Wall, "The Canonical Function of 2 Peter," *Biblical Interpretation* 9.1 (2001): 68.
[185] Davids, *The Letters of 2 Peter and Jude*, 154.
[186] Miller, "The Sociological Category of 'Collective Identity,'" 159. See also Ruth Anne Reese, "Narrative Method and the Letter of Second Peter," in *Reading Second Peter with New Eyes: Methodological Reassessments of the Letter of Second Peter*, ed. Robert L. Webb and Duane F. Watson (London: Bloomsbury, 2010), 130–32.

Combining Miller's analysis to the structure of narrative from Wall, we can summarize 2 Peter's narrative as follows: *conflict* (false teachers: flawed ethics and denial of Jesus' return), *climax* (condemnation and judgment of teachers), and *resolution* (future return and judgment of Christ). For the narrative of 2 Peter, the story remains unresolved as the principal conflict described (the opposition of the false teachers and the conflict of Christian living with the corruptions of the world) will not find its resolution until the *parousia*, wherein the false teachers will be judged and the beloved of God transformed. The unresolved nature of the conflict can be attributed, in part, to the epistolary nature of the work. As Reese notes, in an epistle, we are listening in on one side of a conversation and thus have a limited view of the situation being addressed. A letter is thus, a "slice of bread not the whole loaf,"[187] and so the story that can be told as a result will by necessity be incomplete. We are left to wonder what became of these believers after receiving this letter. Were they reinvigorated in their faith, or did they succumb to the corrupting influence of the false teachers? Were the false teachers removed from the community, or did they grow in their influence? The story ends on a cliff hanger, which we ultimately cannot resolve, though Peter points us forward to the bigger picture and the ultimate resolution of all stories which is to come.

2 PETER AS CHRISTIAN SCRIPTURE

As a part of the Christian canon, 2 Peter does not exist as an isolated text only relevant to a past historical moment. Reading 2 Peter as Christian Scripture means understanding the text to have a place in a larger web of relationships with the canonical texts.[188] In Protestant perspective, this means seeing its connections to the other sixty-five books of the canon, though the intertextual relationships of this text also necessarily take us outside of that canonical boundary. While our goal should always be to understand a text on its own terms and in light of its own authorship, situation, rhetorical strategy, structure, and argument, Christian readers must also think about its canonical relationship. Such thinking in part

---

[187] Reese, "Narrative Method and the Letter of Second Peter," 146.
[188] Here, see Wall, "The Canonical Function of 2 Peter," 64–81.

raises questions about what the canon is and what implications these relationships have for us understanding the canon as Scripture.

2 Peter and Old Testament Literature

While 2 Peter contains some obvious connections to other New Testament texts (e.g., the Transfiguration and various teachings on the return of Christ), its relationship to the Old Testament has raised questions, particularly when compared with 1 Peter. Bauckham, for example, has stated "there is virtually no direct contact between 2 Peter and the Hebrew Scriptures."[189] By direct, Bauckham appears to be referring to quotations of the Old Testament, and on this matter, his assessment is generally correct. The lack of quotations does not, however, indicate an absence of integration of the Old Testament into the letter, and Bauckham himself finds nearly twenty allusions to the Old Testament in 2 Peter in addition to its interactions with noncanonical Jewish texts.[190] He cites probable allusions in 2 Peter 1:17–18 (Ps 2:6–7); 1:19 (Num. 24:17); 2:2 (Isa. 52:5); 2:5 (Gen. 6:17); 2:6 (Gen. 19:29); 2:15–16 (Num. 22:21–35); 2:22 (Prov. 26:11); 3:5 (Gen. 1:1); 3:8 (Ps. 90:4 [LXX 89:4]); 3:9 (Hab. 2:3); 3:10–12 (Isa. 34:4); 3:12 (Isa. 60:22); 3:12–14 (Hab. 2:3); 3:13 (Isa. 65:17),[191] and additional possible allusions in 2 Peter 1:11 (Dan. 7:27); 1:17 (Ps. 8:5 [LXX 6]); Dan. 7:14); 1:19 (Cant. 2:17).[192]

The author of 2 Peter is also quite well acquainted with various Jewish traditions concerning the interpretation of the Old Testament. The significant influence of Jewish textual traditions are present throughout the letter. This indicates, as Werse summarizes, that 2 Peter interprets "several early Jewish literary themes and traditions through interpretive lenses similar to those found in many later pseudepigraphical works."[193] Texts like *1 Enoch*, *Assumption of Moses*, *Testament of the Twelve Patriarchs*, Wisdom of Solomon, and *Sibylline Oracles*, along with traditions found in Philo, Josephus, and the rabbinic writings, all have resonances with different

---

[189] Davids, *The Letters of 2 Peter and Jude*, 129.
[190] Bauckham, *Jude–2 Peter*, 138–40.
[191] Bauckham, *Jude–2 Peter*, 138.
[192] Bauckham, *Jude–2 Peter*, 138.
[193] Nicholas R. Werse, "Second Temple Jewish Literary Traditions in 2 Peter," *CBQ* 78 (2016): 129. See also Peter H. Davids, "What Glasses Are You Wearing? Reading Hebrew Narratives through Second Temple Lenses," *JETS* 55.4 (2012): 763–71.

aspects of the letter. While the letter is often analyzed for its Hellenistic features, it is well informed by the world of Second Temple Judaism as well, and the heavy integration of such Jewish interpretative lenses and traditions seem to make the text more likely the product of the first century than later Christianity.

2 Peter, Pseudonymity, and Truth

Though 2 Peter traveled a difficult path toward canonical acceptance, its acceptance was universal by the fourth century. I have argued that it seems historically impossible with the current data to come to a definitive conclusion about the authorship of this text and have suggested that authenticity within the lifetime of Peter is a possibility, though it faces certain challenges. It is also historically possible, and presently the majority view, that the text was written after Peter's death, whether by an authorized companion or an unacquainted pseudepigrapher. If this is the case, certain challenges arise to a Christian conception of Scripture, particularly those who would hold to a traditional view of the authorship of 2 Peter in relation to a belief in the truthfulness and reliability of the text.

The question pursued here in light of the majority position on authorship is what theological implications emerge when the text is approached as one written in Peter's name but not during the life of, or even by the knowledge of, the apostle. In examining these implications, particularly for how 2 Peter, and other such texts, might function in the life of the church, the theological discussions surrounding canonical inspiration and inerrancy are necessary for discussion.[194]

While the historic position of the church has held that the texts of Scripture are indeed inspired by God, true in what they affirm, and authoritative for the life of the church, these ideas have not taken on uniform or universal expression. While the early church creedalized its teachings on the gospel, Christology, Trinity, and related doctrines, no such creedalization occurred for the doctrine of Scripture. Most theological accounts of inspiration begin with two major texts: 2 Timothy 3:16 and

---

[194] I am aware of hesitations to continuing using this term in light of its many controversies and the "death by qualification" that often comes with it. I use the term here simply in reference to the belief that Scripture, as inspired, is a trustworthy, true, and reliable communication from God to his people.

2 Peter 1:20.[195] These texts state that Scripture is God-breathed, useful for instruction, not the result of a prophet's own independent thought, and comes about by the moving of the Holy Spirit. These affirmations form much of the basis of a Christian doctrine of inspiration.

The early church established much of its discussion of Scripture in relation to its doctrine of God. Cyril of Alexandria affirmed, "It is impossible for God to speak falsely,"[196] meaning that Scripture, being produced of divine direction, likewise must be true. Augustine, in criticizing Jerome's opinion that God could use deception for good purposes, stated, "If so-called white lies are permitted in the Holy Scriptures, what authority can these writings then have?"[197] This line of thought would be echoed later by Calvin, who wrote of 2 Peter specifically, that were 2 Peter pseudonymous, this would make it "a fiction unworthy of a minister of Christ, to have impersonated another individual."[198] Though the early church did not codify a philosophical framework for how inspiration or inerrancy occurred in the divine communicative act, it affirmed that the text was inspired by God and therefore true and authoritative.[199]

While biblical scholars have long wrestled with questions of authorship, textual revision, canon formation, and the copying and preserving of texts, theologians at times formulate their doctrines of Scripture without significant attention to these issues.[200] A model of inspiration that accurately represents the nature of Scripture, must, however, consider how Scripture was produced. One obvious challenge here is that Scripture itself does not attest to a uniform model of its production. Many accounts of inspiration describe the process primarily in terms of a single-author model rather than seeing Scripture's

---

[195] Farkasfalvy recognizes, "It is worth noting ... that the two most important New Testament passages about inspiration ... belong to posthumous ("pseudepigraphic") apostolic letters ... Second Timothy and Second Peter." (Denis Farkasfalvy, *Inspiration & Interpretation: A Theological Introduction to Sacred Scripture* [Washington, DC: Catholic University of America Press, 2010], 59).

[196] Cyril of Alexandria, *Commentary on Isaiah* 1:2–3; see *Cyril of Alexandria: Commentary on Isaiah: Vol. 1: Chapters 1–14*, trans. Robert C. Hill (Brooline: Holy Cross Orthodox, 2008), 21.

[197] Augustine, *Epistle* 40.3; see Carolinne White, *The Correspondence (394–419) between Jerome and Augustine of Hippo* (Lewiston: Mellen, 1990), 76.

[198] John Calvin, *Catholic Epistles*, 363.

[199] See Michael Graves, *The Inspiration and Interpretation of Scripture: What the Early Church Can Teach Us* (Grand Rapids: Eerdmans, 2014), 104–5.

[200] For an attempt to do so, see John H. Walton, *The Lost World of Scripture: Ancient Literary Culture and Biblical Authority* (Downers Grove: IVP Academic, 2013).

production as a communal enterprise.²⁰¹ But for much of Scripture's content, this simply does not work. Consider, for example, the Psalter, in which dozens of poems and hymns were composed, largely independently of one another, and then gathered and shaped into a final collection, the final form of which influences its interpretation. Proverbs 25:1ff. describes itself as a compilation of proverbs of Solomon, compiled by the "men of Hezekiah, king of Judah," whose arrangement of these statements would have undoubtedly shaped their future interpretation. The Synoptic Gospels are likewise complicated due to some type of literary relationship existing between them in which they borrowed from and edited one another in the compositional process. The Gospel of John describes itself as the result of a collective literary effort in some respects (e.g., John 1:14, 16; 21:24). Furthermore, Paul, in his letters, often identifies coauthors and scribes who co-labored with him in the process of production (e.g., Rom. 16:22; Phil. 1:1; Col. 1:1; 1 Thess. 1:1; 2 Thess. 1:1). If Paul is considered the only one inspired, and yet speaks of a collective process of writing, what would this entail for the resulting product? Such processes involve multiple "minds," "wills," "hands," and even "editions" (cf. Jer. 36:32), complicating what we might mean when we discuss the divine influence upon the production of a text.

As John Frame notes, there are instances in Scripture where something like dictation is described, in which God gives a message to a prophet, and they subsequently write it down (cf. Ex. 24:27; Jer. 36:4).²⁰² Most theologians today, however, shy away from a dictation or mechanistic model of inspiration in general since this does not seem to adequately account for what all of Scripture is.²⁰³ What is opted for instead is something referenced as "organic inspiration" (cf. Bavinck),²⁰⁴ "concursive activity" (cf. Packer),²⁰⁵ or "deputized speech" (cf. Wolterstorff).²⁰⁶

---

[201] On this matter, see Stephen B. Chapman, "Reclaiming Inspiration for the Bible," in *Canon and Biblical Interpretation*, ed. Craig Bartholomew et al. [Grand Rapids: Zondervan, 2006], 182).
[202] John M. Frame, *The Doctrine of the Word of God, A Theology of Lordship*, vol. 4 (Philipsburg: P&R, 2010), 141.
[203] Frame, *The Doctrine of the Word of God*, 142.
[204] Herman Bavinck, *Reformed Dogmatics*, vol. 1 (Grand Rapids: Baker, 2003), 387–448.
[205] J. I. Packer, *"Fundamentalism" and the Word of God* (Grand Rapids: Eerdmans, 1958), 80–81.
[206] Nicholas Wolterstorff, *Divine Discourse: Philosophical Reflections on the Claim that God Speaks* (Cambridge: Cambridge University Press, 1995), 46–52.

On these models, God uses the intellect, experiences, style, and personality of the authors in such a way that preserves and even maximizes their own agency in the process.[207] These approaches also often highlight that the text is inspired in both a *verbal* and a *plenary* sense, meaning that the very words of Scripture are inspired, not just their ideas, and that all of Scripture in its fulness should be viewed as the result of this inspiration.[208]

More recent work in inspiration has sought to integrate the communal dimensions of its production within a formulation of the doctrine. Farkasfalvy, for example, suggests "'biblical inspiration' should be conceived as a divine grace guiding all individuals involved in the process and bringing about as its final product the canonical text of the book in question."[209] Likewise, Bloesch articulates that the guidance of the biblical prophets to act as witnesses to revelation encapsulates "all preachers, writers and editors in biblical history who were made the unique instruments of God's self-revealing action."[210] Stephen Chapman offers a "canonically oriented view of inspiration … [which] sees the divine-human encounter as occurring over a lengthier period of time and as including more people than just one author alone."[211]

A communal approach to inspiration, however, raises concerns for some theologians about where the authority and hermeneutical grounding for interpretation might lie. For example, Carl Henry, in his critique of Childs' canonical approach, suggested, "Apostolicity is a more compelling principle than dialectical process to account for the reception of the canonical books as authoritative."[212] For Henry, if the apostles are not involved directly, or perhaps even exclusively, in producing these texts, the textual reliability become suspect. Chapman instead argues that

---

[207] Kevin J. Vanhoozer, *The Drama of Doctrine: A Canonical Linguistic Approach to Christian Doctrine* (Philadelphia: Westminster John Knox Press, 2005), 228.

[208] See Frame, *The Doctrine of the Word of God*, 143.

[209] Farkasfalvy, *Inspiration & Interpretation*, 211. As he continues, "The Catholic truth about the Bible lies in an equal affirmation of its divine and human components, 'unconfused and inseparable,' allowing no material distinction between the parts to be assigned either solely to God or solely to the human author" (Farkasfalvy, *Inspiration & Interpretation*, 219).

[210] Donald Bloesch, *Holy Scripture: Revelation, Inspiration, & Interpretation* (Downers Grove: IVP Academic, 2005), 119-20.

[211] Chapman, "Reclaiming Inspiration for the Bible," 172.

[212] Carl H. F. Henry, "Canonical Theology: An Evangelical Appraisal." *Scottish Bulletin of Evangelical Theology* 8 (Autumn 1990): 86.

"attention to the canon, rather than weakening the notion of inspiration, actually strengthens it by returning to a reformulated version of what still might be termed 'verbal' inspiration – i.e. that the literary features of the text are inspired, too, and not just the concepts."[213] A robust view of the inspiration and reliability of the text must account for what the texts say about their processes of origination.

An obvious correlation exists between one's formulation of inspiration and what they might hold concerning the "degree" of the inerrancy of the text. If the concepts are inspired but not the words, then the concepts are true and reliable but not necessarily every detail. This is at times referred to as a "limited" view of inerrancy, meaning Scripture is reliable in its theological ideas, and particularly those relevant for salvation, but not necessarily in relation to every word of its content.[214] This is usually contrasted to a "full" sense of inerrancy, in which Scripture is seen as true and reliable in all matters on which it speaks.[215] It is often in these matters of qualification that approaches and definitions to inerrancy diverge.

Paul Feinberg, for example, defines inerrancy as follows:

Inerrancy means that when all facts are known, the Scriptures in their original autographs and properly interpreted will be shown to be wholly true in everything that they affirm, whether that has to do with doctrine or morality or with the social, physical, or life sciences.[216]

David Dockery defines the doctrine accordingly:

When all the facts are known, the Bible (in its original writings) properly interpreted in light of which culture and communication means had developed by the time of its composition will be shown to be completely true (and therefore not false) in all that it affirms, to the degree of precision intended by the author, in all matters relating to God and his creation.[217]

Dockery, while similar to Feinberg in many respects, emphasizes the cultural situatedness of the text, and the limitations that it entails, as well

---

[213] Chapman, "Reclaiming Inspiration for the Bible," 194.
[214] This seems to reflect the Catholic position in inerrancy outlined in the Vatican II document Dei Verbum 11.
[215] This would be the position outlined in the Chicago Statement on Biblical Inerrancy.
[216] Paul D. Feinberg, "The Meaning of Inerrancy," in *Inerrancy*, ed. Norman L. Geisler (Grand Rapids: Zondervan, 1980), 294.
[217] David Dockery, *Christian Scripture: An Evangelical Perspective on Inspiration, Authority, and Interpretation* (Nashville: Broadman & Holman, 1995), 64.

as the intention of the authors ("degree of precision"). Both Feinberg and Dockery offer articulations of a form of "full" inerrancy. In contrast, Bloesch defines inerrancy as "the conformity of what is written to the dictates of the Spirit regarding the will and purpose of God ... not conformity of everything that is written in Scripture to the facts of world history or science."[218] Bloesch's definition, more akin to a limited sense of inerrancy, could make allowance, for example, of historical error being present in the text, though not error in the divine revelation that the text communicates. Thus, the spectrum of definitions for both inspiration and inerrancy must be kept in mind while considering the theological implications that might result from the potential pseudonymous authorship of 2 Peter.

For limited accounts of inerrancy, the issue of 2 Peter's authorship may be irrelevant. The author could be erroneously identified as Peter, but the divine revelation that the text communicates could still be accurate and reliable. For those who might affirm a full view of the inerrant nature of Scripture, several further questions must be addressed. For example, in identifying its author as "Peter," would a pseudonymously composed 2 Peter necessarily intend to deceive its audience? This is by no means a straightforward question since it deals with the intentions and motivations of the author, things that we cannot fully access. At face value, there appears to be no need to presuppose deceptive intent in an author utilizing Peter's identity in the composition of the letter, and there are pseudonymous texts thar are written with nondeceptive motivations.[219] Second Peter's contents appear to offer a faithful representation of the apostolic message and do not signal any obvious deceptive intent.

Wolterstorff's concept of "deputized speech" may establish a means by which the issue of pseudonymity and "deception" may be addressed. Wolterstorff uses the concept of "deputized speech" as a means of describing how human authors may speak for God and such speaking be legitimate.[220] In this framework for divine inspiration, God's authorization of the human agent to speak on God's behalf is what legitimizes the speech.

---

[218] Bloesch, *Holy Scripture*, 107.
[219] See again Bruce M. Metzger, "Literary Forgeries and Canonical Pseudepigrapha," *JBL* 92 (1972): 5–12.
[220] Wolterstorff, *Divine Discourse*, 41–52.

By analogy, it would not be unreasonable for a human author to speak for another human in a deputized manner and that speaking be legitimate. Just as God authorizes prophets to speak in his name and on his behalf, it is possible for an associate of Peter to write in Peter's name, even after his death, and produce a faithful and legitimate speech-act on Peter's behalf. This need not involve deception on the part of the author if the author's discourse is somehow "deputized," whether formally or informally, and is a faithful representation of Peter's teachings. It may be that such an individual received such an authorization directly from Peter prior to his death, or even was related to Peter in such a way that they were believed to represent his thought accurately after his passing. Such scenarios fit within the scope of Metzger's taxonomy of pseudonymity previously discussed.[221] While our current evidence does not allow us to conclude that this was indeed the case in the production of 2 Peter, it lies within the realm of possibility. Given its consistency with apostolic teaching, it may indeed be reasonable to assume that, if "pseudonymous," the text arose from someone with direct knowledge of Peter's teaching, whose goal was to apply his teachings to the present situation. This, it would seem, undercuts the major issue for inspiration and inerrancy as it relates to pseudonymity, since the motive of deception or forgery would be nullified, and the possibility of deputized speech may exist.[222]

The recognition of a text as pseudonymous does not necessarily discount it as inspired, true, and authoritative Scripture. This is a possible outcome but not a necessary one. As Stephen Evans argues, "It is possible that some of the books attributed to apostles or close associates of apostles were not in fact written by those people, but yet that God determined that those particular writings were among the writings that God designated as authoritative revelation."[223] Further, Gempf suggests,

We must not take the point or view that anyone who thinks there are pseudonymous books in the NT *necessarily* has something wrong with their view of biblical authority. The books of the Bible were written by specific human beings in specific cultural settings. Being sensitive to these origins, even when features of them

---

[221] Metzger, "Literary Forgeries and Canonical Pseudepigrapha," 5–12.
[222] Perhaps here the name of pseudonymity itself needs reworking as it implies deception.
[223] C. Stephen Evans, "Canonicity, Apostolicity, and Biblical Authority," in *Canon and Biblical Interpretation*, ed. Craig Bartholomew et al. (Grand Rapids: Zondervan, 2006), 157.

appear to conflict with our own cultural expectations, enhances rather than detracts from our understanding of how the Holy Spirit used these people and situations to bring us the book we know as Holy Scripture.[224]

While such a work composed with deceptive intent would contradict a traditional understanding of Scripture, deceptive intent need not necessarily be attached to such works. The evaluation of the presence of deception must be taken on a case-by-case basis, since not all works written pseudonymously had the intention to deceive or mislead.

In the conversation of the relation between inspiration, inerrancy, and pseudonymity, it seems what would challenge at least some Christian conceptions of the truth of Scripture would be for 2 Peter, or any disputed text, to be written in an apostle's name either by someone not authorized to do so or by someone with malicious or deceptive intent. While seeing 2 Peter as a testament may not be a sufficient means by which to hold together pseudonymity and the inspiration and inerrancy of the text, this does not necessarily mean such an affirmation is not possible through other means. The concept of "deputized speech" offers one such possibility for seeing "pseudonymous" texts as legitimate representations of apostolic thought by later authors.

Pseudonymity presents some real theological challenges for the use of Scripture in the life of the church. To affirm that God speaks to his people in Scripture is to likewise understand that the kind of speech Scripture offers says something about what kind of god God is. While truthfulness is not the only characteristic relevant to this discussion, it is a significant one. Can we take God at his word? Does he tell us the truth? Can we read Scripture with confidence in its teachings? These questions, among others, are raised by the question of pseudonymity in Scripture, and in wrestling with pseudonymity, they ought not be a mere afterthought, especially when the conversation intersects with ecclesial life. Many parishioners would be quite surprised, if not disturbed, to hear discussions of pseudonymity in the New Testament among scholars. While such conversations are taken for granted in the academy, it should not be assumed they are well known in local churches. As a result, care must be taken not to weaken the confidence of congregations either in the Scriptures or in the character of

---

[224] Conrad Gempf, "Pseudonymity and the New Testament," *Themelios*, 17.2 (1992): 8–10.

God as a result of such discussions, and the theological implications must be a part of the conversation of pseudonymity when it intersects with ecclesial life.

The correspondence of Scripture's claims to reality is also not the only measure of Scripture's reliability. As Kärkkäinen argues, Scripture can neither be reduced to a set of true propositions, nor can it be divorced from having a propositional nature. It is propositional, relational, and transformative.[225] Orr for example, suggested,

> Proof of the inspiration of the Bible ... is to be found in the life-giving effects which that message has produced ..... It leads to God and Christ; it gives light on the deepest problems of life, death, and eternity; it discovers the way of deliverance from sin; it makes men new creatures; it furnishes the man of God completely for every good work.[226]

The *telos* of Scripture is not merely the conveyance of accurate information but the transformation of the person into the image of Christ. In affirming the inspiration, truthfulness, and authority of 2 Peter as Scripture, its ultimate *telos* must likewise not be an afterthought either from a theological perspective or from the assessment of the text itself. It is perhaps here that our conversation must eventually arrive when questions of pseudonymity or other critical issues in Scripture come about in the life of the church. God is not simply a God who gives us things to know but who invites us into life with himself. Second Peter affirms this notion throughout the text, and quite prominently in 2 Peter 1:3-4, where Peter sees the ultimate goal for humans as partaking in the life of God. Dealing with uncertainty in both life and scholarship ultimately demands our trust, even in the midst of difficulties and challenges, something with which the author of 2 Peter was also well-acquainted. In 2 Peter 1:5-9, the author admonishes his audience to pursue goodness, knowledge, self-control, perseverance, godliness, and love. Recognizing that transformative communion with God is the ultimate goal for the human life communicated by Scripture does not make the truthfulness and reliability of the text irrelevant. But the significance of that question must not overshadow the ultimate purpose of Scripture, which is to draw us into life with the Triune God.

---

[225] Veli-Matti Kärkkäinen, *Trinity and Revelation, A Constructive Christian Theology for the Pluralist World*, vol. 2 (Grand Rapids: Eerdmans, 2014), 71-72.
[226] James Orr, *Revelation and Inspiration*, (New York: Scribner's, 1910), 217-18.

Interpreting 2 Peter

The approach of this volume will be intentionally integrative of a variety of methods of textual analysis and reflection as discussed above. In addition to examining traditional interpretive dimensions such as social, cultural, grammatical, and historical matters, this commentary will seek to situate 2 Peter within the world of the literature of the period, informed both by Greco-Roman and Jewish works. It will also seek to situate the letter canonically, attending to both intertextual connections made by the text, as well as theological reverberations from its teaching to other places in Christian Scripture. Furthermore, in addition to attending to grammatical and syntactical matters in the Greek text, this commentary will integrate insights from Discourse Analysis, a discipline that analyzes Greek texts through the utilization of the insights of linguistics. An additional means of analysis and consideration will come from the overlap of the rhetoric of the letter and narrative theology, which can both provide new and fruitful angles of reflection on the text. Finally, given that such commentaries are quite often read by ministers, both ordained and laity, concerns related to the Christian life and ministry will also be given attention in this work. Much of the foundations of these different layers of textual and interpretive analysis have been laid in the introductory sections, which will inform the analysis of the text which follows.

SUGGESTED READINGS

Below are the major works on 2 Peter that ought to inform one's study of the text. This commentary has been greatly informed by these and other texts, though I consider those listed here as essential for analysis of this letter.

Bauckham, Richard J. *Jude, 2 Peter*. Word Biblical Commentary, vol. 50. Waco: Word Books, 1983.
Davids, Peter H. *The Letters of 2 Peter and Jude*. The Pillar New Testament Commentary. Grand Rapids: Eerdmans, 2006.
Frey, Jörg. *The Letter of Jude and the Second Letter of Peter: A Theological Commentary*. Waco: Baylor University Press, 2018.
Green, Gene L. *Jude and 2 Peter*. Baker Exegetical Commentary on the New Testament. Grand Rapids: Baker Academic, 2008.
Neyrey, Jerome H. *2 Peter, Jude: A New Translation with Introduction and Commentary*. The Anchor Yale Bible, vol. 37C. New Haven: Yale University Press, 1993.
Watson, Duane Frederick. *Invention, Arrangement, and Style: Rhetorical Criticism of Jude and 2 Peter*. SBL Dissertation Series, 104. Atlanta: Scholars Press, 1988.
Witherington III, Ben. *Letters and Homilies for Hellenized Christians: A Socio-Rhetorical Commentary on 1–2 Peter*, vol. 2. Downers Grove: IVP Academic, 2007.

Commentary

Second Peter opens with a brief greeting section, which was customary of ancient letters. Unlike many New Testament letters, but similar in some ways to 1 Peter, it lacks the kind of personal comments that may give the reader some indication of the letter's recipients, location, or their general situation. Where 1 Peter does contain some personal comments in the closing of its letter (cf. 1 Pet. 5:12–14), 2 Peter lacks any mention of specific persons to greet or those who send greetings. This lack of personal comment creates a difficult scenario for both the contextualization of the letter as well as the verification of its authenticity (see Introduction: Authorship and Date as well as Introduction: Audience and Setting). This also means conclusions about the specific nature of the issues Peter addresses must be offered somewhat tentatively. The structure of the outline based on a rhetorical analysis follows the below general scheme:

Greeting (1:1–2)
Exordium (1:3–15)
Probatio (1:16–3:13)[1]
Peroratio (3:14–18a)
Doxology (3:18b)[2]

Here, the *exordium* supplies the topical introduction of the speech, intending to introduce its contents to the reader and establish rapport

---

[1] Neyrey notes a *digressio* present in 2:10b–22 (Neyrey, *2 Peter, Jude*, 111).

[2] Watson, *Invention, Arrangement, and Style*, 141–42; See also Witherington, *Letters for Hellenized Christians*, 274–75. Compare this with Witherington's outline, which follows a combination of rhetorical, thematic, and redactional emphases: Epistolary Prescript (1:1–2); *Exordium* (1:3–11); Quoted Testimony (1:12–21); Beguilers Past and Present (2:1–22); Eschatological Reminders (3:1–13); *Peroratio* (3:14–18a); Concluding Doxology (3:18b). See also Davids, *The Letters of 2 Peter and Jude*, 144–45.

with the audience. The *probatio* contains the main argumentation and evidence of the work, attempting to persuade the audience with logic and emotional appeals. The *peroratio* summarizes the main points of the argument and intends to leave a positive impression with the audience as the presentation is brought to a close.

Deploying the tools of discourse analysis, Fresch organizes the structure differently, seeing δέ, which typically denotes development or a new section, as the marker of the first major break (1:13); the presence of the vocative, a participant shift, and a topic shift as marking the second (3:1); a new frame, a thematic shift, and the presence of οὖν (NA²⁸) as denoting the third (3:11); and the presence of οὖν, with the vocative ἀγαπητοί, and a new frame of reference as denoting the final section (3:17). Fresch's outline thus is structured as follows:

Greeting and Exhortation (1:1–12)
Intent to Remind and Reminder: Beware of False Teachers (1:13–2:22)
Reminder: Beware of Scoffers (3:1–10)
Wait for the Day of the Lord (3:11–16)
Summative Exhortations and Doxology (3:17–18)

While recognizing the merits of such approaches, my own organization will deal somewhat thematically with the contents of the letter, though organizing and examining those contents largely in light of their rhetorical and discourse features from the analysis of the authors presented above:

Greeting (1:1–2)
Life with God (1:3–12)
Prophetic Testimony (1:13–21)
The Description of the False Teachers (2:1–11)
The Fate of the False Teachers (2:12–22)
The Day of the Lord (3:1–13)
Closing Remarks (3:14–18)

2 PETER 1:1–2: GREETING

1 ¹ Simeon Peter, a slave of and apostle of Jesus Christ, to those who obtained a faith equal to us in the justice of our God and Savior Jesus Christ.
² May grace and peace be multiplied to you in the knowledge of God and of Jesus our Lord.

1:1 – Despite the forthright statement in the first line of the letter identifying the author as Simon (here "Simeon") Peter (Συμεὼν Πέτρος), much doubt and disagreement exists in scholarship today over the author of this letter.³ Of interest textually here is the form of the name as Συμεὼν instead of the more common Σίμων. This form is used only seven times in the New Testament and only twice of Peter, here and likely in Acts 15:14. The form used here is closer to the Hebrew name, though both Greek and Jewish authors substitute the more common Greek form Σίμων at times.⁴ Πέτρος is the name given to Simon (Matt. 16:17–18) by Jesus, and is the Greek rendering of the Aramaic name "Cephas" (כֵּיפָא, kêpā'), which both mean "rock" or "stone." First Peter introduces its author simply with Πέτρος rather than the combined name Συμεὼν Πέτρος here.

Peter likewise identifies himself as a "slave and apostle" (δοῦλος καὶ ἀπόστολος) of Jesus Christ. This combination of terms is found elsewhere in Paul's introduction in Romans 1:1 and Titus 1:1, as well as in John 13:16 ("a slave is not greater than his master"; the parallel in Matt. 10:24 has διδάσκολος instead of ἀπόστολος). Slavery in the ancient world was quite common.⁵ The practice meant the legal treatment of humans as property and often carried little ethical hesitation. While some advocated for the humane treatment of slaves, there were abuses to the practice as well. While most slaves were of lower, working classes, slaves could also be found in positions of higher social mobility as well.⁶ To be a slave of a noble could, then, entail a position of honor and even authority.⁷ The adoption of the language of "slave" by Jesus' followers as a self-description

---

³ See Introduction: Authorship and Date for a discussion of the complicated nature of 2 Peter's authorship; I will generally refer to the author throughout as "Peter" for the sake of simplicity.
⁴ William Arndt et al., *A Greek-English Lexicon of the New Testament and Other Early Christian Literature* (Chicago: University of Chicago Press, 2000), 957.
⁵ According to Schumacher, slaves made up somewhere between 15–20 percent of the Roman Empire during the first century (Leonhard Schumacher, *Sklaverei in der Antike: Alltag und Schicksal der Unfreien* [Munich: C. H. Beck, 2001], 42), though other estimates vary.
⁶ For an overview, see J. Albert Harrill, "Slavery," in *Dictionary of New Testament Background*, ed. Craig A. Evans and Stanley E. Porter (Downers Grove: IVP Academic, 2000), 1124–27.
⁷ See Neyrey, *2 Peter, Jude*, 144–45.

likely comes from Jesus' own teachings.[8] Take, for example, Mark 10:44, where Jesus instructs his disciples that "whoever wants to be first among you must be the slave of all." In the book of Acts (2:18), the new covenant prophecy from Joel 2 speaks of God pouring out his Spirit on his male and female slaves (see also Acts 16:17). Likewise, in his letter to the Romans, Paul instructs Roman Christians to consider themselves no longer as slaves to Sin but as slaves to righteousness (Rom. 6:17–19). Peter here reflects this same attitude that being a follower of Jesus means being completely at his service and disposal.

As an "apostle," Peter identifies himself as one commissioned by Jesus for special service in the mission of God. The first apostles were called by Jesus and sent out to herald the message of the kingdom, cast out unclean spirits, and heal every kind of sickness (Matt. 10:1–15; Luke 9:1–10). Luke specifies that twelve of Jesus' collection of disciples were designated with the title (Luke 6:13). Later, the title expands in its usage to include others such as Matthias (Acts 1:23–26, who replaced Judas Iscariot), Barnabas and Paul (cf. Acts 14:14), Andronicus and Junia (Rom. 16:7), James the brother of the Lord (Gal. 1:19), Apollos (1 Cor. 4:6–13), Epaphroditus (Phil. 2:25), Titus (2 Cor. 8:23), and Timothy and Silas (1 Thess. 1:1, cf. 2:6). The term thus expanded in the New Testament beyond the twelve originally commissioned, though the role seems largely the same: to spread the message of Christ. The essence of the role seems to have been akin to what we might call a missionary or church planter today, though "the" apostles, and particularly Paul and the twelve, did seem to hold a unique degree of authority over the churches to which they were connected.

The designation of Jesus as "Christ" (Χριστός, or "Anointed One") is, of course, a nod to his Messianic identity. As Son of David (cf. Matt. 1:1; 21:9–15; Luke 1:32; Rom. 1:1–4), Jesus occupies the eternal throne (Matt. 26:64; Mark 14:62; Luke 22:69; Acts 5:31; 7:55–56; Rom. 8:34; Eph. 1:20; Col. 3:1; Heb. 1:3; 8:1; 10:12; 12:2; 1 Pet. 3:22), which God promised long ago to David's descendants (cf. 2 Sam. 7:8–17). Thus, Jesus rules and reigns as the heavenly King over the "eternal kingdom" (cf. 2 Pet. 1:11).

---

[8] As Reese notes, the term also has a history in the Old Testament (LXX) to describe a relationship with God in texts such as Exod. 32:13, Deut. 34:5, and 1 Sam. 3:9–10 (Ruth Anne Reese, *2 Peter & Jude*, THNTC [Grand Rapids: Eerdmans, 2007], 130).

Unlike most letters in the New Testament, little detail is given in the opening greeting about the recipients of the letter. The recipients are identified as those who received a "faith" (πίστιν) equal in value to "us" (ἡμῖν) "by the justice of our God" (ἐν δικαιοσύνῃ τοῦ θεοῦ ἡμῶν). Peter clearly writes to fellow believers in Christ who share a common commitment of belief and practice. Such is fitting, of course, for the rhetoric of the letter, as it is reminding, motivating, and reinforcing things that the audience already knows.

Several dimensions of this greeting, however, require further consideration. The term "faith" (πίστιν) possesses a wide range of meaning in the New Testament, evoking ideas of "trust," "commitment," "faithfulness," "belief," "a pledge," "confidence," or "a set of ideas/beliefs." Peter may intend the latter meaning here, though with its use in proximity to the use in 1:5, where the term seems to indicate a virtue or character trait, some combination of "commitment" and "faithfulness" is probably more likely. Peter states this faith is "of equal value to ours," indicating by the plural a comparison with a group of some sort. A few suggestions have been offered to the identity of this "us": Peter and the wider Christian community,[9] Peter and the group of apostles,[10] Jewish Christians,[11] or Peter and the authorial group from which the letter derives (which would have at least consisted of Peter and an amanuensis). The identification here should take into consideration other uses of the first person plural throughout the letter (1:4, 8, 11, 14, 16, 18, 19; [2:20]; 3:13, 15, 18). The majority of these uses refer to the wider Christian community (1:4, 8, 11, 14; [2:20]; 3:13, 15, 18). The exceptions to these generic references occur in 1:16–21, where the letter shifts to personal testimony from Peter. Here the "we" and "our" references more likely refer to the apostles and specifically those who were eyewitnesses to the Transfiguration. Since such a narrowing of the reference is not explicit or required in this section, it is probably best to the view "our" here in 1:1–14 as a reference to the wider Christian community, though the secondary option would be Peter and the apostles or Peter and his literary contributors. The phrase here ("of equal value to ours") then indicates that

---

[9] Green, *Jude and 2 Peter*, 174; Norman Hillyer, *1 and 2 Peter, Jude*, New International Bible Commentary (Peabody: Hendrickson, 1992), 157.

[10] Frey, *The Letter of Jude and the Second Letter of Peter*, 251.

[11] Joseph B. Mayor, *The Epistle of St. Jude and the Second Epistle of St. Peter: Greek Text with Introductions, Notes and Comments* (Minneapolis: Klock and Klock, 1978), 81.

the recipients of this letter share in the same standing as believers everywhere, Peter included, as recipients of faith through the justice of Christ.

Justice (ἐν δικαιοσύνῃ) here is the means or "sphere" through which faith is received and is specifically "the justice of our God and Savior Jesus Christ." A few elements of this phrase are striking and worth discussion. First, the term "justice" (δικαιοσύνη), like "faith" (πίστις), carries a range of possible meanings, including "fairness," "righteousness," "justice," "rightness," and "uprightness." Its usage in Paul's letters in particular has been a source of fierce debate among scholars in recent decades.[12] Peter's use of the term and its cognates is much more limited, occurring a handful of times in both letters (1 Pet. 2:24; 3:12, 14, 18; 4:18; 2 Pet. 1:1; 2:5, 7, 8, 21; 3:13) and never in its verbal form (δικαιόω). While echoing some features of Pauline teaching (e.g., 1 Pet 2:24; cf. Rom. 6:13), its use in the Petrine letters typically encodes more of an ethical connotation (see 1 Pet. 3:12, 13, 18; 2 Pet. 2:5, 7, 8, 21; 3:13) than a soteriological one. As Bauckham recognizes, in the context it likely refers "to the fairness and lack of favoritism which gives equal privilege to all Christians."[13] God's justice is unlike human justice in that he executes it impartially, in truth, and with loving and restorative motivations behind it.[14] As Neyrey observes, since God's judgment will be a central theme of the letter, to introduce the concept of God's justice at the outset is fitting.[15]

Peter identifies this justice as that of "our God and Savior Jesus Christ" (τοῦ θεοῦ ἡμῶν καὶ σωτῆρος Ἰησοῦ Χριστοῦ), structured here, as Davids recognizes, as "an example of the Granville Sharp Rule: two nouns (θεοῦ and σωτῆρος) that are personal but not proper names, are in the same case,

---

[12] For an introduction, see James K. Beilby and Paul Rhodes Eddy, *Justification: Five Views* (Downers Grove: IVP Academic, 2011). Some major recent works include David E. Aune, *Rereading Paul Together: Protestant and Catholic Perspectives on Justification* (Grand Rapids: Baker, 2006); Campbell, *The Deliverance of God*; Michael Horton, *Justification* (Grand Rapids: Zondervan, 2018); Bruce L. McCormack, *Justification in Perspective: Historical Developments and Contemporary Challenges* (Grand Rapids: Baker Academic, 2006); Thomas R. Schreiner, *Faith Alone: The Doctrine of Justification and Why It Still Matters* (Grand Rapids: Zondervan, 2015); Stephen Westerholm, *Justification Reconsidered: Rethinking a Pauline Theme* (Grand Rapids: Eerdmans, 2013); N. T. Wright, *Justification: God's Plan and Paul's Vision* (Downers Grove: IVP Academic, 2009).

[13] Bauckham, *Jude-2 Peter*, 168. See also Green, *Jude and 2 Peter*, 174-75.

[14] See particularly Michael J. Gorman, *Participating in Christ: Explorations in Paul's Theology and Spirituality* (Grand Rapids: Baker Academic, 2019), 21-41

[15] Neyrey, *2 Peter, Jude*, 147.

and are preceded by a definite article that is not repeated before the second noun refer to the same person."[16] The thrust of this grammatical arrangement is that here, Jesus is identified as both God and Savior (also Titus 2:13; 1 John 5:20; Rom. 9:5; 2 Thess. 1:12),[17] which, though often considered a marker of the lateness of this letter, can be found in earlier works in the New Testament, most notably (though debated there) in Romans 9:5. Peter's writing, like much of the New Testament, takes on a decidedly Trinitarian shape, giving authority and honor also to God (1:2, 17–18, 21; 2:4–10; 3:5–6, 8–10, 12–13, 15), the Son (cf. 1:2–4, 8, 11, 14, 16–17; 2:20; 3:2, 4, 8–10, 15, 17–18), and the Spirit (1:21). To recognize Jesus as God, Savior, and Lord as Peter does, is undoubtedly to afford him the same position and authority as Israel's God, who bears those same titles throughout the Hebrew Scriptures.[18]

As Savior, as Frey summarizes, this designation "not only refers back to salvation that has already occurred (e.g., through the forgiveness of sins, cf. 1:9), but also implies the power of Christ to save the pious from temptation (cf. 2:9) and ultimately to grant them 'entry into the eternal kingdom of our Lord and Savior, Jesus Christ.'"[19] Christ has saved and will save his people when the day of the Lord comes and the heavens and earth are judged. This title may have struck its original hearers with a note of contrast as well, since "Savior" was also a title attributed to the Roman emperor. This may have offered a subversive critique, then, of Rome's power, claiming instead that it is Jesus who ought to be heralded as "Savior of the world."[20]

1:2 – The greeting of the letter ends with Peter praying that "grace and peace" be multiplied to his recipients in the "knowledge of God and of

---

[16] Peter H. Davids, *II Peter and Jude: A Handbook on the Greek Text* (Waco: Baylor University Press, 2011), 42.
[17] Cf. Bauckham, *Jude–2 Peter*, 168.
[18] For a comparison of early textual witnesses of 2 Peter with particular focus on Christological presentation, see Terrance Callan, "Reading the Earliest Copies of 2 Peter," *Biblica* 93.3 (2012): 427–50.
[19] Frey, *The Letter of Jude and the Second Letter of Peter*, 254. For a study of the titles attributed to Jesus throughout 2 Peter, see Kelly Adair Seely, *A Study of Petrine Christology from Key Texts in 2 Peter* (Eugene: Wipf & Stock, 2021), 7–40.
[20] On attribution to the emperors, see Craig R. Koester, "The Savior of the World (John 4:42)," *JBL* 109 (1990): 665–80. The title was likewise used for the gods in Greco-Roman sources, such as Zeus, Asclepius, Isis, and Serapis (Koester, "The Savior of the World," 666).

Jesus our Lord." "Grace" (χάρις) and "peace" (εἰρήνη) are, of course, frequently used terms in the New Testament and common especially in the introduction of New Testament letters (e.g., Rom. 1:7; 1 Cor. 1:3; 2 Cor. 1:2; Gal. 1:3; Eph. 1:2; Col. 1:2; 1 Thess. 1:1; 2 Thess. 1:2; 1 Tim. 1:2; 2 Tim. 1:2; Titus 1:4; Philem. 3; 1 Pet. 1:2; 2 John 1:3; Rev. 1:4). While the language of grace is familiar in Christian theological circles, its ubiquity can dull its force. Grace is essentially God's posture of giving toward humanity.[21] God's generosity is boundless and overflows to his creation. As James articulates, "every good and perfect gift" comes from this generous God (Jas. 1:17). Peter, in asking for God's grace to be "multiplied," is praying that this boundless generosity overflow especially to his recipients (compare with 1 Pet. 1:2).[22] The peace Peter has in mind is more than simply the absence of conflict, but the state of *shalom* (שָׁלוֹם), that of wholeness and flourishing.[23]

Peter further recognizes that the means by which this boundless generosity and flourishing may be experienced is the "knowledge of God and of our Lord Jesus Christ." The term for knowledge used here (ἐπίγνωσις) is uncommon in the New Testament, used just twenty times in total, and mostly in Pauline letters (Rom. 1:28; 3:20; 10:2; Eph. 1:17; 4:13; Phil 1:9; Col. 1:9–10; 2:2; 3:10; 1 Tim. 2:4; 2 Tim. 2:25; 3:7; Titus 1:1; Philem. 6; see also Heb. 10:26), but it is used four times in 2 Peter (1:2, 3, 8; 2:20; see also the use of γνῶσις in 2 Pet. 3:18). Peter clearly has in mind a personal kind of knowledge, informed by apostolic teaching, as God or Christ is the object of all four of the uses of ἐπίγνωσις. As Frey summarizes, this "is about the knowledge of God and of the Lord Jesus Christ that began in the turn toward Christ, but is to be proved in one's way of life (cf. 2:20–22), and thus continues to deepen (3:18)."[24] In John's Gospel, Jesus describes this type of knowing as the essence of eternal life, knowing the Father and the Christ (John 17:3). It is this kind of life Peter has in mind as he transitions from the greeting of the letter.

---

[21] See especially John M. G. Barclay, *Paul and the Gift* (Grand Rapids: Eerdmans, 2017).
[22] The verb used here (πληθυνθείη) is found in the optative mood, a form used of this verb only in 1 Pet. 1:2; 2 Pet. 1:2; and Jude 2, in each case in the opening greeting of the letter.
[23] See Moisés Silva, *New International Dictionary of New Testament Theology and Exegesis*, vol. 2 (Grand Rapids: Zondervan, 2014), 111–18.
[24] Frey, *The Letter of Jude and the Second Letter of Peter*, 256.

2 PETER 1:3–12: LIFE WITH GOD

³ as all things necessary for life and devotion to God have been presented to us through his divine power through the knowledge of the one who called us by his own glory and virtue,

⁴ through which he has presented to us precious and great promises in order that through these things you may become sharers of the divine nature, and so escape from the corruption in the world because of distorted desires,

⁵ and now for this same reason, by contributing all eagerness, supply with your faith virtue, and with virtue knowledge,

⁶ and with knowledge self-control, and with self-control perseverance, and with perseverance devotion to God,

⁷ and with devotion to God sibling affection, and with sibling affection love,

⁸ for if these things are yours and increasing, they will not make you useless or unfruitful in the knowledge of our Lord Jesus Christ.

⁹ For to the one for whom these things are not present, they are blind, being nearsighted, choosing to forget the cleansing of their former sins.

¹⁰ Therefore, siblings, be even more eager to make your calling and election certain, for in doing these things, you will never ever stumble.

¹¹ For in this way entrance into the eternal kingdom of our Lord and Savior Jesus Christ will be richly supplied to you.

¹² Therefore, I will continually remind you about these things although you know them and are confirmed in the truth you possess.

1:3 – The *exordium* (1:3–15), in which the author gives a preview of the content of the work and attempts to establish good rapport with the audience,[25] opens the body of the letter and focuses on virtuous behavior, something at the heart of the substance of the letter. The purpose of the *exordium* is to make the audience "attentive, receptive, and well-disposed."[26] As an example of epideictic rhetoric,[27] these virtues are reinforced through praise[28] and will also be reinforced with the examples of Jesus and the apostles and then contrasted with the antithetical

---

[25] See Witherington and Myers, *New Testament Rhetoric*, 6, 21.
[26] Watson, *Invention, Arrangement, and Style*, 89.
[27] Watson categorizes the letter as an epistle and testament fashioned in the form of deliberative rhetoric since "it is clearly intended to advise and dissuade the audience with regard to a particular way of thinking and course of action" (Watson, *Invention, Arrangement, and Style*, 85). Watson suggests that the letter also contains portions of judicial rhetoric (1:16–2:10a; 3:1–13) and epideictic rhetoric (2:10b–22) (Watson, *Invention, Arrangement, and Style*, 86).
[28] See Witherington, *Letters for Hellenized Christians*, 298.

behaviors of the false teachers. The style through which Peter delivers these remarks fits the common descriptions of Asiatic Greek. As Witherington notes, "Asiatic Greek was especially compatible with epideictic rhetoric ... [and] when the two were combined, one could expect lengthy and sometimes convoluted sentences, grandiloquent phrases and vocabulary, amplification and redundancy – all to make the honorable look more glorious and the dishonorable look more despicable."[29]

From a discourse analysis perspective, 2 Peter can be defined as a hortatory discourse, since the author is concerned primarily with the behavior of the recipients, wishes to see certain behaviors enacted or terminated, and exhibits tension between present circumstances and future projects.[30] In other words, the transformed inner life, and its subsequent outward effects, is the focal point for 2 Peter. The upholding of Christian virtue, then, acts as the point of cohesion throughout the letter, though 2 Peter is often, because of its varied use of source materials, treated as more of a patchwork assortment of ideas.[31]

Much discussion has occurred noting the Hellenistic origin of many of Peter's terms, including θείας ("divine") here, but, as Bauckham notes, the term also occurs with some frequency in Hellenistic Jewish writers (such as *Sib. Or.*, Philo, and Josephus) as well as in Acts 17:29 and in the LXX,[32] so we must be careful not to characterize 2 Peter's Hellenism on a spectrum of "Jewish" v. "Greek." Hellenistic influences were a reality everywhere in the Roman empire. The language, customs, and beliefs of the Greco-Roman world were part of the cultural landscape within which first-century Jews lived, so Jewish authors who took cues from non-Jewish Hellenistic authors as well as Jewish ones ought not be considered somehow "less Jewish" in their thinking. The LXX, after all, was itself a product of the "Hellenizing" of Judaism. There are times when these influences are more pronounced,

---

[29] Witherington, *Letters for Hellenized Christians*, 298–99.
[30] See Christopher J. Fresch, "2 Peter," in *Discourse Analysis of the New Testament Writings*, ed. Todd A. Scacewater (Minneapolis: Fortress Press, 2020), 622–23.
[31] As Witherington elaborates, "One of the real problems in overconcentrating on the source criticism of this discourse is that one fails to see how skillfully our author has blended this diverse source material into a powerful discourse, which reflects skill especially in the manipulation of style" (Witherington, *Letters for Hellenized Christians*, 299). On reading this section as in the form of a formal decretal, see Frederick W. Danker, "2 Peter 1: A Solemn Decree," *CBQ* 40.1 (1978): 64–82.
[32] Bauckham, *Jude–2 Peter*, 177.

but the presence of those influences does not somehow negate the "Jewishness" of a discourse.

The opening two verses of the *exordium* express a cluster of potent theological realities. Indeed, Peter distills here the essence of the goal of the gospel: *to share in the life of God*. The transition from 1:2 to 1:3, however, is a point of scholarly debate as the new verse begins with a comparative conjunction (ὡς) when a formal comparison is lacking in the syntax of the sentence. The word seems to take on more of a causal sense within the verse.[33] Peter has prayed for grace and peace to be multiplied "in the knowledge of God and of Jesus our Lord" (1:2), and this knowledge acts as the means by which its possessors receive "all things necessary for life and devotion to God" (1:3). Peter clearly intends this knowledge to be understood as more than intellectual assent to a set of ideas. Rather, it represents a deeply personal knowledge of God that transforms one's inner life.

Peter opens the exordium proclaiming, "all things necessary for life and devotion to God" (πάντα ... τὰ πρὸς ζωὴν καὶ εὐσέβειαν) have been presented to believers through God's "divine power" (τῆς θείας δυνάμεως). As Davids recognizes, the term for "devotion to God" (εὐσέβεια) occurs only a handful of times in the NT (once in Acts, ten times in the pastorals, and four times in 2 Peter). Likewise, as Frey argues, the phrase θεία δύναμις "occurs in Greek philosophy for exceptional abilities"[34] (i.e., superhuman deeds of power) and is uncommon in Jewish and early Christian literature,[35] and this may be a further indication that the author is engaging a more Hellenistic context.[36] In keeping with the theme of divine grace, Peter affirms that the power by which the Christian life can be lived can only come from God through Christ. Everything needed (πάντα) for "life and devotion to God" has been given by God as a divine gift (δεδωρημένης).[37] As Willard states, God offers to His people a "life without lack," and the essence of this life of fulness is

---

[33] See Davids, *II Peter and Jude*, 44; Lewis R. Donelson, *I & II Peter and Jude*, New Testament Library (Louisville: Westminster John Knox Press, 2010), 218.
[34] Frey, *The Letter of Jude and the Second Letter of Peter*, 259.
[35] Davids, *The Letters of 2 Peter and Jude*, 169.
[36] Davids, *The Letters of 2 Peter and Jude*, 168.
[37] Philo is close here in stating, "How could the soul have perceived God if he had not inspired it, and touched it according to his power? For human intellect would not have dared to mount up to such a height as to lay claim to the nature of God, if God himself had not drawn it up to himself, as far as it was possible for the mind of man to be drawn

knowing God and living in the light of His presence.[38] God's power (θεία δύναμις)[39] provides the means to sustain believers through the dark days of life as well as the means to draw near to God even, or especially, in the midst of those trying circumstances.

As noted above, the *knowledge* that Peter reemphasizes here from 1:2 underscores the personal nature of knowing that Peter envisions through faith. The object of this knowledge is the *"one who called us,"* which may, again, be taken either as a reference to God, or to Christ, with Christ being the nearest referent in the context. Of course, the divine work, as reflected in the idea of the "divine economy," exists as a cooperative enterprise between the Father, Son, and Spirit who, though, according to orthodox teaching, existing in one unified nature, are divine "persons" distinct from one another, and thus each play a unique "role" in the work of salvation. This diverse participation in the divine work is an outflowing of the distinct relations of the Godhead in which the Son relates to the Father as Son (begotten) and the Spirit relates through the Spirit's procession.[40]

It is by the personal ἰδίᾳ δόξῃ καὶ ἀρετῇ ("glory and excellence of character") that the divine work draws humanity to this knowledge of God. "Glory" throughout Scripture represents both God's majestic splendor (e.g., Matt. 16:27; Luke 9:32; Acts 22:1; Rom. 6:4) as well as His renown and honor (e.g., Heb. 2:7; Rev. 4:11; 5:12). Peter may be offering here a bit of a preview of things to come as well, with the attention he will pay to Jesus' glorious transfiguration in just a few verses.[41] The *"excellence of character"* (ἀρετή) implies "an element of the ethical positivity and integrity of Christ and his actions."[42] This too is foundational for much of what is to come, since the proper beliefs and behaviors of those who claim the name of Christ are of utmost importance in this letter.

---

up, and if he had not formed it according to those powers which can be comprehended" (Philo, *Leg. Alleg.*, 138).

[38] See Dallas Willard, *Life Without Lack: Living in the Fullness of Psalm 23* (Nashville: Thomas Nelson, 2018).

[39] It is unclear in the context whether the power referred to is God's or Christ's, though Christ is the nearest referent. For a discussion, see Frey, *The Letter of Jude and the Second Letter of Peter*, 258.

[40] For the historical roots of this language, see the Athanasian Creed.

[41] As observed by Douglas Harink, *1 & 2 Peter*, BTCB (Grand Rapids: Brazos Press, 2009), 138.

[42] Frey, *The Letter of Jude and the Second Letter of Peter*, 260.

1:4 – Peter's thought continues with a second expression of means indicating how God's promises have come to believers ("through which things"; δι' ὧν). The "things" implied here are either the "knowledge" of God or "his own glory and excellence of character," though it could refer to the cluster of ideas in 1:3 as well. Often Asiatic style is written less for precision than for its effect. The bestowing of "precious and great promises" (τὰ τίμια καὶ μέγιστα ... ἐπαγγέλματα) is also not clarified in the context. The term "promise" (ἐπάγγελμα) occurs in the NT only here and in 3:13 (though cognate terms occur in 3:4, 9 in 2 Pet.).[43] In the scope of the letter, it may reference the future return of Christ, though that would not account for the plural. In 2 Pet. 3:13, the usage connects to the promise of the new heavens and the new earth. Elsewhere in the NT, cognate terms for ἐπάγγελμα are used to refer to the covenantal promises from the Old Testament, the promised salvation through the Messiah (Acts 13:23-33; Eph. 3:6; 2 Tim. 1:1; Titus 1:2-3; Heb. 4:1; 6:12; 8:6; 9:15; 10:36; 11:13, 39; Jas. 1:12; 2:5; 1 John 2:25), the promise of eschatological resurrection (Acts 26:6), the promise of Christ's return (2 Pet. 3:4, 9), and the promise of new creation (Heb. 11:26; 2 Pet 3:13). While Peter could have any range of these ideas in mind, it seems at least that salvation, the return of Christ, and new creation would be at the forefront of his mind in this text.

God's purpose of giving "these things" (τούτων) is that through them believers might "become sharers of the divine nature" (θείας κοινωνοὶ φύσεως). Bauckham suggests that Peter does not have participation in God's nature in mind here and that this partaking most likely happens at death.[44] This seems unlikely on both accounts. Peter expressly connects the divine power (τῆς θείας δυνάμεως αὐτοῦ) in 1:3 and the sharing in the divine (θείας κοινωνοὶ) in 1:4 by proximity and lexical ties. Peter does not, of course, mean that Christians share in the divine nature *en toto*, but rather, based on the context, they share in those "communicable attributes" of God such as his eternality and moral perfections. The use of the perfect and aorist tenses throughout 1:3-4 likewise demonstrate that Peter likely has in mind something that is already a reality, not simply a future endowment. Perhaps here the framework of inaugurated eschatology can better explain the force of this text, in that partaking in the divine nature is

---

[43] Cf. Davids, *The Letters of 2 Peter and Jude*, 171.
[44] Bauckham, *Jude–2 Peter*, 181–82.

something believers already do in their present union with Christ but will also be consummated when they are perfected in the age to come. Since Peter views this sharing in the divine life as the foundation for moral living in the present, it makes sense for this to be also a present reality rather than something only to come in the future.[45] Were it only obtained in the future, it would provide no basis for moral transformation to Peter's audience now, something he clearly intends to reinforce in the letter.

Peter here employs language that would later be categorized under the theological verbiage of *theosis*, becoming "partakers of the divine nature" (θείας κοινωνοὶ φύσεως; cf. 1:4). Indeed, if a prooftext for such a doctrine exists in the New Testament, it is these two verses. A shift has occurred over the last few decades of New Testament scholarship in seeing the idea of "participating" in the life of God as central to New Testament soteriology, with some authors even explicitly adopting the language of *theosis* or deification.[46] Such a concept is often seen as rooted in Eastern Orthodoxy,[47] the patristic predecessors of which are examined in Russell's work on the subject.[48] Such an idea finds expression as early as Irenaeus, who wrote, "the Word of God, our Lord Jesus Christ, who, through His transcendent love, became what we are, that He might bring us to be even what He is Himself."[49] More forceful still is Clement of Alexandria, stating "But let us . . . listen to the Word, and take on the imprint of the truly saving

---

[45] See Frey, *The Letter of Jude and the Second Letter of Peter*, 257–67.

[46] See Constantine R. Campbell, *Paul and Union with Christ: An Exegetical and Theological Study* (Grand Rapids: Zondervan, 2012); Douglas A. Campbell, *The Quest for Paul's Gospel: A Suggested Strategy* (New York: T&T Clark, 2005); James D. G. Dunn, *The Theology of Paul the Apostle* (Grand Rapids: Eerdmans, 1998), 390–441; Michael J. Gorman, *Inhabiting the Cruciform God: Kenosis, Justification, and Theosis in Paul's Narrative Soteriology* (Grand Rapids: Eerdmans, 2009); *Becoming the Gospel: Paul, Participation, and Mission* (Grand Rapids: Eerdmans, 2015); and *Participating in Christ: Explorations in Paul's Theology and Spirituality* (Grand Rapids: Baker Academic, 2019); Richard B. Hays, *The Faith of Jesus Christ: The Narrative Substructure of Gal. 3:1–4:11* (Grand Rapids: Eerdmans, 2002).

[47] See Khaled Anatolios, *Deification through the Cross: An Eastern Christian Theology of Salvation* (Grand Rapids: Eerdmans, 2020); Panayiotis Nellas, *Deification in Christ: Orthodox Perspectives on the Nature of the Human Person* (Yonkers: St. Vladimir's Seminary Press, 1987). Note, however, the Hellenistic parallels, as recognized by Neyrey, in Josephus, *Ag. Ap.* 1.232; *Ant.* 8.107; Philo, *Decal.* 104; *Abr.* 144; Plutarch, *Defectu* 415C (Neyrey, *2 Peter, Jude*, 157).

[48] Norman Russell, *The Doctrine of Deification in the Greek Patristic Tradition* (Oxford: Oxford University Press, 2006; online ed., Oxford Academic, 2011).

[49] Irenaeus, *AH* 5, Praef.

life of our Savior; and meditating on the heavenly mode of life according to which we have been deified, let us anoint ourselves with the perennial immortal bloom of gladness."⁵⁰ Athanasius followed a similar trajectory of thinking, stating of Christ in *De Incarnatione*, "he was made man that we might be made God."⁵¹ The fathers often explicated this notion of deification, or theosis, from their exegesis of Psalm 82, a text referenced in the New Testament in John 10:34–36 and that evidences a type of interplay between the human and the divine. This notion of *theosis*, however, guards against potentially idolatrous implications in that a distinction is maintained between God's nature in itself and that which He shares with humanity. As Russell summarizes, "These attributes belong to God alone; we can only participate in them if God first unites himself to the human race through the incarnation of the Logos. Individual human beings may then be united with Christ through filial adoption, which enables them to participate in the divine attributes of incorruption and immortality."⁵² Rather than understanding Christians as taking on the totality of the divine identity, we might understand this in terms of what Protestant theologians would more commonly call God's "communicable attributes" (e.g., love and holiness are shared but not omnipotence or omnipresence). The fathers also express this notion in the shape of an inaugurated eschatology in that participation in the divine life begins now through an encounter with Christ, baptism, and meditation on Scripture, though it is not fully realized until the new heavens and earth.⁵³

The purpose of this sharing of the divine nature has the additional corollary of escaping "from the corruption in the world because of distorted desires." The "corruption" (φθορά) that Peter describes here can

---

⁵⁰ Clement of Alexandria, *Paed.* 1.98.3. Or Origen, along similar lines, wrote, "May you too be a partaker and ever increase the participation, that you may say not only, 'We have become partakers of Christ' (Heb. 3: 14), but also, 'We have become partakers of God'" (Origen, *Philocalia* 13.4, trans. Norman Russell in *The Doctrine of Deification*, https://doi.org/10.1093/acprof:oso/9780199205974.003.0005).

⁵¹ Athanasius, *De Incarnatione Verbi Dei*, 54.

⁵² Russell, *The Doctrine of Deification*. See also Donelson, *I and II Peter and Jude*, 220; Oliver D. Crisp, *Participation and Atonement: An Analytic and Constructive Account* (Grand Rapids: Baker Academic, 2022), 224; Dietrich Bonhoeffer, *Discipleship* (Minneapolis: Fortress Press, 2015), 269. For a thorough study, see J. M. Starr, *Sharers in the Divine Nature: 2 Peter 1:4 in Its Hellenistic Context*, Coniectanea biblica: New Testament Series (Stockholm: Almquist & Wiksell, 2000).

⁵³ See Russell, *The Doctrine of Deification*.

refer to a kind of material decay but, contextually, more likely he has in mind a moral decay that brings the destruction of a person from the inside out. This moral sense is a common use of φθορά, both in the LXX and the New Testament.[54] As Davids notes, "The 'escape' is not an escape from the world or from physical existence . . . but 'escape from the *corruption* in the world.' Thus at the end of 2 Peter . . . one does not find immortal existence free from a body, but a new (or renewed) heaven and a new (or renewed) earth."[55] This corruption exists "because of distorted desires" (ἐν ἐπιθυμίᾳ), again evoking language common of inward moral corruption in the New Testament.[56] This term (ἐπιθυμία) takes on an almost entirely negative sense in the New Testament.[57] While this text has an eschatological dimension,[58] it need not be seen as one exclusively so, since, again, 2 Peter grounds present moral commitments in these realities as well.

1:5 – The transition from 1:2-4 to 1:5-7 is bridged by an assumed causal idea ("and now *for* this same reason"; καὶ αὐτὸ τοῦτο δὲ),[59] creating a bridge to the virtue catalog that follows. Virtue lists are well known in antiquity, both within the New Testament and outside of it.[60] The form adopted here, as Witherington describes, is *sorites* or *gradatio*, which creates "an ascending chain of virtues that leads to the supreme virtue – Christian love. It is a device which involves repetition, something near to the heart of Asiatic rhetoricians."[61] The form was known to other authors (Philo, *Sacrif. Abel.* 27; Philo, *Leg. Alleg.*, 1.64; *Wisd.* 8:7; *m. Sot.* 8:15; 1QS 4:2-6),[62] though the substance of those lists shares some differences with the content of the lists in the NT.

---

[54] LXX: Exod. 18:18; Ps. 102:4; Odes 6:7; Wis. 14:12, 25; Ps. Sol. 4:6; Mic. 2:10; Jonah 2:7; Isa. 24:3; Dan. 3:92; 10:8; NT: Rom. 8:21; 1 Cor. 15:42, 50; Gal. 6:8; Col. 2:22; 2 Pet. 2:12, 19.
[55] Davids, *The Letters of 2 Peter and Jude*, 175. See also, Harink, *1 & 2 Peter*, 140.
[56] E.g., Rom. 7:7ff.; Gal. 5:24; Col. 3:5; 1 Thess. 4:5; 1 Tim. 6:9; 2 Tim. 2:22; Jas. 1:14ff.; 1 Pet. 4:3.
[57] Exceptions would include texts like Mark 4:19; Phil. 1:23.
[58] E.g., Bauckham, *Jude-2 Peter*, 182
[59] Or an accusative of respect, per Davids, *II Peter and Jude*, 46.
[60] Compare Rom. 5:1-5; 2 Cor. 6:6-7; 8:7; Gal. 5:22-23; Eph. 6:14-17; Phil. 4:8; Col. 3:12-14; 1 Tim. 3:2-3; 6:11; Titus 1:7-8; Jas. 3:17-18; Rev. 2:19; *Ep. Barn.* 2.2.3; 1 Clem 62:2; m. Sotah 9.15; Wis. 6:17-20; Philo, *Sacr.* 27; *Leg.* 1.64. See also See J. D. Charles, *Virtue Amidst Vice: The Catalog of Virtues in 2 Peter 1*, JSNTSup, 150 (Sheffield: Sheffield Academic Press, 1997).
[61] Witherington and Myers, *New Testament Rhetoric*, 263. See also Green, *Jude and 2 Peter*, 191.
[62] See Davids, *The Letters of 2 Peter and Jude*, 178-79 for a comparison.

The link between this section and the previous one reinforces that the transformation that Peter grounds in participation in the divine life must, through both divine gift and human response,[63] develop into Christ-like character. Maximus the Confessor describes this connection in stating, "Our Lord Jesus Christ himself is the substance of all the virtues . . . . It is evident that every person who participates in virtue as a matter of habit participates in God, the substance of the virtues."[64] Personal and participatory knowledge of God necessarily results in the reworking of the inner person. Or, as Donelson puts it, "Theology not only leads to ethics; it requires it."[65] Effort is required on the part of Peter's recipients in order that, "by contributing all eagerness, [you must] supply" (σπουδὴν πᾶσαν παρεισενέγκαντες ἐπιχορηγήσατε) these virtues. "Supply" (ἐπιχορηγήσατε) here ought to be seen as emphasized, since imperatives are prominent in hortatory discourses.[66] This verb also serves as the focal point of 1:5–11 (and possibly 12–15 also), since the thematic focus of the entire section is upon the development of Christian virtue.

It seems unlikely that Peter intends a logical progression to the virtues here, since a developmental relationship progressing from faith to virtue to knowledge to self-control to perseverance, etc., lacks clarity, explanation, or development by the author.[67] In keeping with Asiatic rhetoric, the intended outcome is likely the effect achieved by such a list rather than its logical progression. The bookends of the list, however, probably bear some significance. Likely faith (πίστις) is understood in a foundational sense and love (ἀγάπη) in a climactic one, with the other virtues in between

---

[63] As Davids states, "We do not automatically become more virtuous as if God infused virtue into us intravenously; we need to make plans and expend effort" (Davids, *The Letters of 2 Peter and Jude*, 179).

[64] *Ambiguum 7*, in St. Maximus the Confessor, *On the Cosmic Mystery of the Jesus Christ: Selected Writings from St. Maximus the Confessor*, Popular Patristics Series, 25, trans. Paul M. Blowers and Robert Louis Wilkin (Crestwood: St. Vladamir's Seminary Press, 2003), 58. This presents a contrast of sorts with the Stoic pursuit of virtue. As Charles summarizes, "According to Stoic doctrine, one suppresses the passions of the flesh by a rigorous cultivation of the virtues. Being virtuous, however, is an entirely rational rather than 'spiritual' exercise" (J. Daryl Charles, "The Language and Logic of Virtue in 2 Peter 1:5–7," *BBR* 8 [1998]: 62).

[65] Donelson, *I & II Peter and Jude*, 220.

[66] Fresch, "2 Peter," 624.

[67] Contra Charles, "The Language and Loic of Virtue in 2 Peter 1:5-7," 58–59.

simply also emerging from participating in the life of God rather than from one another.⁶⁸

Though virtue and vice lists could contain much longer enumerations,⁶⁹ the cardinal virtues in the Greco-Roman world, originating with Socrates and Plato, are wisdom (φρονησις), temperance (σωφροσυνη), justice (δικαιοσυνη), and courage (ἀνδρεια), with corresponding vices often accompanying them.⁷⁰ Hoag suggests that these cardinal virtues were maintained as an organizing principle of sorts for the more extensive virtue and vice lists through the period of the Roman Republic and into the Empire,⁷¹ as noted by Cicero.⁷² Vices were often categorized around the concepts of folly (ἀφροσύνη), licentiousness (ἀκολασία), injustice (ἀδικία), and cowardice (δειλία), which were seen as cardinal vices and also the opposites of the cardinal virtues.⁷³ Concerning the purpose of these lists, Charles summarizes, "Rhetorically speaking, the ethical list has an epideictic function; that is, as a form of speech it is intended to instill praise or shame in the hearer or listener."⁷⁴ Peter's inclusion of this virtue list likely serves the same rhetorical purpose.

The first virtue in the list, πίστις ("faith" or "faithfulness"), often bears the idea of "loyalty" in Greco-Roman contexts, particularly loyalty to one's family or the Empire.⁷⁵ The term shows up with some frequency in NT virtue lists as well (2 Cor. 8:7; Gal. 5:22–23; Eph. 6:14–17; 1 Tim. 6:11; Rev. 2:19). While πίστις can carry the idea of "belief" (e.g., Jas. 2:14–26) or "trust" (e.g., 1 Cor. 2:5) in the New Testament, it often also carries this idea of "loyalty" or "faithfulness" (e.g., Rom. 3:3), as directed to God

---

⁶⁸ Cf. Donelson, *I & II Peter and Jude*, 220.
⁶⁹ For examples of ancient virtue/vice lists, see Pseudo-Aristotle, *Virt. Vit.*; Cicero, *Tusc.* 4.11–27; *Inv.* 2.53–54, 159, 164; Pseudo-Diogenes, *Ep.* 28; Dio Chrysostom, *Or.* 1.4, 6, 13; 2.75; 3.5, 39–41; 4.83–96; 8.8; 23.7; 44.10; 49.9; 62.2; 66.1; 69.6, 9; Diog. Laer., 7.92–93, 110–12; Epictetus, *Diatr.* 2.8.23; 3.20.5–6; 14.8; 16.14; *Diss.* 2.22.30; 4.3.7; Maximus of Tyre, *Or.* 36.4c; Seneca the Younger, *Brev. Vit.* 10.2–4; 22.11; Musonius Rufus 16; Plutarch, *Mor.* 12B; 465D; 523D; Virgil, *Aen.* 6.732; Lucian, *Pisc.* 15–17.
⁷⁰ Plato, *Resp.* 4.427–45.
⁷¹ Gary G. Hoag, *Wealth in Ancient Ephesus and the First Letter to Timothy: Fresh Insights from Ephesiaca by Xenophon of Ephesus* (University Park: Penn State University Press, 2015), 103.
⁷² Cicero, *De Inventione*, 2.53.159–2.54.163.
⁷³ John T. Fitzgerald, "Virtue/Vice Lists," in *The Anchor Bible Dictionary*, ed. David Noel Freedman (New Haven: Yale University Press, 1992), 857–59.
⁷⁴ Charles, "The Language and Loic of Virtue in 2 Peter 1:5–7," 57.
⁷⁵ Davids, *The Letters of 2 Peter and Jude*, 161.

through Jesus Christ.[76] Though πίστις is used only here and in 1:3 in the letter, the relational emphases thus far in the letter likely indicate that Peter also has this idea of "faithfulness" or "loyalty" in mind here, which would make a more fitting interpretation in a virtue list than "belief." Green supports this thought in stating,

> Insofar as Peter's fundamental concern is to caution the church against the error of the heretics, placing "faithfulness" at the head of the virtue catalog is a strategic move. They are called to maintain this loyalty to their benefactor [i.e., God] (1:3-4, 11), as anyone in ancient society would have understood. To violate loyalty to the one into whose *fides* one had come would be considered a most serious moral breach.[77]

Ἀρετή ("virtue"; see also 1:3) is rare in New Testament virtue lists (elsewhere only in Phil. 4:8,[78] but it occurs with frequency in Hellenistic lists and often serves therein "as an umbrella term for ethically positive characteristics."[79] As Harink notes, it has been defined already by Peter "*with direct reference to Jesus Christ . . . and it is his* excellence [or 'virtuousness'] that has both called us and is that to which we are called."[80] The virtues Peter has in mind, then, are not simply the kinds of things Greco-Roman culture would have considered virtuous but rather those character traits grounded in the person of Christ that must be formed in the life of every believer. Though there is overlap between Greco-Roman (particularly Stoic) concepts of virtue and early Christian ones, there are divergences as well.

1:6 - "Knowledge" (γνῶσις) also finds its place in pagan virtue lists and often designates religious or philosophical knowledge,[81] though Peter's emphasis, again, appears to be upon personal knowledge of Jesus Christ (see 1:2-3, 8; 2:20; 3:18). The term also shows up in Paul's virtue lists in 2 Cor. 6:6-7 and 8:7. It is through this knowledge of Christ that true

---

[76] See, for example, Nijay K. Gupta, *Paul and the Language of Faith* (Grand Rapids: Eerdmans, 2020).
[77] Green, *Jude and 2 Peter*, 192.
[78] Note, however, also its use in the LXX in 2 Macc. 6:31; 10:28; 15:12, 17; 3 Macc. 6:1; 4 Macc. 1:2, 8, 10, 30; 2:10; 7:22; 9:8, 18; 10:10; 11:2; 12:14; 13:24, 27; 17:12, 23; Odes 4:3; Wis. 4:1; 5:13; 8:7; Hab. 3:3; Zech. 6:13; Isa. 42:8, 12, 21; 63:7.
[79] Frey, *The Letter of Jude and the Second Letter of Peter*, 272.
[80] Harink, *1 & 2 Peter*, 148.
[81] Frey, *The Letter of Jude and the Second Letter of Peter*, 273.

knowledge of God arises, which itself is the catalyst for moral transformation (cf. 1:3–4). It is such a knowledge that Peter's opponents lack, since they deny the Lordship (2:1) and the future return and judgment (and, subsequently, authority) of Jesus the Messiah.

"Self-control" (ἐγκράτεια) is a standard virtue in Hellenistic thought, particularly among Stoics, though Philo too adopts this notion.[82] The term also occurs in Paul's virtue list in Gal. 5:22–23. Self-mastery was an important concept in Greco-Roman moral frameworks and particularly in Aristotle and those whom he influenced.[83] According to Xenophon, ἐγκράτεια was foundational to all other virtues, for it is only through one's ability to control their desires that they can then turn toward accomplishing what is good.[84] To have self-control was to possess power to restrain one's emotions, impulses, or desires, particularly, as Green notes, in relation to food, speech, and sexuality.[85] This kind of self-control will be found as lacking among Peter's opponents, whose behavior at Christian meals (2:13), distorted speech (2:1–3, 11, 18–19), and lack of sexual restraint (2:10, 13–15, 18–19) demonstrate the absence of earnestness concerning the virtuous life.

"Endurance" (ὑπομονή) is a frequent term in NT virtue lists (Rom. 5:3–4; Col. 1:11; 1 Thess. 1:3–4; 1 Tim. 6:11; 2 Tim. 3:10; Titus 2:2; Jas., 1:3–4) and is a quality that Paul understands both God and Christ to possess (cf. Rom. 15:5; 2 Thess. 3:5). Defined by BDAG as the "the capacity to hold out or bear up in the face of difficulty,"[86] it is easy to see why the term would be significant for Peter's audience, since early Christians often faced social pressures from both pagans and non-Christian Jews. Such pressures become evident later in this letter, and so the opening section can be seen as foundational to the later themes that the author will address. This kind of endurance also holds fast to the hope of the future return of Christ, which must be awaited with great patience (3:4–15a). In contrast, this kind of endurance against external pressures is absent among Peter's opponents, who give into temptation and

---

[82] On Philo, see, for example, *Mos.* I.154, I.161, I.303; II. 185; *Spec.* I.149–50, I.173–75, I.186, I.193; II.195; III.22; *Virt.* 127, 180.
[83] E.g., Aristotle, *Eth. nic.*, 7.1145–54.
[84] Xenophon, *Memorabilia*, 1.5.4.
[85] Green, *Jude and 2 Peter*, 193.
[86] Arndt et al., *A Greek-English Lexicon*, 1039. See, for example, 4 Macc. 7:9; Rom. 2:7.

practice greed (2:3, 14), sexual indulgence (2:10, 13-15, 18-19), and are instead enslaved by their desires (2:19).

"Devotion to God" (εὐσέβεια; cf. 1:3; see also 3:11) also occurs in Hellenistic virtue lists, generally with reference to "reverence for the gods."[87] In the Greco-Roman world, as Cicero attests, the practice of εὐσέβεια was relevant in a broad number of settings: "They refer to what happens in fear and worship of the gods as religion and the tasks which duty tells us to perform towards our native land or to parents or to others linked to us by blood relations as piety."[88] Though the term has prominence in Greco-Roman literature, it also finds usage across the LXX, particularly in 2 and 3 Maccabees, but also in Proverbs, Wisdom of Solomon, Sirach, and Isaiah. While the expression of devotion in Greco-Roman contexts would have relevant parallels, the obvious difference would be the object of their devotion and the specific practices by which such devotion would be enacted. This kind of devotion to God finds its opposite in Peter's opponents, who deny the Lord (2:1-2) and are drawing others away to do the same (2:17-22)

1:7 – "Sibling affection" (φιλαδελφία) finds usage also in 1 Pet. 3:8 and is used in a metaphorical sense here and in other places in the NT wherein the early church understood itself as a "fictive kinship," having been made into a divine family in Christ.[89] Natural sibling affection was a central social bond in the ancient world; that the church adopted this language to speak of its communal relationships indicates the intensity in which those relational bonds existed.[90] As Davids notes, the early church was known for its inclination to treating one another as family, which was notable to outsiders (e.g., Lucian, *Peregrinus* 13; Minucius Felix, *Oct.* 31.8; Tertullian, *Apology*, 39).[91]

---

[87] Frey, *The Letter of Jude and the Second Letter of Peter*, 274.
[88] Cicero, *De invention rhetorica*, 2.66. Quoted in Hoag, *Wealth in Ancient Ephesus and the First Letter to Timothy*, 166.
[89] See, for example, Joseph H. Hellerman, *Jesus and the People of God: Reconfiguring Ethnic Identity*, New Testament Monographs (Sheffield: Sheffield Phoenix Press, 2007); *The Ancient Church as Family* (Minneapolis: Fortress Press, 2001).
[90] On a more practical and pastoral level, see Joseph H. Hellerman, *When the Church Was a Family: Recapturing Jesus' Vision for Authentic Christian Community* (Nashville: B&H, 2009).
[91] Davids, *The Letters of 2 Peter and Jude*, 183.

"Love" (ἀγάπη) stands at the pinnacle of the list (see also Rom. 5:3–5; 1 Cor. 8:7) and serves as primary evidence of knowledge of God for Peter, as it does also for Paul (Gal. 5:22; Rom. 13:10; 1 Cor. 13:13; Col. 3:14), James (Jas. 2:8–13), John (1 John 2:5; 3:11–17, 23; 4:7–5:4), and, of course, Jesus (Matt. 5:43–44; Mark 12:30–31). As Louw-Nida notes, though at times the distinctions between φιλός/φιλέω and ἀγάπη/ἀγαπάω are exaggerated, one such distinction may be that φιλός/φιλέω is rooted in interpersonal relatedness while ἀγάπη/ἀγαπάω focuses more on holding others (possibly regardless of such relatedness) in high regard.[92] Peter's inclusion of both here would indicate the appropriateness of both within a Christian understanding of love. Such a concept of love for "outsiders" finds its grounding in Christian theology in the love of God for humanity in spite of their enmity against him (e.g., John 3:16; Rom. 5:8). Such love, which seeks the good of others, and is not self-serving, is clearly absent from Peter's opponents as well.

Excursus: The Love of God and Christian Identity
Love is a term that permeates our culture. In the top ten Spotify songs of 2023, the word was used some forty-one times.[93] From slogans like "Love is love" or "Love wins," to the warm fuzzies of "falling in love," to talk of loving movies, food, and video games, there is an undoubtedly broad understanding of the term in the late modern world, so one artist can proclaim, "'I love you,' ain't that the worst thing you ever heard?"[94] Some conceptions of love might see it primarily as an emotion, as "confluent" (i.e., open or not exclusive), or even as evidence of structural inequities in late modern culture.[95]

For Christians in the late modern world, cultural conceptions of love can easily become entangled in our theological conceptions, particularly with the extent to which the late modern world consumes media.[96] According to Forbes, the average

---

[92] Johannes P. Louw and Eugene Albert Nida, *Greek-English Lexicon of the New Testament: Based on Semantic Domains* (New York: United Bible Societies, 1996), 293.
[93] Top 10 according to Newsweek. See Kelly Lyons, "Spotify Wrapped 2023: Top Songs, Artists, Podcasts and Listening Trends," www.newsweek.com/spotify-wrapped-2023-listening-trends-1848048. Miley Cyrus' hit song "Flowers" alone sings the word 22 times.
[94] Taylor Swift, "Anti-Hero," released October 2022, on *Midnights*, Republic Records.
[95] See, for example, Katie Barclay, "Love and Violence in the Music of Late Modernity," *Popular Music and Society* 41.5 (2018): 539–55.
[96] According to Gallup, teens spend an average of 4.8 hours on social media per day (Jonathan Rothwell, "Teens Spend Average of 4.8 Hours on Social Media Per Day," https://news.gallup.com/poll/512576/teens-spend-average-hours-social-media-per-day.aspx). In 2017, according to Forbes, the average American spent 32 hours per week listening to music (Hugh McIntyre, "Americans Are Spending More Time Listening To Music Than Ever Before," www.forbes.com/sites/hughmcintyre/2017/11/09/americans-are-spending-more-time-listening-to-music-than-ever-before/?sh = 471de9c92f7f.

American spends over thirteen hours a day partaking of digital media,[97] which means that, inevitably, cultural impressions about love and identity become entwined, even unwittingly, in our theological beliefs. The term "expressive individualism" has become a widespread designation for late modern cultural beliefs about identity, particularly in the West. "Expressive individualism" conveys that authenticity and self-expression stand at the center of our ideas of identity. As Goldstein and Rayner summarize, "The question of 'Who am I?' [has become] increasingly difficult to answer. The new concept of authenticity... announces that each individual is his or her own measure, and if I am not true to myself, I miss the significance of my life."[98] As a result, the late modern world understands identity both as internal and as mutable, meaning we enter into an endless cycle of self-reflection and are constantly reforming our understanding of self-identity.[99] The sources that factor into this sense of identity include gender, race, ethnicity, sexual orientation, political ideology, vocation, religious and spiritual beliefs and experiences, and social relations, all as interpreted and integrated by the self.

Such an understanding of self-identity is not simply a secular phenomenon but something Christians easily fall prey to as well. Take, for example, the intense way in which political identity has become central, especially in the United States, to the extent that political affiliation has become for many, a mark of "true Christianity," rather than the historical commitments of the Christian faith. As Alan Noble warns of expressive individualism in the Church, "by adopting these ephemeral cultural expressions, we may signal to our neighbors that Christianity is merely another consumer preference in the endless sea of preferences we use to define ourselves as individuals."[100]

A theological understanding of love, rooted in the texts and traditions of Christianity, can help us to arrive at a better starting point concerning conceptions of identity. To reach such a place, however, requires us to define more precisely what exactly we mean by "love" in Christian theology. Though some recent, important work has been done on this topic,[101] it is one that needs more

---

[97] Ana Durrani, "The Average American Spends Over 13 Hours A Day Using Digital Media - Here's What They're Streaming," www.forbes.com/home-improvement/internet/streaming-stats/.
[98] Jonah Goldstein and Jeremy Rayner, "The Politics of Identity in Late Modern Society," *Theory and Society* 23.3 (1994): 368. See also Charles Taylor, *The Malaise of Modernity* (Toronto: House of Anansi Press, 1991), 20.
[99] Goldstein and Rayner, "The Politics of Identity in Late Modern Society," 370.
[100] Alan Noble, *Disruptive Witness: Speaking Truth in a Distracted Age* (Downers Grove: IVP, 2018), 28
[101] A few recent volumes include Oliver D. Crisp, James M. Arcadi, and Jordan Wessling, eds., *Love, Divine and Human: Contemporary Essays in Systematic and Philosophical Theology* (New York: Bloomsbury Publishing, 2019); Jon D. Levenson, *The Love of God:*

careful thought and pervasive reflection, for Christians everywhere, since the ideas and actions of love are so central to Christian belief and practice. In my own conception, there are five fundamental dynamics in God's love for which our theological reflection must account.[102] First, God's love if *covenantal*, meaning God's love is reliable, responsible, and committed. God's love as covenantal both obligates God to His people and obligates God's people to Him. The relationship that divine love creates comes with obligations, both for God and for His people.[103] Though there are emotive dimensions to God's love, a Christian conception of love cannot reduce it to an emotional state. Love is a commitment. Second, God's love is *reciprocal*, or *relational*, meaning that God actual enters into a real, dynamic, living relationship with His people, both individually and corporately.[104] God loves without reciprocity (e.g., Rom. 5:8), meaning He does not only extend love to those who love Him, but God's love is intended for and idealized with reciprocity. This idea of God's committed love being reflected in and reciprocated by His people is at the heart of the Old Testament's understanding of the dynamic between God and His people (e.g., Deut. 6:4). Third, God's love is *benevolent*, meaning that in His love, God seeks the good of humanity. His desires, as the Joseph narrative and Paul both illustrate (Gen. 50:20; Rom. 8:28), is to seek the good of His people, even in the midst of the evil that permeates the world. And this seeking-of-the-good-of-humanity is not simply directed at those already in covenant with God but, as John (John 3:16) and Paul (Rom. 5:8) bear witness, the world of sinners as well. Fourth, God's love is *sacrificial*. Since the cross stands at the center of a Christian understanding of God's purpose and mission for the world, and acts as a demonstration of God's love (here again, Rom. 5:8), sacrifice is obviously at the heart of a Christian understanding of love. Fifth, and finally, God's love is *unconditional*. God does not offer His love to those who measure up or are deserving (see, again, Rom. 5:8)[105] but rather to the whole sweep of humanity. Putting all of this together, we may offer a definition of sorts along these lines: Love is *an unwavering* (unconditional) *commitment* (covenantal) *to seek the good of another* (benevolent), *toward deep, relational union* (reciprocal), *even at a great cost to oneself* (sacrificial).

Divine Gift, Human Gratitude, and Mutual Faithfulness in Judaism (Princeton: Princeton University Press, 2015); John C. Peckham, *The Love of God: A Canonical Model* (Downers Grove: IVP, 2015); Jordan Wessling, *Love Divine: A Systematic Account of God's Love for Humanity* (Oxford: Oxford University Press, 2020).

[102] See in particular the work of Levenson (*The Love of God*) and Peckham (*The Love of God*) for overlapping approaches.
[103] See Levenson, *The Love of God*, 1–58.
[104] See Peckham, *The Love of God*, 142–64.
[105] See here, Barclay, *Paul and the Gift*.

To return, now, to the question of identity, my suggestion would be that our ideas of self-conception should find as their starting point what likely served as the center of Jesus' own conception of self-identity. This may be observed from the two places where the Father speaks audibly to Jesus in the Gospels (his baptism and transfiguration). Here the Father says to the Christ, "You are My beloved Son" (Mark 1:11; Matt 3:17; Luke 3:22; Mark 9:7; Matt. 17:5; Luke 9:35; 2 Peter 1:17). Jesus understood himself as one completely secure in the unconditional, covenantal, benevolent, reciprocal, and sacrificial love of God.[106] This was fundamental to his identity. For believers, the New Testament resoundingly speaks the same reality: we are God's beloved children.[107] This is the only thing about God's children that is unchanging, because it is rooted in the life of God, not in our own merits, achievements, activities, or worth. No one can take it away from us, and God's enduring commitment is to love us. This became central to Henri Nouwen's own self-understanding, evidenced when he says:

Jesus came to share his identity with you and to tell you that you are the beloved sons and daughters of God ... God says, "I have loved you with an everlasting love." This is a fundamental truth of your identity. This is who you are whether you feel it or not. You belong to God from eternity to eternity. Life is just an opportunity during a few years to say, "I love you too."[108]

God's love does not change. It is eternally true and present because it is who God is. It is fundamental to His nature. This is the only thing about God's children that is eternally constant, and therefore, the essence of their identity. Identity is not for our own making. It belongs, eternally, to God.

The reality of such a belief may be readily adopted on intellectual terms, but the real transformative effect comes in its internalization. It is one thing to assent to the reality of God's love as grounding our identity, it is another to live in it. Such a process requires both intellectual and emotional growth and is a work that necessarily takes place in a person's interior life. This will cause one to wrestle with the pains and disappointments of their past experiences, which are powerful, shaping forces in our lives. Wilder describes salvation as "the creation of a

---

[106] For a discussion of Jesus' self-identity, see Thomas H. West, *Jesus and the Quest for Meaning: Entering Theology* (Minneapolis: Fortress Press, 2001), 59–69.

[107] As God's children: Matt. 5:9, 45; 8:18; 13:38; Luke 6:35; 20:36; John 1:12; 11:52; 12:36; Rom. 8:14–19, 21, 23; Gal. 3:26; 4:1–6; Eph. 1:5; 5:1; 1 Thess. 5:5; Heb. 2:10; 12:5–8; 1 John 3:2, 10; 5:2. As beloved: Luke 11:42; John 3:16; 5:42; Rom. 5:5, 8; 15:30; 2 Cor. 13:11, 14; Col. 3:12–14; Gal. 2:20; Eph. 2:4; 3:19; 5:2; 2 Thess. 3:5; Titus 3:4; 1 John 4:9–11, 19.

[108] Henri J. M. Nouwen, *Finding My Way Home: Pathways to Life and the Spirit* (New York: Crossroad, 2001), 103.

new attachment with Jesus."[109] Such love requires the involvement and surrender of our entire selves, including our internal life and its desires,[110] and must be both recognized and experienced. In that love is at the core of human desires and identity, rightly ordering our understanding, experience, and pursuit of love toward God and his beliefs about and desires for us creates a transformative effect producing healing and wholeness in our inner lives. It is no wonder, then, 2 Peter sees love as the climax of his virtue catalog. All else Christians believe and live hangs on this reality (Matt. 22:40).

1:8 – Verse 8 begins with an explanatory conjunction (γάρ, "for"), meaning it elaborates on the material in the preceding section. Most translations and commentators interpret the two participles (ὑπάρχοντα, "are," and πλεονάζοντα, "increasing"), which introduce the main verb of the clause (καθίστησιν, "to make"), as conditional ("if these things are yours and increasing"), and so the fulfillment of the action ("this does not make you . . .") is dependent on the condition being met. Possessing and increasing in "these things" prevents one from being "useless" (ἀργούς) and "unfruitful" (ἀκάρπους) in their Christian life. "Useless" (ἀργούς) occurs elsewhere in the New Testament to describe inactivity or unemployment (Matt. 20:3, 6; 1 Tim. 5:13; Titus 1:12). James famously uses the term to describe belief in God without "works," which is lifeless, "useless," and dead (Jas. 2:20). Such an idea in Peter's context means that the engine that drives Christian productivity is Christian virtue. To lack this transformative power is to simply be spinning one's wheels. "Unfruitful" (ἀκάρπους) finds its origination in agricultural language, describing those plants or crops that fail to yield a harvestable product (see Matt. 13:22; Mark 4:19; Jude 12), but can be used in a metaphorical sense as well (see 1 Cor. 14:14; Eph. 5:11; Titus 3:14) as Peter does here.

To connect to the previous section, to avoid being "useless" (ἀργούς) and "unfruitful" (ἀκάρπους), Peter's audience must apply all diligence (1:5) to pursue the virtues in his list in increasing measure (see also 1 Clem. 34:4). Peter emphasizes the goal of progressive transformation into the character of God in Christ. As Chrysostom says, "These things, as well

---

[109] Jim Wilder, *Renovated; God, Dallas Willard, and the Church That Transforms* (Colorado Springs: NavPress, 2020), 104.
[110] Wilders, *Renovated*, 105.

as those already mentioned, namely, virtue, knowledge, continence, patience, godliness, brotherly love and charity, must not only be present in us, they must be present to overflowing. For if their presence is a good thing, how much more their abundance!"[111] As Chrysostom recognizes, the sense of the participle πλεονάζοντα is to increase to the point of excess. These virtues ought not simply to be present in the Christian life but to overflow beyond measure.

This abundant overflow of Christian virtue is again grounded by Peter "in the knowledge of our Lord Jesus Christ," which, as argued previously (see comments on 1:3, 6), is not simply a catechetical or doctrinal knowledge of facts about God but an intimate, personal knowledge of the living Christ. It is union with God through Christ that provides the context and power in which such a transformative encounter can take place. Reuschling summarizes the reality of Peter's ethical framework well in stating:

> This means that the Christian moral life is not automatic but must be attended to, practiced, and habituated. We learn to be good by living well; we learn to be self-controlled by exercising self-control; and we learn mutual affection for others by living in communities where we must practice kindness and love for others. And ironically, we need accompanying virtues to do this. Learning to love requires endurance; practicing godliness requires growth in knowledge; and exercising self-control also means exercising faith. We become these things while we "make every effort" to practice these virtues. And as we do so, we participate in God's life and embody God's own goodness.[112]

1:9 – The inverse of such moral flourishing is described next as a means of contrasting the moral vision that Peter has laid out. This sentence is also constructed as an explanatory clause (γὰρ, "for") describing the one who lacks these qualities. To parallel the two descriptors (ἀργοὺς, "useless," and ἀκάρπους, "unfruitful") in 1:8, the terms here (τυφλός, blind, and μυωπάζων, "nearsighted") offer a metaphorical description of the impaired spiritual vision of the one lacking Christian virtue. While τυφλός is common in the NT (used fifty times, though predominantly in the

---

[111] Chrysostom, in J. A. Cramer, ed., *Catena in Epistolas Catholicas* (Oxford: Clarendon, 1840), 86.
[112] Wyndy Corbin Reuschling, "The Means and End in 2 Peter 1:3–11: The Theological and Moral Significance of Theosis," *Journal of Theological Interpretation* 8.2 (2014): 294.

Gospels), μυωπάζων is not, occurring only here. While the move from blindness to nearsightedness seems to lessen the force of what Peter says, Green argues that the verbal form used here, μυωπάζω, described a more serious eye condition that produced a discharge and led to the eye no longer opening (cf. Pseudo-Zonaras, *Lexicon* 711.11; Suda, *Lexicon*, 1065.1), making it comparable to blindness.[113] The metaphor for blindness as a refusal to see the truth is common in early Christian literature (as Bauckham details, cf. Matt. 15:14; 23:16, 24; Luke 6:39; John 9:40–41; 12:40; Rom. 2:19; 2 Cor. 4:14; *Gos. Thom.* 28; cf. *T. Sim.* 2:7; *T. Dan* 2:4; *T. Jud.* 18:3, 6; 19:4).[114] This metaphor is also found in the Old Testament, particularly in the prophets (e.g., Isa. 42:18–19; 43:8; 56:10; 59:10; Lam. 4:14; Zeph. 1:17; see also Wis. 2:21). While those who possess the virtues Peter describes are useful and fruitful to God, those who lack them are spiritually blind and therefore useless and fruitless.

The participle that follows (λαβών, "having") is probably best taken temporally, describing the circumstances around this lack of virtue, though it could also be taken causally, giving the reason for why these virtues are not present. At focus here is the "forgetting" (λήθην) of one's cleansing of their former sins. The clause offers a bit of a challenge for translators, as can be seen in the variety of how it is handled.[115] The challenge comes from the syntax of the sentence, which, if woodenly translated, would read something like "having forgetfulness of the cleansing of their past sins." The verb here (λαμβάνω) can also mean "to choose" (e.g., Heb. 5:1; also in the LXX Num. 8:6; Amos 2:11), and a volitional notion here would make more sense of the context since Peter's focus is on intentionality on the part of the believer. To forget can certainly be accidental, but forgetting something as significant as what Peter mentions here takes more than a slip of the mind. What Peter warns of is "choosing to forget the cleansing of their former sins," something reiterated by his desire to stir their memory in 1:12–13.

---

[113] Green, *Jude and 2 Peter*, 198.
[114] Bauckham, *Jude–2 Peter*, 189.
[115] NIV: "forgetting that they have been cleansed from their past sins"; ESV: "having forgotten that he was cleansed from his former sins"; NET: "he has forgotten about the cleansing of his past sins"; NRSV: "is forgetful of the cleansing of past sins."

"Although 'cleansing' (τοῦ καθαρισμοῦ) commonly recalls a religious ritual or ceremonial act (Mark 1:44; Luke 2:22; 5:14; John 2:6; 3:25; 2 Macc. 2:16; Josephus, *Ag. Ap.* 1.31§282; *m. Ṭohar., in toto*), the link with 'sin' here points to the idea of moral purification (Heb. 1:3; Job 7:21; and the verbal form in Acts 15:9; 2 Cor. 7:1; Eph. 5:26; Titus 2:14; Heb. 9:14; James 4:8; 1 John 1:7, 9). The reference is most likely to Christian baptism, which, as the Christian rite of initiation, is often described as the event in which divine cleansing occurs (Acts 22:16; Rom. 6:1–14; 1 Cor. 6:9–11; Eph. 5:26; Col. 2:11–13; Titus 3:5; Heb 10:22)."[116] This act appears to have happened in close proximity to the event of one's "conversion" among the earliest Christians, and so one's conversion and baptism are often viewed as one in the same.

1:10 – The conclusion of this subsection is begun here with the conjunction διὸ ("therefore"), which is emphasized and highlighted with μᾶλλον ("even more"). This is followed by the vocative ἀδελφοί ("siblings"), the first term of direct address in the letter (see also 3:1, 8, 14, and 17, which are all ἀγαπητοί, "loved ones"). The use of the language of familial love (see also 1:7) indicated more than just friendship in the ancient world, in contrast to how we might use the term "brother" or "sister" today. Blood-related siblings, as traced primarily through the patriline,[117] were viewed in the first-century Mediterranean world as the strongest social bonds of society[118] and were central to the maintenance or procuring of honor for one's household. As Cicero described, "shared blood binds men together in goodwill and affection" (*On Duties* 1.54). Peter's addressing his audience as "siblings" thus presents a "constructed kinship" in which their social bonds have been rearranged around a new patriline, where God is their Father and they are siblings, demanding a new set of loyalties.[119]

What Peter asks of his siblings is to "be even more eager" (σπουδάσατε) to "make certain" (βεβαίαν ποιεῖσθαι) their "calling" (κλῆσιν) and "election" (ἐκλογή). The command "make every effort," prominent in the

---

[116] Green, *Jude and 2 Peter*, 199. See also Bauckham, *Jude–2 Peter*, 189.
[117] Bruce J. Malina, *The New Testament World: Insights from Cultural Anthropology* (Louisville: Westminster John Knox Press, 2001), 138.
[118] Malina, *The New Testament World*, 138.
[119] See, again, Hellerman, *The Ancient Church as Family*.

discourse as Peter's second imperative,[120] indicates both intentionality and a willingness to expend concentrated energy to perform the required action. Effort and focus will be required. "Making certain" (βεβαίαν ποιεῖσθαι) entails a sense of validity or confirmation, or to be sure of something, in this case the "calling" and "election" of these believers. "Calling" (κλῆσιν) finds usage only occasionally in the New Testament and mostly in Paul's letters (Rom. 11:29; 1 Cor. 1:26; 7:20; Eph. 1:18; 4:1, 4; Phil. 3:14; 2 Thess. 1:11; 2 Tim. 1:9; Heb. 3:1).[121] The calling of believers is an activity performed by God[122] or Christ.[123] Jesus describes the activity as a summons of sorts (e.g., Matt. 22:3-14; Luke 14:15-24), and most references to God's calling of believers in the New Testament fit this general sense, though some have more narrow vocational implications (such as Paul in Gal. 1:15). To have God's calling, then, is to have received and responded to the summons to join in life with God through Jesus Christ. "Election" (ἐκλογή) is also rare in the NT, and is found, again, primarily in Paul (Acts 9:15; Rom. 9:11; 11:5, 7, 28; 1 Thess. 1:4).[124] In a Jewish context, the language of election relates to communal belonging and vocation more so than with later theological concepts of a divine decision to save and condemn certain humans to a predetermined eschatological fate.[125] This notion of belonging (being truly counted among God's people) and vocation (transformative participation in the life of God) fits Peter's imperative contextually quite well and thus asks these believers to "certify," with great eagerness and attention, their own calling and election, through their progressing in Christian virtue. Such a notion may seem to call in to question "salvation

---

[120] Cf. Fresch, "2 Peter," 624.
[121] The verbal form (καλέω) is much more common, used 148 times in the NT.
[122] See Rom. 8:30; 9:7, 12, 24-26; 11:29; 1 Cor. 1:9, 26; 1 Cor. 7:15-24; Gal. 1:6, 15; 5:8, 13; Eph. 1:18; 4:1, 4; Phil. 3:14; Col. 3:15; 1 Thess. 2:12; 4:7; 5:24; 2 Thess. 1:11; 2:14; 1 Tim. 6:12; 2 Tim. 1:9; Heb. 3:1; 9:15; 11:8; 1 Pet. 1:15; 2:9, 21; 3:9; 5:10; Rev. 19:9.
[123] See Mark 1:20; 2:17; Luke 5:32.
[124] Though note the verbal form ἐκλέγομαι is found in Mark 13:20; Luke 6:13; 9:35; 10:42; 14:7; John 6:70; 13:18; 15:16, 19; Acts 1:2, 24; 6:5; 13:17; 15:7, 22; 1 Cor. 1:27, 28; Eph. 1:4; Jas. 2:5.
[125] For a discussion, see my *The Chosen People: Election, Paul, and Second Temple Judaism* (Downers Grove: IVP Academic, 2013). For a condensed overview, see my "Election and Predestination," in *The Dictionary of Paul and His Letters: A Compendium of Contemporary Biblical Scholarship*, ed. Lynn Cohick, Nijay Gupta, and Scot McKnight (Downers Grove: IVP Academic, 2022).

by grace through faith." There are clear participatory dimensions to the New Testament's theology of salvation that place a significant role and responsibility on the believer themself. As Davids summarizes well:

This teaching may sit uncomfortably with some people's theology, but it is the other side of the coin that has on one side that God makes us firm and on this side that we make our own salvation firm. And it is our side of the coin that the believers 2 Peter addresses need to hear, for they have among them some who think that their salvation is firm enough without their pursuing any of the virtues our author recommends.[126]

Peter further explains (γὰρ, "for") the effects of pursuing these virtues in stating "if you are doing these things, you will never ever stumble." The participle here (ποιοῦντες) is adverbial and could be taken as causal (*"because you are doing* these things"), means (*"by doing* these things"), or conditional (*"if you are doing* these things") in force, though most translations and commentators opt for the conditional sense. Since the participle is an imperfective form (present tense) of an activity verb ("doing"), it also has an ongoing sense to it, further underscoring the progressive pursuit of growing in virtuous Christian living, which Peter has described.[127] The result of the condition being fulfilled is that one "will never ever stumble" (οὐ μὴ πταίσητέ ποτε). The combination here of οὐ μὴ with the subjunctive (πταίσητέ) indicates "emphatic negation," an intense form of denial in New Testament Greek, which is heightened further by the addition of ποτε ("ever"). There is a reminiscence here of Gal. 5:16, where Paul states, "Walk by the Spirit, and you will never (οὐ μὴ) fulfill the desires of the flesh." Peter wants his audience to be sure that the pursuit of life with God and the virtues entailed therein will result in eternal reward. Bauckham appears to be correct that "stumble" (from πταίω) more likely has final reward in mind than simply the avoidance of sin given what Peter

---

[126] Davids, *The Letters of 2 Peter and Jude*, 188.
[127] Further, as Frey notes, "The repetition of words or word stems frames these verses between σπουδήν (v. 5) and σπουδάσατε (v. 0) as well as ἐπιχορηγεῖν (vv. 5, 11). This repetition strengthens the admonition to eagerness and emphasizes the correspondence between the 'supply' or development of virtues in life and the final 'supply' or provision of entry into eternal salvation" (Frey, *The Letter of Jude and the Second Letter of Peter*, 269-70).

states in the clause to come. According to Bauckham, this description "pictures the Christian walking the road which will lead him into the eternal kingdom; if he does not stumble on the road he will reach his destination."[128]

1:11 – The last explanatory statement (γάρ, "for") of this subsection (1:8-11) describes the ultimate result of pursuit of life with God in Christ: "entrance into the eternal kingdom of our Lord and Savior Jesus Christ." The phrase "eternal kingdom" (τὴν αἰώνιον βασιλείαν) is unique in the NT, occurring only here, but echoes both the eternal Messianic kingdom of Daniel 7:14 (ἐξουσία αἰώνιος) and the promises of an eternal kingdom to David in his royal covenant in 2 Sam. 7:12-16.[129] The "kingdom of God" or "the kingdom of heaven" is a stock phrase in the Gospels and Acts, which mention the kingdom dozens of times. Kingdom language is less common outside of those writings (Rom. 14:17; 1 Cor. 4:20; 6:9-10; 15:24, 50; Gal. 5:21; Eph. 5:5; Col. 1:13; 4:11; 1 Thess. 2:12; 2 Thess. 1:5; 2 Tim. 4:1, 18; Heb. 1:8; 12:28; Jas. 2:5; Rev. 1:6, 9; 5:10; 11:15; 12:10;), though anywhere we find mention of Messiah/Christ or Lord, the concept of "kingdom" is echoing not far away,[130] so much so that the kingdom of God may be thought of as one and the same as the kingdom of the Messiah (see Matt. 13:41; 16:28; 20:21; John 18:36; Eph. 5:5; Col. 1:13; Heb. 1:8; 2 Tim. 4:1).

The "kingdom" is a phrase also ubiquitous in many Christian circles to the extent that it often loses significance for modern readers.[131] When we see kingdom described and embodied in the New Testament, we find, as McKnight describes, that it has a king (Messiah Jesus), a rule (the authority given to Jesus), a people (redeemed Jews and Gentiles together in the

---

[128] Bauckham, *Jude-2 Peter*, 191.
[129] There is a threefold repetition in the LXX of an "eternal throne" (τὸν θρόνον αὐτοῦ ἕως εἰς τὸν αἰῶνα), and "eternal house and eternal kingdom" (ὁ οἶκος αὐτοῦ καὶ ἡ βασιλεία αὐτοῦ ἕως αἰῶνος ἐνώπιον ἐμοῦ).
[130] For a helpful development of the connection between kingdom and gospel, see N. T. Wright, *How God Became King: Getting to the Heart of the Gospels* (New York: HarperOne, 2012); Scot McKnight, *The King Jesus Gospel: The Original Good News Revisited* (Grand Rapids: Zondervan, 2016); and Matthew Bates, *Salvation by Allegiance Alone: Rethinking Faith, Works, and the Gospel of Jesus the King* (Grand Rapids: Baker Academic, 2017).
[131] For a brief canonical overview, see Patrick Schreiner, *The Kingdom of God and the Glory of the Cross*, Short Studies in Biblical Theology (Wheaton: Crossway, 2018).

people of God), a land (eschatologically speaking, the entirety of creation), and a law (Jesus' authoritative interpretation of Torah).[132] The kingdom is thus a political reality that requires a new set of allegiances, customs, values, and behaviors. Christians become citizens of this new kingdom (Phil. 3:20), which demands allegiance to King Jesus, his character, and his commands. It is clear in the larger context that it is this broad, all-encompassing reality that Peter has in mind as he calls these early Christians into life lived with God, in pursuit of transformative union with Christ, inhabiting and practicing the virtues of Christ in preparation for life in the eternal kingdom to come. This is what Peter means when he asks them to diligently seek the virtuous Christian life as a means of preparation for entrance into the eternal kingdom of our Lord and Savior Jesus Christ.[133] It is through this pursuit (οὕτως, "in this way") that entrance[134] into this glorious kingdom will be "richly supplied" (πλουσίως ἐπιχορηγηθήσεται). It will be abundantly awarded if they belong to God through personal, transformative union with Christ, diligently seeking to live this reality each day as they journey on the perilous road toward the eternal kingdom.[135]

---

[132] Scot McKnight, *Kingdom Conspiracy: Returning to the Radical Mission of the Local Church* (Grand Rapids: Brazos Press, 2014), 205. As Bauckham notes, "The eternal kingdom here is not simply 'heaven,' but looks forward to the cosmic reign of God in righteousness in the new heaven and new earth (3:13)" (Bauckham, *Jude-2 Peter*, 192).

[133] As Donelson observes, "The language of entry in the kingdom recalls that of the Gospels (e.g., Matt. 5:20; 18:3; Mark 10:23; Luke 18:17; John 3:5)" (Donelson, *I & II Peter and Jude*, 223).

[134] It is clear that a wordplay exists here where εἴσοδος is used to describe the eschatological entrance into the heavenly kingdom and ἔξοδος in the LXX can describe both Israel's exit from Egypt (e.g., Exod. 19:1; Ps. 113:1) and possibly exile as well (cf. Isa. 37:28) or "departure" from life, as in Sir. 38:23 or Wis. 3:2 or, in the immediate context here, 2 Pet. 1:15. So, Peter's "exit" from this present life will be met with "entrance" into the kingdom.

[135] This is underscored by Donelson in stating: "2 Peter focuses more on the positive role of virtue. These verses insist that living the righteous life is central to the narrative of salvation. Without the presence of these virtues, there is no promise of final blessing.... In 2 Peter the announced necessity of virtues explains the dangers of the immoral life that the false prophets lead and promote" (Donelson, *I & II Peter and Jude*, 223). See also Dennis D. Sylva, "A Unified Field Picture of Second Peter 1.3-15: Making Rhetorical Sense Out of Individual Images," in *Reading Second Peter with New Eyes: Methodological Reassessments of the Letter of Second Peter*, ed. Robert L. Webb and Duane F. Watson (New York: Bloomsbury, 2010), 109.

1:12 – This verse acts as the summation of this first major unit, introduced here with the conjunction διό ("Therefore"), which serves as an inferential marker from what has come before it. Though a person change is introduced here (from "you" to "I"), the presence of δέ in 1:13, which typically marks a new section or development, along with the shift in tense from 1:12 to 1:13 (present to future), which is maintained in what follows, along with the fact that διό does not typically serve to introduce new material, indicates that this verse should be taken with what precedes it, though it does serve as a transition to the next major unit as well.[136]

The "I will continually remind" (μελλήσω ἀεὶ) here is the first use of first-person address in the letter, which will occur a number of times in 1:12–19, and then again in 3:1 and 3:13. This resurfaces the question of authorship addressed in the introductory material.[137] For those who hold that the author is Peter, writing during his lifetime, this would be taken as a matter of a natural use of Peter's own perspective in this letter. If 2 Peter is composed after Peter's lifetime, it would necessitate that either the letter's author is impersonating Peter, which the early church was quite wary of recognizing as a legitimate means of producing scriptural texts, or that an associate of Peter, writing on Peter's behalf, possibly even after his death, has integrated here Peter's own testimony as a part of his composition.

Peter's statement here that he "will continually remind you" offers a bit of a grammatical difficulty, leading Kelly, for example, to state the section is "clumsily and pretentiously composed."[138] What Peter might mean by a future persistent reminder here has led to several different suggestions by interpreters. Davids notes three possibilities: (1) it refers to some future letter from Peter, (2) it refers to the production of Mark's Gospel,[139] or (3) "the reference is to 2 Peter itself viewed as future with respect to its arrival."[140] This latter option is most likely and best fits the context of the unit. Further, it was not uncommon for ancient letters to adopt different deployments of past, present, and future time to describe things

---

[136] See Fresch, "2 Peter," 631.
[137] See Introduction: Authorship and Date.
[138] Kelly, *The Epistles of Peter and Jude*, 315.
[139] Eusebius, referencing Papias, suggests the Gospel of Mark was sourced from Peter's teaching (*Eccl. Hist.* 2.15.1).
[140] Davids, *The Letters of 2 Peter and Jude*, 197.

already happening or anticipated in the future. Tense choice could be descriptive of the author's past, present, or future action in writing the document, or of the audiences anticipated response of its future receipt.[141] Further, since ancient letters were at times believed to facilitate the presence of the author, the ongoing presence of the letter in the community could act, by extension, as Peter's ongoing presence and thus ongoing reminding.[142]

Concerning the need to remind of "these things" (τούτων), Peter likely has in mind both the larger unit of 1:3–11, which focuses on life with God and its transformative results, as well as other things entailed by that theme, which may be expanded by his mention of their being "confirmed in the truth you possess" (ἐστηριγμένους ἐν τῇ παρούσῃ ἀληθείᾳ). The act of reminder in rhetoric was seen as a means of instruction that honored the knowledge of recipients rather than shamed or demeaned them. As Davids remarks, in classical rhetoric it was deemed good custom to remind readers as if they knew the information already even if they did not.[143] Our author may be following this custom or may have known the audience already knew these things, but regardless of which option is most likely, the act of reminder underscores the importance with which these matters are viewed by 2 Peter's author.

2 PETER 1:13–21: PROPHETIC TESTIMONY

[13] Now, I consider it right, as long as I inhabit this body, to awaken you by reminder,

[14] knowing that the laying aside of this habitation is coming soon, just as our Lord Jesus Christ revealed to me,

[15] so I will also make every effort at all times to have you, after my departure, make recollection of these things.

[16] For we did not make known to you the power and presence of our Lord Jesus Christ by following cleverly created myths but by becoming eyewitnesses of that man's majesty.

---

[141] Green likewise notes this phenomena (*Jude and 2 Peter*, 208).
[142] See Donelson, *I & II Peter and Jude*, 226; Michael Trapp, ed. *Greek and Latin Letters: An Anthology with Translation* (Cambridge: Cambridge University Press, 2003), 39. See also Bauckham, *Jude-2 Peter*, 195–96.
[143] Davids, *The Letters of 2 Peter and Jude*, 192.

¹⁷ For when he received honor and glory from God a voice such as this was brought to him by the Majestic Glory, "This is my son, my beloved, this is one with whom I take delight,"

¹⁸ and we heard this voice brought from heaven when we were with him on the holy mountain.

¹⁹ and we have the utmost reliable prophetic word, to which you do well to pay attention as to a lamp shining in a dark place, until the day dawns and the morning star rises in your hearts,

²⁰ knowing this first, that every prophecy of Scripture does not come from one's own interpretation;

²¹ for it was not by the will of a human that a prophecy was ever produced, but people brought along by the Holy Spirit spoke from God.

1:13 – The presence of δέ ("Now") here likely signals the beginning of a new unit and the transition from Peter's exhortation to his personal remarks concerning his present state of affairs and his desire for the community he addresses.[144] This section is primarily what has led Bauckham and others to identify 2 Peter as a testament,[145] since the testamentary features that the letter shares are primarily found in 1:13–21. As was argued in the Introduction,[146] however, it is better for us to see 2 Peter as a letter that has some testamentary features, but not as a formal testament, since formal testaments also include a narrative framework and a description of the figure's death, which 2 Peter lacks.[147] As such, some of the arguments that Bauckham makes concerning 2 Peter based on its testamentary nature do not hold up since the letter does not conform to the standard elements of the genre and little evidence exists of the form of a testamentary letter or testaments as "transparent fictions."

This section does share, however, the major elements of a farewell speech, as Davids outlines.[148] Farewell speeches contain five major features: (1) prediction of death (cf. 1:14), (2) prediction of future crises (cf. 2:1), (3) exhortation to virtue (cf. 1:12–15), (4), blessing or commission (cf. 1:12–13, 15, 19), and (5) reference to the legacy of the dying person.[149] For 2 Peter,

---

[144] Fresch, "2 Peter," 631.
[145] See Bauckham, *Jude–2 Peter*, 131–38, 194–203.
[146] See Introduction: Reading Scripture as Ancient Texts.
[147] Donelson concludes similarly (Donelson, *I & II Peter and Jude*, 224).
[148] See, for example, Gen. 49; Deut. 31–33; Josh. 24:1–28; 1 Kgs 2:1–9; Luke 22:14–36; John 13–17; Acts 20:17–35
[149] Davids, *The Letters of 2 Peter and Jude*, 191–92.

the crisis is not only future but also present, though the other features of a farewell speech may be found here.

This section also evidences a break in the style of writing observed so far in the letter, in addition to the sustained transition to first-person material. As Witherington notes, "Here we do not find the long-convoluted sentences that characterize Asiatic style at its most florid. Rather, the style here is more like what we find in 1 Peter."[150] Furthermore, numerous similarities exist between this unit and 1 Peter 1:10-12,[151] which may indicate, as Witherington suggests, that we have presented here the testimony of Peter integrated into the letter by its composer or compiler. Indeed, portions of the section conform even to the general patterns by which we recognize creedal or traditional material, which may mean these traditions had been formalized and were well known to churches acquainted with Peter by this time.[152] This would further fit with the repetition of words of reminder in this section, as the author here indicates that little new information is being conveyed but is rather a call to remember things formerly received.

The evoking of the first person here, "I consider it right . . .," gives direct address to the audience from the apostle Peter. It is difficult to say how the original recipients would have perceived this material if it were composed after the apostle's death, but the purpose here is to evoke both the apostolic memory and authority for the present moment. Indeed, we find little in the letter that might distinguish it from the early apostolic teaching we see in other texts of the New Testament, which no doubt contributed in large part to the inclusion of the letter in the canon. The letter reads as a faithful deposit of the apostolic witness.

Another invoking of remembrance ("to awaken you by reminder"; διεγείρειν ὑμᾶς ἐν ὑπομνήσει) occurs here, underscoring both that the text preserves and applies the apostolic message already received and that what is being offered is not a new revelatory event but a retrieval of things already delivered to these believers. Peter wants to "wake them up" (διεγείρω; also 2 Pet. 3:1), just as the disciples woke Jesus, who was asleep in the boat during the storm (Mark 4:38; Luke 8:24). The storm of the false

---

[150] Witherington, *Letters for Hellenized Christians*, 317.
[151] Mayor, *The Epistle of St. Jude and the Second Epistle of St. Peter*, lxix-xxiv.
[152] See comments below on 1:17-18.

teachers is upon them, and Peter, fearing for their safety, wants to rouse them from the complacency into which they may have settled. The purpose of such a reminder, as Green suggests, is to deepen further the commitment and virtue of the recipients: "Reminders are part of the fabric of moral instruction (1 Thess. 2:9; 3:4; 4:1; 5:1–2; 2 Thess. 3:5, 10), and Peter's purpose in the present (1:13; 3:1) and future (vv. 12, 15) is to remind his readers of the apostolic teaching that they had ... His aim is to exhort them to maintain Christian virtue."[153]

The end of 1:13 provides the first indication that Peter's death may be impending ("as long as I inhabit this body"). The analogy that Peter uses here of "habitation" (ἐν τούτῳ τῷ σκηνώματι) invokes a term uncommon in the New Testament, though not a hapax. The cluster of terms related to σκήνωμα (σκηνή "tent"; σκηνοπηγία "Festival of Booths/Tabernacles"; σκηνοποιός "tent maker"; σκῆνος "tent"; σκηνόω "take up residence") all convey similar images of a temporary or humble dwelling place.[154]

1:14 – What was implied in the previous verse is stated plainly here. Peter declares that the "laying aside of this habitation is coming soon" (ταχινή ἐστιν ἡ ἀπόθεσις τοῦ σκηνώματός μου). Speaking of a body as a temporary location, and especially as a "tent," was not uncommon in Jewish literature. Such an image is offered by Hezekiah as he reflected on his impending death, which the Lord postponed, stating, "like a tent (σκηνὴν), my life has departed and been taken from me" (Isa. 38:12, LXX). Paul, similarly, mourns, "we who are in this tent (ἐν τῷ σκήνει) groan" while waiting for a heavenly dwelling/body (2 Cor. 5:4).

The language of escaping a temporary body may call to mind here debates about substance dualism and the material and spiritual composition of human nature.[155] Theological discussions surround the question of the relationship of body and soul and the relationship of the present body to existence in the intermediate and eternal states. Such debates exist, at least in part, because a clear and descriptive metaphysic of such realities is never given by the biblical authors. It does not seem such a clarification is

---

[153] Green, *Jude and 2 Peter*, 211.
[154] See Gen. 4:20; 12:8; 13:3, 5, 12; 18:1; Num. 24:6; Deut. 16:16; 31:10; 33:18; Josh. 3:14; Judg. 5:17; 19:9; 2 Sam. 7:23; 1 Kgs. 8:4; Zech. 14:16, 18, 19; Wis. 9:15; 2 Macc. 10:6; John 1:14; Acts 7:46; 2 Cor. 5:4; Rev. 13:6; 21:3.
[155] For a comparison of views, see Joel B. Green and Stuart L. Palmer, *In Search of The Soul: Four Views of The Mind-body Problem* (Downers Grove: IVP Academic, 2005).

intended by Peter here, and though some of the imagery he employs resonates with Greek philosophical systems, it does not really seem his intention here to stake out a position on such matters. As Green suggests, "We should not over press Peter's language to conclude that he viewed the body as nothing more than the temporary dwelling of the soul. His choice of anthropological terms at this point is governed by his desire to stress the transitory nature of his existence and his imminent demise."[156]

The second major question that arises from this verse is what Peter means in stating that his imminent departure will happen "just as our Lord Jesus Christ revealed to me." The language of "revealing" (ἐδήλωσέν) here insinuates a prophetic revelation, as other occurrences of the verb (δηλόω) in the NT similarly allude (Luke 20:37; 1 Cor. 3:13; Heb. 9:8). The question, then, is to what prophecy does this refer? Bauckham suggests five possibilities: (1) John 13:36–38, (2) John 21:18–19, (3) *Apoc. Pet.* R, (4) *Acts Verc.* 35, (5) Epistle of Clement to James 2.[157] Of these options, the last three are likely after the composition of 2 Peter and thus not good candidates for influence. The possibility of a reference to John 13:36 or John 21:18 would depend on the dating of the two documents and whether or not John's Gospel comes first. Bauckham strongly favors John 21:18 as the likely candidate, though it is also a possibility that the text refers to a revelation from Jesus to Peter that does not appear in the surviving literature or perhaps was never even written down but was known to Peter personally or transmitted orally among early Christians in Peter's network of influence.[158] John 21:18–19 also focuses on the manner of Peter's death, rather than the timing, which is the facet primarily in view here.

1:15 – How Peter intends to have his audience recall these things "at all times" (ἑκάστοτε) after his departure is not explicitly stated in the text but would likely be describing the function of the letter itself.[159] As letters often did in the ancient world, the composition stands, as Green states, "for the apostle's presence before the church both now and in the future. The

---

[156] Green, *Jude and 2 Peter*, 211.
[157] Bauckham, *2 Peter-Jude*, 200–201.
[158] Frey prefers the *Apocalypse of Peter* as the prophecy of literary inspiration of the author, but this would require that text be earlier than 2 Peter, which is still a matter of some dispute (Frey, *The Letter of Jude and the Second Letter of Peter*, 289–91). On this matter, see the Introduction: Authorship and Date.
[159] Bauckham, *2 Peter-Jude*, 202.

author does not see himself divorced from the message of this composition even after his 'departure.' Authors continue to speak through their texts long after they have passed away, and their texts should never be separated from their person."[160]

The urgency of the message is affirmed by Peter making "every effort" for this message to be before the recipients' hearts and minds. The verb used here (σπουδάζω) occurs four times in the letter (1:10, 15; 3:14; the noun σπουδή is used in 1:5), here in its third use. The other uses refer to the urgency of developing moral virtue, and, though the object of effort is different here, the urgency is likely connected to that development here. As Green notes, "Peter's concern is that 'these things' will be available to them after his departure, and these have to do with the moral life."[161]

The "departure" (ἔξοδος) that Peter speaks of concerns his impending death, referenced previously in 1:14. Though language of "exodus" (ἔξοδος) may recall for biblically informed readers the events of Moses and Israel in Egypt, the term became used at times in other Jewish literature (Luke 9:31; also Josephus, *Ant.* 4.189; Wis. 7:6) as an analogy for death as it is here. The use of "exodus" here also contrasts with the journey of the reader seeking "entrance" (εἴσοδος) into the heavenly kingdom in 1:11. As Sylva notes in his study,[162] the language of "journeying" dominates the imagery used in 1:3–15 (examples include "escaping" [1:4], "blindness" [1:9], "stumbling" [1:10], and "entrance" [1:11]). Sylva summarizes,

> Peter functions as leader of the recipients, who are on the same journey, marking the trail for them and sending word back that the trail is the right one. His situation is analogous to theirs. Rhetographically, Peter can speak effectively to those whose goal is the "entrance into the eternal kingdom" because he himself is at that point, referred to by his own "exodus." Finally, he "intends" (μελλήσω; v.12) to make sure that the recipients "always" (ἀεί; v. 12) hear his words, both before and after his death (vv. 12, 15). The rhetorical effect of this multiple blend is to highlight the importance of the knowledge that the recipients have received, as written about in vv. 3–11. At the end of his own personal journey, Peter is envisioned as focusing not on the goal ahead, but rather on the goal of looking back, both before and after the completion of this journey, to insure that this knowledge is transmitted.[163]

---

[160] Green, *Jude and 2 Peter*, 214.
[161] Green, *Jude and 2 Peter*, 214.
[162] Sylva, "A Unified Field Picture of Second Peter 1.3–15," 91–118.
[163] Sylva, "A Unified Field Picture of Second Peter 1.3–15," 111.

1:16 – Verse 16 opens with the explanatory conjunction γάρ ("for"). As Fresch notes, "Contrary to expectation, the author does not move directly to the stirring reminder. Verse 16 is introduced by γάρ, signaling the content as background information ... the author discerns the need first to defend their authority and credibility, presumably to ensure that the readers do in fact listen."[164] The author overall, however, is less concerned with their own personal credibility than with the reliability of the testimony about the transfiguration of Jesus and what it implies for His future return and judgment. The broadening of the subject here from singular to plural insinuates that this is about the reliability of apostolic testimony rather than being only about the author's reliability, though the two are obviously related.

Bauckham, following Neyrey, recognizes the form οὐ ... ἀλλά, which occurs here (as well as 1:21 and 3:9) as offering a response to an objection, likely sourced from Peter's false-teaching opponents.[165] This would be the reader's first glimpse into what kind of trouble the false teachers are causing, namely in suggesting that the apostolic teaching concerning the incarnation and future return of Christ could be dismissed as "cleverly created myths" (σεσοφισμένοις μύθοις).[166] Green agrees, noting, "Here we likely have an echo of the heretics' own *vituperatio* against apostolic theology."[167] The device of *vituperatio* functioned to both denounce the wicked and to teach the character of the moral life by examples of vice in addition to virtue.[168]

The focus here concerns what the apostles (represented as "we") "made known" to the recipients concerning the "power and presence" of the Lord Jesus Christ. Green notes that the "making known" that Peter describes here (ἐγνωρίσαμεν) often describes the activity of disclosing divine

---

[164] Fresch, "2 Peter," 638.
[165] Bauckham, *Jude–2 Peter*, 204–5; cf. Jerome H. Neyrey, *The Form and Background of the Polemic in 2 Peter* (unpublished doctoral dissertation, Yale University, 1977), 18–19, 22, 24.
[166] As Donelson summarizes, three suggestions are offered to what "myths" the author refers: (1) the opponents are arguing based upon myths, (2) the opponents accuse the apostolic tradition of being founded upon myths, or (3) the distinction is rhetorical rather than historical (Donelson, *I & II Peter and Jude*, 231). Based upon the reading suggested above, option 2 is most likely.
[167] Green, *Jude and 2 Peter*, 217.
[168] See Green, *Jude and 2 Peter*, 18–26.

revelation (cf. John 15:15; 17:26; Acts 2:28; Rom. 9:22–23; 16:26; Eph. 1:9; 3:3, 5, 10; Col. 1:27) or specifically relates to apostolic testimony (cf. 1 Cor. 12:3; 15:1; 2 Cor. 8:1; Gal. 1:11; Eph. 6:19).[169] Such is doubly the case here (divine revelation proclaimed through apostolic testimony).

The terms "power and presence" (δύναμιν καὶ παρουσίαν) form a hendiadys (i.e., "powerful presence"), and the event that they disclose is clarified in 1:17–18 as the Transfiguration. While, as Bauckham notes, the term παρουσία typically refers to Christ's future (i.e., "second") coming,[170] the immediate context indicates that the first coming is in mind here, confirmed by the explanatory connector γάρ at the beginning of 1:17. It is specifically the power displayed in his transfiguration that is in focus for the author, though this event clearly foreshadows his second coming in glory and for judgment.[171] Such a link between the Transfiguration and the Second Coming was already established in the Gospels, wherein Jesus states that the Son of Man will come again with his angels in the glory of his Father (cf. Matt. 16:27–28; Mark 8:38–9:1; Luke 9:26–27).[172] Further, this description of a future return immediately precedes the event of the Transfiguration in each of the Synoptic Gospel accounts.[173]

The modes of information transfer contrasted here are "cleverly created myths" (σεσοφισμένοις μύθοις), which is apparently how the false teachers described the apostolic testimony, and the "eyewitness" (ἐπόπται) account of the apostles of "that man's majesty" (τῆς ἐκείνου μεγαλειότητος). Both of the terms used in the phrase "cleverly created myths" have negative connotations. The term μυθοί occurs often in ancient literature, including Jewish literature, as something that contrasts true

---

[169] Green, *Jude and 2 Peter*, 219.
[170] Bauckham, *Jude–2 Peter*, 215. LSJ defines παρουσία as "presence"; "arrival"; "especially a visit of a royal or official personage" (Henry George Liddell and Robert Scott, *A Greek-English Lexicon* (Oxford: Clarendon Press, 1940), www.perseus.tufts.edu/hopper/morph.jsp?la=greek&l=PAROUSI%2FA#lexicon).
[171] Neyrey recognizes the presence of both interpretations in the early Christian tradition, but it may be that Peter has both in mind here rather than one or the other (Jerome H. Neyrey, "The Apologetic Use of the Transfiguration in 2 Peter 1:16–21," *CBQ* 42:4 (1980): 504–19. See also Witherington, *Letters for Hellenized Christians*, 315–16.
[172] On this point, see Harink, *1 & 2 Peter*, 158.
[173] For a recent theological exploration of the Transfiguration, see Patrick Schreiner, *The Transfiguration of Christ: An Exegetical and Theological Reading* (Grand Rapids: Baker Academic, 2024).

information.¹⁷⁴ While the contrasting term, ἐπόπται ("eyewitnesses"; compare also with ἐποπτεύσαντες in 1 Pet. 2:12 and 3:2), was used in relation to advancement in the mystery religions,¹⁷⁵ Peter's use here simply describes one who observed an event attentively (e.g., Esth. 5:1a; 2 Macc. 3:39; 7:35; 3 Macc. 2:21). Rather than inventing fictive legends about the Messianic glory of Jesus, Peter asserts that the testimony of the apostles is credible because they were observers of these events.¹⁷⁶ From the Gospel accounts, we are told that Peter, James, and John were the only disciples to accompany Jesus to the Mount of Transfiguration, and so the "we" represented here would naturally constitute that particular trio.

1:17-18 - The account of the Transfiguration given here, while sharing certain overlap with the Gospel accounts, does not quite match the details of any of those documents. In terms of differences, while the Synoptic accounts describe Jesus and the disciples ascending "the mountain" (τὸ ὄρος; Luke 9:28) or "a high mountain" (ὄρος ὑψηλὸν; cf. Matt. 17:1; Mark 9:2), Peter has "the holy mountain" (τῷ ἁγίῳ ὄρει). In the Synoptic accounts, where the divine voice comes from "the cloud" (ἐκ τῆς νεφέλης), Peter describes the voice coming from the "Majestic Glory" (μεγαλοπρεποῦς δόξης) and "heaven" (ἐξ οὐρανοῦ). The quotation of the heavenly voice in 2 Peter matches most closely with Matthew's version, though differences between the two exist, primarily in syntax, and Matthew includes the phrase "Listen to him!" where Peter does not:

2 Pet. 1:17: "This is my son, my beloved, this is one with whom I take delight" (**Ὁ υἱός μου ὁ ἀγαπητός** μου **οὗτός ἐστιν** εἰς ὃν ἐγὼ **εὐδόκησα**)

Matt. 17:5: "This is my beloved Son, with whom I take delight. Listen to him!" (**Οὗτός ἐστιν ὁ υἱός μου ὁ ἀγαπητός**, ἐν ᾧ **εὐδόκησα**· ἀκούετε αὐτοῦ)

In examining the parallels, Bauckham suggests, "We may conclude that the evidence is strongly in favor of the view that in his account of the Transfiguration the author of 2 Peter was not dependent on the synoptic

---

¹⁷⁴ See Plato, *Tim.* 26e; Philo, *Opif.* 1; *Exsecr.* 162; Josephus, *Ant.* 1.22; *Ag. Ap.* 2.256; Plutarch, *Is. Os.* 20; cf. Kelly, *The Epistles of Peter and of Jude*, 316.
¹⁷⁵ See Green, *Jude and 2 Peter*, 220-21.
¹⁷⁶ The "eyewitness" nature of the apostolic proclamation was an important feature of the witness of the early church (e.g., 1 Cor. 15:3-8; Gal. 1:11-17). For a study related to eyewitness testimony in the ancient world, see Richard J. Bauckham, *Jesus and the Eyewitnesses: The Gospels as Eyewitness Testimony* (Grand Rapids: Eerdmans, 2008).

Gospels but on independent tradition, which could perhaps be his own knowledge of Peter's preaching."¹⁷⁷ Frey, in contrast, considers the direction of influence to go from the Synoptic tradition, through the *Apocalypse of Peter*, into 2 Peter, noting from Gründstäudl that "clear differences from Matt are found in 2 Pet only where 2 Pet agrees with [*Apoc. Pet.* Version] E."¹⁷⁸ The primary parallels that Frey cites between 2 Peter and the *Apocalypse of Peter* (E), which are absent in the Gospels, are the reference to the "holy mountain" (ἐν τῷ ἁγίῳ ὄρει), the voice coming from heaven (ἐξ οὐρανοῦ) instead of the cloud (ἐκ τῆς νεφέλης), the receipt of "honor and glory" (τιμὴν καὶ δόξαν). For the first parallel, the phrase "holy mountain" occurs extensively in Jewish literature (e.g., Ps. 2:6; 3:5; 14:1; 42:3; 47:2; 86:1; 98:9; Joel 2:1; 4:17; Obad. 16–17; Hab. 3:3; Zeph. 3:11; 8:3; Isa. 11:9; 27:13; 56:7, 13; 65:11; 65:25; Jer. 38:23; Ezek. 20:40; 28:14; Dan. 9:16–17, 20; 11:45; 1 Macc. 11:37; Wis. 9:8), and one could simply explain the presence of the phrase as from the influence of Jewish traditions. Concerning the second parallel, the occurrence of the phrase "from heaven" is so common in Old Testament literature, one could see how such a substitution may naturally occur, whereas "from the cloud" occurs in biblical literature only in the Synoptic accounts. Concerning the ascribing of "honor and glory" to Christ in 2 Pet. 1:17, Frey notes that in *Apoc. Pet.*, it is those who pursue God's righteousness, not Jesus, who are promised honor and glory. While the occurrence of the phrase in this ordering is uncommon (only in 1 Tim. 1:17; Rev. 5:12–13 in the NT), it also finds parallels in Jewish literature (Exod. 28:2, 40; Dan. 2:37; 4:30) as well as Greco-Roman works (e.g., Thucydides, *Hist.* 4.17.4; Plutarchus, *Fab. Max.*, 27.4.5; Isocrates, *Mytil.*, 6.3; Demosthenes, *De pace*, 21.2–3). Likewise, "glory" is present in the context of Matthew (16:27) and in the text of Luke (9:31–32). With the date of *Apoc. Pet.* being uncertain (and generally postulated as mid-second century), it seems more compelling evidence would be required to support this possibility based on the somewhat generic parallels suggested, which are not exact and may be found in other Jewish literature.¹⁷⁹ As Foster

---

¹⁷⁷ Bauckham, *Jude–2 Peter*, 210.
¹⁷⁸ Gründstäudl, *Petrus Alexandrinus*. 120, quoted in Frey, *The Letter of Jude and the Second Letter of Peter*, 296.
¹⁷⁹ For interactions with Frey's thesis, see Jörg Frey, Matthijs den Dulk, Jan G. van der Watt, eds., *2 Peter and the Apocalypse of Peter: Towards a New Perspective* (Leiden: Brill, 2019).

summarizes, "These points of contact are slight and brief ... [and] are not sufficient to establish a strong argument for literary dependence."[180] Furthermore, as Bauckham argues, the account in *Apoc. Pet.* is an apocalyptic encounter with Jesus before an ascension event, not an account of the Transfiguration, which makes it all the less likely that it is the source for 2 Peter's Transfiguration description.[181] Bauckham thus concludes, quite forcefully, "In my view, Frey has hugely exaggerated the significance of the coincidence between these two texts."[182] While the Gospel of Matthew is the most likely text of influence, it is unlikely 2 Peter draws from *Apoc. Peter* in this passage and uncertain if the Synoptic texts are influential at all.

Also of interest, the passage shares certain features of New Testament creeds and hymns, which suggest perhaps this was even a formalized piece of testimony from a preexistent source. As Gordley summarizes, creeds and hymns are often marked by the following criteria:

1) contain words like "deliver," "believe," or "confess"; 2) marked by contextual dislocation; 3) do not fit the context syntactically; 4) exhibit unique terminology or style; 5) repeat the same formula; 6) exhibit simple syntax and proceeds by thesis rather than argument; 7) stand out; 8) contain rhythm; 9) arranged in lines and strophes; 10) marked by appositions and noun predicates; 11) favor participles and relative clauses; 12) refer to elementary truth or salvation history as normative.[183]

This text in 2 Pet. 1:17 appears to meet criteria 1, 2, 3, 4, 6, 7, 9, 11, and 12, meaning this formulation of the Transfiguration event may have been formalized for memorization and transmission in the early church, possibly by the apostles themselves.

This verse is framed as an explanatory comment on 1:16, describing how Peter and the apostles witnessed the coming and power of Christ and his

---

[180] Paul Foster, "Does the Apocalypse of Peter Help to Determine the Date of 2 Peter?," in *2 Peter and the Apocalypse of Peter: Towards a New Perspective*, ed. Jörg Frey, Matthijs Dulk, and Jan van der Watt (Leiden: Brill, 2019), 256.
[181] Richard J. Bauckham, "2 Peter and the Apocalypse of Peter Revisited: A Response to Jörg Frey," in *2 Peter and the Apocalypse of Peter: Towards a New Perspective*, ed. Jörg Frey, Matthijs Dulk, and Jan van der Watt (Leiden: Brill, 2019), 269.
[182] Bauckham, "2 Peter and the Apocalypse of Peter Revisited," 272. As he continues, "In 1998, I concluded only that a literary relationship is 'somewhat probable ....' So I have changed my mind and have concluded that the case for a literary relationship is actually very weak" (277).
[183] Summarized in Matthew Gordley, *New Testament Christological Hymns: Exploring Texts, Contexts, and Significance* (Downers Grove: InterVarsity Press, 2018), 21.

majesty. The episode here, contrary to the depiction in *Apoc. Pet.* clearly has the Transfiguration in view, which gives explanation then to the "honor and glory" (τιμὴν καὶ δόξαν) that Peter witnessed Jesus receiving from God. It is possible Peter is also framing this account in line with a Christological reading of Psalm 2:6–8. Lexical similarities between the two texts consist both of the descriptor "holy mountain" (ὄρος τὸ ἅγιον / τῷ ἁγίῳ ὄρει) and "You are/this is my son" (Υἱός μου εἶ σύ / Ὁ υἱός μου ὁ ἀγαπητός μου), as well as the parallel of the heavenly voice (ἐν οὐρανοῖς / ἐξ οὐρανοῦ), as well as possible overtones of the intertexts of Matt. 3:17; Mark 1:11; and Luke 3:22 with Isa. 42:1, though the lexical similarities to the LXX are absent here.[184]

The voice here in 2 Pet. 1:17 is said to be "brought" to Christ "from heaven" (1:18) as well as by the "Majestic Glory" (μεγαλοπρεποῦς δόξης; 1:17), a phrase unparalleled in biblical literature, though it bears some resemblance to constructions found elsewhere (Deut. 33:26 [LXX]; 2 Macc. 8:15; 15:13; see also ἡ μεγάλη δόξα, "great glory," cf. *T. Levi* 3:4; *1 En.* 102.3; Isa. 11:32; Heb. 1:3). This may demonstrate again the penchant of the author of 2 Peter to use more verbose and grand language whenever possible, though this section is generally more "toned down" than others, and particularly when compared with chapter 2.

A clear emphasis on the divine activities in these events is conveyed not only from the heavenly voice speaking but from the fourfold repetition of φέρω (ἐνεχθείσης [1:17]; ἐνεχθεῖσαν [1:18]; ἠνέχθη [1:21]; φερόμενοι [1:21]) in this passage.[185] The heavenly voice speaks at the Transfiguration (emphasized through two occurrences in 1:17 and 18) and the prophetic word is not "brought" from the will of the human prophet (1:21) but rather through the Holy Spirit "bringing along" those chosen human messengers. This lexical play is used to clearly stitch together the divine utterance given to Christ (and those present) at the Transfiguration with the prophetic utterances given to God's chosen instruments, to which the previously mentioned apostles belong.

---

[184] On connections between the Transfiguration and Sinai typology, particularly from Exodus 20, see A. D. A. Moses, *Matthew's Transfiguration Story and Jewish-Christian Controversy*, JSNT Supp 122 (Sheffield: Sheffield Academic Press, 1996).

[185] I am grateful for my PhD student, Noah Fate-Cloud, for alerting me to this.

The Transfiguration is, perhaps, an underappreciated dimension of the Gospel narratives. The revelatory act that takes places there, occurring strategically near the midpoint of the Gospels of Matthew and Mark, was no doubt an event of emphasis for the Evangelists. Peter sees this as an essentially revelatory act, an apocalyptic unveiling about the heavenly reality of Jesus' identity.[186] As Hart summarizes, the transfiguration "offers us a glimpse of the eschatological horizon of salvation; for the same light that the three disciples were permitted to see break forth from the body of Christ will, in the fullness of time, enter into and transform all of creation, with that glory that the Son had with the Father before the world began."[187] This dual dimension of the Transfiguration, which the Gospels themselves develop, in which a present, as well as future, reality is revealed is precisely the purpose of Peter's words here. And such an event was fitting to employ for his audience considering the dangers that the false teachers among them were posing. As Harink describes, "When we deny or diminish the significance of the apocalyptic enthronement of Jesus Christ, and of his coming in power, we are attempting to live in some other world, a world that does not exist by the word and judgment and action of the one creator God."[188] Such was the world of the false teachers, where Christ was not Lord (cf. 2 Pet. 2:1) or the soon coming judge (2 Pet. 3:3-4), and the present world was therefore one that could be lived in without concern for future consequence. Such an ideation, however, was a direct affront to the apostolic teachings concerning the gospel of Jesus Christ, who is the once revealed and now ascended Lord of heaven and earth, coming again to judge the living and dead.

1:19 – The next few verses (1:19-21) contain several matters of debate in interpretation that lead to several different outcomes of possible meaning for the text. Important for our purposes is to judge these interpretive issues by the larger context of 1:16-21 in which they occur rather than to treat them in isolation. The first concerns the phrase often translated "we have the more reliable prophetic word." Such a translation prompts the question, "more reliable than what?" and seems to leave the interpreter with the

---

[186] See Harink, *1 and 2 Peter*, 155.
[187] David Bentley Hart in Solrunn Nes, *The Uncreated Light: An Iconographical Studie of the Transfiguration in the Eastern Church* (Grand Rapid: Eerdmans, 2007), xiii–xiv.
[188] Harink, *1 & 2 Peter*, 158.

option of viewing apostolic testimony as more reliable than the OT Scriptures or more reliable than the revelation of the Transfiguration, unless the comparison extends back to 1:16, in which the "more reliable" would be a reference to the "cleverly created myths" discussed in 1:16. The first two options are undesirable for many interpreters and also seem to undercut the point being developed in this passage, which is the continuity and reliability of divine revelation. The third option, though making more sense in the context, requires the reader to jump back to the beginning of the section and to a phrase that is not clearly explained or developed in the context. A better option is likely to see the form βεβαιότερον here,[189] which is in the comparative (indicated by τερ) as an occurrence of the comparative used as superlative.[190] This resolution better fits the overall context of the passage and the development of thought up to this point and is rendered as such by the 2011 NIV ("We also have the prophetic message as something completely reliable"), in comparison with other translations that retain the comparative sense.

The second question here is to what the "prophetic word" (προφητικὸν λόγον) referenced might refer. Bauckham notes six possibilities suggested by scholars:

1) OT messianic prophecy (Bigg, Mayor, Moffatt, Wand, Chaine; Käsemann, "Apologia," 187); 2) the whole OT understood as messianic prophecy (Schelkle, Spicq, Kelly, Grundmann); 3) one specific OT prophecy (Fornberg, *Early Church*, 82–83); 4) OT and NT prophecies (Plumptre, Sidebottom); 5) 2 Pet. 1:20–2:10 (Robson, *Studies*, 44–48); 6) the Transfiguration itself as a prophecy of the Parousia (Neyrey, *CBQ* 42 [1980] 514–16).[191]

The use of the phrase (προφητικὸν λόγον) in relevant literature (e.g., Philo, *Plant.*, 118; *Sobr.*, 68) generally points in the direction of the second option (the whole OT), though perhaps some emphasis on specific OT messianic prophetic texts may be inferred from the previous context (see the use of the phrase, e.g., 2 Chr. 15:8; 2 Esd. 16:12 [LXX]; Philo, *Leg. All.*, 3.43).

---

[189] For a recent analysis of βεβαιότερον, see Travis B. Williams, "Confirming Scripture through Eyewitness Testimony (2 Peter1.19a): Resolving a *Crux Interpretum*," *JSNT* 43.4 (2021): 605–24.

[190] On this category, see Daniel B. Wallace, *Greek Grammar: Beyond the Basics (An Exegetical Syntax of the New Testament)* (Grand Rapids: Zondervan Academic, 1996), 299–300.

[191] Bauckham, *Jude–2 Peter*, 224.

What follows in 1:20 seems to point in the direction of the broader sense of the phrase.[192] Thus, a form of the second option seems likely, as Bauckham suggests, with a possible focus on the cluster of Ps. 2:7 ("you are my son"), Dan. 7:13-14 ("coming on the clouds" with "authority, glory, and power" and an "everlasting dominion"), Num. 24:17 ("a star will come out of Jacob"), and other relevant texts in mind.[193] The conceptual connection seems to indicate, as Frey suggests, that "the truth of Christ's glory seen at the transfiguration (which should itself be understood as a fulfillment of biblical promises) strengthens the reliability of the scriptural prophecies,"[194] providing a supremely reliable message of prophetic truth.

Peter again calls his audience to attend to this message (1:12, 13, 15, 16), noting that in doing so they "will do well" (καλῶς ποιεῖτε). Two metaphors follow Peter's call for attention. The first relates to the "utmost reliable prophetic word," which Peter describes as a "lamp shining in a dark place" (λύχνῳ φαίνοντι ἐν αὐχμηρῷ τόπῳ). The image of a lamp or light being associated with divine revelation and guidance is relatively common in biblical literature (2 Sam. 22:29; Job 29:3; Ps. 18:28; 119:105; Prov. 6:23; Sir. 48:1; Wis. 18:4; 2 Apoc. Bar. 77:13-15; Bib. Ant. 9:8; 15:6; 19:5; Matt. 5:15; Mark 4:21; Luke 8:16; Luke 11:33; Rev. 21:23; 22:5). Peter adapts this metaphor here for the purpose of illustrating the illuminating qualities of the reliable revelation that God has given through Christ and particularly his Transfiguration. This shining light may also offer a previewing contrast to the "gloomy darkness" that Peter will describe in 2:4 as he turns to the false teachers and their corresponding judgment.

The second metaphor is less contextually clear. The text states that this lamp of prophetic revelation will shine "until the day dawns" (ἕως οὗ ἡμέρα διαυγάσῃ) and "the morning star rises in your hearts" (φωσφόρος ἀνατείλῃ ἐν ταῖς καρδίαις ὑμῶν). The "day" that will dawn, though not specified here, is most likely the day of the Lord and second coming of

---

[192] According to Bauckham, "All other known occurrences of the phrase refer to OT Scripture, except 2 Clem. 11:2, which refers to an apocryphon which the writer presumably regarded as part of OT Scripture (cf. 1 Clem. 23:3)" (Bauckham, Jude–2 Peter, 224).

[193] Bauckham, Jude–2 Peter, 224. See also Williams, "Confirming Scripture through Eyewitness Testimony," 620.

[194] Frey, The Letter of Jude and the Second Letter of Peter, 303.

Christ.¹⁹⁵ The dual nature of that day, which will be a day of judgment for the enemies of God and a day of deliverance for God's people, echoes throughout the biblical texts. Such an emphasis is also clarified later in the letter, where Peter speaks of the "day of judgment" (εἰς ἡμέραν κρίσεως) that awaits the unrighteous (2:9; 3:7), and the day of the Lord (ἡμέρα κυρίου; 3:10) and "day of God" (θεοῦ ἡμέρας; 3:12), which bring both destruction and deliverance. Since Peter sees a close connection between the Transfiguration and the Second Coming/day of the Lord, it is likely a reference to that future event in mind here, which will reveal Christ's glory to the whole world. The rising of the "morning star" (φωσφόρος) is more difficult to situate for several reasons. First, the term is used only here in biblical literature (though a parallel exists to some extent in Rev. 22:16; ὁ ἀστὴρ ὁ λαμπρὸς ὁ πρωϊνός) and occurs sparingly in Jewish literature (e.g., Philo, *Ebr.* 44). In Greco-Roman literature, the word usually describes the planet Venus.¹⁹⁶ While a different word is employed here, the imagery of a star "rising" may be echoing Num. 24:17 ("a star will come out of Jacob") or Mal. 3:20 LXX ("sun of righteousness"), with Num. 24 in particular having established Messianic connections (see also *T. Levi* 18:3; *T. Jud.* 24:1; 1QM 11:6-7; CD 7:18-20). As Green notes, the verb for "rising" "becomes a rich metaphor with eschatological coloring in Scripture as it speaks of the rising of the glory of the Lord (Isa. 60:1; cf. Luke 1:78)."¹⁹⁷ With the previous reference of "the day" likely pointing to the return of Christ/day of the Lord, which again finds connection in the Gospels with the Transfiguration, this seems a likely interpretive option. The addition of the phrase "in your hearts," however, adds an element of difficulty since that event is typically described as a publicly visible one that brings dramatic consequences for the world and its inhabitants. As Green further suggests, since this event, though publicly visible, will clearly have an "effect on the inner life of the Christian (Kelly 1969: 321),"¹⁹⁸ it need not be seen in 2 Peter as an exclusively existential event but a public and existential one, with the emphasis here on the existential element. Davids

---

¹⁹⁵ See Isa. 13:6, 9; Ezek. 7:19; 13:5; 30:3; Joel 1:15; 2:1, 11, 31; 3:14; Amos 5:18, 20; Obad. 15; Zeph. 1:7-8, 14, 18; 2:2-3; Zech. 14:1; Mal. 4:5; Acts 2:20; 1 Cor. 5:5; 2 Cor. 1:14; 1 Thess. 5:2; 2 Thess. 2:2; 2 Pet. 1:19.
¹⁹⁶ Arndt et al., *A Greek-English Lexicon*, 1073.
¹⁹⁷ Green, *Jude and 2 Peter*, 229.
¹⁹⁸ Green, *Jude and 2 Peter*, 229.

comments along similar lines on the personal impact that this even entails via analogy: "One treasures a love letter while the beloved is absent, but once he or she is present, the letter is laid aside and exchanged for the personal contact."[199] As such, when Christ returns, the testimony about him will be set aside for that which the testimony draws attention, the person and presence of Christ, which will be a moment of intense reunion and communion.[200]

1:20 – This verse extends the previous chain of thought that was begun in 1:19 and further explains the possession of the "prophetic word," which, again, should be understood as a revelation of the glory of Christ, specifically in his Transfiguration and future return. The participle here ("knowing," γινώσκοντες) thus functions dependently, further elaborating on the main clause of 1:19 ("we have the utmost reliable prophetic word") by giving a sense of priority ("this first")[201] to the presupposition about to be stated. This therefore undergirds the absolute confidence in the prophetic word. The presupposition is this: "that every prophecy of Scripture does not come from one's own interpretation." Two questions arise here: what does Peter mean by "every prophecy of Scripture" and who is referenced with the phrase "one's own" interpretation?

On the first question, "every prophecy of Scripture" here in the context likely references to the Old Testament. Scripture (γραφῆς) denotes something written, and though portions of the New Testament were written and circulating by this time, the whole had not been completed, collected, or authorized yet by the early Church.[202] While it is possible Peter may have had knowledge of certain writings that would come to form the New Testament (and specifically comments on knowledge of at least some of Paul's letters in 3:15), it could not have been the whole

---

[199] Davids, *The Letters of 2 Peter and Jude*, 210.
[200] Augustine reflects the interpersonal dimension of the event in his consideration: "For what sort of love of Christ is it to fear his coming? Brothers, do we not have to blush for shame? We love him, yet we fear his coming. Are we really certain that we love him? Or do we love our sins more? Therefore, let us hate our sins and love him who will exact punishment for them" (Augustine, *Exposition on Psalm 95*, New Advent, www.newadvent.org/fathers/1801096.htm).
[201] On reading this phrase as a disclosure formula, see Stanley E. Porter and Andrew W. Pitts, "τοῦτο πρῶτον γινώσκοντες ὅτι in 2 Peter 1:20 and Hellenistic Epistolary Convention," *JBL* 127.1 (2008): 165–71, which responds to Terrance Callan, "A Note on 2 Peter 1:19–20," *JBL* 125.1 (2006): 143–50.
[202] See also discussion on 2 Pet. 3:14–16.

corpus of twenty-seven books that Peter speaks of here. Contextually, it was noted that Peter's remarks on the "prophetic word" (1:19) likely refer to the Old Testament, with specific attention on particular Messianic texts, and it would be natural for such a focus to carry over into this statement as well.

On the second question, of who the "interpreter" might be, the two major interpretations suggested are that "one's own" (ἰδίας) refers (1) to the prophet or (2) to the interpreter of prophecy/Scripture.[203] As Bauckham summarizes, "The question is whether it means 'one's own' or 'the prophet's own,' i.e. whether the ἐπίλυσις ('interpretation') is that of the contemporary exegete or that of the original author of the prophecy."[204] The term "interpretation" (ἐπιλύσεως) only occurs here in the NT and occurs sparingly elsewhere in Jewish literature (see *Jub.* 11:8; Philo, *Contempl.* 75.8). Both the context and discussion of prophetic interpretation in nonbiblical literature (e.g., Philo, *Her.* 259; *Mos.* 1.281–83; *Spec.* 1.65; 4.49; *QG.* 3.10; Jer. 23:16 [LXX]; Ezek. 13:3 [LXX], Josephus, *Ant.* 4.121) point toward the first use, meaning that it is the origin of prophecy that Peter has in mind here and not its interpretation, and a majority of commentators read it through this lens.[205] The Old Testament gives a harsh standard for divine prophets in that those who may speak oracles that are not from the LORD as if they were should be put to death (cf. Deut. 18:20). This did not prevent false prophets from arising in Israel (e.g., Jer. 14:14; 23:16; Ezek. 13:3), but it does indicate the seriousness that came with speaking on behalf of God. The Old Testament also portrays the prophetic impulse as one that carried divine inspiration to the extent that the prophet had difficulty resisting the word of the LORD (though Jonah is something of an exception). Jeremiah, for example, states, "But if I say, 'I will not mention his word or speak anymore in his name,' his word is in my heart like a fire, a fire shut up in my bones. I am weary of holding it in; indeed, I cannot'" (Jer. 20:9, NIV). Peter's insistence here is that when a prophet truly speaks on behalf of God, the words of his utterances are not his own invention but truly a message from the LORD.

---

[203] Kelly, *The Epistles of Peter and of Jude*, 324.
[204] Bauckham, *Jude–2 Peter*, 229.
[205] See Bauckham, *Jude–2 Peter*; Frey, *The Letter of Jude and the Second Letter of Peter*, 309–10.

1:21 – The final verse of the first chapter offers an explanatory description (γάρ) of what has preceded. That Peter has in mind throughout the inspiration of prophetic utterances is clear from both 1:19 and what is contained here in 1:21, as well as the larger context of the passage (1:16–21). The explanation is that "for it was not by the will of a human that a prophecy was ever produced." Peter uses here the same verbal root (ἠνέχθη) as in 1:17 (ἐνεχθείσης; from φέρω), where the divine voice was brought from heaven to the beloved Son. Here, the divine voice is brought, not by the will of a human but by being "carried along" (φερόμενοι).[206] The consistent use of the passive of φέρω throughout this section emphasizes through semantic and pragmatic ties that it is the divine will that has revealed the message about Christ to the prophets, to the Son, and to the apostles. The continuity of revelation, and therefore its reliability, is the paramount emphasis of this unit. The Spirit of God is the catalyst of prophetic inspiration and divine revelation throughout Scripture,[207] and that role is emphasized here as well. The two major activities of the Spirit in the biblical text are the bringing about of life and the revelation of truth, and it is the latter that Peter emphasizes here, though the two are never disconnected.[208] Peter's defense of the reliability of the revelation concerning Christ,[209] to both the prophets (OT) and apostles (the revealing of Christ himself, but chiefly in context the Transfiguration/Second Coming), serves as an important theological foundation. He now turns his attention squarely in chapters 2 and 3 to the false prophets and their denial of this revelation in both their teaching and their pattern of living.

---

[206] So Davids, "One should understand that no scriptural prophecy came about by the prophet's own interpretation of the prophetic phenomena that he received because of two things: (1) the prophecy did not originate in the human will, and (2) the prophets spoke from God as the Holy Spirit 'carried them along'" (Davids, *The Letters of 2 Peter and Jude*, 213).

[207] See Num. 11:25–26, 29; 1 Sam. 10:6, 10; 19:20, 23; 2 Sam. 23:2; Neh. 9:30; Isa. 61:1; Joel 2:28; Zech. 4:6; 7:12; Mark 12:36; Luke 1:67; Acts 1:16; 2:17–18; 19:6; 28:25; Eph. 3:5; 2 Tim. 3:16; Heb. 3:7; 10:15–16; 1 Pet. 1:11. See also Philo, *Mos.* 1.283; *Spec. leg.* 1.65; Josephus, *Ant.* 4.119.

[208] On this, see my essay "Does the Spirit Have a Story? A Narrative Theology of the Holy Spirit," *Journal of Theological Interpretation* 14.2 (2020): 246–66.

[209] On a theological assessment of Scripture, revelation, and authority, see John Douglas Morrison, *Has God Said? Scripture, the Word of God, and the Crisis of Theological Authority* (Eugene: Pickwick, 2006).

2 PETER 2:1–11 THE DESCRIPTION OF THE FALSE TEACHERS

2 ¹ Now false prophets came among the people, just as there will also be false teachers among you, who will introduce destructive beliefs, even denying the Master who bought them, bringing upon themselves swift destruction.

² And many will follow their immoral ways, because of whom the way of truth will be slandered,

³ and in greed, they will buy you with fake words, for whom condemnation is not idle and their destruction is not asleep.

⁴ For if God did not spare the angels who sinned, but held them captive in Tartarus in chains of darkness [and] handed over those being kept for judgment,

⁵ and [if he] did not spare the ancient world but preserved eight, including Noah, a herald of righteousness, when he brought a great flood upon the world of the ungodly,

⁶ and [if] he condemned the cities of Sodom and Gomorrah [to destruction], reducing them to ashes, having appointed them as an example for those who were going to be ungodly,

⁷ and [if] he rescued righteous Lot, who was worn down by the behavior of lawless persons in immorality,

⁸ for that righteous man, while living day after day among them, was torturing his righteous soul by seeing and hearing their lawless deeds,

⁹ [so] the Lord knows how to rescue the devout from trials, and how to keep the unrighteous who are going to be punished for the day of judgment,

¹⁰ and especially those who are following after the flesh in defiling desire and who are despising the One Who Rules. Bold, arrogant, while defaming glorious beings, they are not trembling,

¹¹ whereas angels, being greater in strength and power, are not bringing against them a judgment of defamation from/with the Lord.

2:1 – In chapter 2, we find 2 Peter's Asiatic style become most pronounced. The chapter is riddled with loquaciousness, scrupulous reiterations, anomalous phraseology, and impassioned disquisition. The previous sentence may give indication of the effect of Asiatic style. It would be more straightforward to say that chapter 2 contains wordiness, structured repetitions, uncommon vocabulary, and emotionally charged speech, but Asiatic style is not interested in the simple but rather in the impactful. As my former colleague John Morrison was fond of saying, an apparent fan of such rhetorical flourishes, "If it can be said simply, it isn't worth being said." A translation that emphasizes such style could read 2:1 as follows: "Now false prophets came among the people, just as also there will be false teachers among you, who will stealthily establish destructive dogmas, even loathing the Lord who liberated them, establishing upon themselves devastating destruction." The vocabulary and style communicate the point of the discourse but with an obvious and, by the judgment of some ancient rhetors, unnecessary flair. This penchant for flair at times obscures the meaning, particularly near the end of the chapter, where the use of rare terms and employing of complex style creates unclear images for the reader.

The second chapter of 2 Peter also contains the bulk of Peter's use of the letter of Jude. While a comparison of the two documents does not yield an obvious trajectory of "who used whom," when their differences are compared, a majority of instances favor the theory of Peter's inclusion and revision of Jude rather than the reverse. While it is possible the overlap is incidental, it does not seem likely based upon the evidence. As one point of illustration, the verbal parallels between the two documents, in roughly the same order of presentation, are provided in the comparison below.

2 Peter 2:1–2 δεσπότην ἀρνούμενοι … ταῖς ἀσελγείαις	**Jude** 4 εἰς ἀσέλγειαν … δεσπότην … ἀρνούμενοι.
2:4 ἀγγέλων … ζόφου … τηρουμένους,	6 ἀγγέλους … τηρήσαντας … ζόφον τετήρηκεν,
2:6 πόλεις Σοδόμων καὶ Γομόρρας … ὑπόδειγμα	7 Σόδομα καὶ Γόμορρα … πόλεις … δεῖγμα
2:10 σαρκὸς … μιασμοῦ … κυριότητος … δόξας … βλασφημοῦντες,	8 σάρκα … μιαίνουσιν κυριότητα … δόξας … βλασφημοῦσιν.
2:11 οὐ φέρουσιν … βλάσφημον κρίσιν.	9 κρίσιν ἐπενεγκεῖν βλασφημίας
2:12 οὗτοι … ὡς ἄλογα ζῷα … φυσικὰ … ἀγνοοῦσιν βλασφημοῦντες … φθαρήσονται	10 οὗτοι … οὐκ οἴδασιν βλασφημοῦσιν, φυσικῶς ὡς τὰ ἄλογα ζῷα … φθείρονται.
2:15 ἐπλανήθησαν … τοῦ Βαλαὰμ … μισθὸν	11 τῇ πλάνῃ τοῦ Βαλαὰμ μισθοῦ
2:17 Οὗτοί … ἄνυδροι … ὁ ζόφος τοῦ σκότους τετήρηται.	12–13 οὗτοί … ἄνυδροι … ὁ ζόφος τοῦ σκότους … τετήρηται.
2:18 ὑπέρογκα … ἐπιθυμίαις	16 ἐπιθυμίας … ὑπέρογκα
3:1–2 ἀγαπητοί … μνησθῆναι τῶν προειρημένων ῥημάτων … τῶν ἀποστόλων … τοῦ κυρίου	17 ἀγαπητοί, μνήσθητε τῶν προειρημένων ὑπὸ τῶν ἀποστόλων τοῦ κυρίου
3:3 ἐπ᾽ ἐσχάτων … ἐμπαῖκται … ἐπιθυμίας	18 Ἐπ᾽ ἐσχάτου … ἐμπαῖκται … ἐπιθυμίας

While Peter does adapt the material to work within his own discourse, the lexical similarities here are clear, and, generally speaking, 2 Peter's modified reliance upon Jude seems the most likely explanation.

The δὲ ("now") that opens the chapter marks a new development, transitioning to the next phase of the discourse.[210] The opening warning here, which connects the prophecy of the Old Testament ("false prophets came among the people") with the revelation of the apostles ("there will be false teachers among you"), is echoed in Justin's *Dialogue with Trypho* (82.1; c. AD 155), suggesting 2 Peter can be pushed no later than the early second century based on its reception by Justin.[211] Witherington notes three common markers of false prophets in the Old Testament, which will be evident with the false teachers Peter targets: (1) they lacked divine authority, (2) they preached peace when judgment was imminent, and (3) they demonstrated, in belief and behavior, being worthy of condemnation.[212] The Old Testament contains numerous examples of false prophets being present within Israel (e.g., Deut. 18:20; Jer. 6:13; 14:14; 23:16; Ezek. 13:3; Zech. 13:2), and the New Testament warns about false teachers among Christians as well, whose numbers will increase in the "last days" (Matt. 7:15-21; 24:11, 24; Mark 13:22; Luke 6:26; Acts 13:6; 2 Cor. 11:13; 1 Tim. 1:3; 1 John 4:1; Rev. 16:13; 19:20; 20:10).

The term here "false teachers" (ψευδοδιδάσκαλοι) first appears in extant literature in this letter, so subsequent use in the writings of the early church would appear to be influenced by Peter's invention.[213] Peter's statement that these false teachers "will be among you" (ἐν ὑμῖν ἔσονται) is the subject of much discussion among commentators, with some believing this indicates these false teachers were not yet present but only predicted to be so. Bauckham sees the use of the future here as representing a prophecy from Peter about the arrival of the false teachers.[214] In his discourse analysis of 2 Peter, Fresch, however, suggests that "The

---

[210] See O'Brien, *II Peter and Jude*, 64.
[211] See Bauckham, *Jude-2 Peter*, 237. It is, of course, possible 2 Peter post-dates Justin, but this seems less likely as Bauckham articulates.
[212] Witherington, *Letters for Hellenized Christians*, 347.
[213] Though see also a similar conception ("not to teach other doctrines") in 1 Tim. 1:3. Green notes that other ψευδο- compounds occur with infrequency in the NT (ψευδάδελφος; 2 Cor. 11:26; Gal. 2:4; ψευδαπόστολος; 2 Cor. 11:13; ψευδομαρταρία/ψευδόμαρτυς; Matt. 15:19; 26:59 / Matt. 26:60; 1 Cor. 15:15; ψευδόχριστος; Matt. 24:24; Mark 13:22) (Green, *Jude and 2 Peter*, 237-38).
[214] Bauckham, *Jude-2 Peter*, 239, 245.

prediction of false teachers among the letter's readers is placed within a comparison, thereby backgrounding it and indicating that it is known, or assumed to be known, information."[215] This is confirmed, as Davids recognizes, by the later context of the chapter where it is clear the false teachers are indeed already present[216] and further by Witherington in noting that this warning of false teachers coming is predicted by Jesus himself.[217]

The false teachers are said to "bring in" (παρεισάξουσιν) destructive teachings. Peter's description here may offer a revision of Jude's description of "certain people" who "slipped in stealthily" (cf. Jude 4, παρεισέδυσαν) in order to spread immoral behavior among believers.[218] While Jude's opponents have "snuck into" the community of believers, it seems the false teachers in 2 Peter were more deeply integrated (cf. especially 2 Pet. 2:13). The "destructive beliefs" (αἱρέσεις ἀπωλείας) that these false teachers introduce seem to consist of a twofold departure from apostolic teaching: they live without proper moral restraint and they deny the coming judgment of God through Jesus Christ. The term for "beliefs" (αἱρέσεις; *haireseis*) used here came later to signify "heresies" and thus can carry a pejorative sense. In the New Testament, the term is typically used to describe "groups" or "factions" that are divided by certain beliefs or practices (cf. Acts 5:17; 15:5; 24:14; 26:5; 1 Cor. 11:19; Gal. 5:20). The term in Peter's time did not yet have the predominantly negative connotation that it would come to develop in later centuries, but it is denoted as negative here by Peter with its modification by the genitive noun ἀπωλείας. The construction here (αἱρέσεις ἀπωλείας) could be taken to mean that the beliefs lead to destruction[219] or that they are destructive,[220] and the larger context of chapter 2 will demonstrate that both are true regardless of which emphasis the author may have intended here.

Peter demonstrates the extent of the distortion of the false teachers in stating that they are "even denying the Master who bought them" (καὶ τὸν ἀγοράσαντα αὐτοὺς δεσπότην ἀρνούμενοι). "The Master" (δεσπότην; see

---

[215] Fresch, "2 Peter," 640.
[216] Davids, *II Peter and Jude*, 65.
[217] Cf. Mark 13:22 (Witherington, *Letters for Hellenized Christians*, 348).
[218] Donelson, *I & II Peter and Jude*, 237.
[219] Cf. Bauckham, *Jude–2 Peter*, 240; Green, *Jude and 2 Peter*, 240.
[220] See Peter H. Davids, *II Peter and Jude*, 65.

also Acts 4:24) here most likely represents Christ (see also Jude 4), and his "buying" (ἀγοράσαντα) of them recalls the redemptive imagery found elsewhere in the New Testament often used to describe the work of Christ in his death and resurrection. The imagery used here of a "master buying" takes us to the metaphor of the purchase of slaves in the ancient world, which, as Green notes, "was absorbed into the church as a metaphor of Christian salvation (1 Cor. 6:20; 7:23; Rev. 5:9; 14:3–4),"[221] frequently summarized in theological discourse with a term like "redemption" or "liberation." Though Peter does not specify it here, elsewhere in the New Testament (e.g., Rom. 6:17–18), the old, oppressive owners of the believer are identified as Sin and Death, and Christ's redemptive work bought the Christian's freedom and placed them under a new Master.[222] The concept of salvation as freedom from slavery is rooted in the deliverance of Israel from Egypt in the exodus, which was God's paradigmatic act of salvation in the Old Testament. This act of deliverance in the New Testament then serves as a typology of a new exodus.[223] The implication, then, is as Perkins describes, "The Master who purchased the slaves in the household should be treated with obedience and respect,"[224] something that the false teachers clearly reject. Such a denial (ἀρνέομαι) is framed by Jesus as a rejection of God himself (Matt. 10:33; Luke 12:9).[225] Peter himself famously committed this kind of denial on the night Jesus was betrayed (Matt. 26:70, 72; Mark 14:68; Luke 22:57; John 13:38; 18:25, 27). In Peter's own experience, such a denial could be reversed (cf. John 21:15–19), which perhaps is echoed in 2 Pet. 3:9 where God's great patience seeks to bring all to repentance.[226]

As it stands now, however, this denial means the false teachers are "bringing upon themselves swift destruction" (ἐπάγοντες ἑαυτοῖς ταχινὴν

---

[221] Green, *Jude and 2 Peter*, 241. See also Mark 10:45; Rom. 6:17–18; 1 Pet. 1:18–19.

[222] Chang argues that the language here of the false teachers being bought by the master supports the concept of an unlimited atonement (Andrew D. Chang, "Second Peter 2:1 and the Extent of the Atonement," *BibSac* 142 [1985]: 52–63).

[223] See Bryan D. Estelle, *Echoes of Exodus: Tracing a Biblical Motif* (Downers Grove: InterVarsity Press, 2018).

[224] Perkins, *First and Second Peter, James, and Jude*, 181.

[225] As Green notes, "Christian as well as Jewish theology even predicted an 'apostasy' from the faith before the final consummation (Matt. 24:11–13; 2 Thess. 2:3; 1 Tim. 4:1; *1 En.* 93.9; 90.26; 2 Esd. [4 Ezra] 5:1–13; 2 Bar. 41.3; 42.4; G. Green 2002: 307)" (Green, *Jude and 2 Peter*, 242).

[226] See also the dynamic which exists in Paul's thought Romans 11 concerning Israelites who have been "cut off" from covenant belonging due to their rejection (ἀπιστίᾳ) of Christ.

ἀπώλειαν). Just as their teachings are "destructive" (ἀπωλείας) so too their consequence is "destruction" (ἀπώλειαν). The use of the present tense here (ἐπάγοντες) could be taken to mean that they are experiencing a type of destruction now, but since participles generally derive their time from the main verb to which they connect, and the verbs that preceded it are future (ἔσονται), it is likely that eschatological destruction is what is in mind. The "swiftness" (ταχινὴν) then refers not to the relative timing of the destruction but to the speed with which it will occur once it begins. As Green clarifies,

> The term speaks of what will happen soon, and any notion of "suddenness" is only suggested because of the speed of the occurrence (BDAG 992; MM 627; LSJ 1762; cf. the adjective ταχύς, tachys, which always refers to that which happens swiftly: James 1:19; Matt. 5:25; 28:7; Luke 15:22; John 11:29; Rev. 2:16; 3:11; 11:14; 22:7, 12, 20; so, too, the adverb ταχέως, tacheōs, speedily).[227]

As such, the statement here does not contradict Peter's understanding of the "delay" of the παρουσία (3:8-10) since it is not the timing in focus but how quickly the judgment will occur once it begins. Their rejection of Christ's coming judgment and subsequent immoral behavior is a rejection of God.[228]

2:2 – The conjunction καὶ that begins v. 2 marks a continuation of the previous thought. A result of the spreading of these destructive beliefs of the false teachers is that many (πολλοὶ), presumably within the faith community, "will follow their immoral ways" (ἐξακολουθήσουσιν αὐτῶν ταῖς ἀσελγείαις). The genitive modifier αὐτῶν ("their") here is "dislocated," meaning it is out of its normal position where it would typically follow the noun it modifies. This draws additional focus to the possessor of the immorality that Peter describes: the false teachers. As noted in the previous verse, the use of the future here (ἐξακολουθήσουσιν) does not require in the context that this is only a problem yet to come. Indeed, Peter's repetition of the term later in the chapter (2:15), where it describes the false teachers, indicates this is also a present problem for the believing community, since the tense form there is present. The language of

---

[227] Green, *Jude and 2 Peter*, 241.
[228] Thus Neyrey notes, "But as Pss 9, 10, and 13 LXX indicate, when people 'denied God,' they also denied God's coming judgment. Thus 'denial of the Lord' may be understood as a cryptic remark which implies a fuller denial of theodicy" (Neyrey, *2 Peter, Jude*, 189).

"following" (ἐξακολουθήσουσιν; from ἐξακολουθέω / ἀκολουθέω) occurs on three occasions in the letter: first of Peter's denial that the apostles followed "cleverly created myths" (1:16), here of believers who are following the false teachers (2:2), and finally of the false teachers following the way of Balaam (2:15), all three tying into the contrasts that Peter develops. "Immoral" (ἀσελγείαις) here, as defined by BDAG, indicates "lack of self-constraint which involves one in conduct that violates all bounds of what is socially acceptable."[229] The term often carries the connotation of lack of restraint with regard to sexual desires in particular,[230] a reality that will be further attributed to the false teachers later in chapter 2.[231] This restraining of sexual desires was a message no more popular in the first century than it is today.[232] Schooping elaborates helpfully here:

> The passions are the disordered energies within the soul of man that darken his mind, misdirect his emotions, and confuse his will. Whereas in his ontological composition he is made to find his fulfillment in God as his ultimate referent ... in his basic and rightful urge towards this infinite fulfillment (i.e., God) he is tragically and constantly attaching it to the unreliable fluctuations of material reality.[233]

The moral vision developed by 2 Peter concerns virtuous flourishing through pursuit of life with God. A rejection of God (and Christ) cannot but mean a rejection of moral flourishing. Here again, Peter draws a clear link here between this denial and embracing moral vice.[234]

The activities of the false teachers cause (δι' οὕς) "the way of truth" (ἡ ὁδὸς τῆς ἀληθείας) to be slandered. The phrase "way of truth" is not pervasive in Scripture (see LXX Ps. 118:30; Wis. 5:6), but descriptions of following Israel's God, with some reference to his character, are quite common (compare "the way of the Lord/God," Gen. 18:19; Prov. 10:29; Judg. 2:22; Jer. 5:4–5; Ezek. 18:25, 29; 33:17, 20; Matt. 22:16; Mark 12:24; Luke

---

[229] Arndt et al., *A Greek-English Lexicon*, 141.
[230] Louw and Nida, *Greek-English Lexicon of the New Testament*, 770.
[231] Green affirms: "Sexual license is a distinguishing mark of their heresy (2:10, 12, 14; 3:3)" (Green, *Jude and 2 Peter*, 243).
[232] Achtemeier et al., *Introducing the New Testament*, 431.
[233] Joshua Schooping, *A Manual of Theosis: Orthodox Christian Instruction on the Theory and Practice of Stillness, Watchfulness, and Ceaseless Prayer* (Olyphant: St. Theophan the Recluse Press, 2020), 13.
[234] Bauckham suggests: "If the hypothesis is correct that the false teachers' denial of future eschatology was influenced by pagan skepticism, it may be that their immorality also should be seen as primarily a relapse into pagan ways" (Bauckham, *Jude–2 Peter*, 241).

20:21; "the way of the righteous/righteousness," Ps. 1:6; Prov. 8:20; 12:28; 16:31; Isa. 26:7; Matt. 21:32; "the way of faithfulness," Ps. 119:33; "the way of wisdom," Prov. 4:11; "the way of life," Prov. 5:6; Jer. 21:8; "the way of peace," Isa. 59:8). The connection of "the way" here with "truth" stands in contrast against the errors that the false teachers promote.

The slandering (βλασφημηθήσεται) that occurs because of their departing from the way of truth should be understood in the context as a "slandering," or "reviling," of God and his ways and may therefore echo Isaiah 52:5, which states, "And all day long my name is constantly blasphemed" (see also 1 Tim. 6:1; Titus 2:5). The activity of disparaging is directed in 1 Pet. 3:16 against believers themselves, who are maligned for their good conduct. The denigration of Christians and their beliefs was not an uncommon occurrence in the Roman empire. As Green summarizes:

Tacitus (Annals 15.44.2-8) called Christianity a "deadly superstition," and the charge laid against the Christians during Nero's persecution was "hatred of the human race." Christians were "hated for their abominations," and their faith was deemed "hideous and shameful." Suetonius (Nero 16.2) echoed the sentiment by calling Christianity "a new and wicked superstition.[235]

The shame being brought here upon the Christian community, however, did not result from their blameless conduct but rather from some embracing the shameful behaviors of the false teachers, which not only caused their faith to be maligned but would have also harmed the effectiveness of their Christian witness. The mission of the Church and the transformation of the Church into a Christlike character must always go together.

2:3 – Verse 3 is likewise joined with a conjunction marking continuation (καὶ) as Peter continues to elaborate on the activities of the false teachers. Having condemned their dangerous beliefs and lack of moral restraint, he now charges them with motivations of "greed" (ἐν πλεονεξίᾳ). The false teachers are selling the community a false bill of goods,[236] deceiving them with "fake words" (πλαστοῖς λόγοις). No doubt Peter here contrasts his denial of the apostles following "cleverly created

---

[235] Green, *Jude and 2 Peter*, 244.
[236] The verb here (ἐμπορεύσονται) has commercial/economic overtones that I have retained in my translation.

myths" (σεσοφισμένοις μύθοις) with the false teachers constructing falsified representations of reality.²³⁷

Peter assures his audience that the "condemnation from long ago" (τὸ κρίμα ἔκπαλαι) of these false teachers "is not idle" (οὐκ ἀργεῖ) and that "their destruction is not asleep" (ἡ ἀπώλεια αὐτῶν οὐ νυστάζει). His words here serve as a bridge of transition between his description of the activities of the false teachers in 2:1–3 to his illustration of their condemnation through historical examples in 2:4–11. Peter's wording here is a bit unusual but likely envisions the agent of activity in the verse as "the condemnation." In doing so, Peter personifies the condemning judgment, which he describes as "not idle" and "not asleep." As Bauckham notes, however, "Behind the personification ... lies, of course, the personality of God whose judgment they represent."²³⁸ God himself is the one who "will neither slumber nor sleep" (Ps. 121:4), and so those who are deserving of condemnation will not escape his notice.

Peter's description here resonates with denials of divine judgment elsewhere in Greco-Roman literature,²³⁹ a topic that will explicitly surface in chapter 3. As Neyrey summarizes, these denials often consist of four major propositions: (1) the world was made by chance, (2) the idea that divine providence destroys moral freedom, (3) unfulfilled prophecy disproves divine foreknowledge, and (4) the absence of justice in the present demonstrates God does not punish or reward.²⁴⁰ Green illustrates this phenomenon by way of example:

> In his treatise *De sera numinis vindicta* (On the Delays of the Divine Vengeance), Plutarch dialogues with Patrocleas, Timon his brother, and Olympichus. At one point Patrocleas replies, "The delay and procrastination of the Deity in punishing the wicked appears to me the most telling argument by far," and then he quotes Euripides, who said, "Apollo lags; such is the way of Heaven (548C–D)."²⁴¹

Such may represent the attitude of the false teachers, who in denying divine judgment, deny divine authority, the divine Messiah, and so cut

---

[237] On possible connections here with the sophistics, see Burge, "A Sub-Christian Epistle?," 310–32.
[238] Bauckham, *Jude–2 Peter*, 247. See 2 Kgs. 18:28; Ps. 44:23; 120:4 (LXX); Isa. 5:28 (LXX).
[239] On the denial of judgment as a challenge to God's honor, see Neyrey, *Jude, 2 Peter*, 189–200.
[240] Neyrey, "The Form and Background of the Polemic in 2 Peter," 409.
[241] Green, *Jude and 2 Peter*, 246–47.

themselves off from the community of the redeemed. In his opening of chapter 2, which is the focus of the letter's *probatio*,[242] Peter levies the charges of dangerous beliefs, immoral behavior, and greed against the false teachers, and so has offered a preview of things to come, as these three issues will form his major critique in the examples of judgment he offers (2:4–11). He will then return to further develop the accusations against the false teachers in 2:12–22.

2:4 – The transition to a new subunit is marked here by the introduction of the section with γὰρ ("for"), which indicates Peter is now providing explanation of the previous opening material on the false teachers. The explanation comes by way of an extended conditional sentence, which is composed of two major parts, a complex protasis ("if . . ."; 2:4–8), which contains four conditions/examples, and a simpler apodosis ("then . . ."; 2:9–10a), which offers the result. The structure can be visualized as follows:

Condition 1 (2:4)	"if God did not spare . . . but handed over . . ."	Εἰ . . . ὁ θεὸς . . . οὐκ ἐφείσατο . . . ἀλλὰ . . . παρέδωκεν
Condition 2 (2:5)	"and [if God] did not spare . . . but preserved . . ."	καὶ . . . οὐκ ἐφείσατο ἀλλὰ . . . ἐφύλαξεν
Condition 3 (2:6)	"and [if God] condemned . . ."	καὶ . . . κατέκρινεν
Condition 4 (2:7)	"and [if God] rescued . . ."	καὶ . . . ἐρρύσατο
Fulfillment (2:9)	"then the Lord knows . . . how to rescue . . . and to keep . . ."	οἶδεν κύριος . . . ῥύεσθαι . . . δὲ . . . τηρεῖν

Peter's first condition/example is that "God did not spare the angels who sinned" (ὁ θεὸς ἀγγέλων ἁμαρτησάντων οὐκ ἐφείσατο). Peter offers no biblical quotations in his examples here and so expects some knowledge of these well-known stories among his audience. We again find significant overlap with Jude, and Jude's descriptions more readily call to mind the text of Gen. 6:1–4, particularly as received through the interpretations found in *1 En.* 6–12.[243] Where Jude expresses that these angels "did not keep to their own domain but deserted their proper dwelling place" (6), Peter only states that they "sinned" (ἁμαρτησάντων). The sin in question

---

[242] See the introduction to the Commentary section for discussion.
[243] On the importance of 1 Enoch for these authors, see Frey, *The Letter of Jude and the Second Letter of Peter*, 119–22.

here is most likely the narrative of the "sons of God"[244] having sexual relations with "the daughters of men," the offspring of whom were known as the Nephilim.[245] While the Genesis narrative contains only cryptic details of this episode, Jewish writers, including 1 Enoch, expanded upon this story extensively and often saw these "fallen angels" as the major corrupting force at work in the world and in the affairs of humans.[246] Where there is an implicit connection in the biblical text between the fall of the "sons of God" and the increasing of evil among humans (Gen. 6:5), Jewish authors made this implicit development explicit.[247]

A description of the punishment for these rebellious "sons of God" is not stated in Genesis 6 but is found in Jewish traditions. First Enoch 10:4-6 describes the archangel Raphael binding the wicked angel Azazel, who had given corrupting knowledge to humans, by casting him into a dark pit, covering him with rocks and darkness, and leaving him there until the day of judgment when he will be cast into fire. Such a description is similar to that of the Greek Titan Prometheus, who defied the gods of Olympus and was condemned to eternal torment.[248] Josephus noted the similarities between the Greek myths and Jewish traditions of the Watchers and sons of God in stating, "The deeds that tradition ascribes to them resemble the audacious exploits told by the Greeks of the giants."[249] This background helps to make sense of Peter's description of the fate of the sinful angels whom God "did not spare" (οὐκ ἐφείσατο) but "held captive in Tartarus in chains of darkness [and] handed over those being kept for judgment"

---

[244] "Angelic beings" or "lesser gods." It is clear Peter and Jude do not interpret this text as referring to human beings and neither did their Jewish contemporaries. On the use of "sons of Gods" as heavenly figures, see also Job 1:6; 2:1; 38:7; Deut. 32:8 (LXX); Ps. 29:1; Ps. 89:6.

[245] For an exploration of this narrative throughout Scripture, see Michael S. Heiser, *The Unseen Realm: Recovering the Supernatural Worldview of the Bible* (Bellingham: Lexham Press, 2015). See also Annette Yoshiko Reed, *Fallen Angels and the History of Judaism and Christianity: The Reception of Enochic Literature* (Cambridge: Cambridge University Press, 2005).

[246] In addition to 1 Enoch, see also *Jub.* 4-4; 1QapGen. See Hannah K. Harrington, "Sin," in *Eerdmans Dictionary of Early Judaism*, ed. John J. Collins and Daniel C. Harlow (Grand Rapids: Eerdmans, 2010), 1230.

[247] 1 Enoch 10:8, for example, states, "And the whole earth has been corrupted through the works that were taught by Azazel: to him ascribe all sin." See also *Jub.* 7:21-24.

[248] See George W. E. Nickelsburg, "Apocalyptic and Myth in 1 Enoch 6-11," *JBL* 96.3 (1977): 399-404.

[249] Josephus, *Ant.* 1.73. See also LXX Ezek. 32:27; Sir. 16:7.

(σειραῖς ζόφου ταρταρώσας παρέδωκεν εἰς κρίσιν τηρουμένους). Peter gives three descriptive actions here in the form of a verb and two participles. The first construction, an aorist participle (ταρταρώσας) followed by an aorist verb (παρέδωκεν), qualifies as an attendant circumstance construction, meaning the actions are portrayed as a sequence ("[God] held them captive in Tartarus in chains [and] handed over"). The final participle (τηρουμένους; "those being held for judgment") functions as the object of the clause, referring back to the "angels who sinned" at the beginning of 2:4.

While "Tartarus" (here in the verbal form ταρταρώσας) may be unfamiliar to many biblical readers, the term does occur in the LXX (Job 40:20; 41:24; Prov. 30:16 [LXX]) as well as in noncanonical Jewish literature (1 En. 20.2; Philo, Embassy, 7.49; 14.103; Josephus, Ag. Ap., 2.33.240; Sib. Or. 2.303). Those familiar with Greek mythology will recognize Tartarus as "the deepest gulf beneath the earth"[250] where the gods sent those most deserving of eternal torment. Plutarch describes it as a place "teeming with frightful streams and wind, intermingled with burning fire and corpses."[251] The Titans were consigned to Tartarus after their defeat by the gods.[252] The fate of Ixion, who sought to seduce Hera, is described as follows: "Zeus ordered Hermes to bind Ixion to a wheel of fire which would spin forever through the air."[253] Prometheus' torture is described as follows: "Bound with inextricable bonds, cruel chains, and drove a shaft through his middle, and set on him a long-winged eagle, which used to eat his immortal liver; but by night the liver grew as much again everyway as the long-winged bird devoured in the whole day."[254] The Sibylline Oracles similarly describe the fate of the Watchers: "Nevertheless they went under the dread house of Tartarus guarded by unbreakable bonds, to make retribution, to Gehenna of terrible, raging, undying fire."[255] Peter's imagery here of the sinful angels being held in "chains of darkness in Tartarus" (σειραῖς ζόφου

---

[250] Homer, *Iliad*, 8.13–14.
[251] Plutarch, "Dinner of the Seven Wise Men," in *Loeb Classical Library*, vol. 2 (Cambridge, MA: Harvard University Press, 1928), 159.B.6, 421.
[252] Apollodorus, *Bibl.* 1.1.2; Virgil, *Aen.* 4.580–85.
[253] Apollodorus, *Bibl.* 1.8.2.
[254] Hesiod, *Theo.*, 521–25.
[255] *Sib. Or.* 1.98–103.

ταρταρώσας)²⁵⁶ thus finds comparable conception in Greek and Jewish texts. These rebellious heavenly beings have experienced a judgment of sorts already in their bondage, though they are awaiting a final judgment that will likewise be severe.

2:5 – Peter moves now to his second condition/example, which focuses on "the ancient world" (ἀρχαίου κόσμου) and "Noah," and is a departure from the examples given in Jude.²⁵⁷ Peter's ordering here (fall of angels then flood) follows the narrative order in Genesis but also reinforces the connection made in Jewish texts between the two events as noted above. This example also involves the first contrast that Peter presents, where God's action is both judgment against the ancient world and rescue of Noah and his family. Several features of his description of Noah are noteworthy. First, Peter describes Noah as "eighth" (ὄγδοον) but does so without explanation of the significance of the number. Jensen catalogs three major interpretations of Noah's association here with the number eight: (1) Noah is the eighth person saved (cf. 1 Pet. 3:20; see Kelly, Grundmann, Neyrey, Arichea, Vögtle, Moo, Richard, Senior and Harrington, Davids, Green, Donelson, Watson and Callan, Schreiner), (2) eight symbolizes eschatological salvation and new creation (cf. Bauckham, Kraftchick, Skaggs, Keating), and (3) eight references the number of generations from Adam to Noah (cf. Gen. 4:17-24; Jude 14; see Bigg), while Jensen suggests instead that Noah is "understood to be the eighth proclaimer of righteousness in the line of Adam as counted from Enosh."²⁵⁸ Given 2 Peter's penchant for modifying sources, it may be that his cryptic description here represents his reliance on 1 Pet. 3:20, which he has modified for his purposes. In 1 Peter, the number eight signifies the number of people saved on the ark and could be 2 Peter's intended reference as well.

---

²⁵⁶ While some texts follow the reading "chains" (σειραῖς) of darkness others follow the reading "pits" (σιροῖς) of darkness. The UBS4 committee, as noted by Metzger, saw "pits" more likely as a correction to the text, in spite of its support in ℵ A B C 81 h vg^ms; Aug Cass (Bruce M. Metzger, *A Textual Commentary on the Greek New Testament*, 2nd ed. [London: United Bible Societies, 1994], 632). "Chains" is also represented in the earliest witness P72. See cf. *1 En.* 10:4-12; 18:11; 21:7; 88:1-3; *Jub.* 5:10.
²⁵⁷ Bauckham, *Jude-2 Peter*, 247.
²⁵⁸ Matthew D. Jensen, "Noah, the Eighth Proclaimer of Righteousness: Understanding 2 Peter 2.5 in Light of Genesis 4.26," *JSNT* 37.4 (2015):458-69.

The second noteworthy description is Noah as a "herald of righteousness" (δικαιοσύνης κήρυκα).²⁵⁹ The phrase could be taken to mean either that Noah was a "righteous herald" (descriptive genitive) or that the message that Noah heralded was about righteousness (objective genitive). The biblical texts describe Noah in several places as a righteous man (Gen. 6:9; 7:1; Ezek. 14:14, 20; Heb. 11:7), but the text of Genesis does not describe Noah as one who was preaching. Indeed, Noah does not utter a single word in the biblical narrative until after the flood has receded and he awakens from a drunken stupor after planting a garden (Gen. 9:20–28). Here again 2 Peter echoes ideas from Jewish interpretive traditions that expand upon the flood narrative. In the *Sibylline Oracles*, Noah is instructed to "preach repentance to all people so that they may all be saved" (1.155), which Noah is described as doing in some detail (1.215–44).²⁶⁰ Second Peter is likely influenced by these traditions in his description here.

Second Peter then clarifies for the reader the result of God not sparing the ancient world, which was that "he brought a great flood upon the world of the ungodly." In the Jewish imagination, the flood became a stock image for eschatological judgment and salvation (see Isa. 54:9; 1 En. 93:4; Sib. Or. 1.195–270; 2.196–213; Ant. 1.70–71; Matt. 24:37–38; 1 Pet. 3:20).²⁶¹ This "great flood" (κατακλυσμὸν; cf. Gen. 6:17 LXX), which is described in Genesis 6–8 and retold in numerous Jewish texts, was the instrument of God's judgment on the "world of the ungodly" (κόσμῳ ἀσεβῶν). The charge of "ungodliness" (ἀσεβής; 2 Pet. 2:5, 6; 3:7) contrasts in 2 Peter with "devotion to God" (εὐσέβεια; 2 Pet. 1:3, 6–7; 2:9; 3:11) and divides humanity into those opposed to God and his ways and those who embrace them.

2:6 – The third condition/example that Peter offers is Sodom and Gomorrah and Lot, and these examples again provide a contrast between

---

[259] The genitive modifier in the construction (δικαιοσύνης) precedes the head noun (κήρυκα), which is not common in Koine Greek but does occur with some frequency in 1 Peter (e.g., 1 Pet. 1:11; 17; 3:1, 4, 20; 4:4; 4:14).

[260] See also Josephus, *Ant.*, 1.3.1; 1.74; *Jub.* 7:20; as well as *Eccles. Rab.* 9:15; *Pirqe R. El.* 22; *b. Sanh.* 108. Hafemann argues that though the title "preacher of righteousness" is not ascribed to Noah in the biblical text, his designation as "righteous" and his proclamation of blessings and curses (Gen. 9:24–27) could account for where the post-biblical traditions arise (Scott Hafemann, "Noah, the Preacher of (God's) Righteousness": The Argument from Scripture in 2 Peter 2:5 and 9," *CBQ* 76 [2014]: 306–20).

[261] See Daniel A. Machiela, "Flood," in *Eerdman's Dictionary of Early Judaism*, ed. John. C. Collins and Daniel C. Harlow (Grand Rapids: Eerdmans, 2010), 646.

God's judgment (Sodom and Gomorrah) and God's salvation (Lot). Peter also again here modifies what he receives from Jude in adding the contrasting example of Lot, where Jude focuses only on scenes of judgment. Here the contrasting actions are God "condemning" (κατέκρινεν) Sodom and Gomorrah and God "rescuing" (ἐρρύσατο; 2:7) Lot. The verb here for "condemning" (κατέκρινεν) carries with it a judicial connotation, the noun form of which (κρίμα) was used in 2:3 to describe God's judgment of the false teachers. As with the flood, Sodom and Gomorrah became frequently associated with divine judgment.[262] The goal of the condemnation here is "destruction" (καταστροφῇ), a word that is omitted in some manuscripts, including early witnesses (P72 B C* 945 1241 1243 1739 1881 al), but included in a number of others (ℵ A C² K Ψ 049 056 0142 33 81 614 al).[263] That "destruction" was intended, though, is clarified both in the phrase that follows (τεφρώσας; "reducing them to ashes") and in the account of Genesis 19. Hillyer notes the imagery of burning to ashes here was used elsewhere "by Dio Cassius (66) in his account of the eruption of Vesuvius in A.D. 79, which buried Pompeii and Herculaneum in lava."[264]

The "sin of Sodom" is a hotly debated element of the biblical text among modern interpreters.[265] One of the first mentions of Sodom in the biblical narratives describes it as a city full of wicked people who "were sinning greatly" (Gen. 13:13). Abraham famously pleaded with God not to destroy the city following the grievous incident with the angelic visitors, the men of Sodom, and the daughters of Lot (Gen. 19:1–11). It is then that Lot's angelic visitors declare that the Lord is about to destroy the city, dragging Lot and his family in flight (Gen. 19:12–29). The reception of the sins of Sodom and Gomorrah in biblical intertexts reinforces several elements from the Genesis story. Isaiah remarks that the sin of Sodom and Gomorrah was done in defiance against the Lord, "parading their sin" without shame (Isa. 3:9). Ezekiel describes Sodom and Gomorrah's sins as committing "detestable practices" (16:47), being "arrogant, overfed and unconcerned,"

---

[262] E.g., Deut. 29:23; 32:32; Isa. 1:9–10; 3:9; 13:19; Jer. 23:14; 49:18; 50:40; Lam. 4:6; Ezek. 16:46–56; Amos 4:11; Zeph. 2:9; 2 Esd. 2:8–9; Matt. 10:15; 11:23–24; Luke 10:12; 17:29; Rom. 9:29; Jude 1:7; Rev. 11:8.
[263] See Metzger, *A Textual Commentary on the Greek New Testament*, 632.
[264] Hillyer, *1 and 2 Peter, Jude*, 194.
[265] On interpretations ancient and modern, see Ed Noort and Eibert Tigchelaar, eds., *Sodom's Sin: Genesis 18–19 and Its Interpretations* (Leiden: Brill, 2021).

and not helping the poor and needy (16:49).²⁶⁶ In Jewish traditions, these basic elements from Genesis are reinforced. *Jubilees* condemns Sodom and Gomorrah because "they defile themselves and commit fornication in their flesh, and work uncleanness on the earth" (*Jub.* 16:5; also 20:5; see also Philo, *Vit. Mos.*, 2.58). The *Testament of Naphtali* connects the sin of the Watchers with the sin of Sodom and Gomorrah, similar to 2 Peter, describing both of their acts as "wicked" (see also Wis. 10:6) and as "changing their nature" (*T. Naph.* 1:26–27; compare Jude 6). Like Ezekiel, Sirach charges Sodom and Gomorrah with "arrogance" (Sir. 16:8). Peter's source text of Jude describes the sin of Sodom and Gomorrah as "sexual immorality" and "pursuing other flesh" (Jude 7), likely alluding to desiring intercourse with angels, which is a reversal of sorts of the incident in Genesis 6:1–4. Second Peter's integration of Sodom and Gomorrah follows a similar trajectory to the biblical and Jewish traditions. Second Peter charges the false teachers with sexually immoral behavior (2:2, 14), greediness (2:3, 14–15), ungodliness (2:5–6), arrogance (2:10), and reveling in sin (2:13), all sins that Sodom and Gomorrah are charged with in these textual traditions.

Peter asserts the destruction of Sodom and Gomorrah was completed "as an example" (ὑπόδειγμα), again seeing the judgment of these cities as a paradigm of divine judgment, similar to his Jewish contemporaries. The participle "having appointed" (τεθεικώς) occurs in the perfect tense, marking it as prominent in the discourse and thus making it prominent in this unit. These sorts of stock examples of judgment were commonly recalled in Jewish literature. Wisdom of Solomon 10 recounts numerous such examples, framed there as those who have rejected wisdom, and includes both examples of judgment (Cain, the Five Cities, and Egypt) and deliverance (Noah, Abraham, Lot, Jacob, Joseph, and Israel).²⁶⁷ Sodom and Gomorrah and the Watchers, both included by 2 Peter, frequently find mention as examples of judgment in Jewish texts.²⁶⁸ These examples of

---

[266] Steinmann summarizes, "The sins of these Cities of the Plain are described by Ezekiel as pride and haughtiness, having plenty but not taking care of the poor and needy, and committing abominable acts before God (Ezek. 16:49–50; cf. Lev. 18:5–30)" (Andrew E. Steinmann, *Genesis: An Introduction and Commentary*, TOTC [Downers Grove: IVP Academic, 2019], 195).

[267] See also Philo, *Vit. Mos.*, 2.53–65.

[268] E.g., *T. Naph.* 3.4–5; *1 En.* 6–16; Sir. 16:7–8; 3 Macc. 2:4–5; 1 Pet 3:19–20.

judgment are to serve as warnings "for those who were going to be ungodly" (μελλόντων ἀσεβεῖν[269]), offering a caution to those would live in disregard to the way of truth.

2:7 – Verse 6 completes the triad of warnings of judgment that Peter offers. The Watchers, the ancient world that they corrupted, and the cities of Sodom and Gomorrah all stand as examples of what happens when the way of truth is discarded and people live in error, committing shameful deeds, denying the authority of Christ, and promoting false ideologies. In 2:7, Lot appears as the second illustration of divine salvation (along with Noah) amidst these three examples of divine judgment. The syntax of the verse frontloads the situation of Lot, and the verb that conveys the divine action of rescue (ἐρρύσατο) ends the sentence. Our author refers to his example here as "righteous Lot" (δίκαιον Λώτ). For the reader who is familiar with the Genesis account, an obvious question may arise: How could our author possibly consider Lot as righteous? As Lyons summarizes:

> The principal flaw with viewing Lot as a wholly righteous man is that it does not deal with the increasingly negative characterization of Lot in the preceding narratives ... and in his subsequent actions concerning his daughters (19:30–38). In each of these texts Lot is portrayed as selfish and as increasingly absent from the promise made by YHWH to Abraham.[270]

Or, as Hillyer summarizes:

> Lot appears as self-centered, an opportunist (Gen. 13:10–14) who had strayed from the God of his fathers. True, he offers hospitality (Gen. 19:1–3), but he is so depraved (Gen. 19:8) that he lost the power of moral choice (Gen. 19:14). He is weak-willed (Gen. 19:16) and preyed upon by drink (Gen. 19:33). He has so settled into the life of Sodom that force has to be used to drag him to safety (Gen. 19:16).[271]

The portrayal of Lot as righteous, however, finds parallels in Jewish interpretation. The Wisdom of Solomon states Lot was "a righteous man" (Wis. 10:6; 19:17) and a servant of wisdom (10:9). Philo describes

---

[269] The variant reading here (ἀσεβέσιν) is supported by P[72] B P 614 syr[ph,] (cop[sa,] τοῖς ἀσεβέσιν) arm, while the reading followed by NA28 (ἀσεβεῖν) is supported by ℵ A C K Ψ 33 81 1739 Byz (it[h]) vg.

[270] William John Lyons, *Canon and Exegesis: Canonical Praxis and the Sodom Narrative* (Sheffield: Sheffield Academic Press, 2002), 222.

[271] Hillyer, *1 and 2 Peter, Jude*, 189–90.

Lot as one who, though not having attained the perfection of wisdom, did not "join the multitude" in their indulgent behaviors (Philo, *Vit. Mos.*, 2.58).[272]

Second Peter's presentation of Lot does not lack at least some negative characterization. Though Lot is said to be "worn down by the behavior of lawless persons in immorality" (καταπονούμενον ὑπὸ τῆς τῶν ἀθέσμων ἐν ἀσελγείᾳ ἀναστροφῆς) and portrayed in imperfective aspect (καταπονούμενον) so as to show the ongoing disorder he experienced, he is also described as contributing to the situation, noting in v. 8 that "he was torturing his righteous soul" (ψυχὴν δικαίαν ... ἐβασάνιζεν). For Peter's purposes, Lot may be said to be righteous insofar as he took the judgment of God seriously, which is our author's main concern in this section. The false teachers who deny the future coming judgment by the Lord Jesus can expect to be dealt with swiftly like Sodom and Gomorrah. Peter's audience, like Lot, must heed the divine warning, avoiding "lawless" (ἀθέσμων) and "immoral" (ἀσελγείᾳ) behaviors and heeding the divine warnings as did Lot, even reluctantly so.

2:8 – Verse 8 begins with the conjunction γάρ ("for"), meaning Peter here further explains his previous statements about Lot and how he was worn down by lawless and immoral persons. Our author first reiterates the "righteous" (ὁ δίκαιος) status of Lot. As in the previous verse, the tenses here (a present participle, ἐγκατοικῶν ["living"], and an imperfect indicative, ἐβασάνιζεν ["was tormenting"]) encode the imperfective aspect, emphasizing the ongoing nature of Lot's distress. This came about through the "lawless deeds" (ἀνόμοις ἔργοις) that Lot was "seeing" (βλέμματι) and "hearing" (ἀκοῇ) "day after day" (ἡμέραν ἐξ ἡμέρας). By "lawless deeds," Peter likely has in mind those things that transgress divine instruction in the Torah and particularly the kinds of immoral behaviors either previously described or which will be visited in the latter half of chapter 2. These actions include sexually immoral behavior (2:2, 14; cf. Exod. 20:14; Lev. 18–20; Deut. 22:22–30), greediness (2:3, 14–15; cf. Exod. 20:17; Lev. 19:9–10; Deut. 5:21; 15:7–11; 24:14–15), ungodliness (2:5–6; Lev. 26:18–19; Deut. 8:11–18;

---

[272] See also *Gen. Rab.* 49:13 and *Pirqe R. El.* 25. On an analysis of some of the issues involved with this text and its development of the LXX and Jewish interpretation, see John Makujina, "The 'Trouble' with Lot in 2 Peter: Locating Peter's Source for Lot's Torment," *Westminster Theological Journal* 60.2 (1998): 255–69.

Deut. 30:15–20), arrogance (2:10; Deut. 8:11–18), and reveling in sin (2:13; Lev. 18:24–30; 19:2; Deut. 29:18–21).

As indicated above, the "torturing of his righteous soul" (ψυχὴν δικαίαν ... ἐβασάνιζεν) is an action that it appears Lot himself is performing.[273] As the Genesis account indicates, Lot's living in Sodom was a choice entirely of his own selfish discretion when the conflict over land arose between Lot's herdsmen and Abram's (Gen. 13:1–14). Afterwards, Lot is temporarily carried off over conflict with the region's coalitions of kings (Gen. 14:1–12) and is eventually returned to Sodom as a result of Abram's intervention (Gen. 14:16). We next read of Lot in Genesis 19, when he encounters the angelic visitors, offers his daughters in place of these "men," reluctantly flees the city before its destruction, and drunkenly impregnates his daughters (Gen. 19). While Lot's "distress" in the text of Genesis arises primarily from the men of the city pressuring him to hand over his visitors to them (Gen. 19:9), this episode appears to be viewed as a window into a larger pattern of wicked deeds, as other texts in Genesis (e.g., Gen. 13:13) would allude.

2:9 – Peter now moves to the apodosis of his conditional statement (class 1, marked by εἰ with the indicative in 2:4). It is clear from the context that Peter judges that the conditions he has given are true and that his "fulfillment" clauses thereby obtain as well. The Lord did not spare the angels but held them captive. He did not spare the ancient world but rescued Noah. He condemned Sodom and Gomorrah and rescued Lot. Because of these examples of judgment and deliverance, he assures his audience that "the Lord knows how to rescue the godly" (οἶδεν κύριος εὐσεβεῖς ... ῥύεσθαι) and how "to keep the unrighteous for punishing" (ἀδίκους δὲ ... κολαζομένους τηρεῖν).

Peter now begins to bridge concretely from his historical examples to his audience and their situation. The "devout" (εὐσεβεῖς) here are not only Noah and Lot, but Peter's audience as well, at least those among them who continue to follow the way of truth. This term (εὐσεβεῖς) occurred several times in Peter's introduction (1:3, 6, 7; see also 2 Pet. 3:11), where Peter's audience was reminded that "all things necessary for life and devotion to

---

[273] So, Donelson recognizes in stating, "Lot makes his own life miserable ... by living among these impious people, by witnessing and hearing their deeds, by surrounding himself with lawlessness" (Donelson, *I & II Peter and Jude*, 245).

God (εὐσέβειαν)" have been provided for them, and so they are called to a life of devotion to God. They are assured that just as the Lord rescued Noah and Lot (ἐρρύσατο; cf. 2:7), so too he is capable of "rescuing" (ῥύεσθαι; cf. 2:9) them "from trials" (ἐκ πειρασμοῦ ῥύεσθαι). Our author may here echo the words of Jesus in Matt. 6:13, where he teaches the disciples to pray for the Father to not bring them "into temptation" (εἰς πειρασμόν) but "deliver" (ῥῦσαι) them from evil. Noah and Lot no doubt faced trials/temptations[274] of their own, and just as they were called to trust and follow God in the midst of the societal ills that surrounded them, so too Peter's audience must heed this call to faithfulness. While Peter may have in mind a rescue from present trials, his allusion at the end of the verse to the "day of judgment" certainly contains an eschatological focus as well. It may be that both are in view here, as the inaugurated eschatology of the New Testament often combines present and future elements.[275]

The second half of Peter's apodosis/fulfillment moves from divine rescue to divine judgment. The second clause in v. 9 is introduced with δέ, a preposition that shows "new development" but here introduces both a new implication along with a sense of contrast.[276] The contrast is clear enough: while the devout are being rescued, the unrighteous are not. The new element is that "the unrighteous" (ἀδίκους), who have been connected to the "fallen angels," the "ancient world," and Sodom and Gomorrah, and now will be identified with the false teachers who are contemporary to Peter's audience, are being "kept for punishing" (κολαζομένους τηρεῖν). The language here particularly connects them to the fate of the sinful angels in 2:4 who are "being kept for judgment" (εἰς κρίσιν τηρουμένους). The phrasing is noteworthy as both verbal forms are in the present tense and encode imperfective aspect. The statement is that the Lord "knows ... how to keep those being punished on the day of judgment" (οἶδεν κύριος ... εἰς ἡμέραν κρίσεως κολαζομένους τηρεῖν). While the "keeping" as an ongoing, even present-time event makes good enough

---

[274] On the distinction, see Bauckham, *Jude–2 Peter*, 253.
[275] For an introduction, see Benjamin L. Gladd and Matthew S. Harmon, *Making All Things New: Inaugurated Eschatology for the Life of the Church* (Grand Rapids: Baker, 2016). For the foundational work on the concept, see George Eldon Ladd, *The Presence of the Future; The Eschatology of Biblical Realism* (Grand Rapids: Eerdmans, 1974).
[276] See David L. Mathewson and Elodi Ballantine Emig, *Intermediate Greek Grammar: Syntax of Students of the New Testament* (Grand Rapids: Baker, 2016), 263. See also Fresch, "2 Peter," 641.

sense, the present tense of the participle ("those being punished," κολαζομένους) raises the question as to whether Peter has in mind present punishment or future punishment.[277] The tense of the participle would seem to lean toward the present, since it connects temporally to the verb οἶδεν, which has a present sense. The attachment, however, of the phrase "day of judgment" (ἡμέραν κρίσεως), which would seem to imply the "day of the Lord" and final, eschatological judgment, leans toward a future sense.[278] As Witherington notes, Peter's language here "could either imply that (1) the unrighteous are being punished now as well as on judgment day, or (2) they are being held under (the prospect) of punishment on judgment day, or (3) they are being kept to be punished at judgment day."[279] Bauckham notes that some Jewish texts describe various forms of suffering taking place among the wicked in the intermediate state (e.g., 1 En. 22:10–11; 4 Ezra 7:79–87; Luke 16:23–24), which would make sense in the case of the "sinful angels" but not as much for the false teachers, whose future judgment would seem to be in mind.[280] Green's summary is also worth considering, noting:

> The present participle may convey a future sense, and so the punishment in view is more likely that which the unrighteous will experience in the future "day of judgment" (Bauckham 1983: 254; M. Green 1987: 114; Kraftchick 2002: 131–32). Since the future participle is rare in the NT and since the time of the participle is relative to that of the main verb with its temporal reference determined from the context ... this is certainly a possible interpretation (BDF §§339, 65; Porter 1989: 377–79).[281]

This interpretation accords with the discussion of the judgment of the false teachers that will occur in chapter 3 as well. Indeed, the only present

---

[277] A relevant question here would be the classification of the action "to punish" and whether it represents a state, activity, achievement, or accomplishment, which likely raises questions that would partly be answered by one's eschatological framework more than the word itself. For a discussion as it relates to law practice, see Raffaele Rodogno "Shame, Guilt, and Punishment," *Law and Philosophy* 28 (2009): 438–41. This is an area where more reflection is needed related to the Greek verb and linguistic analysis. For discussion related to Greek verbs, see Christopher J. Thomson, "What Is Aspect? Contrasting Definitions in General Linguistics and New Testament Studies," in *The Greek Verb Revisited: A Fresh Approach for Biblical Exegesis*, ed. Steven E. Runge and Christopher J. Fresch (Bellingham: Lexham Press, 2016), especially 48–70.
[278] For a discussion of the "day of the Lord," see comments on 3:10–12.
[279] Witherington, *Letters for Hellenized Christians*, 354.
[280] Bauckham, *Jude–2 Peter*, 254.
[281] Green, *Jude and 2 Peter*, 264–65.

consequences that the false teachers seem to be experiencing is their enslavement to sin (cf. 2:19–21), though this also has implications for their future judgment.

2:10 – This verse begins perhaps the most complex section of the letter, grammatically speaking, arranged no doubt for rhetorical effect.[282] The use of δέ here indicates a second new development as our author extends his historical examples to the situation of his audience. As Fresch notes, the δέ here "is not necessary, but its use makes good sense. The presence of δέ correlates well with topic shifts, and the content of v. 10a does constitute one, although it is not characterized by high discontinuity."[283] The presence of μάλιστα ("especially") heightens the intensity and the focus as Peter begins to explicitly shift from his historical examples back to the activities of the false teachers. He identifies "those going after flesh in defiling desire" (τοὺς ὀπίσω σαρκὸς ἐν ἐπιθυμίᾳ μιασμοῦ πορευομένους) as the ones who are especially the objects of divine punishment in the coming day of judgment.[284] The "flesh" (σαρκὸς) here represents, similar to Pauline usage,[285] the desires of the inner person that are prone to sinful expression. Peter's use in this letter occurs only here and in 2:18, where it likewise represents a bent toward sinful indulgence (ἐν ἐπιθυμίαις σαρκὸς; "in the desires of the flesh").[286]

---

[282] As Witherington summarizes, "The Greek in 2 Peter 2:10b–22 is extremely difficult and convoluted, full of hapax legomena and imponderables" (Witherington, *Letters for Hellenized Christians*, 355). Neyrey has recognized the presence of assonance throughout this section: "As the audience hears the passage, they are aided in holding its complex sentences together by the repetition of words and patterns of assonance. The initial remarks are linked by the catchword 'insult' (*blasphēmountes*, v 10b ... *blasphemon*, v 11 ... *blasphēmountes*, v 12). This evil leads to 'destruction' (*phthoran* ... *en phthorai* ... *phtharēsontai*, v 12). The *lex talionis* continues this: 'they will suffer wickedly the wages of their wickedness' (*adikoumenoi* ... *adikias*, v 13). The impurity of the opponents is stressed through repeated synonyms ('blots, blemishes') and by repetition of the charge of 'dissipation' (*tryphēn* ... *entryphōntes*, v 13). Truth and falsehood are contrasted in the juxtaposition of the 'straight way' and the 'way of Balaam'" (v 15)" (Neyrey, *2 Peter, Jude*, 206).

[283] Fresch, "2 Peter," 641–42.

[284] For parallels to πορεύθεσαι ὀπίσω see LXX: Deut. 4:3; 6:14; 28:14; 3 Kdgms. 11:10; Isa. 65:2; Hos. 11:10; also *T. Jud.* 13:2.

[285] See Dunn, *The Theology of Paul the Apostle*, 62–70. Dunn summarizes σάρξ as the weakness of humanity which is "always vulnerable to the manipulation of its desires" (70).

[286] On the Old Testament background of the flesh/spirit contrast, particularly as relevant to Genesis 6 and Joel 2, see my "Does the Spirit Have a Story?," 246–66.

The phrase "defiling desire" (ἐπιθυμίᾳ μιασμοῦ; lit. "in desire of defilement") possesses an interesting construction. Davids refers to the phrase as a "double Hebraism."[287] While it is possible to read this as an objective genitive, meaning the false teachers desire defilement,[288] it is probably better to read it with an attributive sense, meaning "desire that defiles." Though cultic defilement can be described with μιασμός, Green notes that the notion of moral defilement better fits the context.[289] This defilement is a serious matter, not only because of the implications for the final judgment but also because, as Neyrey notes, such defilement contaminates the group as well as the individual.[290]

The second charge against those who will especially be punished at the day of judgment is that they are "despising the One Who Rules" (κυριότητος καταφρονοῦντας). While most translations render the phrase as "despising authority" or something similar (e.g., LEB, NIV, NASB, RSV, ESV), the use of the adjective κυριότης in light of the previous uses of κύριος throughout 2 Peter (1:2, 8, 11, 14, 16; 2:9, as well as 2:20; 3:2, 8, 9, 10, 15, 18), all taken as likely references to the Lord Jesus, make it reasonable that the "authority" that is being despised is specifically Christ's.[291] In that the false teachers despise the One to whom the highest honors and reverence are to be ascribed, an action which resonates with their denial of the Master in 2:1, Peter illustrates the depth of their waywardness.

Such an astonishing act of scorn leads Peter to name-call, an act of *vituperatio* in ancient rhetoric, analogous, perhaps, to the modern day "diss track" in hip hop culture.[292] Such a rhetorical strategy was designed to impugn the character of one's adversary in order to discredit their position.[293] Peter calls the false teachers "bold" and "arrogant." While "bold" (Τολμηταί; another NT hapax) does not necessarily represent a vice or

---

[287] Davids, *II Peter and Jude*, 75.
[288] See Kelly, *The Epistles of Peter and Jude*, 336.
[289] Green states, "This is the pollution in the heart that is closely associated with sexual desire (T. Benj. 8.2–3; cf. T. Levi 17.8. BDAG 650; F. Hauck, *TDNT* 4:647)," noting other parallels in see, e.g., *Let. Aris.* 141–66; 1QS 5.13; Josephus, *J.W.*, 4.5.2, 323; *Jub.* 7:20–21 (Green, *Jude and 2 Peter*, 267).
[290] See Neyrey, *Jude, 2 Peter*, 201.
[291] See Green, *Jude and 2 Peter*, 267.
[292] This would be represented, for example, in the feud between 2Pac and Notorious B.I.G. in the 90s or more recently between Kendrick Lamar and Drake.
[293] See Luke T. Johnson, "The New Testament's Anti-Jewish Slander and the Conventions of Ancient Polemic," *SBL* 108.3 (1989): 422.

character defect and can be indicative of courage (compare with τολμηρός in Rom. 15:15 or τολμάω in Mark 15:43; Phil. 1:14), Peter clearly means it here as a kind of reckless audacity. "Arrogant" (αὐθάδεις) does present a more inherently negative depiction. Clement, for example, writes, "Boldness and arrogance and audacity are for those who are cursed by God; but graciousness and humility and gentleness are with those who are blessed by God" (1 Clem. 30:8).

Their reckless arrogance is demonstrated in that "while defaming glorious beings" (δόξας ... βλασφημοῦντες), the false teachers "are not trembling" (οὐ τρέμουσιν). Here Peter's rhetoric struggles to provide a clear frame of reference for the reader. Those familiar with Jude's text would notice a similar remark in v. 8 ("these ... defile the flesh and reject authority and defame majestic beings"; οὗτοι ... σάρκα μὲν μιαίνουσιν κυριότητα δὲ ἀθετοῦσιν δόξας δὲ βλασφημοῦσιν). Whereas Jude gives some explanatory context, relating the scene from Michael and Satan disputing over the body of Moses (cf. the *Assumption of Moses*), Peter provides no elaboration on δόξας ... βλασφημοῦντες.[294] As Hillyer notes, δόξας, particularly when used in the plural as here in 2 Pet. 2:10, can be "used to describe a class in the angelic hierarchy (Eph. 1:21; Col. 1:16),"[295] and thus "majestic beings" here refers to angels (as also in Exod. 15:11 [LXX]; *T. Jud.* 25:2), as 2:11 clarifies. As Bauckham notes, two possible interpretations exist in that the δόξας are either sinful angels or holy angels, with Bauckham preferring the former interpretation. If 2 Peter is assuming some of Jude's meaning, it is possible that a condemnation of divination of sorts is intended,[296] but none of this can be gathered from Peter's remarks on their own. Neither interpretation can be definitively proven from the context, but what is clear is the disregard that the false

---

[294] As Green helpful notes on Peter's omission of this story, "It need not suggest that the author does not understand his source (Bauckham 1983: 261), that he calculates that his readers would be unfamiliar with the Michael/Moses/devil story (Fornberg 1977: 54), or that he omits the apocryphal story 'to preclude any suggestion that these works should be considered as authoritative Scripture' (Schreiner 2003: 348). Perkins (1995: 184) is likely correct that the omission of the story is 'because it is not relevant to the argument of the letter'" (Green, *Jude and 2 Peter*, 272–73).

[295] Hillyer, *1 and 2 Peter, Jude*, 195.

[296] See Rodolfo Gavan Estrada III, "Blaspheming Angels: The Presence of Magicians in Jude 8–10," *JETS* 63.4 (2020): 739–58.

teachers have for the authority of Christ and the heavenly realm, both of which they hold in contempt.

2:11 – That Peter intends "heavenly beings" by δόξας in 2:10 is reinforced by the clarification that begins in 2:11 (ὅπου ἄγγελοι; "whereas angels"). The comparison here could either be that angels do not bring defaming judgments against other angels or that angels do not bring defaming judgments against the false teachers, depending on how one reads the referent κατ' αὐτῶν ("against them"). The two characteristics that Peter ascribes here to these angels are a greater "strength" (ἰσχύϊ) and "power" (δυνάμει), both of which could be said either of sinful or holy angels, offering little clarification to 2:10, though one might expect more negative characterization to be present if he were referring to demons or sinful angels. These angels, in contrast to the false teachers, are not bringing "a defaming judgment" (βλάσφημον κρίσιν) against their target, be it other angels or false teachers.[297] That these angels have authority to offer judgment may again point in the direction that they are holy rather than sinful angels. Such a role is played, for example, by the archangels in 1 Enoch, with each angel having a specific realm of authority and the angel Phanuel presiding over the eternal judgment of humanity (1 En. 40:9).[298] That Peter intends a comparison is clear not only from the structure of the verse but through his repetition of terms in 2:10–12. It is also clear, as Bauckham notes, that the false teachers are being rebuked for their slighting of the "glorious ones."[299] Peter's adaptation illustrates his apparent freedom to create his own message even with his use of other source material.[300] If the false teachers are rebuking the authority of the archangels over the spheres that God has assigned them, and particularly those that have authority to preside over the judgment of

---

[297] The phrase "with the Lord" is a variant reading, deemed as likely original based on ℵ B C P 1175. 1243. 1448ᶜ. 1739. 1852. 2492 Byz, though sometimes represented in the genitive (παρα κυριου), as in 𝔓⁷² 5. 307 vgᵐˢˢ syᵖʰ mss.ʰ** (cf. Eberhard Nestle and Erwin Nestle, *Nestle-Aland: NTG Apparatus Criticus*, ed. Barbara Aland et al., 28. revidierte Auflage [Stuttgart: Deutsche Bibelgesellschaft, 2012], 711).

[298] So, Green suggests, "We may assume that their rejection of angelic authority is linked to the common understanding of the angelic role in the execution of the final judgment (Neyrey 1993: 213; Perkins 1995: 184). These are not the 'fallen angels' (contra Bauckham 1983: 261) but those who accompany the Lord in the great assize (Matt. 13:39, 41, 49; 16:27; 24:31; 25:31; 2 Thess. 1:7; Rev. 7:2; 8:2, 6, 13; 9:15)" (Green, *Jude and 2 Peter*, 271).

[299] Bauckham, *Jude-2 Peter*, 262.

[300] See Green, *Jude and 2 Peter*, 272–73.

humanity, this would indeed connect to the larger denial they make concerning the Parousia, final judgment, and the reliability of the message of the prophets and apostles.[301]

2 PETER 2:12–22: THE FATE OF THE FALSE TEACHERS

¹² But these people are like irrational animals, born by nature for capturing and killing, are ignorant concerning things which they are defaming, and in their destruction, they will be destroyed.

¹³ suffering harm for the wages of their harmful ways, considering self-indulgence during the daytime a pleasure, they are stains and blemishes, delighting in their deception while feasting together with you,

¹⁴ having eyes full of adultery and unceasing sin, enticing weak souls, having a heart which has been trained for greediness, they are accursed children;

¹⁵ having forsaken the proper way, they went astray, having followed the way of Balaam of Bosor, who loved the wages of his harmful ways

¹⁶ but received a rebuke for his own lawlessness; a speechless donkey, speaking with a human voice, restrained the prophet's madness.

¹⁷ These people are dry fountains and mists driven by a hurricane, for whom the gloom of darkness has been reserved.

¹⁸ For by speaking arrogant, empty words, they are enticing with the desires of the flesh and immoralities those who are barely escaping from the ones living in deception,

¹⁹ promising them freedom though themselves being slaves of depravity; for to whatever one succumbs, by this they are enslaved.

²⁰ For, if after escaping the impurities of the world through the knowledge of [our] Lord and Savior Jesus Christ, but, having again become entangled in these things, succumbing to them, the last things have become worse than the first ones.

²¹ For it would have been better for them to have not known the way of righteousness than, having known it, to turn back from the holy commandment which had been delivered to them.

²² What the true proverb says has happened to them, "A dog returns to its own vomit," and "A sow, having washed, returns to wallowing in the mud."

2:12 – While Peter has begun his shift from the historical examples of 2:4–9 to the situation of his audience and the false teachers in 2:10–11, the shift is

---

[301] As noted by Frey, *The Letter of Jude and the Second Letter of Peter*, 341.

largely completed now in 2:12.³⁰² Peter again places here the conjunction δέ ("but"), which is now accompanied with a topic shift and clarification of his referent (οὗτοι), which was implicit in 2:10–11 but is now made explicit in the text. As Fresch notes here, δέ signals a new "distinct block."³⁰³ Though Fresch does not see a separate discourse unit here, he notes that several elements of focal prominence occur along with a change in referent and topic renewals via οὗτοι in 2:12 and 2:17, justifying seeing 2:12–22 as a distinct unit.³⁰⁴ One can also observe the shift in mainline verbs here from the use of past tenses in 2:4–10a (primarily the aorist) to the present in 2:10:b–12a to the future in 2:12b. Our author then strings a long change of dependent clauses and phrases, mostly composed of participles, from 2:13–15a, before offering another historical example (Balaam), by way of aorist tense verbs in 2:15b–16. Chapter 2 then closes with an amplified set of charges against the false teachers (2:17–22), composed mostly of perfect tense verbs, which heighten the intensity and prominence of the discourse in this section and offer a climax of sorts to the chapter.³⁰⁵

This section is also home to a host of text-critical issues, stemming primarily from the fact that our author has continued to borrow from Jude yet has also revised his words and at times removed Jude's explanations of his images or replaced them altogether. While some of the discrepancies between the texts may be conceived in terms of Jude borrowing from 2 Peter, the majority continue to point in the opposite direction, as shall be illustrated in what follows.³⁰⁶

Peter begins his heightened condemnation of the false teachers with a comparison: these people are "like irrational animals" (ὡς ἄλογα ζῷα). Having charged the false teachers with slandering divine beings, Peter spells out the state that could afford such a striking offense. To commit such "blasphemy" requires that one lack proper epistemic functioning.

---

³⁰² Note the example of Balaam will be introduced to reinforce Peter's condemnation of the false teachers in 2:15.
³⁰³ Fresch, "2 Peter," 642.
³⁰⁴ Fresch, "2 Peter," 642–43. This text division is followed by the NA27/28 as well.
³⁰⁵ His change of tenses here ought to be seen primarily as rhetorical rather than shifting from prophetic prediction in 2:1–3 to present reality, contra Bauckham, *Jude–2 Peter*, 245. See Witherington, *Letters for Hellenized Christians*, 267.
³⁰⁶ In 2:12, two major issues surface, concerning the arrangement of γεγεννημενα φυσικα and the difference in the verbal forms φθαρήσονται / καταφθαρήσονται, both of which have little material difference in interpretation.

They are incapable of reasoning (ἄλογος). The charge is reminiscent of the words of Jeremiah, who observes that the birds, by their nature, know the times of migration, but the people of God, contrary to their nature, do not know the commands of the Lord (Jer. 8:4–7). The Wisdom of Solomon connects irrationality among humans with worshiping "dumb creatures" (Wis. 11:15), and other ancient authors note that part of what distinguishes humans from animals is the ability to reason (Aristotle, *Pol.* 1.20; Philo, *Leg. Alleg.* 3.9. 30; Josephus, *Ag. Ap.* 2.29–31; *Ant.* 10.11.6 262; Plutarch, *Mor.* 493D; Epictetus, *Diss.* 4.4–11).[307] These false teachers are acting beneath their nature, which is ironic given their resentful treatment of heavenly beings.[308]

Peter offers further description of the "irrationality" of the false teachers, stating they are "born by nature for capturing and killing" (ἄλογα ζῷα γεγεννημένα φυσικὰ εἰς ἅλωσιν καὶ φθορὰν). Peter's comments here further the comparison of the false teachers to irrational animals. Plutarch records such a disposition toward animals by Alexander the Great, who believed that animals exist for use by humans.[309] Aristotle, also speaking of animals, states that "in some cases things are marked out from the moment of birth to rule or to be ruled."[310] Peter states that this being born for capturing and killing is in accordance with the false teachers' "nature" (φυσικὰ) as irrational animals. Here, Frey observes, "The lexeme φυσικός also creates a link with the letter opening: according to 1:4 the faithful will escape perishability or destruction (φθορά) and acquire a share in the 'divine nature' (φύσις), while the opponents demonstrate in their behavior a similarity with animal 'nature.'"[311] The participation in the divine nature by the faithful in Peter's audience directs them toward the *telos* of human destiny: to become like God in Christ (see also Rom. 8:28). The false

---

[307] On the comparison of humans to animals in ancient literature, see Terrence Callan, "Comparison of Humans to Animals in 2 Peter 2,10b–22," *Biblica* 90.1 (2009): 101–13.
[308] So, Davids states they "are behaving in a subhuman, not a superhuman manner" (Davids, *The Letters of 2 Peter and Jude*, 237).
[309] Plutarch. *Mor.*, "On the Fortune or the Virtue of Alexander," trans. Frank Cole Babbitt, Loeb Classical Library, 1927, Section 1, 329a. On Plutarch's own defense of enacting justice toward animals, see Damian Miszczyński, "Justice for Animals According to Plutarch," *Mare Nostrom* 10.1 (2019): 54–76. Epictetus compares the capture of animals to the slavery of humans (Epictetus, *Diss.*, 4.1).
[310] Aristotle, *Pol.* 1.20.
[311] Frey, *The Letter of Jude and the Second Letter of Peter*, 343.

teachers, in rejecting participation in the divine nature, have descended to the nature of lower creatures. As a result of this degradation of nature, the false teachers are "ignorant concerning things which they are defaming" (ἐν οἷς ἀγνοοῦσιν βλασφημοῦντες). Peter here extends the description in 2:12a with a second main verb (ἀγνοοῦσιν ["being ignorant"], with a stative verb inferred in the opening comparison) and a participial descriptor (βλασφημοῦντες). The lexical link here with 2:10–11 continues (βλασφημοῦντες; βλάσφημον; βλασφημοῦντες). The ignorance (ἀγνοοῦσιν; lit., "not knowing") of the false teachers means they don't even understand the significance of their slanderous actions. Their embracing of a lower nature has left them in clueless contempt.

Peter's final clause of 2:12 contains a perplexing construction, stating, "in their destruction, they will be destroyed" (ἐν τῇ φθορᾷ αὐτῶν καὶ φθαρήσονται). While scholars have debated the specific syntactical force of the arrangement here,[312] the sense, compounded with the repetition of φθορ- terms (φθοράν; φθορᾷ; φθαρήσονται; as well as φθορᾶς in 2:19), is to relay the inevitable "destruction" of the false teachers. As Frey notes, "Because they resemble animals in their irrationality, they also share their fate: they have no future, but are doomed to destruction."[313] Peter also creates another lexical link with the letter's opening. Where his audience, through participation in the divine nature by means of knowledge of Christ, has escaped "the corruption" (φθορᾶς) of the world, the false teachers will be "destroyed in their destruction" (ἐν τῇ φθορᾷ αὐτῶν ... φθαρήσονται).[314] Peter gives his audience a clear picture of the consequences of rejecting the authority and lordship of Christ in contrast to the blessing that awaits those who know him. That commitment to Christ is the essence of the issue at hand is affirmed by Neyrey, who helpfully

---

[312] On major approaches to this phrase, see Bauckham, *Jude-2 Peter*, 263–64. See also Davids, *II Peter and Jude*, 79. This phrase offers a contrast to Jude, whose language is more straightforward ("But these persons slander all that they do not understand, and all that they understand by nature, like the irrational animals, by these *things* they are being destroyed"), and which Peter seems to have stylized.

[313] Frey, *The Letter of Jude and the Second Letter of Peter*, 342.

[314] As Reese notes, "The word 'ruin/destruction' (φθορά, *phthora*) is repeated three times (twice in noun form, once as a verb) in the space of eleven words.... This repeated use of the word *ruin* is followed by a double use of the word *wrongdoing/injustice* (ἀδικία, *adikia*). The false teachers suffer wrong because they engage in doing wrong ('injustice'). They reap the harvest of the seed that they have sown, and it is a set of seeds that will, in the end, bring suffering, darkness, and ruin" (Reese, *2 Peter & Jude*, 155).

contextualizes this dispute in light of the honor/shame dynamics of the first-century Mediterranean world. He states:

> The honor of Jesus is challenged and must be defended. New members of the group once "acknowledged" the Lord; that is, they pledged loyalty to him, acclaimed his sovereignty as Lord and Judge, and swore to follow his Way. The honor of Jesus increased as he was thus publicly acclaimed. But now that honor is challenged and denied, for these same disciples no longer follow his Way, no longer fear his judgment, and no longer expect his triumphal arrival. The teachers of these folk have themselves denied the Master (2:1), thus shaming him; and now recent disciples follow their shameful example.[315]

While late modern sensibilities may be challenged and made uncomfortable by the sharpness of Peter's rhetoric in this section, it is indeed the perception of the honor of Christ that is at stake in the conflict, which our author seeks to defend fiercely.

2:13 – Peter's *vituperatio* continues in this verse, which extends the charges of 2:12 by way of four participial phrases (ἀδικούμενοι …; ἡγούμενοι …; ἐντρυφῶντες …; συνευωχούμενοι …). The participles in this section (2:12–14; with the exception of γεγυμνασμένην in 2:14) all encode imperfective aspect, meaning the charges are likely presented as "ongoing" activities by the false teachers. These are not "one off" misdeeds but a pattern of enduring behavior. It is possible to read the participial phrases here as adverbial or attributive, so the focus of the functions is not straightforward. This is not uncommon, however, in Asiatic rhetoric, with Eph. 1:3–14 as a notable text of comparison. Often the grammatical arrangement has been composed more for effect than syntactical precision. Peter first states the false teachers are "suffering harm for the wages of *their* harmful ways" (ἀδικούμενοι μισθὸν ἀδικίας). Similar to the φθορᾷ … φθαρήσονται construction above, Peter gives a repetition of similar terms (here ἀδικούμενοι; ἀδικίας). The terms can convey the ideas of wrongdoing, injury, harm, mistreatment, and injustice, and the word play that Peter produces if often lost here in translation, whereas it would have been clear to the original audience. The phrase "wages of their harmful ways/ unrighteousness" finds some parallel in 2 Macc. 8:33 and Acts 1:18 (and inversely in Wis. 2:22 ["wages of holiness"]; 10:17), where it similarly

---

[315] Neyrey, *2 Peter, Jude*, 218–19.

conveys the negative idea of being "rewarded" for one's wrongdoing. As Frey also notes, "the phrase "wages of unrighteousness" (μισθὸν ἀδικίας) points ahead to the example of Balaam introduced in v. 15."[316] The "harm" they receive is not an act of ἀδικίας ("wrongdoing") on God's part but rather the consequences that they are reaping for their misdeeds.[317] Rejection of divine authority comes with serious results.

Next, Peter observes the false teachers are "considering self-indulgence during the daytime a pleasure" (ἡδονὴν ἡγούμενοι τὴν ἐν ἡμέρᾳ τρυφήν). As Perkins notes, "Carousing in midday (v. 13b) was considered particularly reprehensible in antiquity (Isa. 5:11; Juvenal, *Satires*, 1:103; Cicero, *Disc.* 2.41, 104)."[318] Isaiah 5:11, for example, states, "Woe to those who rise early in the morning to run after their drinks." To behave in such a way meant to either have no worthy obligations, a vice in and of itself, or to ignore one's obligations to give in to the pleasures of the present moment. This way of life was something for which the Epicureans were well known in the ancient world. In his *Lives*, Diogenes Laertius states that Epicurus asserted, "Wherefore we call pleasure the alpha and omega of a blessed life. Pleasure is our first and kindred good."[319] Whether this means one ought to identify the false teachers as Epicureans is debatable, but the resonances of the ideas for which the Epicureans were known are clearly present in Peter's accusations. Such a worldview, though popular still in late modernism, is in clear conflict with early Christian belief and practice.

Peter now asserts "they are stains and blemishes" (σπίλοι καὶ μῶμοι), which seems a sudden interjection in the flow of thought. Our author's irritation with the corrupting influence of these false teachers is clear. As Witherington observes, Peter's remarks here stand in direct contrast to how he describes the calling of the faithful, which is to be "without blot or blemish" (cf. 3:14).[320] "Stains" (σπίλοι; used elsewhere in the NT only in Eph. 5:27) refers to a blotch or unwanted spot and may be Peter's

---

[316] Frey, *The Letter of Jude and the Second Letter of Peter*, 344.
[317] So Bauckham, *Jude–2 Peter*, 265, who notes the challenge in translating the wordplay.
[318] Perkins, *First and Second Peter, James, and Jude*, 185. See also Bauckham, who cites examples from Eccl. 10:16; Isa. 5:11; *T. Mos.* 7:4 (Bauckham, *Jude–2 Peter*, 265).
[319] Diog. Laert., 10.128. So, Frey states, "The phrase ἡδονὴν ἡγούμενοι locates the opponents – rightly or wrongly – in proximity to the Epicureans, or to the moral depravity they are broadly presumed to embrace" (Frey, *The Letter of Jude and the Second Letter of Peter*, 346).
[320] Witherington, *Letters for Hellenized Christians*, 358.

augmentation of Jude's "hidden reefs" (σπιλάδες). "Blemishes" (μῶμοι; used only here in the NT, though the negative form ἄμωμος is used in Eph. 1:4; 5:27; Phil. 2:15; Col. 1:22; Heb. 9:14; 1 Pet. 1:19; 2 Pet. 3:14; Jude 24; Rev. 14:5) describes a defect, either physically (such as LXX Lev. 21:17-23; 22:20-25; 24:19-20; Num. 19:2; Deut. 15:21; 17:1, where it is used of sacrifices; or of human appearances in LXX 2 Kgdms 14:25; Song. 4:7) or morally (such as LXX Sir. 20:24; 33:23; 47:20). The false teachers are corrupting influences on the pure garment of the Church.

Peter continues that the false teachers are "delighting in their deception" (ἐντρυφῶντες ἐν ταῖς ἀπάταις αὐτῶν). They do not merely deceive the vulnerable but find a distorted sense of joy in doing so. Here again, Peter echoes Jude's terminology (Jude 12) but has altered it. Where Jude describes the false teachers feasting together "at your love feasts" (ἐν ταῖς ἀγάπαις ὑμῶν), Peter states they delight in "their deceptions" (ἐν ταῖς ἀπάταις αὐτῶν). Bauckham sees these parallels in ἀγάπαις / ἀπάταις as evidence of a deliberate pun on Peter's behalf.[321] Peter in the context also states that this delight in deception occurs "while feasting together with you" (συνευωχούμενοι ὑμῖν), replicating Jude's description of their "feasting together" (συνευωχούμενοι; cf. Jude 12). Part of the challenge of the eucharist meal in the early church was that the cultural symbols of Greco-Roman feasts at times influenced the practice of the meal in ways contrary to Christian ethics (e.g., 1 Cor. 11:17-34). Greco-Roman meals were places of important social interaction and events in which social hierarchies and social excesses were often displayed.[322] Peter's audience seems to be no exception to these challenges. Since bread and wine were a part of the Christian observation of the eucharist, the potential to revert to cultural norms of revelry and intoxication had to be resisted. The potential of the false teachers performing pleasure-seeking activities in the midst of the Christian communal meals would certainly cause a corrupting influence in the community.[323]

---

[321] Bauckham, *Jude-2 Peter*, 266.
[322] See R. Alan Streett, *Subversive Meals: An Analysis of the Lord's Supper Under Roman Domination During the First Century* (Eugene: Wipf & Stock, 2013).
[323] As Reese writes, "When meals are shared in the context of the community it should be one of the intimate places where truth and encouragement are shared with all the members of the community. This makes its distortion and use for deceit even more ugly as the false teachers twist this precious resource to their own ends" (Reese, *2 Peter & Jude*, 156).

2:14 – Our author's stringing together of participles continues in this verse, with three participial clauses (ἔχοντες …; δελεάζοντες …; ἔχοντες …) and one participial modifier (γεγυμνασμένην) framing the verse. Structurally, this thought continues to extend the main verb construction that ended 2:12 ("they will be destroyed"), describing the state and behaviors that determine their future destruction. The next main verb clause from 2:12b does not appear until 2:15.

The castigation of the false teachers continues with the accusation of "having eyes full of adultery and unceasing sin" (ὀφθαλμοὺς ἔχοντες μεστοὺς μοιχαλίδος καὶ ἀκαταπαύστους ἁμαρτίας). The phrase "eyes full of adultery" offers a vivid description of the false teachers. Their lust consumes their thinking to the extent that all they see are opportunities for sexually immoral behavior. An oft-cited parallel in Plutarch gives a similar analogy: "The shameless person had not pupils (κόρας) in his eyes, but harlots (πόρνας)."[324] The connection between the eyes and lustful intent was, of course, addressed by Jesus in the Sermon on the Mount, where he challenged that "everyone who looks at a woman in order to lust for her has already committed adultery with her in his heart" (Matt. 5:28). First John similarly speaks about the "lust of the eyes" as a desire that stems from love of the worldly system (1 John 2:16). While a Jewish sexual ethic was often more restrained than Greco-Roman counterparts, adultery was often viewed as shameful among both Jews and Gentiles, though many Greco-Roman authors complain that the practice was widespread.[325] The false teachers seem to lack this basic sense of shame and restraint for their urges.

Furthermore, the false teachers are accused of "enticing weak souls" (δελεάζοντες ψυχὰς ἀστηρίκτους). The lexeme represented in the participle here (δελεάζω; "lure" or "entice") is used elsewhere in the New Testament only in Jas. 1:14 and again in 2 Pet. 2:18. James warns that sin comes through one being "enticed by their own desires" (ὑπὸ τῆς ἰδίας ἐπιθυμίας … δελεαζόμενος). Peter will specify in 2:18 that the false teachers are enticing with the "desires of the flesh" (ἐν ἐπιθυμίαις σαρκὸς), again

---

[324] Plutarch, *Mor.*, 528E.
[325] Craig S. Keener, "Adultery, Divorce," in *Dictionary of New Testament Background*, ed. Craig A. Evans and Stanley E. Porter (Downers Grove: IVP Academic, 2000), 6–8.

reinforcing the sexual nature of their motivations. They direct their luring at "weak" or "unstable" (ἀστηρίκτους) souls, a descriptor used in the New Testament only here and in 2 Pet. 3:16, with the positive counterpart (στηριγμός) used in 2 Pet. 3:17, which contrasts the faithful of Peter's audience with the false teachers and those they lead astray. Our author references the "soul" of humans in only one other place in the letter, when he writes of Lot torturing "his righteous soul" (ψυχὴν δικαίαν). It is difficult, therefore, to draw a clear picture of 2 Peter's concept of the "soul" from these two depictions, though the context of both has to do with the inner moral life of the person and therefore, to some extent, their relation to God.[326]

The next accusation against the false teachers is their "having a heart which has been trained for greediness" (καρδίαν γεγυμνασμένην πλεονεξίας ἔχοντες). Peter has levied the charge of greediness (πλεονεξίᾳ; 2:3) already against the false teachers and will expand on this charge in his comparison of their actions with Balaam in 2:15–16. Not only are the false teachers greedy, but they have "trained" (γεγυμνασμένην) their hearts for such a disposition. The language here, echoed also elsewhere in the NT,[327] reflects the imagery of athletic training as would occur in the ancient *gymnasium*. In other ancient literature, as Green describes, this concept was "applied to the training of the whole person, especially the moral training someone would receive either via philosophers (Epictetus, *Diss.*, 1.26.3) or through the circumstances of life ('I am long trained in the athletics of life,' Philo, *Joseph* 5.26; Isocrates, *Demon.*, 21)."[328] Rather than training for the pursuit of virtue, the false teachers have committed themselves to a disciplined pursuit of their vices.

Our author punctuates this long sentence, spanning from 2:12b–14, with an abrupt invective, calling the false teachers "accursed children" (κατάρας τέκνα). The language of blessing and cursing is prevalent in the OT and particularly Deuteronomy (e.g., Deut. 11:26–28; 23:6; 28:15, 45; 30:1, 19), where it serves an important covenantal function. Such an invective occurs

---

[326] On the concept of the soul in 1 Peter, and Platonic influences in its presentation, see Reinhard Feldmeier, *The First Letter of Peter: A Commentary on the Greek Text* (Waco: Baylor University Press, 2008), 87–92.
[327] See Heb. 5:14; 12:11; 1 Tim. 4:7–8.
[328] Green, *Jude and 2 Peter*, 283.

elsewhere in the OT (e.g., "children of adultery"; Hos. 2:4),[329] as well as in Sirach ("born under a curse"; Sir. 41:9; see also Eph. 2:3), and contrasts with the positive identity of being "children of God" (Matt. 5:9, 45; Luke 6:35; John 1:12; 11:52; Rom. 8:14, 19, 21; 9:26; Gal. 3:26; Phil. 2:15; 1 John 3:1-2, 10; 5:2; see also Eph. 5:8; 1 Pet. 1:14). Peter's discussion here also offers a transition to his example of Balaam in 2:15-16, who was commissioned to curse Israel at the behest of the king of Moab (Deut. 23:4-5; Josh. 24:9-10; Neh. 13:2).[330]

Peter's accusations against the false teachers in 2:12-14 charge them with slandering heavenly beings, pursuing unrighteousness, drinking and reveling in the daytime, committing harmful deceit, seeking adulterous interactions, drawing weak persons into sin, and committing themselves to greed. Their actions do damage to marriages, the sacred meal, and the community itself, and the seriousness of their behavior should not be underestimated.[331]

2:15 - A participial phrase introduces 2:15 (καταλίποντες εὐθεῖαν ὁδὸν; "having forsaken the proper way")[332] and connects to the new main verb introduced in the following clause (ἐπλανήθησαν; "they were led astray"). The change in tense here from present and perfect forms to the aorist, which continues through 2:16 (ἐξακολουθήσαντες, ἠγάπησεν, ἔσχεν, φθεγξάμενον, ἐκώλυσεν), indicates the author is framing this material as background information, connecting the behavior of the false teachers to the historical example of Balaam.[333] The verbal concepts here also resume the "journeying" theme observed in 1:11-15. Where Peter prepared for his departure and sought to ensure his recipients completed their entry into

---

[329] As Gruber describes the use in Hosea, they are called "children of adultery because they represented the typically idolatrous Israelites of the time of our prophet" (Mayer I. Gruber, *Hosea: A Textual Commentary* [New York: Bloomsbury T&T Clark, 2017], 117).

[330] As Frey notes, citing Deut. 23:5-6; Josh. 24:9-10; Neh. 13:2; Philo, *Migr.* 113-14; and *Conf.* 159 as support, "The reference to the curse [cf. 2:14] creates an associative bridge to the following passage, since the Balaam pericope aims at the cursing of Israel and later traditions reckon with an actual curse" (Frey, *The Letter of Jude and the Second Letter of Peter*, 349).

[331] Donelson, *I & II Peter and Jude*, 253.

[332] On parallels to the "proper" or "straight way," see LXX 1 Kgdms. 12:23; Ps. 106:7; Prov. 2:13, 16; Isa. 33:15; Hos. 14:10; Wis. 5:6; also Acts 13:10.

[333] Second Peter drops the negative examples of Cain and Korah cited by Jude and includes only the example of Balaam in his characterization of the false teachers.

the eternal kingdom, the false teachers have forsaken the path to the kingdom and instead gone a different and destructive way.

The path they follow (ἐξακολουθήσαντες) is not the way of Christ but "the way of Balaam of Bosor" (τῇ ὁδῷ τοῦ Βαλαὰμ τοῦ Βοσόρ). Balaam figures prominently in Numbers 22–24,[334] where he is summoned by the king of Moab to curse Israel. Balaam travels to the king and on the way finds himself opposed by the angel of the Lord, with his donkey refusing to pass. This results in Balaam beating the donkey until Balaam's own eyes are opened and he himself sees the angel of the Lord. Balaam eventually appears before the king and instead blesses Israel and prophesies destruction upon Israel's enemies, Moab included. When Balaam is further mentioned, however, in the Old Testament, he is described as one who enticed Israel to sin against the Lord at Peor (Num. 31:16; cf. Num. 25), one who practiced divination (Josh. 13:22), and one who could be hired to curse Israel (Mic. 6:5).

These negative portrayals of Balaam resulted in the development of further critiques of the figure in Jewish tradition, particularly related to his greed, practice of divination, and sexual immorality. While the narrative in Numbers portrays Balaam as rejecting the payment for cursing offered to him by the king of Moab, Jewish traditions (Jude 11; *b. Sanh.* 106a; *Num. Rab.* 20:20; 22:5; *Sipra Numbers* 137; *Tgs.* Num. 22:7; Philo, *Mos.* 1.48, 266–68; 1.45, 295–304; *Mig.* 114; *Abot R. Nat.* 1.29; *Num. Rab.* 20:10) depict him as desiring such gifts.[335] Philo is representative, stating that Balaam was "allured by the gifts" offered to him (Philo, *Mos.* 1.48, 268). When Peter casts Balaam as one who "loved the wages of *his* harmful ways" (ὃς μισθὸν ἀδικίας ἠγάπησεν), he represents agreement with the portrayal of Balaam in these traditions.

Peter's phrasing that Balaam was "of Bosor" (τοῦ Βοσόρ) is the subject of debate. In the Old Testament, Balaam is the son of Beor (Βεώρ; בְּעוֹר; cf. Num. 22:5), not Bosor (Βοσόρ). While some manuscripts read Βεώρ instead (B vg^{mss} sy^{ph} sa; Aug), the evidence indicates this is a scribal correction. Several possibilities for the use of τοῦ Βοσόρ exist. First, our

---

[334] See also Num. 31:8, 16; Deut. 23:4–5; Josh. 13:22; 24:9–10; Neh. 13:2; Mic. 6:5; Jude 11; Rev. 2:14; cf. *Tg. Ps.-J.* on Num. 22:30.

[335] As Bauckham summarizes, "Jewish tradition remembered Balaam primarily as a man of greed, who for the sake of reward led Israel into debauchery and idolatry" (Bauckham, *Jude–2 Peter*, 81).

author could be in error in his recollection of the name of Balaam's father. Second, as Bauckham has suggested, it is possible Peter altered the spelling as a play on words of the Hebrew word *bāśār*, meaning "flesh."[336] This would accord with some of the charges levied against both Balaam and the false teachers, as the language of "flesh" is often associated with sexual immorality. Third, as Green has suggested, the reference to "of Bosor" may refer to where Balaam lived rather than his lineage. As he writes, "Peter may be referring not to Balaam's father but to the place from which he came. A city called Bosor was located in Syria ... and according to Num. 23:7, Balaam came from Aram, the state around Damascus. Likewise, Num. 22:5 locates Balaam at Pethord 'near the river, in his native land.'"[337] Regardless of which option is to be preferred, the focus of Peter's rhetoric here is not greatly impacted by this question.

2:16 – The critical comparison of the false teachers to Balaam continues with Peter's note that Balaam "received a rebuke for his own lawlessness" (ἔλεγξιν δὲ ἔσχεν ἰδίας παρανομίας). Just as the inhabitants of Sodom and Gomorrah committed "lawless deeds" (ἀνόμοις ἔργοις), so too Balaam, and the false teachers, are guilty of violating divine expectations. As noted previously, Jewish traditions surrounding Balaam portray him as one who was sexually immoral. Numbers 31:16 indicates that it was Balaam who led Israel astray into sexually immoral and idolatrous behavior with the Midianites (cf. Num. 25), and Jewish texts frequently make similar connections (*Bib. Ant.* 18:13; *Tg. Ps. J.*; Philo, *Mos.* 1.295–300; Josephus, *Ant.*, 4.126–30; *y. Sanh.* 10.28d; *b. Sanh.* 105a; Rev. 2:14) even at times accusing Balaam with bestiality.[338]

Balaam's disordered behavior is contrasted with an ironic comparison: "a speechless donkey" (ὑποζύγιον ἄφωνον). Though donkeys, of course, naturally are speechless, capable of only contentless grunts and brays, Balaam's donkey inquires of his master, "What have I done to you to make you beat me these three times?" (Num. 22:28) and then, sarcastically, asks, "Am I not your own donkey, which you have always ridden, to this day? Have I been in the habit of doing this to you?" (Num. 22:30). Thus, the

---

[336] Bauckham, *Jude–2 Peter*, 267–68. On development from textual shifts in the LXX, see Frey, *The Letter of Jude and the Second Letter of Peter*, 351.
[337] Green, *Jude and 2 Peter*, 289. See also 1 Macc. 5:25, 36.
[338] As Bauckham notes, "Jewish tradition sometimes accused Balaam of this (bestiality with his ass: *Tg. Ps.-J.* Nu. 22:30)" (Bauckham, *Jude–2 Peter*, 82).

donkey speaks in Numbers as "with a human voice" (ἐν ἀνθρώπου φωνῇ). The irony of the account in Numbers is thickened in 2 Peter as Balaam, rebuked by a talking donkey naturally compares with the false teachers who act like "irrational animals" (ἄλογα ζῷα). Just as Jewish tradition understood Balaam to be ignorant and filled with vice, so too the false teachers whom Peter opposes.

Our author clarifies the source of the rebuke Balaam received in stating it was the donkey who "restrained the prophet's madness" (ἐκώλυσεν τὴν τοῦ προφήτου παραφρονίαν). In addition to the vice of greed and sexually immoral conduct, Balaam is depicted in the Old Testament as one who practiced divination (Num. 22:7; 23:23; 24:1; cf. Lev. 19:26). The practice involved the use of oil and water, smoke, animals, astrology, casting lots, dreams, pouring of blood, communication with the dead, and other practices, in order to determine messages from the gods.[339] Though Balaam receives his words from the Lord in Numbers 22–24 without such activity, the Old Testament acknowledges that he was apparently prone to use such methods at other times. This may be what Peter has in mind with referring to Balaam's donkey as restraining "the prophet's madness" (τὴν τοῦ προφήτου παραφρονίαν). These more ecstatic forms of prophetic illumination, which were condemned in the Old Testament (cf. Lev. 19:26; Deut. 18:10–14), likewise contribute to the negative characterization of Balaam. Balaam's "madness" is depicted with a word coined here (παραφρονίαν), which Witherington notes is so construed "so that it will rhyme with the word for transgression: *paranomia*."[340] This rhetorical flourish, a further demonstration of the author's Asiatic style, is one of a number of such creative formulations arranged by our author in his tirade against the false teachers.

Our author's depiction of the figure of Balaam serves the purpose of highlighting the condemnation of the false teachers. The charges of greed (2:3, 14), sexual immorality (2:2, 10, 13–14), and improper interaction with spiritual beings (2:10–11) has already been levied against the false teachers by way of the examples of the Watchers, the flood generation, and Sodom

---

[339] See D. P. O'Mathúna, "Divination, Magic," in *Dictionary of the Old Testament: Pentateuch*, ed. T. Desmond Alexander and David W. Baker (Downers Grove: IVP Academic, 2002), 457–65.

[340] Witherington, *Letters for Hellenized Christians*, 359.

and Gomorrah. The use of the figure of Balaam reinforces these negative aspects of the false teachers and serves as a springboard for their further condemnation, which follows in 2:17–22.

2:17 – Peter returns to present tense verbs from the background material of Balaam that served as a comparative critique of the false teachers. The change both in subject and verbs here (comprising mostly present and perfect verbal forms, with a few aorist participles, which provide more background material) indicates a return to the focus of the critique of the false teachers. "These people" (οὗτοί), he writes, "are dry fountains and mists driven by a hurricane" (εἰσιν πηγαὶ ἄνυδροι καὶ ὀμίχλαι ὑπὸ λαίλαπος ἐλαυνόμεναι). Peter's language here again echoes Jude while modifying his imagery and language. Where Jude writes of his opponents that they are "dry clouds carried away by winds" (νεφέλαι ἄνυδροι ὑπὸ ἀνέμων παραφερόμεναι) and "wild waves of the sea" (κύματα ἄγρια θαλάσσης), Peter's modifications make his imagery less clear at times. Augustine remarks that "Peter calls these people dry springs – springs, because they have received knowledge of the Lord Christ, but dry, because they do not live in accordance with that knowledge."[341] Indeed, 2:20 will suggest that Peter envisions these teachers as those who have been initiated into the way of Christ and have now departed from it, making them apostates.[342] To be a "dry fountain," particularly in regions where water was a precious commodity, represents not just a useless but a terribly disappointing state of affairs.[343] Water in biblical texts is often representative of life, comfort, and flourishing (e.g., Prov. 13:14; Matt. 10:42; Mark 9:41; Luke 13:15; 16:24; John 4:13–15; 7:38; Rev. 7:17), and the absence of water is a cause for mourning (cf. Jer. 14:3). Such is the state of the inner life of the false teachers. They are dried up and without life.

As "mists driven by a hurricane" (ὀμίχλαι ὑπὸ λαίλαπος ἐλαυνόμεναι), the false teachers obscure the vision of those around them. As Green notes, they are not "pleasant morning mists ('mist' in Wis. 2:4; Sir. 24:3; 43:22); instead, they are mists that produce foreboding darkness (Job 38:9; Joel 2:2;

---

[341] Augustine, "On Faith and Works," in *Fathers of the Church: A New Translation* (Washington DC: Catholic University of America Press, 1947), 25 (46).

[342] Donelson writes, "2 Peter gives what is probably the fullest account of apostasy in the NT" (Donelson, *I & II Peter and Jude*, 256).

[343] See Kelly, *The Epistles of Peter and Jude*, 345.

Isa. 29:18; Amos 4:13; Zeph. 1:15)."³⁴⁴ They bring chaos, confusion, destruction, and disorder because of their rejection of the reality of the future coming and judgment of Christ and their lack of moral restraint. Like the rebellious angels who rejected divine authority (cf. 2:4), the false teachers are likewise those "for whom the gloom of darkness has been reserved" (οἷς ὁ ζόφος τοῦ σκότους τετήρηται). This phrase lexically reproduces the statement in 2:4 where those angels are held in chains of "darkness" (ζόφου) and "being kept" (τηρουμένους) for judgment, creating another obvious link between these past examples of divine judgment and the judgment awaiting the false teachers. This also contains the first verb in a cluster of perfect tense forms that will come in 2:17-22 (τετήρηται, ἥττηται, δεδούλωται, γέγονεν, ἐπεγνωκέναι, συμβέβηκεν). Since the perfect tense creates heightened intensity or focus within the text, the presence of this many perfect tense verbs in this short section packs a punch of prominence within the text.³⁴⁵ The castigation of the false teachers is both artfully constructed, with many interconnections woven within the chapter and into the discourse as a whole, and forcefully delivered. Our author wants his readers to make no mistake about the fate that awaits those who have forsaken the lordship of Jesus Christ.

2:18 – Our author continues with an explanatory comment ("for"; γάρ) as to why he has accused the false teachers of bringing danger, disappointment, and confusion. Their means of deception is "speaking arrogant, empty words" (ὑπέρογκα ... ματαιότητος φθεγγόμενοι). As Witherington notes, the description of their rhetoric as ὑπέρογκα ("boastful"), sometimes translated as "bombastic" (HCSB, NRSV), was a phrase sometimes used to describe Asiatic rhetoric, a style our author has adopted, but also had its critics.³⁴⁶ Though Peter's words here have a "bombastic" flair, they differ from the false teachers in that they cannot be described as empty. The apostolic teaching, as our author has already defended, contains the true, "contentful,"³⁴⁷ revelation from God and Christ.

---

³⁴⁴ Green, *Jude and 2 Peter*, 292.
³⁴⁵ See Mathewson and Emig, *Intermediate Greek Grammar*, 111–18.
³⁴⁶ Witherington, *Letters for Hellenized Christians*, 360.
³⁴⁷ A term I first learned in relation to revelation from John Morrison, though I'm not sure of its origins in theological circles. See John D. Morrison, "Scripture as Word of God: Evangelical Assumption or Evangelical Question?," *Trinity Journal* 20.2 (1999): 165–90.

Their empty and arrogant words "are enticing with the desires of the flesh and immoralities" (δελεάζουσιν ἐν ἐπιθυμίαις σαρκὸς ἀσελγείαις). The present tense in the verb here (δελεάζουσιν; and the participles in this verse as well) shows the ongoing nature of the abuses of the false teachers. Their "enticing" or "luring" may invoke a fishing metaphor, enticing unsuspecting victims with false goods in order to set the hook in them.[348] There is a pattern to their manipulation and exploitation. Though "flesh" (σαρκὸς) occurs only twice in 2 Peter (here and in 2:10), it carries a negative connotation in both and is paired in both places with ἐπιθυμία ("desire") as well. The "desires of the flesh" occurs also in Pauline literature (Rom. 13:14; Gal. 5:16; Eph. 2:3), where it carries similar negative connotations. The combination likely hints at sexual immorality, which Peter has addressed numerous times throughout the chapter, and contrasts with the "self-control" (ἐγκράτειαν) he admonished his audience to pursue in 1:6. The "immoralities" (ἀσελγείαις) of the false teachers have a similar focus, a term already used also in 2:2 of the false teachers and in 2:7 of the lawless residents of Sodom and Gomorrah, and indicates a lack of moral restraint.[349]

The objects of their enticement are "those who are barely escaping" (τοὺς ὀλίγως ἀποφεύγοντας). The compound ἀποφεύγω used here occurs only in 2 Peter in the NT, though the verb φεύγω is more common (twenty-nine times). The adverb attached here (ὀλίγως; "barely") is only used here in the NT.[350] Second Peter's affinity for more obscure words is a reflection of its adoption of Asiatic style. These objects are attempting escape "from the ones living in deception" (τοὺς ἐν πλάνῃ ἀναστρεφομένους). The syntax here is a bit strained, as both participles (ἀποφεύγοντας, ἀναστρεφομένους) are in the accusative case, but are not functioning as two objects, particularly since they lack a connective like καί. As Biggs notes, ἀναστρεφομένους could be taken to refer either to the false teachers, which would be grammatically awkward since they are the subject of the sentence (δελεάζουσιν), or to pagan unbelievers in general, which would subsequently include the false teachers by default, and

---

[348] Green, *Jude and 2 Peter*, 295.
[349] See Arndt et al., *A Greek-English Lexicon*, 141.
[350] This follows the text of the NA27, supported by 𝔓⁷² ²ℵ A B Ψ 33. 436 latt sy co over the NA28 reading of ὄντως based on ℵ* C P 048. 5. 81. 307. 442. 642. 1175. 1243. 1448. 1611. 1735. 1739. 1852. 2492 Byz.

dissolves the difficulty.³⁵¹ The compounding of the verbal form (φεύγω) with the preposition ἀπό causes the verb to indicate separation, so the second participle (ἀναστρεφομένους) functions as the object of the first (ἀποφεύγοντας), indicating the group from which the believers ought to be fleeing.³⁵² The pagan world in which these believers formerly lived was one of "error" (πλάνη). Peter creates another lexical connection here, as he has described the false teachers as those who have gone astray (ἐπλανήθησαν; 2:15). He will warn his audience once again in 3:17 of those who would lead them away in error (πλάνη), with the essence of their error being their denial of future judgment and their selfish, sinful behavior.

2:19 – Peter's explanation (γάρ; "for"; cf. 2:18) continues in 2:19, further describing the way in which the false teachers are enticing some within Peter's audience to abandon the way of truth. In addition to "enticing with desires" (δελεάζουσιν ἐν ἐπιθυμίαις; cf. 2:18), the false teachers are "promising them freedom" (ἐλευθερίαν αὐτοῖς ἐπαγγελλόμενοι), and the use of the present tense of the participle here again underscores the persistent nature of their activity. This verse is the only place in the letter where the subject of freedom (ἐλευθερίαν) arises, and scholars debate what is entailed by Peter's evoking of the concept. Bauckham details five approaches to the question of what this freedom entailed: (1) freedom from the moral law, (2) freedom from the archons or the demiurge (cf. Gnosticism), (3) freedom from "perishability," (4) political freedom, (5) freedom from fear of judgment.³⁵³ One's answer depends, in part, on the imagined background of the letter and the specific socioreligious context inhabited by the false teachers.³⁵⁴ Given the background and development of this discourse, it seems the fifth option is most likely. The two major features that the letter attributes to the false teachers are denial of the lordship and future return and judgment of Christ and embracing moral corruption. As Bauckham suggests, "freedom from moral restraint is a consequence of freedom from fear of judgment."³⁵⁵

---

³⁵¹ Bigg, *A Critical and Exegetical Commentary on the Epistles of St. Peter and St. Jude*, 285. See also Green, *Jude and 2 Peter*, 295; Neyrey, *2 Peter, Jude*, 221.
³⁵² See O'Brien, *II Peter and Jude*, 87.
³⁵³ Bauckham, *Jude–2 Peter*, 275.
³⁵⁴ On the history of interpretation concerning the social/philosophical source of this notion of freedom among the false teachers, see Frey, *The Letter of Jude and the Second Letter of Peter*, 356–57.
³⁵⁵ Bauckham, *Jude–2 Peter*, 275.

The irony of the state of the false teachers is that though they promise freedom, they themselves are "slaves of depravity" (αὐτοὶ δοῦλοι ... τῆς φθορᾶς). Peter introduced himself in the letter as a slave (δοῦλος) of Jesus Christ and one on his way to entrance into his eternal kingdom (cf. 1:10–15). The false teachers, having rejected the lordship of Christ (cf. 2:1), are instead enslaved to depravity (φθορᾶς). As Watson comments, "*Phthora* is personified and portrayed in the common imagery of a victor in war who seizes those defeated as slaves and booty."[356] Whereas Christ is portrayed as liberator (cf. 2:1), "Depravity" is that which enslaves.

A note of explanation (γάρ; "for") of the enslavement of the false teachers is given in the clause that follows, which states, "for to whatever one succumbs, by this they are enslaved" (ᾧ γάρ τις ἥττηται, τούτῳ δεδούλωται). The change here to the perfect tense provides "front grounding" for this statement while also giving it a sort of gnomic force.[357] As Hilary of Arles comments on this verse, "A man is a slave of whatever vice controls him."[358] Peter paints an image here similar to Paul in Romans 6 (see also John 8:34), where Sin and Death are portrayed as the enslavers who pay their slaves with death, while God, in Christ, has slaves of righteousness who are rewarded with eternal life. Jesus casts a similar image as well when he contrasts the inability to serve two masters: God or wealth (cf. Matt. 6:24)

There is a great irony present in the interchange between the pursuit of pleasure and its ultimate inability to provide any sense of lasting fulfillment. As Schooping expresses, "Desire ... is a present pain ceaselessly oriented towards fleeting sensory pleasure and away from inevitable pain, and is thus unable to ever either truly escape its painful precondition or rest form its own miserable motivations. Pleasure and pain are thus inextricably linked."[359] Christian freedom must not be seen only as a "freedom from" but also as a "freedom for." As Paul states in Rom. 6:20, life apart from Christ is a life absent of righteousness. It is a life without the

---

[356] Watson, *Invention, Arrangement, and Style*, 120.
[357] On the saying as a possible noncanonical saying of Jesus, preserved orally and recorded by the author of 2 Peter, see Wolfgang Grünstäudl, "'On Slavery': A Possible *Herrenwort* in 2 Pet. 2:19," *Novum Testam* 57 (2015): 57–71.
[358] Hilary of Arles, "Introductory Commentary on 2 Peter," in *Patrologiae Latinae Supplementum*, ed. A. Hamman (Paris: Garnier Frères, 1958), 3:113.
[359] Schooping, *A Manual of Theosis*, 20.

possibility of flourishing, since true flourishing is found in Christ alone. Bonhoeffer, in his Sermon on John 8:32, expresses this poignantly:

> God's truth is God's love and God's love makes us free from ourselves for others. To be free means nothing less than to be in love. And to be in love means nothing less than being in the truth of God. The person who loves because he has been made free by God is the most revolutionary person on earth. He challenges all values. He is the explosive material of human society. He is a dangerous person. For he recognizes that the human race is in the depths of falsehood. And he is always ready to let the light of truth fall upon his darkness; and he will do this because of his love . . . . It is also true that a people cannot find truth and freedom unless it stands under the law of God's truth. A people remains in lies and in slavery until it receives and wants to receive truth and freedom from God alone; until it knows that truth and freedom will lead it into love; yes, until it knows that the way of love leads to the cross. If a people would really know this, then it would become the only people who could rightly be called a free people, the only people which does not become a slave to itself, but the slave of the truth of God and therefore free.[360]

Such is a freedom that the false teachers, having forsaken life in Christ, cannot know and that the unstable within this congregation are at risk of losing should they find themselves aligning with the false teachers' empty words.

2:20 – A new sentence is begun in 2:20 that offers an explanatory comment (γάρ; "for") on the previous sentence (2:18–19). This explanatory comment is framed as a first-class condition (εἰ; "if"), often described as "assumed true for the sake of argument." The first part of the protasis of the condition (a participial clause) reads as follows: "For, if, after escaping the impurities of the world" (εἰ γὰρ ἀποφυγόντες τὰ μιάσματα τοῦ κόσμου). The language here harkens back to 2 Pet. 1:4 ("escape from the corruption in the world because of distorted desires"), replicating both the verbal form (ἀποφυγόντες / ἀποφυγόντες) and object (ἐν τῷ κόσμῳ / τοῦ κόσμου), though the modifier (ἐν ἐπιθυμίᾳ φθορᾶς / τὰ μιάσματα) has changed.[361] This language in the context functioned to describe

---

[360] Dietrich Bonhoeffer, *Dietrich Bonhoeffer's Christmas Sermons*, trans. and ed. Edwin H. Robertson (Grand Rapids: Zondervan, 2011).

[361] On the comparison of this verse and 1:2-4, see also Davids, *The Letters of 2 Peter and Jude*, 248.

participation in the divine life (i.e., "salvation"), which was contrasted with participation in the corruption of the world.

The means of "escape" also resonates with 1:4 in that in both places it is the "knowledge of [our] Lord and Savior Jesus Christ" (ἐν ἐπιγνώσει τοῦ κυρίου [ἡμῶν]³⁶² καὶ σωτῆρος Ἰησοῦ Χριστοῦ; cf. 2 Pet. 1:2, 3) which makes escape is possible. As noted previously, this knowledge in 2 Peter does not simply contrast with Gnosticism,³⁶³ nor is it simply cognitive knowledge but rather a personal and revelatory knowledge which unites believers with God through the righteous work of Jesus Christ (see comments on 1:2–4).

The second part of the protasis (another participial clause) reads: "but, having again become entangled in these things" (τούτοις δὲ πάλιν ἐμπλακέντες). The "these things" being referenced are the corruptions/impurities of the world, which those with knowledge of Christ have escaped. The main verb of the protasis details that those who previously escaped and become re-entangled are then also "succumbing to them" (ἡττῶνται; cf. also 2:19).

With the protasis complete, the result (apodosis) of the condition is that "the last things have become worse than the first ones" (γέγονεν αὐτοῖς τὰ ἔσχατα χείρονα τῶν πρώτων). For those who have experienced knowledge of Christ and yet return to the corruptions of the world, our author views a dire result. With 2 Peter's focus on eschatological judgment, it seems the way in which the state of this person would be worse off would relate to their, as Hebrews states, inability "to renew again to repentance" (Heb. 6:4, 6). A similar teaching occurs in the Gospels of Matthew and Luke, wherein Jesus describes a person who, having been freed from an unclean spirit, finds the spirit returning and seven others reenter the person and, thus, "the last state of that person becomes worse than the first" (cf. Matt. 12:45; Luke 11:26), though the focus there is not upon eschatological judgment. While our text does not explain how the second state is more severe, the impossibility of again possessing knowledge of Christ would certainly fit as a "worse state."

---

[362] While the NA27 includes the pronoun in brackets on the basis of support from following 𝔓⁷² ℵ A C P Ψ 614 1739 *al*, the NA28 removes it and the SBLGNT omits it as well.

[363] Contra Kelly, *The Epistles of Peter and Jude*, 251.

One difficulty with this verse is the referent being described, with the two major options being (1) the false teachers[364] or (2) some susceptible believers within the community Peter addresses.[365] The majority of commentators read the verses as continuing the *vituperatio* against the false teachers rather than changing the focus. Though those affected by the false teachers are mentioned in 2:18 and 19, they are addressed there as the objects of the discourse rather than the subjects. It would be expected, therefore, for some grammatical marker to be present to indicate the attention has shifted from the teachers to their followers, and no such shift is present in this section. However, whether referring to the false teachers or to those within the community who have fallen away, the result of the action is clear. Those formerly possessing knowledge of Christ and participation in the divine nature, having returned to the world and rejected their participation in the divine life, have reached a more dreadful state.[366]

2:21 – Another explanatory clause (γὰρ; "for") follows, which adds description to the previous explanatory condition. This clause is structured as a comparison, with the first clause stating, "it would have been better[367] for them to have not known the way of righteousness" (κρεῖττον γὰρ ἦν αὐτοῖς μὴ ἐπεγνωκέναι τὴν ὁδὸν τῆς δικαιοσύνης). Our author again depicts the Christian life as a journey,[368] with the term "way" (ὁδός) having occurred throughout the discourse (1:11, 15; 2:2, 15) and various modifiers attached throughout ("entrance into the kingdom," cf. 1:11; "way of truth," cf. 2:2; "straight way," cf. 2:15; "way of Balaam," cf. 2:15; "way of righteousness," cf. 2:21). "Knowing" (ἐπεγνωκέναι) is also a key term in the discourse (cf. 1:2, 3, 5, 6, 8, 16, 20; 2:20, 21; 3:3, 17, 18), and knowledge of God in Christ is the quintessential condition of salvation for 2 Peter. To have "known the way of righteousness," particularly with the use of the perfect tense here

---

[364] Bauckham, *Jude-2 Peter*, 277; Davids, *The Letters of 2 Peter and Jude*, 249; Green, *Jude and 2 Peter*, 300-302; Witherington, *Letters and Homilies*, 361.

[365] Kelly, *The Epistles of Peter and of Jude*, 347-48; Neyrey, *2 Peter, Jude*, 218-19.

[366] For comparison, see the famous "warning passages" in Hebrews 2:1-4; 3:7-4:13; 5:11-6:12; 10:19-39; 12:14-29.

[367] On parallels to "it would be better" as a judgment statement (sometimes referred to as a *Tobspruch* or *Tobsprüche*), see Mark 9:42-47; 14:21, cf. Witherington, *Letters for Hellenized Christians*, 356.

[368] See comments on 1:11-15, as well as Sylva, "A Unified Field Picture of Second Peter 1.3-15," 91-118.

(ἐπεγνωκέναι), would seem to indicate those who had some form of genuine knowledge of God in Christ.[369]

The second clause of the comparison follows and states, "than, having known it, to turn back" (ἢ ἐπιγνοῦσιν ὑποστρέψαι[370]). The image of traveling/journeying continues here, with those who had begun on the "way of truth/righteousness/the kingdom" having made an about-face and returning to the corruptions of the world. What they are turning away from is further described as "the holy commandment which had been delivered to them" (ἐκ τῆς παραδοθείσης αὐτοῖς ἁγίας ἐντολῆς). In what way would they be better off not knowing? Oropeza suggests "The author may be influenced here by the Jesus saying that the one who knows the Lord's will and does not do it will be judged more severely than the one who did not know the Lord's will (Luke 12:47–48)."[371]

A further question of Peter's wording here is what the substance of this "holy commandment" (ἁγίας ἐντολῆς) might be? Suggestions include the Christian communal way of life,[372] the way of Jesus,[373] or a body of ethical teaching.[374] While there are only shades of differences between these descriptions, we likely should view this "commandment" as encompassing both the essential Christian teachings (e.g., Jesus is the risen Lord) and the essential ethical conduct that follows from such a commitment. The use of the singular "commandment" (ἐντολή) as a collective or "umbrella" term for a larger body of material occurs elsewhere in relevant literature (e.g., Matt. 15:3; Rom. 7:12; 1 Cor. 14:37; 1 Tim. 6:14; Heb. 9:19; 2 Pet. 3:2; 1 John

---

[369] So Green writes, "This is genuine apostasy, from which there is no escape (Heb. 6:4–8; 10:26 …). The heretics have turned from the 'holy commandment' (2:21) and denied 'the Master who bought them' (2:1)" (Green, *Jude and 2 Peter*, 302). Kelly agrees, noting "the deliberate and eye-opened spurning of God's gift seemed a peculiarly appalling evidence of a man's doomed state" (Kelly, *The Epistles of Peter and Jude*, 348).

[370] There are a cluster of alternate readings at this point in the text ([παλιν] επιστρεψαι εκ| εις τα οπισω επιστρεψαι απο| υποστρεψαι εις τα οπισω απο| εις τα οπισω ανακαμψαι απο; cf. NA²⁸), though several significant witnesses support the text as offered above (𝔓⁷² B C P 307. 442. 1175. 1739).

[371] B. J. Oropeza, *Churches under Siege of Persecution and Assimilation: Apostasy in the New Testament Communities, Volume 3: The General Epistles and Revelation* (Eugene: Wipf and Stock, 2012), 146.

[372] Kelly, *The Epistles of Peter and of Jude*, 350; Neyrey, *2 Peter, Jude*, 224; Witherington, *Letters and Homilies*, 361.

[373] Davids, *The Letters of 2 Peter and Jude*, 251; Green is similar referring to the "substance of Christian instruction" (Green, *Jude and 2 Peter*, 305).

[374] Bauckham, *Jude-2 Peter*, 278; Frey, *The Letter of Jude and the Second Letter of Peter*, 362; Donelson, *1 & II Peter and Jude*, 350.

2:7-8; 3:22-24). In 2 Peter, theological belief and ethical behavior go hand in hand.³⁷⁵ This commandment being "delivered to them" (τῆς παραδοθείσης αὐτοῖς) likely describes the transmission of apostolic teaching (cf. 1:16-21), as the verb here (παραδίδωμι) at times functions in the New Testament to refer to the formal transmission of tradition (see Mark 7:13; Acts 16:4; Rom. 6:17; 1 Cor. 11:2, 23; 15:3; Jude 3).

2:22 – The final verse of the chapter, which concludes the focused *vituperatio* of the discourse,³⁷⁶ offers two proverbial statements ("What the true proverb says has happened to them" [συμβέβηκεν αὐτοῖς τὸ τῆς ἀληθοῦς παροιμίας]) in support of Peter's description of the resultant state of those who have rejected knowledge of Christ for the corruption of the world. The first, a paraphrase of Prov. 26:11,³⁷⁷ states, "A dog returns to its own vomit" (Κύων ἐπιστρέψας ἐπὶ τὸ ἴδιον ἐξέραμα). The second, of less clear origin, though comparable to other ancient sayings (e.g., Philo, *Spec.*, 1.29, 148; *Agr.*, 32, 144; Heraclitus, *All.* 53; *Ahikar* 8:15-18) reads, "and 'A sow, having washed,³⁷⁸ returns to wallowing in the mud'" (καί Ὗς λουσαμένη εἰς κυλισμὸν βορβόρου). Neyrey's comment here is instructive:

> According to Jewish classification, pigs are inherently "unclean," that is, unfit as sacrifice to God or as food for humans (Lev 11:7; Deut 14:8); they are "unclean" not for biological reasons but because they violate the definition of a "clean" animal according to Jewish notions (Mary Douglas, *Purity and Danger* [London: Routledge and Kegan Paul, 1966], 41-57). Dogs, too, were unclean: they were scavengers, haunting streets and refuse dumps and eating unclean things (Exod 22:31; *m. Bek* 5.6), even human flesh (1 Kgs 14:11; 16:4; 2 Kgs 9:10).³⁷⁹

The action described of both animals is returning to a state of filth (vomit and mud), which no doubt represents the return of the false teachers to the "moral filth" of their past pagan life. Vomit and mud thus serve as metaphorical descriptions of the corruptions and impurities of the world. Such language also evokes Peter's past descriptions of the false teachers as

---

³⁷⁵ As Green helpfully reminds, "Healthy Christian living comes when God's commands are seen as the kerbstones on His highway of love, the hedge encompassing His garden of grace" (Green, *2 Peter*, 117-18).
³⁷⁶ Cf. Green, *Jude and 2 Peter*, 306.
³⁷⁷ Prov. 26:11 reads: "Like a dog returning to his vomit *is* a fool reverting to his folly."
³⁷⁸ Kelly suggests this may be a covert reference to baptism, though this is not brought out in the text (Kelly, *The Epistles of Peter and Jude*, 350-51).
³⁷⁹ Neyrey, *2 Peter, Jude*, 221-22.

"irrational animals" (cf. 2:11) as well as Balaam's rebuke by a "speechless donkey" (cf. 2:16).[380] With his *vituperatio* complete, Peter has demonstrated a clear contrast between the excesses of pagan life, embodied by the false teachers, and the "way of righteousness," embodied by Christ as Lord. With this criticism concluded, he now returns his attention directly to his audience, and the implications that this conflict carries for them.

2 PETER 3:1–13: THE DAY OF THE LORD

3 ¹ Loved ones, this is already the second letter I am writing to you, through which I am stirring up your sincere thinking through remembrance.

² to remember the words spoken beforehand by the holy prophets and the commandment of the Lord and Savior through your apostles,

³ knowing this especially, that in the last days mockers will come with ridicule, following according to their own desires

⁴ and saying, "Where is the promise of his coming? For from the time since our fathers died, all things are continuing on as they have since the beginning of creation."

⁵ For it is deliberately suppressed by those who maintain this, that the heavens existed a long time ago and the earth has been established from water and through water by the word of God.

⁶ through which the world at that time, being flooded by water, was itself then destroyed.

⁷ Now by the same word now the heavens and the earth are being reserved for fire, being kept for the day of the judgment and destruction of ungodly people.

⁸ Now do not let this one thing escape you, loved ones, that one day with the Lord is like one thousand years, and one thousand years like one day.

⁹ The Lord of the promise is not slow as some regard slowness, but is being patient for you, not wanting any to lose out, but all to come to repentance.

---

[380] On implications of the comparison, Callahan writes, "Such negative comparison of humans to animals can be rather dangerous. Richard Sorabji has shown in detail how the idea that animals are irrational supported the conclusion that humans could make any use of animals they chose. Comparing humans to animals might support a similar conclusion about those humans. The author of 2 Peter is certainly not drawing such conclusions himself, and his comparison of humans to animals is nuanced and complex. However, his comparison of his opponents to animals could provide the foundation for such a conclusion by others" (Callahan, "Comparison of Humans to Animals," 113).

¹⁰ Now the day of the Lord will come as a thief, in which the heavens will pass away with a rushing noise, and the celestial bodies will be destroyed by burning away, and the earth and the deeds done upon it will be disclosed.

¹¹ Since all these things are going to be destroyed in this way, what kind of people should you be in holy behaviors and godly actions,

¹² while looking for and hastening the coming day of God because of which the heavens will be destroyed by being burned up and the celestial bodies are being dissolved by burning,

¹³ Now according to His promise, we are waiting for new heavens and a new earth, in which righteousness resides.

3:1 – Peter returns to direct address of his recipients here with the vocative "Loved ones" (ἀγαπητοί). Cognates of the term have already been used in 1:7 (ἀγάπην) in the virtue list and in 1:17 (ἀγαπητός) of Christ. This word of address will be used four times in the final chapter of the letter, as well as once in reference to "our brother Paul" (3:14). Similar to the language of "sibling affection" (φιλαδελφία) in 1:17, addressing his audience here as "loved ones" indicates a significant bond of affection that became notorious among early Christians. As Tertullian famously wrote in later centuries, "But it is mainly the deeds of a love so noble that lead many to put a brand upon us. 'See,' they say, 'how they love one another,' for they themselves are animated by mutual hatred; 'see how they are ready even to die for one another,' for they themselves will sooner put to death."³⁸¹ Likewise, Green comments, "The use of 'loved ones' within the early church was a marker of the familial relationship between the disciples of Christ, who call on one Father (Acts 15:25; Rom. 1:7; 1 Cor. 4:17; Eph. 5:1)."³⁸² Such an arrangement was seen as a "fictive kinship," which drew believers into familial relations despite not sharing a biological patriline.³⁸³

Following this introductory appellation, our author comments that "this is already the second letter I am writing to you" (Ταύτην ἤδη . . . δευτέραν ὑμῖν γράφω ἐπιστολήν). Much discussion has occurred over this note, with three major proposals being offered among scholars. As Bauckham summarizes, the three major suggestions are (1) an unknown letter, (2) the

---

³⁸¹ Tertullian, *Apology*, 39.7.
³⁸² Green, *Jude and 2 Peter*, 309.
³⁸³ See note on 1:7 for further discussion.

letter of Jude (cf. Robinson),[384] or (3) 1 Peter, with a majority of scholars favoring this third option.[385] In spite of the author's apparent attempt to connect this letter to 1 Peter, most scholars, however, are not convinced that the author made any use of the original letter. Bauckham is representative, stating, "Second Peter in fact provides no evidence that its author was influenced by or made any use of 1 Peter when writing 2 Peter."[386] While this opinion is widespread, and for some compelling reasons, particularly given the stylistic and hermeneutical differences between the two documents, it is an overstatement to state that there are no connections that can be established.[387] Boobyer, summarizing Mayor's work, notes the following parallels:

coincidences in language in spite of prevailing differences (2 Pet. 1:2 and 1 Pet 1:2; 2 Pet. 3:14 and 1 Pet. 1:19 are examples from a longer list); the prominence of the second-advent theme in both; the mention of Noah and seven others saved from the flood (2 Pet. 2:5, cf. 3:5 ff. and 1 Pet. 3:19 ff.); the μακροθυμία of God related in 2 Pet. 3:15 to the coming conflagration and in 1 Pet. 3:20 to the flood; and the accounts in 2 Pet. 1:16-21 and 1 Pet. 1:10-12 (cf. 2 Pet. 3:1f.) of prophecy as a divinely inspired foretelling of Gospel events now announced by apostles.[388]

As Boobyer notes further:

In 1 Peter, exhortation to turn from evil and live holy lives occupies most of the epistle; and in 1 Peter, as in 2 Peter, the second advent, the incorruptible inheritance in heaven thereafter, and God's coming judgment, unsparing of sinners, are all prominent subjects, not to mention lesser parallels.[389]

---

[384] J. A. T. Robinson, *Redating the New Testament* (London: SCM Press, 1976), 195.

[385] Bauckham, *Jude–2 Peter*, 285-86. Bauckham also mentions a fourth approach, that it treats the "first letter" as the first two chapters of 2 Peter, but this has not gained much scholarly support.

[386] Bauckham, *Jude–2 Peter*, 286. See also Rudolf Knopf, *Die Briefe Petri und Juda*, Kritisch-exegetischer Kommentar über das Neue Testament 12 (Göttingen: Vandenhoeck & Ruprecht, 1912), 254; Hans Windisch, *Die Katholischen Briefe*, 3rd ed., Handbuch zum Neuen Testament 15 (Tübingen: J. C. B. Mohr [Paul Siebeck], 1951), 99.

[387] For a comparison of 2 Pet. 3 to Matt. 24:33-51, see Evald Lövestam, "Eschatologie und Tradition im 2 Petrusbrief," in *The New Testament Age: Essays in Honor of Bo Reicke*, vol. 2, ed. William C. Weinrich (Macon: Mercer University Press, 1984), 287-300. Witherington also notes the stylistic similarities between this section and 1:12-15 (Witherington, *Letters and Homilies*, 364).

[388] Boobyer, "The Indebtedness of 2 Peter to 1 Peter," 35

[389] Boobyer, "The Indebtedness of 2 Peter to 1 Peter," 38. Boobyer further points to parallels specifically in 1 Pet. 1:10-12.

Of the 788 unique words found in both 1 and 2 Peter, 155 are shared in common between the two documents (nearly 20 percent of all terms, and 39 percent of those in 2 Peter). While this includes common terms shared in most NT writings (ἀγάπη, εἰρήνη, etc.), it also includes less common terms, such as ἀεί, ἀναστρέφω/ἀναστροφή, etc. A few terms are also found only in 1 and 2 Peter in comparison to the whole NT (ἀπόθεσις), as well as some that occur rarely in the NT but are found in both (e.g., ἀρετή, προγινώσκω, συμβαίνω, φιλαδελφία, etc.). When the area of lexical overlap is expanded to include cognate terms, roughly 70 percent of the unique words found in 2 Peter are found in 1 Peter through either the same lemma or a cognate term of that lemma.[390] This includes a few uncommon terms as well, such as:

ἄγνοια (noun; 1 Pet.) and ἀγνοέω (verb; 2 Pet.)
ἀθέμιτος (1 Pet.) and ἄθεσμος (2 Pet.)
ἄμωμος (1 Pet.) and ἀμώμητος (2 Pet.)
ἕκαστος (1 Pet.) and ἑκάστοτε (2 Pet.)
ἐκλεκτός (1 Pet) and ἐκλογή 2 Pet.)
ἐμπλοκή (1 Pet.) and ἐμπλέκω (2 Pet.)
ἐπίλοιπος (1 Pet.) and λοιπός (2 Pet.)
ἐποπτεύω (1 Pet.) and ἐπόπτης (2 Pet.) (both NT *hapaxes*)
καθαρός (1 Pet.) and καθαρισμός (2 Pet.)
κηρύσσω (1 Pet.) and κῆρυξ (2 Pet.)
μάταιος (1 Pet.) and ματαιότης (2 Pet.)
ὀλίγος (1 Pet.) and ὀλίγως (2 Pet.)
φυλακή (noun; 1 Pet.) and φυλάσσω (verb; 2 Peter)[391]

While other possible explanations can be offered, an examination of these layers of connections creates more plausibility that the author of 2 Peter was familiar with 1 Peter than is often accepted. Indeed, with our author's penchant for taking Jude's material and making it his own, it shouldn't surprise us that he might do the same with 1 Peter, so that the absence of precise verbal parallels need not indicate no knowledge of the document. There is clearly a common shared base of vocabulary, with some instances of words unique to the Petrine corpus. First Peter also

---

[390] See Introduction: Dissimilarity to 1 Peter for further discussion.
[391] See Appendix for list of all overlapping vocabulary.

contains elements of Asiatic style as well, pulling the two documents closer together stylistically.[392] So, while the two letters contain obvious variations, it seems an overdetermination of the data to declare there are no commonalities between these two texts.

If our author indicates overlap between these audiences, we may further postulate an overlap of the location of the audience of 2 Peter. Indeed, it would be strange for its original recipients to be outside of the range of reception indicated in 1 Peter 1:1 (the provinces of Pontus, Galatia, Cappadocia, Asia, and Bithynia – roughly equivalent to modern day Turkey) given that the author calls attention to their receipt of (most likely) 1 Peter. Given the obvious adoption of Asiatic style, which was most prominent in the province of Asia Minor, it would seem that Asia Minor would be an obvious candidate for its location of receipt.[393]

The author continues, commenting on this "second letter," "through which I am stirring up your sincere thinking" (ἐν αἷς διεγείρω ὑμῶν ... τὴν εἰλικρινῆ διάνοιαν). The "stirring up" (διεγείρω) here (occurring also in 2 Pet. 1:13) is often used of attempting to wake someone who is asleep (e.g., Mark 4:38–39; Luke 8:24), though it can be used also in the case of the waters of the sea being made rough ("stirred up"; cf. John 6:18). To have "sincere thinking" (τὴν εἰλικρινῆ διάνοιαν) is to possess honest, genuine, and earnest understanding of the main issues at hand. Green suggests, "Peter seeks to preserve the singularity and simplicity of their understanding and does not want to see it sullied in any way by the persuasion of the heretics and their error."[394] The means by which he seeks to generate this sincere thinking is "through remembrance" (ἐν ὑπομνήσει), a notion that has occurred already in the letter (cf. 2 Pet. 1:12–13, 15) and will be reinforced again in 3:2 and in 3:17. This reminder was signaled previously in 1:12–15, though our author was sidetracked with his *vituperatio* against the false teachers. The reminder has reached its substance here, which, as in 1:16–21, contains as its focus the prophetic utterances of the Scriptures

---

[392] See Craig S. Keener, *1 Peter: A Commentary* (Grand Rapids: Baker Academic, 2021), 34.

[393] Kelly suggests the possibility, though not firmly (Kelly, *The Epistles of Peter and of Jude*, 353). Contra Davids, who surmises, "We would never have imagined that 2 Peter was written to the northwest quadrant of Asia Minor unless we had 1 Peter" (Davids, *The Letters of 2 Peter and Jude*, 259). Given the author's adoption of Asiatic style, the style alone could lead one in this direction.

[394] Green, *Jude and 2 Peter*, 311.

(i.e., Old Testament) and the teachings of Jesus as delivered through the apostles. Such reminders, as Green notes, are an important part of ethical instruction, building upon the knowledge already held by the audience, affirming it, and calling them to recommit themselves to living by those ideals.[395]

3:2 – Our author now makes clear the substance of this reminder: "to remember the words spoken beforehand by the holy prophets" (μνησθῆναι τῶν προειρημένων ῥημάτων ὑπὸ τῶν ἁγίων προφητῶν). The phrase "holy prophets" is uncommon in biblical literature, occurring only here and in Luke 1:70 and Acts 3:21 (in a speech by Peter).[396] This section again echoes the words of 1:19–21, where the "prophetic word" and "prophecy of scripture" held some focus and referenced the Old Testament prophets and writings and their divine inspiration alongside the eyewitness testimony of the apostles of the Lord (see also 1 Pet. 1:10–12).[397] What words of the "holy prophets" was the audience expected to remember? As in chapter 1, most likely our author has in mind the major ethical teachings of the Old Testament, which held importance for both Jewish and Gentile Christians in the early church, and the texts that were seen as prophetic foresight into the coming of the Messiah.

Our author continues with also commending the remembrance of "the commandment of the Lord and Savior" (καὶ τῆς . . . ἐντολῆς τοῦ κυρίου καὶ σωτῆρος). The content of the commandment here is not specified, but as in 2:21, it likely refers to the ethical content of Christian teaching from which the false teachers had departed.[398] This commandment is further described as coming "through your apostles" (τῶν ἀποστόλων ὑμῶν),[399] a phrase occurring only here in the New Testament.[400] A number of commentators

---

[395] Green, *Jude and 2 Peter*, 211.
[396] See also Wis. 11:1; 2 Bar. 85:1, and possibly Eph. 3:5.
[397] That some commentators take this to refer to Christian prophets, the content of chapter 3 and the previous references in 1:16–21 make that unlikely (cf. E. M. Sidebottom, *James, Jude, 2 Peter* [Grand Rapids: Eerdmans, 1982], 118). See Davids, *The Letters of 2 Peter and Jude*, 260.
[398] Bauckham, *Jude–2 Peter*, 288.
[399] Some manuscripts (Ψ 5. 1448. 1611. 1735^c. 1852 sy, cf. NA28) read "ἡμῶν" here instead, possibly indicating some scribes saw the phrase as problematic.
[400] On an argument for reading the reference as the written works of the apostles, see Margaryta Teslina, "'Apostles' in 2 Peter 3.2: Literal Predecessors in Faith or Literary Records of their Witness?," *JSNT* 44.1 (2021): 170–93.

see this as an obvious indication that we are dealing with a post-apostolic writing, since it recognizes the apostles as a "distinct group" as occurs in post-apostolic writings, and so our pseudepigrapher has "slipped up" in his work of imitation.[401] It seems, however, another legitimate reading can be suggested here in taking the phrase as simply referring to those apostles who brought the message of Christ to this community, which Peter was, perhaps, not among. So, Witherington suggests, "'Your apostles' simply means the ones who founded your church, and Peter is looking back on the recent past when the churches were formed, not the distant past, as if all the apostles were now deceased."[402] The mention of a collective of apostles need not indicate a fully developed and ensconced view of apostolic authority associated with later second-century Christianity. Furthermore, the recognition of the apostles as a distinct, authoritative group within the early Christian movement can be found as early as the writings of Paul.[403]

There is a parallelism of sorts then of two streams of tradition here noted by the author: the words of the OT prophets and the commandment of Jesus Christ that came to the audience through the apostolic missionaries who carried it to them.[404] This "duality" of streams of teaching is evidenced in other places in the New Testament, such as Eph. 2:20 ("having been built upon the foundation of the apostles and prophets, Christ Jesus himself being the cornerstone"). That the early church understood there to be a kind of continuity between the writings of the Old Testament and the teachings of Jesus and the apostles is evidenced by such explanations and should caution those who would drive to hard a wedge between Judaism and the early Christian

---

[401] E.g., Frey, *The Letter of Jude and the Second Letter of Peter*, 373. As Green notes, the group of "apostles" in the New Testament is wider than the Twelve, Peter, and Paul (cf. Acts 14:14; Rom. 16:7; 1 Cor. 15:5, 7; 2 Cor. 8:23; Gal. 1:19; Eph. 4:11; Phil. 2:25; 1 Thess. 1:1; 2:7) (Green, *Jude and 2 Peter*, 313).

[402] Witherington, *Letters for Hellenized Christians*, 366–67. See also Davids, *The Letters of 2 Peter and Jude*, 262.

[403] One might compare with the varied use of the term in the book of Acts, or Paul's comments in Rom. 16:7; 1 Cor. 4:9; 9:5; 12:28–29; 15:7, 9; Gal. 1:17, 19; Eph. 2:20; 3:5; 4:11; 1 Thess. 2:6. Compare also with Jude 17.

[404] So Zerwick and Grosvenor suggest the translation "the commandment of the Lord and Savior transmitted by the apostles to you" (Max Zerwick and Mary Grosvenor, *Grammatical Analysis of the Greek New Testament*, vol. 2, *Epistles-Apocalypse* [Rome: Biblical Institute Press, 1979], 723).

movement or Christian interpreters today who might seek to disconnect the teachings of Jesus from the Old Testament.[405]

Peter here heralds Jesus as "Lord" and "Savior," a combination used a number of times throughout the letter (see 2 Pet. 1:1–2, 11; 2:20; 3:18). To recognize Jesus as Lord is to understand him to possess unique authority and to bear the "name" attributed to Israel's God himself.[406] To hail him as "Savior" is to recognize not only the soteriological significance of his death and resurrection but also to see him as the deliverer of Israel and humanity. Both titles were attributed at various times to Caesar and so the sociopolitical implications of these designations go beyond mere religious symbolism.[407] Davids' reminder here is helpful:

> In Jesus, the rule of God became manifest in this world, and this manifestation of the rule of God brings with it a demand that people turn from their way and submit to God's way, that is, obey the good news and submit to the way of life that it proclaims. While often missing from contemporary preaching, this is the message of the New Testament.[408]

Such a recognition of the sovereign authority of Jesus Christ, and of submission of the entirety of one's being to his "way," is clearly on the mind of 2 Peter, particularly as our text moves toward discussion of the return of Christ and the coming judgment that he will bring.

3:3 – The importance of the reminder receives attention first, as our author states "knowing this especially" (τοῦτο πρῶτον γινώσκοντες). The author's words here do not necessarily indicate that this is the most important thing to know from all possible knowledge but rather that this is what is most important as it relates to this situation and discourse. As Witherington notes, rhetorically it was common to save one's most

---

[405] On the significance of Peter's distinction between prophets and apostles as a consideration for a "bi-covenantal" canon, see Michael J. Kruger, "2 Peter 3:2, the Apostolate, and a Bi-Covenantal Canon," *JETS* 63.1 (2020): 5–24.

[406] See, perhaps most dramatically, Phil. 2:6–11. The Greek title κύριος was frequently used to translate the divine name in the Septuagint. On variations, see Martin Rösel, "The Reading and Translation of the Divine Name in the Masoretic Tradition and the Greek Pentateuch," *Journal for the Study of the Old Testament* 31 (2007): 411–28.

[407] See, for example, Scot McKnight and Joseph B. Modica, *Jesus Is Lord, Caesar Is Not: Evaluation Empire in New Testament Studies* (Downers Grove: InterVarsity Press, 2013).

[408] Davids, *The Letters of 2 Peter and Jude*, 261. For an unpacking of this notion, see also Bates, *Salvation by Allegiance Alone*.

pressing point for last in the discourse,[409] and so the central issue facing Peter's audience is a denial, on the part of the false teachers, of the *parousia*. Such a denial is, therefore, the focus and climax of 2 Peter's discourse.

This recognition of importance is followed by the content (ὅτι) of the reminder, "that in the last days mockers will come with ridicule" (ὅτι ἐλεύσονται ἐπ' ἐσχάτων τῶν ἡμερῶν [ἐν] ἐμπαιγμονῇ ἐμπαῖκται).[410] The "last days" here refers to the period of time on the cusp of the *eschaton* but ought to be placed in the larger framework evidenced in the New Testament, and in 2 Peter,[411] of inaugurated eschatology.[412] Since the resurrection of the dead was anticipated as an eschatological event in the framework of Second Temple Judaism, the resurrection of Jesus and inauguration of his Messianic reign was understood by the New Testament authors as already bringing about the "end times" in some sense, while also awaiting a fuller consummation that would begin with the return of Jesus (Matt. 4:17; 22:44; Mark 1:15; Luke 10:11; Luke 17:20-21; Acts 2:33; Rev. 3:21). Such language can be found in the Old Testament prophets as well, often connected to the day of the Lord or similar eschatological events (Isa. 2:2; Hos. 3:5; Mic. 4:1; see also Acts 2:17; 2 Tim. 3:1; Heb. 1:2; Jas. 5:3), and these ideas are at the forefront of the mind of our author in this section and connected to the return of Christ.[413]

That "mockers will come with ridicule" (ἐμπαιγμονῇ ἐμπαῖκται; "mockers will come with mocking") is constructed as a play on words, giving emphasis to the phrase. The proclamation of the Old Testament prophets was also at times met with mocking (Isa. 5:18-20; Jer. 5:12-24; Ezek. 12:22; Amos 9:10; Zeph. 1:12; Mal. 2:17), and, similar to Jude, Peter sees the mocking of the false teachers as a sign that the last days have arrived.[414]

---

[409] Witherington, *Letters and Homilies*, 367.
[410] Bauckham suggests Peter follows an unknown Jewish apocalypse as his source here, which is also picked up in 1 and 2 Clement (Bauckham, *Jude-2 Peter*, 283-85). For a critique, see Davids, *The Letters of 2 Peter and Jude*, 264-65; and Frey, *The Letter of Jude and the Second Letter of Peter*, 365-86.
[411] See previous comments on 2 Pet. 1:4.
[412] See, again, Gladd and Harmon, *Making All Things New*; Ladd, *The Presence of the Future*. See also N. T. Wright, *Surprised by Hope: Rethinking Heaven, the Resurrection, and the Mission of the Church* (New York: HarperOne, 2008).
[413] See also Isa. 27:6; 30:8; Jer. 23:20; 30:24; 48:47; 49:39; Ezek. 38:16; Dan. 2:28 where "days to come" contains a future prophetic force.
[414] See Acts 2:17; 2 Tim. 3:1; Heb. 1:2; James 5:3; Jude 18; cf. Green, *Jude and 2 Peter*, 315.

Mocking is an act of ridicule, attempting to demean and mischaracterize its targets. As Green notes, "Mocking is a supreme act of dishonor in an attempt to bring shame upon a person (see Herodotus 4.134; Epictetus, *Diss.*, 1.4.10)."[415] The mocking of the false teachers brings dishonor not only upon the community and its leaders but also upon the Lord Jesus whom they have come to despise (cf. 2 Pet. 2:1, 10).

In addition to their scoffing, our antagonists are described as "following according to their own desires" (κατὰ τὰς ἰδίας ἐπιθυμίας αὐτῶν πορευόμενοι). This depiction fits the characterization offered in the *vituperatio* of chapter 2, where chief among the charges levied against the false teachers were their lack of self-control, particularly in matters of sexual desires. The prediction language here may derive from Jesus' words about false teachers coming in the last days (e.g., Mark 13:22-23), though the specific language of mocking or scoffing does not occur there and is likely derived from Jude 18.

3:4 – The primary content of the mockers of concern to our author is now set forth: saying, "Where is the promise of his coming?" (καὶ λέγοντες· ποῦ ἐστιν ἡ ἐπαγγελία τῆς παρουσίας αὐτοῦ;). We have here an example of the rhetorical device of diatribe or "speech in character," where the position of the mocking false teachers is laid out in their own words.[416] What is being mocked here is the very idea of the return of Christ, particularly related to the coming judgment that he will bring. The return of Christ is described here as "the promise of his coming" (ἡ ἐπαγγελία τῆς παρουσίας αὐτοῦ), reminiscent of language used both in 1:4 ("which he has presented to us precious and great promises" [ἐπαγγέλματα]) and in 2:19 ("promising [ἐπαγγελλόμενοι] them freedom though themselves being slaves of depravity"). Such mocking questions can be observed in the Old Testament prophets, such as Jeremiah recounting, "They keep saying to me, 'Where is the word of the Lord? Let it now be fulfilled!'" (Jer. 17:15). As Donelson notes, "The form and content of the question are reminiscent of the frequent questions about God's absence in the OT . . . . 'Where is your God?' ([Ps] 42:10; cf. 79:10; Joel 2:17; Mal 2:17)."[417]

---

[415] Green, *Jude and 2 Peter*, 315.
[416] Watson, *Invention, Arrangement, and Style*, 128-29.
[417] Donelson, *I & II Peter and Jude*, 267.

Naturally this mocking retort raises the question of the "delay of the *parousia*," something often discussed in scholarly literature.[418] The New Testament authors at times speak of the wait for the return of Jesus as requiring an exercise in patience (e.g., Luke 12:45; Heb. 10:36–37; Jas. 5:7–8), while at other times express the immediacy of the event in a way that envisions very near fulfillment (compare Matt. 10:23; 16:28; 24:29–34; 25:1–46; Mark 9:1; 13:30; John 21:22–23). The tension created by those two affirmations will surface through this section of 2 Peter as well. Furthermore, as Bauckham notes, "The problem of delay is the apocalyptic version of the problem of evil."[419] Rather than eschatology being an unimportant or abstract matter, Peter pursues response to this mocking with a sense of urgency toward his audience.[420]

We next find a phrase of explanation (γὰρ) from the false teachers concerning their derision of the notion of Christ's return: "For from the time since our fathers died" (ἀφ' ἧς γὰρ οἱ πατέρες ἐκοιμήθησαν), "all things are continuing on as they have since the beginning of creation" (πάντα οὕτως διαμένει ἀπ' ἀρχῆς κτίσεως). The first part of this statement gives a temporal direction to their explanation and has been much discussed by scholars, with two major opinions emerging: (1) the "fathers" referenced here are the first generation of Christian followers, which would include the apostles, and (2) the "fathers" referenced here are the ancestors of those speaking. Frey suggests it must refer to the first Christian generation since the fathers of Israel would have little to do with the promise of the second coming of Christ.[421] This argument, however, can be inverted, since one could likewise ask what significance the passing of a few decades might be in the grand scheme of the timetable of the universe and the *eschaton* in particular. As noted above, a tension can be observed, even in the earliest texts of the New Testament (i.e., Hebrews and James, which are at times dated as early as the 60s) concerning the timing of the return of

---

[418] For a recent treatment that covers the history of the question, see Christopher M. Hays, ed., *When the Son of Man Didn't Come: A Constructive Proposal on the Delay of the Parousia* (Minneapolis: Fortress Press, 2016).

[419] Richard J. Bauckham, "The Delay of the *Parousia*," TB 31.1 (1980): 7.

[420] On reading apocalyptic expectations related to Jesus in early Christianity, see Tucker S. Ferda, *Jesus and His Promised Second Coming: Jewish Eschatology and Christian Origins* (Grand Rapids: Eerdmans, 2024).

[421] Frey, *The Letter of Jude and the Second Letter of Peter*, 382.

Christ and the need for patience concerning his arrival.⁴²² Bauckham also notes that this usage of "fathers" for the first Christian generation is unattested elsewhere.⁴²³ As he states,

> Those who wish to maintain that "the fathers" are the OT patriarchs or prophets (Bigg, Lumby, Green) have the weight of usage on their side. In early Christian literature, continuing Jewish usage ... οἱ πατέρες ("the fathers") means the OT "fathers," i.e. the patriarchs or, more generally, the righteous men of OT times (John 7:22; Acts 13:32; Rom 9:5; Heb 1:1; *Barn.* 5:7; 14:1; *Apoc. Pet.* E 16; *Ep. Apost.* [Coptic] 28).⁴²⁴

The larger context of our author's response to the words of the false teachers, which begins in 3:5, also includes reference to the events of creation and the flood, which likewise seems out of place if the false teachers are concerned with the first Christian generation.

The second part of the explanation ("all things are continuing on as they have since the beginning of creation" [πάντα οὕτως διαμένει ἀπ' ἀρχῆς κτίσεως]) denies a place for divine involvement in the state of worldly affairs. Here, a number of scholars, following Neyrey,⁴²⁵ see the likely influence of Epicureanism in the opinions of the false teachers.⁴²⁶ As Reese summarizes, the Epicurean denial of providence was based upon the beliefs that there was not an involved creator in creation, providence destroys freedom, the world exists by chance, and the gods are not engaged in punishment or reward.⁴²⁷ As Lucretius writes, "Nature is seen to be free at once and rid of proud masters, herself doing all by herself of her own accord, without the help of the gods."⁴²⁸ Similarly, Diogenes Laertius quotes Epicurus as saying, "Death, therefore, the most awful of evils, is nothing to us, seeing that, when we are, death is not come, and, when death is come, we are not. It is nothing, then, either to the living or to the dead, for with the living it is not and the dead exist no longer."⁴²⁹ The argument

---

[422] In his recent work, Bernier dates James to AD 62 and Hebrews to between 50 and 70 (Bernier, *Rethinking the Dates of the New Testament*, 185–212).
[423] Bauckham, *Jude–2 Peter*, 291.
[424] Bauckham, *Jude–2 Peter*, 290.
[425] Neyrey, *2 Peter, Jude*, 231.
[426] See Introduction: Audience and Setting for further discussion.
[427] Reese, *2 Peter & Jude*, 164.
[428] Lucretius, *De Rerum Natura*, 2.1090–92.
[429] Diog. Laert., 10.125.

of the mockers, then, is that the universe lacks evidence that any sort of divine intervention has occurred in human history, and so the expectation of the God-man's return can be dismissed simply as a "cleverly created myth" (cf. 2 Pet. 1:16).

Excursus: Divine Hiddenness
The question of "where is your God?" asked here by the false teachers, and echoing similar questions throughout the Old Testament, strikes at one of the core difficulties of navigating faith in a world full of death, suffering, loss, and loneliness. Like the psalmists who beg God to come to their aid (e.g., Ps. 35:23; 44:23–24), our late modern world is full of such pleas. The question of divine hiddenness is intimately connected to the problem of evil, both of which attempt to make sense of belief in a good God in the midst of the horrors and traumas of human life.[430] When our faith questions hit us on an emotional and personal level, theoretical ideas and abstractions can become insurmountable walls of fear, sadness, or depression. Since we are persons existing as integrated composites of social, moral, emotional, physical, psychological, and spiritual dimensions of personhood, our experiences, relationships, stressors, and traumas affect how we understand, view, and relate to God.[431]

In such circumstances, a person may tell themselves that God is distant or doesn't care, and this struggle often creates "feelings of aloneness or separateness … [growing] to feel very separate and cut off from other people, life, and God."[432] Such an experience can spiral where one's lack of experience of God can lead to denial of any presence of God in their life, even when such evidence may exist. Guiness observes, "The pressure is painful because of the feeling that God is not guiding us at the very moment when so much is at stake."[433]

One may not even question God's existence in such moments but instead question God's sincerity or love. Crump confirms this, stating, "Our natural

---

[430] For an existential reflection, see my "Emotional Doubt and Divine Hiddenness," *Eleutheria* 1.2 (2014): 1–18, which has informed this section.

[431] See, for example, Bruce Hunsberger, Susan Alisat, S. Mark Pancer, and Michael W. Pratt, "Religious Fundamentalism and Religious Doubts: Content, Connections and Complexity of Thinking," *International Journal for the Psychology of Religion* 6.3 (July 1996): 201–20; Neal Krause, Berit Ingersoll-Dayton, Christopher G. Ellison, and Keith M. Wulff, "Aging, Religious Doubt, and Psychological Well-Being," *Gerontologist* 39.5 (1999): 525–33; Kathleen Galek et al., "Religious Doubt and Mental Health Across the Lifespan," *Journal of Adult Development* 14.1-2 (June 2007): 16–25. For a more recent look at how emotional trauma and psychological and physical well-being interrelate, see Bessel van der Kold, *The Body Keeps the Score: Brain, Mind, and Body in the Healing of Trauma* (London: Penguin Books, 2015).

[432] David J. H. Hart, *Christianity: A New Look at Ancient Wisdom* (Kelowna, BC: Wood Lake, 2005), 90.

[433] Os Guinness, *God in the Dark: The Assurance of Faith Beyond a Shadow of Doubt* (Wheaton: Crossway Books, 1996), 175.

assumption ... [is] that our life situation is somehow the result of God's disposition towards us .... If I feel unloved by God, it must be because God does not love me."[434] Our experiences may even lead to a mistrust of God's promises or self-revelation. In his *Disappointment with God*, Philip Yancey recalls an encounter with a young man who abandoned his faith when his prayers were unanswered. He had even prayed for a sign from God that he was real, and when this was not received, he determined to "forget God and get on with life."[435]

Such an experience was known by the author of Psalm 88.[436] The psalmist recounts his persistent seeking of God, pleading for God to intervene in his troubles. He sees his circumstances as the result of the divine hand: "*You* have put me in the lowest pit, in the darkest depths. *Your* wrath lies heavily on me; *you* have overwhelmed me with all your waves. *You* have taken from me my closest friends and have made me repulsive to them. I am confined and cannot escape; my eyes are dim with grief" (Ps. 88:6-9). As the psalm ends, the psalmist's cry remains unanswered, and he complains that the Lord's terrors have caused him to be "numb with pain" (Ps. 88:15, NET).

A startling lesson emerges from the psalmist's agony that, in spite of his feelings of abandonment and despair, he does not abandon his pursuit of God. As Brueggemann has noted, "The speaker never entertains the possibility of withdrawing from conversation with God, never considers the prospect that such talk is futile or that help must be sought elsewhere."[437] This psalm demonstrates that feelings of divine abandonment are not beyond the Christian Scriptures, nor beyond the concerns of God. Such laments of suffering contain great pastoral and personal significance when dealing with the darkness that can enter into our lives. Psalm 88 is a reminder that unresolved suffering may be a part of the life of the righteous on this side of the eschaton. Such suffering need not be assumed to be the result of divine judgment or abandonment. Indeed, the sufferings of Christ demonstrate the willingness of God to enter into the sufferings of his creatures.[438]

---

[434] David Crump, *Feeling Like God: A Spiritual Journey to Emotional Wholeness* (Toronto: Clements, 2005), 142.
[435] Philip Yancey, *Disappointment with God* (Grand Rapids: Zondervan, 1988), 35.
[436] For an analysis, see my "A Theology of Psalm 88," *EQ* 87.1 (2015): 45-57. Some of my thoughts here are drawn from this essay.
[437] Walter Brueggemann, *The Psalms and the Life of Faith* (Minneapolis: Fortress Press, 1995), 51.
[438] For further reading, see James Keating and Thomas Joseph White, *Divine Impassibility and the Mystery of Human Suffering* (Grand Rapids: Eerdmans, 2009); Robert J. Matz and A. Chadwick Thornhill, *Divine Impassibility: Four Views of God's Emotions and Suffering* (Downers Grove: IVP Academic, 2019); Jürgen Moltmann, *The Crucified God: The Cross of Christ as the Foundation and Criticism of Christian Theology* (Minneapolis, MN: 1993); Joshua D. Chatraw and Jack Carson, *Surprised by Doubt: How Disillusionment Can Invite Us into Deeper Faith* (Grand Rapids: Brazos Press, 2023).

3:5 – Our author now picks up his own explanation (γάρ; "for") of the situation with his assessment of the critiques of the false teachers (αὐτοὺς; "they"), beginning a *refutatio* against the claims of the false teachers summarized in 3:4.[439] He states, "For it is[440] deliberately suppressed by those who maintain this" (λανθάνει γὰρ αὐτοὺς τοῦτο θέλοντας).[441] Translations differ on how to treat the verb here (LEB, NASB: "escapes notices"; compare NIV: "deliberately forget"; NET: "deliberately suppress"; RSV: "deliberately ignore"). While it is clear the false teachers have intentionally rejected apostolic teaching, it is less clear whether they are unaware of the biblical traditions concerning the creation and sustaining of the world by God or whether they are deliberately ignoring them, though the larger context of the letter may lean in the direction of intentional avoidance.[442]

Our author embarks on a series of assertions to develop his explanation, beginning "that the heavens existed a long time ago" (ὅτι οὐρανοὶ ἦσαν ἔκπαλαι), which he seems to take as self-evident, though no doubt grounded in the narratives of the biblical text, particularly from places like Genesis 1–2, Job 38:4-7, Ps. 148:2-5, and Isa.45:12. The second assertion in the explanation is that "the earth has been established from water and through water" (καὶ γῆ ἐξ ὕδατος καὶ δι' ὕδατος συνεστῶσα). The language of "from water" (ἐξ ὕδατος) and "through water" (δι' ὕδατος) likely harkens to the framing of the creation narrative in Genesis 1, where the primordial waters (Gen. 1:2) are separated into waters above and below the sky (1:6-9; see also Ps. 24:2; 136:6).[443] Such a view is affirmed among Jewish interpreters as well (e.g., 4 Ezra 6:42; 2 En. 47:5; *Jub.* 2:2-7; see also Gen. 7:11).[444]

---

[439] Cf. Frey, *The Letter of Jude and the Second Letter of Peter*, 384.

[440] Bauckham suggests that the "present tense in v 5a shows that the author has again abandoned the 'testament' convention of prophecy, in favor of direct present-tense argument with his contemporaries" (Bauckham, *Jude-2 Peter*, 296). Given the number of such "abandonments" that occur throughout our text, it is better for us to simply not call the text a testament.

[441] The are two ways, grammatically, to take the presence of the demonstrative pronoun τοῦτο in this clause: (1) as the subject of the verb λανθάνει ("this escapes notice") or (2) as the object of the participle θέλοντας ("while maintaining this"). Most translations and commentators opt for the first. See Donelson, *I & II Peter and Jude*, 265.

[442] So Neyrey, comments, "The scoffers ignore or forget (3:5), whereas the author remembers and reminds (1:13-15; 3:1-3)" (Neyrey, *2 Peter, Jude*, 234).

[443] For a discussion of how such language functioned in ancient Israelite understanding, see John H. Walton, *The Lost World of Genesis One: Ancient Cosmology and the Origins Debate* (Downers Grove: InterVarsity Press, 2010).

[444] See also Bauckham, *Jude-2 Peter*, 297.

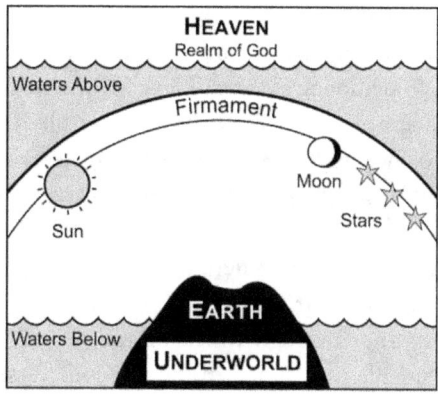

Ancient Near Eastern Cosmology.[445]

Frey notes that the language deployed here also resonates with Hellenistic discourses on cosmogony, particularly with the use of συνίστημι (here συνεστῶσα; "the earth has been established"),[446] which was taken up into Jewish and Christian vocabulary (cf. Plato, *Tim.* 31b, 69c; Philo, *Plant.* 6; *Her.* 281, 311; *Aet.* 4; and elsewhere).[447] The language of the verse is terse, yet the basic idea seems to be that water was the substance that creation was drawn from and upon, though sustained and mediated through the creative and powerful word of God (τῷ τοῦ θεοῦ λόγῳ). The "word of God" (i.e., God's speaking) as the force that organizes and animates creation finds frequent expression in numerous biblical texts (Gen. 1:3–30; Ps. 33:6; 148:5; Wis. 9:1; 4 Ezra 6:38; John 1:1–3; Heb. 11:3).

Our author has likely introduced the waters of Genesis in creation to contrast the kind of destruction to come in the final judgment, which will differ from God's judgment exercised upon humanity in the Genesis flood narrative (cf. 2 Pet. 2:4–5). The emphasis, as Green observes, is to underscore, contrary to the false teachers, that "divine agency ensures the

---

[445] From Denis Lamoureux, "The Ancient Science in the Bible," *BioLogos*, August 21, 2009, https://biologos.org/articles/the-ancient-science-in-the-bible.

[446] Though active, I have translated this verb passively because of the agent ("by the word of God") attached to it. Since "earth" (γῆ) is the subject, rendering it actively ("the earth has established by the word of God") does not make much sense.

[447] Frey, *The Letter of Jude and the Second Letter of Peter*, 389.

continued existence of all things."[448] The primary emphasis is not, then, to create a precise and scientific cosmogony but rather, through incorporating biblical traditions, to demonstrate that the very existence of the universe is dependent upon the power and will of God. As a result, if God was active at the origin of the cosmos and is the agent active in sustaining its existence, even now, it should be no surprise that he will be active at the end of this present age.

3:6 – The explanation continues here with a series of phrases and clauses that connect the author's affirmation of God's activity in creation to the Genesis flood. In stating "through which things" (δι' ὧν),[449] continuity is drawn with the elements mentioned in the previous verse as the principle agents at work in the flood. The vagueness of the phrase "through which things" (δι' ὧν) has generated different suggestions on what the author has in mind, with suggestions including (1) the heavens and the earth (Reicke and Marín), (2) the heavens (James), (3) out of water and through water (two different categories of water) (Plumptre, Spiffa, Moffatt, Chaine, Sidebottom), (4) water and the word of God (by his word and water God created and destroyed (Bauckham). Bauckham's suggestions seems most likely, since the flood did not come simply through the activity of the heavens, earth, or waters alone but rather through the divine word that initiated the movement of the waters (cf. Gen. 7:4, 11). The waters "above and below" (cf. Gen. 7:11) as well as the creative and powerful "word of God" are also the nearest referents to the relative pronoun.

These waters and the divine word were the means by which "the world at that time, being flooded by water, was itself then destroyed" (ὁ τοτέ κόσμος ὕδατι κατακλυσθεὶς ἀπώλετο). The destruction of the world "at that time" refers to the antediluvian world, and the Genesis story indicates several changes in the constitution of that world as a result of the flood, including reduced human lifespan (cf. Gen. 6:1–4; illustrated by 11:10–32) and population dispersion (cf. Gen. 11:1–9). The destruction of the "world" described here, however, would not be an indication that the planet itself was obliterated (or otherwise Noah would need a newly created world to

---

[448] Green, *Jude and 2 Peter*, 319.
[449] This follows the reading of the NA27 and SBLGNT, which follows this reading on the strength of its evidence (ων 𝔓[72] ℵ A B C Ψ 048. 5. 33. 81. 307. 436. 442. 642. 1448. 1611. 1735. 1739. 1852. 2344. 2492 Byz lat sy co) as opposed to δἰ ὅν in the NA28 (P 1175 t vg[mss]).

dwell on) but rather that the "way of life" or "system" of the world was destroyed and started anew. Witherington affirms this in stating, "The notion of a whole new world would hardly comport with the Genesis story. Rather, it is a whole new *human* world, and all its organization and facets begin again after the flood."[450] The purpose of this destruction was to exercise judgment upon the sinful human and angelic agents who had spread corruption across the earth.[451] The use of language here will be important to keep in mind as we encounter 2 Peter 3:10–11.[452]

3:7 – A new development ("So"; δὲ) in the explanation is presented here, which again focuses upon the agency described ("So by the same word now" [... δὲ νῦν ... τῷ αὐτῷ λόγῳ]) and connects the divine word active in creation and the flood to the present day ("now"; νῦν). The continuity here ("the same word"; τῷ αὐτῷ λόγῳ) shows that principally it is the word of God that is the agent in focus, in creation, the flood, and in the coming judgment. The elements of water and fire serve as secondary agents that function at the direction of God's word.

By this "same word,"[453] we are told, "the heavens and the earth are being reserved for fire" (οἱ ... οὐρανοὶ καὶ ἡ γῆ ... τεθησαυρισμένοι εἰσὶν πυρί). Our author may have in mind here in the background the promise of Gen. 9:11, that God would never flood the earth with water again as a form of judgment. The coming judgment, then, must be of a different sort than the judgment of the flood, though no less serious and devastating in its effects.[454] Many scholars note that this begins an apocalyptic focus in the letter (3:7–13), which connects with various images of eschatological judgment from Judaism and the Greco-Roman world. Donelson's statement that "readers have long noted that the imagery is more Jewish than

---

[450] Witherington, *Letters for Hellenized Christians*, 374. See also Bauckham, *Jude–2 Peter*, 374.
[451] See Davids, *The Letters of 2 Peter and Jude*, 271; Green, *Jude and 2 Peter*, 320.
[452] Against the view that Peter has the complete annihilation of the cosmos in mind, see Matthew Y. Emerson, "Does God Own a Death Star? The Destruction of the Cosmos in 2 Peter 3:1–13," *SWJT* 57.2 (2015): 281–93. See also Gale Z. Heide, "What Is New about the New Heaven and the New Earth? A Theology of Creation from Revelation 21 and 2 Peter 3," *JETS* 40.1 (1997): 37–56.
[453] Some mss. read "by his word," though the referent of the divine word would be the same.
[454] Josephus speaks of "Adam's prediction that the world was to be destroyed at one time by the force of fire, and at another time by the violence and quantity of water" (*Ant.* 1.2.3).

Christian"[455] offers a false dichotomy on the text. The world of first-century Christianity was the world of first-century Judaism, and it is not until the second century that a more definitive separation between the two movements develops.[456] It is doubtful that any of the apostles would have seen their ministries as a part of a "new religion," but rather as continuing in the trajectory of the Old Testament and the Jewish traditions that sprang from it.[457] On the other hand, a number of scholars see the primary influence of Greco-Roman traditions here. As Frey states:

> With regard to its contents, 2 Peter is the only New Testament document to refer to a cosmic conflagration, a burning of the world in fire, which is a well-known element of Greco-Roman, particularly Stoic cosmology, but almost completely unattested in ancient Judaism, with the notable exception of the Sibylline Oracles.[458]

It is probably best for us to take a reading somewhere in between, recognizing that there are both Jewish and Greco-Roman influences that have factored into how our author frames his discussion here. Judgment by fire is a frequent theme within Jewish literature.[459] Deuteronomy 32:22, speaking of the covenantal curses, states "For a fire will be kindled by my wrath, one that burns down to the realm of the dead below. It will devour the earth and its harvests and set afire the foundations of the mountains" (NIV). This theme is picked up steadily in the prophets, with God himself depicted as a consuming fire (cf. Isa. 32:27; 33:14; Zeph. 1:18; 3:8; see also Heb. 12:29). Isaiah 65, in particular, combines a number of the images present here in 2 Peter 3, dealing with God's patience in waiting for repentance, a coming fiery judgment, and the creation of a new heavens and new earth.

---

[455] Donelson, *I & II Peter and Jude*, 264.
[456] See James D. G. Dunn, *The Partings of the Ways: Between Christianity and Judaism and Their Significance for the Character of Christianity* (Norwich: SCM Press, 2006); Annette Yoshiko Reed, ed., *Jewish-Christianity and the History of Judaism: Collected Essays* (Tübingen: Mohr Siebeck, 2018).
[457] See Paula Fredericksen, *When Christians Were Jews: The First Generation* (New Haven: Yale University Press, 2018); Oskar Skarsaune and Reidar Hvalvik, eds., *Jewish Believers in Jesus: The Early Centuries* (Grand Rapids: Baker Academic, 2017).
[458] Frey, "Second Peter in New Perspective," 13.
[459] Deut. 32:22; Isa. 29:6; 30:27–33; 33:14; 66:15–24; Joel 2:30; Nah. 1:6; Zeph. 1:18; 3:8; Mal. 4:1; Acts 2:19; 2 Thess. 1:8; Rev. 9:17–18; 16:8; 20:9; also *Sib. Or.* 2.196–213; 3.80–93; 4.171–82; 5.155–61, 206–13; *Ps. Sol.* 15.4; *1 En.* 1.6–7; 52.6; 1QH 3.29–36; 11.19–36; Josephus, *Ant.*, 1.2.3.

Though the heavens and earth are affected by this judgment, the focus of the judgment is upon God's creatures: "being kept for the day of the judgment and destruction of ungodly people" (τηρούμενοι εἰς ἡμέραν κρίσεως καὶ ἀπωλείας τῶν ἀσεβῶν ἀνθρώπων).[460] As Davis comments, "the judgment is not of the creation but of human beings, just as the flood was not about the creation but about human evil."[461] This judgment on humanity will no doubt include heavenly creatures as well, as alluded to in 2 Pet. 2:4, language that is repeated here (2:4: ἀλλὰ σειραῖς ζόφου ταρταρώσας παρέδωκεν **εἰς κρίσιν τηρουμένους**; 3:7: **τηρούμενοι εἰς ἡμέραν κρίσεως** καὶ ἀπωλείας τῶν ἀσεβῶν ἀνθρώπων). Though destruction by fire is also found in Stoic traditions, such a judgment is seen in Stoicism as a cyclical event, which is not the case here with Peter's language.[462] Diogenes Laertius, for example, suggests that God periodically "absorbs into himself the whole of substance [of the cosmos] and again creates it from himself."[463] Cicero, similarly, writes,

> the entire world will be set on fire when all moisture is consumed, and neither the earth can be nourished nor the air can return, since its origin, water, will be entirely exhausted; thus, nothing will remain except fire, from which the renewal of the world, living and divine, will take place, and the same order will arise again.[464]

While Peter's audience may have heard echoes here of Stoic teaching, and even employed some of the language found therein, the notion of judgment by fire, even of the whole world, is found in Jewish texts and traditions. His focus, moreover, is not necessarily even on what will happen to the cosmos, which he will return to in 3:10-13 (where the language used contains several debatable elements), but rather on the divine judgment that will take place of God's creatures and humans in particular. He refutes the proclamation of the false teachers that the Lord will not return and no judgment is pending. Peter assures his audience that the Lord's return is imminent and

---

[460] On a metaphorical interpretation of this section, see Clifford D. Winters, "A Strange Death: Cosmic Conflagration as Conceptual Metaphor in 2 Peter 3:6-13," *Conversations with the Biblical World* 33 (2013): 147-62.

[461] Davids, *The Letters of 2 Peter and Jude*, 274.

[462] On a comparison with the Stoic conception of cosmic conflagration, with implications for dating 2 Peter, see Carsten Peter Thiede, "A Pagan Reader of 2 Peter: Cosmic Conflagration in 2 Peter 3 and the *Octavius* of Minucius Feux," *JSNT* 26 (1986): 79-96.

[463] Diog. Laert., 7.137.

[464] Cicero, *Nat. d.*, 2.118. See also Heraclitus, *All.*, 20-26; Ovid, *Metamorphoses*, 1.253-61; Plato, *Tim.* 22C-E; Lecretius, DNT, 5.

the judgment of humanity is certain, being ushered in by the very utterances of God.

3:8 – A new development ("now"; δέ) in the argument is now introduced, along with another direct address of the audience ("loved ones"; ἀγαπητοί).[465] On discourse principles, one could see a textual break here on this basis, though, for sake of the development of the argument, it is treated here with the previous material. The direct address also does not introduce a new audience but rather readdresses those already addressed in 3:1, adding some emphasis. The discussion of the divine activity in creation and the flood, which segued to the coming "day of judgment and destruction" (ἡμέραν κρίσεως καὶ ἀπωλείας) in 3:7 served to establish the focal point of this section, which is the author's discussion of the coming of the "day of the Lord" (cf. 2 Pet. 3:10).

Similar to the statement in 2 Pet. 3:3 ("above all knowing this"; τοῦτο πρῶτον γινώσκοντες), our author draws focus to the central topic of chapter 3 in stating, "Now do not let this one thing escape you" (Ἓν δὲ τοῦτο μὴ λανθανέτω ὑμᾶς). There is an implicit contrast here with 3:5, where the author rebuked the false teachers for "deliberately suppressing" or "it escaping their notice" (λανθάνει) that God created and sustains the universe, and the audience is being advised to not repeat this error. As Fresch notes, imperatives are prominent in hortatory discourses,[466] and we find here only the third such form (see also 2 Pet. 1:5, 10) used in the letter, though several more will soon follow (cf. 3:14, 15, 17, 18). This clustering of commands indicates that our author is "getting down to business" and arriving to a pointed and focused conclusion in his efforts to persuade the audience about the central significance of the return of Christ and coming judgment he will bring.

The author begins his rhetorical point of focus stating "that one day with the Lord is like one thousand years" (ὅτι μία ἡμέρα παρὰ κυρίῳ ὡς χίλια ἔτη). This demonstrates that part of the dispute with the false teachers concerned the timing of Jesus' return, likely arguing that an apparent delay was reason to reject that it would happen at all (in their own words): "Where is the promise of his coming? ... all things are continuing on as they have since the beginning of creation" (cf. 3:4). The statement that "one

---

[465] On the address, see previous comments on 2 Pet. 3:1.
[466] Fresch, "2 Peter," 624.

days is like a thousand years" comes from Ps. 90:4,[467] which itself is a psalm of divine judgment. The psalm contains an interplay on the themes of "days" and "years" (cf. 90:4, 9–10, 15), recognizing that human life is brief and full of troubles, and like dust in comparison with God, who is "from everlasting to everlasting" (90:2). The psalm took on a hermeneutical role in Jewish interpretation, becoming a central text in the calculation of divine timelines. Second Enoch 33.1, for example, states,

And I appointed the eighth day also, that the eighth day should be the first-created after my work, and that revolve in the form of the seventh thousand, and that at the beginning of the eighth thousand there should be a time of not-counting, endless, with neither years nor months nor weeks nor days nor hours.

b. Sanh. 97a states that Eliyahu taught:

Six thousand years is the duration of the world. Two thousand of the six thousand years are characterized by chaos; two thousand years are characterized by Torah, from the era of the Patriarchs until the end of the mishnaic period; and two thousand years are the period of the coming of the Messiah.[468]

This line of interpretation also found its way into the church fathers. Across various texts and traditions, we find this framework of one-thousand-year periods applied to creation and the history of the world (*Barn.* 15:4; Irenaeus, *Adv. Haer.*, 5.28.3; *b. Sanh.* 97a), the messianic rule (Justin, *Dial.*, 81; *b. Sanh.* 99a; *Midr. Ps.* 90:17; *Pesiq. R.* 1:7), and the preexistence of Torah (*Gen. Rab.* 8:2; 19:8; 22:1; *Lev. Rab.* 19:1; *Cant. Rab.* 5:11).[469]

Our author, however, also inverts this saying from Ps. 90:4, stating, "and one thousand years like one day" (καὶ χίλια ἔτη ὡς ἡμέρα μία), which is unique among other interactions with this text. Bauckham sees four parallels of significance that relate to our author's interpretation: *Pirqe R. El.* 28; Sir. 18:9–11; *2 Apoc. Bar.* 48:12–13; *Bib. Ant.* 19:13a.[470] The first text, which connects the activity of Abraham chasing away birds of prey (cf. Gen. 15:11) to the four eschatological kingdoms of the Gentiles, concludes that the kingdoms "will only last one day according to the day of the Holy One." Bauckham infers here a connection to Ps. 90:4, which, like our

---

[467] See also Sir. 18:9–11; *Jub.* 4.30; 2 Bar. 48:13.
[468] See also *Gen. Rab.* 8:2; 19:8; 22:1; *Lev. Rab.* 19:1; *Cant. Rab.* 5:11.
[469] cf. Bauckham, *Jude–2 Peter*, 306–7.
[470] Bauckham, *Jude–2 Peter*, 308–9. See also Davids, *The Letters of 2 Peter and Jude*, 277.

author, reverses the statement so that a lengthy period may be viewed, from divine perspective, as quite short. Like Ps. 90:4, Sir. 18:9–11 contrasts the brevity of human life with the eternal life of God, stating "Like a drop of water from the sea and a grain of sand, so are a few years among the days of eternity." This text shares affinity also with 2 *Apoc. Bar.* 48:12–13, which states, "For in a little time are we born, and in a little time do we return. But with you hours are as a time, and days as generations." Lastly, *Bib. Ant.* 19:13a states, "this age shall be in my sight as a fleeting cloud, and like yesterday when it is past." As Bauckham summarizes, these various traditions, like 2 Peter, "indicate that although a period may seem long by human reckoning, in God's eternal perspective it is short."[471]

Peter's purpose here, then, was to demonstrate that the divine timeline cannot be judged from a human perspective.[472] To some extent, at least as humans are concerned, time is relative from God's perspective, which undercuts the critiques of the false teachers. As Malina argued, in the New Testament, written in an "operational time" framework rather than a "historical time" framework, the present and its experiences take precedence over temporal forward-thinking and task-oriented life.[473] The implications of such a cultural situation would mean that a question of first importance concerning eschatological and apocalyptic texts would be "what significance does this have for the present time?," rather than "how does this help anticipate the events of the future?" It is clear from what follows that Peter's aim, though concerned with a theological denial about the future, has a primary focal point on the effects that such a denial would have on the behavior of his Christian audience. He does not seek to implant their lives in events yet to come but rather to influence their present life in anticipation of those realities. The commands of this letter (2 Pet 1:5: "supply with your faith virtue"; 1:10 "be even more eager to make your calling and election certain"; 3:8 "do not let this one thing escape you"; 3:14 "make every effort to be found at peace"; 3:15 "regard the patience of our Lord as salvation"; 3:17 "keep guarding yourselves in order that you might not lose your own steadfastness"; 3:18 "keep growing in the grace and knowledge of our Lord Jesus Christ") focus upon the present behaviors and

---

[471] Bauckham, *Jude–2 Peter*, 309.
[472] See Green, *Jude and 2 Peter*, 326.
[473] Bruce J. Malina, "Christ and Time: Swiss or Mediterranean?" *CBQ* 51.1 (1989): 1–31.

beliefs of the audience, which ought to be shaped by their confident expectation in the coming again of Jesus Christ. This is the chief danger of the false teachers, that in leading these believers astray concerning the rule and reign of Christ (cf. 2 Pet. 2:1), they draw them away from their present participation in the life of God (cf. 1:3-4).

3:9 – A new sentence begins here that further develops the point made in the previous verse by connecting it specifically to the return of Christ. Though most translations take the genitive here as the object of the verb βραδύνει,[474] it is more naturally read as modifying κύριος, thus serving as a subject phrase, "The Lord of the promise" (κύριος τῆς ἐπαγγελίας).[475] The defense offered is that the Lord of the promise "is not slow as some regard slowness" (οὐ βραδύνει … ὥς τινες βραδύτητα ἡγοῦνται). The "promise" in mind here in the context is clearly the promised coming of the Son (cf. 2 Pet. 3:4).[476] The combination here of the verb βραδύνει and the noun βραδύτητα may seem redundant but serves to intensify the phrase. This question of slowness or delay related particularly to the problem of evil in the ancient world. As Davids summarizes, "Plutarch in his work *De sera numinis vindicta* (*Moralia* 548-68) begins his critique of the Epicureans with, 'The delay and procrastination of the Deity in punishing the wicked appears to me the most telling argument by far.'"[477] The apparent lack of divine intervention was argued as evidence for the absence of any form of divine providence. Peter's words here share affinity with both Hab. 2:3 ("For the revelation awaits an appointed time; it speaks of the end and will not prove false. Though it lingers, wait for it; it will certainly come and will not delay"; NIV) and Sir. 35:22 ("Indeed, the Lord will not delay …"; NRSV).[478]

In contrast ("but"; ἀλλὰ) to this claim of delay or slowness, we are told "but is being patient for you" (ἀλλὰ μακροθυμεῖ εἰς ὑμᾶς). The "you" here would seem most likely directed at Peter's audience, relating to the "loved ones" of 3:8, though it is possible that it carries a broader sense as well. The primary question here would be if there are those within the community of

---

[474] Or a "genitive of reference," cf. Davids, *II Peter and Jude*, 101.
[475] This is how Watson and Callan take the phrase (Duane F. Watson and Terrance D. Callan, *First and Second Peter*, PCNT [Grand Rapids: Baker, 2012], 208).
[476] See Bauckham, *Jude-2 Peter*, 311.
[477] Davids, *The Letters of 2 Peter and Jude*, 278.
[478] See also Isa. 13:22; 51:14; Sir. 32:22.

Peter's audience in need of repentance as it relates to the deceptions of the false teachers. This also relates to whether Peter has in mind some in his audience or only the false teachers in 2:18–22 and as 3:17 may indicate as well.

The reason specified for the act of divine patience is "not wanting any to lose out but all to come to repentance" (μὴ βουλόμενός τινας ἀπολέσθαι ἀλλὰ πάντας εἰς μετάνοιαν χωρῆσαι).[479] The posture of divine patience toward sinners is prevalent in biblical texts and traditions. Exodus 34:6–7 is pronounced in this respect:

The Lord, the Lord, the compassionate and gracious God, slow to anger, abounding in love and faithfulness, maintaining love to thousands, and forgiving wickedness, rebellion and sin. Yet he does not leave the guilty unpunished; he punishes the children and their children for the sin of the parents to the third and fourth generation. (NIV)[480]

That the Lord specifically takes joy in the repentance of the wicked is made clear in Ezek.18:23: "'Do I take any pleasure in the death of the wicked?' declares the Sovereign Lord. 'Rather, am I not pleased when they turn from their ways and live?'" (NIV).[481] Indeed, throughout the Old Testament, a pronouncement of divine judgment may even be withheld if the people, in hearing the word of the Lord, turn and repent. As Fuhr and Yates state, "The prophets present a God who is quick to relent of judgment; this is even stated propositionally in texts such as Joel 2:13 and Jonah 4:2."[482] Joel 2:13 describes the Lord as "gracious and compassionate, slow to anger and abounding in love, and he relents from sending calamity" (NIV), phrases repeated almost verbatim in Jonah 4:2. As Fuhr and Yates continue, however, "God's mercies should not be taken for granted; there is a line that, once crossed, cannot be

---

[479] Watson and Callan explain the verse as an enthymeme, and lay out the explicit premises as follows: "One can say that the Lord is slow to keep his promises only if there is no sufficient reason for delay in keeping them. But the Lord delays out of patience, giving all the opportunity for repentance. Therefore, the Lord is not slow to keep his promises" (Watson and Callan, *First and Second Peter*, 208).

[480] This refrain is repeated elsewhere in Num. 14:18; Neh. 9:17; Ps. 86:15; 103:8; 145:8; Joel 2:12–13; Jonah 4:2; Nah. 1:3; see also Sir. 5:4–7; Wis. 11:23; 15:1; 4 Ezra 3:30; 7:32–34; 2 Bar. 12:4; also Rom. 2:4. See also Mark J. Boda, *The Heartbeat of Old Testament Theology: Three Creedal Expressions*, Acadia Studies in Bible and Theology (Grand Rapids: Baker Academic, 2017).

[481] See also Ezek. 33:11; 1 Tim. 2:4.

[482] Richard Alan Fuhr Jr. and Gary E. Yates, *The Message of the Twelve: Hearing the Voice of the Minor Prophets* (Nashville: B&H, 2016), 138.

retraced."[483] Such an understanding of divine judgment certainly relates to the depiction here in 2 Peter, where God's patience and mercy is for the purpose of repentance but has its limits as well.

One matter of debate in this text revolves around the scope of the "all" (πάντας) at the end of the verse and whether it is limited by the "you" (ὑμᾶς) earlier in 3:9.[484] Two questions here relate. First, is Peter's audience, or at least a portion of them, in need of repentance, as possibly suggested by 2:18–22 and 3:17? If this is the case, then the "all" here may indeed be limited to Peter's recipients. Second, are the false teachers beyond repentance, as possibly indicated in 2:21?[485] Witherington, for example, suggests, "Elsewhere in the New Testament (cf. Acts 17:30–31; Rom. 11:32; 1 Tim. 2:4; Ezek. 18:23, 32; 33:11) we certainly find the thought that God wants all to come to know Christ, but that is not the point here. The focus here is more narrowly on Christians who stand in danger of perishing if they do not forsake the false teachers' ways and repent."[486] Oropeza, among others, notes it is also possible to read this point as being broadened in the contrast, stating:

> The author might have in mind the scoffers when mentioning in 3:9 that "some" think the Lord is delaying his promise. If so, then it would seem that they too are able to repent and avoid perishing. Certain scholars interpret the emphatic "all" (πάντας) in this verse to mean all people. In short, the "all" may be a call for everyone to repent – those who are Christians, those who are apostates, and those who have never been converted. It is also evident from other Christian traditions that God desires all humanity to be saved (e.g., 1 Tim 2:4– 6; 4:10; Titus 2:11).[487]

---

[483] Fuhr and Yates, *The Message of the Twelve*, 138.
[484] There are two variant readings of significance as well: (1) εις ημας ("for us"; supported by 307. 442. 642. 2492 Byz); (2) δι υμας ("because of you"; supported significantly by ℵ A Ψ 5. 33. 436. 1611. 1852 latt sy sa).
[485] Compare, for example, Heb. 6:4–8.
[486] Witherington, *Letters for Hellenized Christians*, 378. See also Frey, *The Letter of Jude and the Letter of Second Peter*, 405. Bauckham is in agreement, noting, "πάντας ('all') is clearly limited by ὑμᾶς ('you') . . . . Here it is for the sake of the repentance of 2 Peter's Christian readers. No doubt repentance from those sins into which some of them have been enticed by the false teachers (2:14, 18; 3:17) is especially in mind. We need not suppose that the author put the false teachers themselves entirely beyond possibility of repentance and salvation" (Bauckham, *Jude–2 Peter*, 313).
[487] Oropeza, *Churches Under Siege*, 150. See also Karl Kuhn, "2 Peter 3:1–13," *Interpretation: A Journal of Bible and Theology* 60.3 (2006): 310–12; Earl J. Richard, *Reading 1 Peter, Jude, and 2 Peter: A Literary and Theological Commentary* (Macon: Smyth and Helwys, 2013), 380–81.

Regardless of which options better fits the context, the prevalence of the God's desire of repentance for all occurs sufficiently throughout Scripture to hold to a belief in such a doctrine. While there are points at which it seems repentance is no longer possible, it is not entirely clear if the apostates in Peter's audience are there or not. It is God's love that motivates his patience, desiring to restore all who would come to him through the Son.[488]

3:10 – The author continues with a new development ("Now"; δὲ), which adds further detail to the author's discussion and description. Though in this chapter, our author has referenced the "last days" (ἐσχάτων τῶν ἡμερῶν; cf. 3:3), the "day of judgment" (ἡμέραν κρίσεως; cf. 3:7), and compared "one day" (μία ἡμέρα) to a thousand years in the sight of the Lord, he now focuses in on "the day of the Lord" (ἡμέρα κυρίου), which he will refer to again as the "day of God" (τῆς τοῦ θεοῦ ἡμέρας) in 3:12. These three days ("day of judgment," "day of the Lord," and "day of God") are clearly eschatological in focus and likely refer to the cluster of events envisioned by the New Testament authors as occurring at the end of this age and the beginning of the age to come (cf. 3:18).

The day of the Lord is a frequent topic of focus in the prophetic material of the Old Testament (e.g., Isa. 13:6, 9; Ezek. 7:19; 13:5; 30:3; Joel 1:15; 2:1, 11, 31; 3:14; Amos 5:18, 20; Obad. 15; Zeph. 1:7–8, 14, 18; 2:2–3; Zech. 14:1; Mal. 4:5), and the language is carried over into the New Testament as well (Acts 2:20; 1 Cor. 5:5; 2 Cor. 1:14; 1 Thess. 5:2; 2 Thess. 2:2; 2 Pet. 1:19). The gospels (Matt. 24:29; Mark 13:24–25; Luke 21:25–26), drawing from OT sources concerning the day of the Lord (Isa 13:10; 34:4; Ezek. 32:7–8; Joel 2:10, 31; 3:15), indicate that celestial signs (sun and moon darkened, stars falling from heaven, etc.) would accompany the return of the Son of Man. The day is viewed in the NT as a point of transition that ends the present world and ushers in the eschaton (Isa. 34:4; 51:6; *1 En.* 91:16; Matt. 5:18; 24:35; Mark 13:31; Luke 16:17; 21:33; Rev. 20:11; 21:1). Throughout the biblical texts, the day of the Lord serves as an event of extensive impact, bringing redemption and salvation for the righteous and judgment and humiliation for the wicked.

In keeping with Jesus' teachings on the return of the Son of Man (cf. Matt. 24:44; Luke 12:40), 2 Peter asserts that this day "will come as a thief"

---

[488] On this point, see especially Peckham, *The Love of God*, 97–121.

(Ἥξει δὲ ... ὡς κλέπτης), language reminiscent also of 1 Thess. 5:2; Rev. 3:3; 16:15, though Bauckham argues the phrasing here is more likely the result of oral tradition than textual dependence.[489] Witherington notes that the emphatic position of the verb ἥξει ("will come") further emphasizes the suddenness of this event.[490] Our author has asserted that the day ought not be understood as delayed, for the divine timeline is imperceptible to humans, and now asserts that the event will be unpredictable as well. While many have attempted to prognosticate the time of the return of Christ, it is safe to say that if the angels and the Son do not know the day or hour (cf. Matt 24:36), the best guesses of humans will also fall short. Such is part of the point of Jesus comparing the time of his return to the breaking in of a thief. Robberies are rarely predictable, thus the need for "constant vigilance"[491] in preparation for the Son's return.

Several descriptions of the events of the day of the Lord follow the statement of its suddenness, the first of which being "in which the heavens will pass away with a rushing noise" (ἐν ᾗ οἱ οὐρανοὶ ῥοιζηδὸν παρελεύσονται). This unusual representation of sound, used only here in the NT, may be described as "the noise made by something passing swiftly through the air."[492] The presence of the Lord, along with the coming of his judgment, is often described as being accompanied by thunderous noises, along with other phenomena (cf. 1 Sam. 2:10; 7:10; Job 40:9; Ps. 18:13–15; 77:18; 104:7; Isa. 29:6; 33:3; Jer. 25:30; Joel 3:16; 4:16; Amos 1:2; *Sib. Or.* 4.175b; 1QH 3:32–36). Such may be the sound in mind by the author. "The heavens" (οἱ οὐρανοί) here could be descriptive of the heavenly dwellings or of the "sky." The word is frequently in the plural in the New Testament, perhaps following the common construction of שָׁמַיִם (shamayim) in the Old Testament, and could be used to refer to the sky or atmosphere, as well as "heaven" itself, which is often described as a tiered domain in Jewish literature (i.e., "first heaven," "third heaven," etc.; see, 2 En. 3–22; *T. Levi* 2–5; 2 Cor. 12:2–4; Hagigah 12b). It is unclear which of these realms is in mind by our author, and, as the next phrase will demonstrate, scholars are divided on what may be in focus.

---

[489] Bauckham, *Jude–2 Peter*, 306.
[490] Witherington, *Letters for Hellenized Christians*, 379.
[491] Cf. "Mad-Eye" Moody, from J. K. Rowling, *Harry Potter and the Goblet of Fire* (New York: Scholastic Press, 2000), 217.
[492] Louw and Nida, *Greek-English Lexicon of the New Testament*, 180.

The second descriptive phrase is "the celestial bodies will be destroyed by burning away" (στοιχεῖα δὲ καυσούμενα λυθήσεται). Several features of this phrase require comment. First, the term used here for "the celestial bodies" (στοιχεῖα) can be variously interpreted. As Donelson lays out, it could be taken as a description of (1) the elements of the universe (earth, air, fire, and water), (2) heavenly beings/fallen angels (cf. Gal. 4:3; Col 2:8, 20), or (3) heavenly objects (sun, moon, stars, etc.).[493] Given the apocalyptic focus here, each is a possibility, and some combination could be envisioned as well. The stars and heavenly beings, for example, are often closely associated in biblical texts, as Isa.34:4 illustrates: "All the stars in the sky will be dissolved and the heavens rolled up like a scroll; all the starry host will fall like withered leaves from the vine, like shriveled figs from the fig tree" (NIV). Job 38:6–7 is similar: "On what were its bases sunk? Or who laid its cornerstone, when the morning stars were singing together and all the sons of God [i.e., angels] shouted for joy?" (LEB). Second Peter has already described the judgment awaiting the fallen angels (cf. 2:4) and could have such events in mind here, though his focus seems broader and related to the major changes that the realms of both heaven and earth will experience as the new age is fully ushered in.

As noted above, the "burning away" (καυσούμενα) of these entities need not necessarily be taken as their complete destruction (compare Heb. 6:8). Just as the flood "destroyed" the earth but did not annihilate it entirely (cf. 2 Pet. 3:6), so the burning here, clearly couched in apocalyptic language, need not be seen as a total annihilation either. As Middleton observes, the earth is also not the object of the "burning" described but rather the heavens and στοιχεῖα.[494] Fire is a common symbol of judgment in biblical literature, possibly originating with the Sodom and Gomorrah judgment (cf. Gen. 19:24–25), already alluded to in 2 Pet. 2:6. The imagery of divine fire occurs in various narratives of the Old Testament (e.g., Lev. 10:1–2; 2 Kgs. 1:10), as well as frequently in the OT prophets (Isa. 66:15–16; Mic. 1:4; Nah. 1:6; Zeph 1:18; Mal. 3:2, 19), though often in clearly metaphorical ways. This imagery is found elsewhere in the NT as well (Matt. 3:11–12; Acts 2:19;

---

[493] Donelson, *I & II Peter and Jude*, 276–77.
[494] J. Richard Middleton, *A New Heaven and a New Earth: Reclaiming Biblical Eschatology* (Grand Rapids; Baker Academic, 2014), 190.

2 Thess. 1:7-9; Rev. 9:18; 18:8; 20:9-10; see also *1 En.* 90; 108; 1QHodayot[a] 3:29-33; *Lev. Rab.* 7:6).

The final description given is "the earth and the deeds done upon it will be disclosed" (καὶ γῆ καὶ τὰ ἐν αὐτῇ ἔργα εὑρεθήσεται).[495] The difficulty of the verb here (εὑρεθήσεται; lit. "will be found") appears to have initiated a number of textual variants (ευρεθησεται λυομενα, "will be found as destroyed"; αφανισθησονται, "will disappear"; κατακαησεται, "it will be burned"; κατακαησονται, "they will be burned"), along with a number of proposed conjectural emendations.[496] As Metzger noted, "The oldest reading, and the one which best explains the origin of the others that have been preserved, is εὑρεθήσεται, which is attested by ℵ B K P 424[c] 1175 1739[txt] 1852 syr[ph,] arm Origen."[497] Though a number of commentators find the reading nonsensical, the idea of "being found" is associated with judgment in various places in the OT and NT (Exod. 22:8; Deut. 22:22, 28; Ezra 10:18; Jer. 50:24; Matt 24:46/ Luke 12:43, Mark 13:36, Luke 12:37-38; 23:4; John 18:38; 19:4; Acts 13:28; 23:9; 2 Cor. 5:3; Rev. 14:5).[498] As Neyrey summarizes, "In the context of judgment, rewards, and punishments, then, 'being found' suggests forensic investigation of the heart, a quality regularly credited to God."[499] In the context of 2 Pet. 3:10, this would be taken to mean that the earth and the deeds done within them will be "found out," "disclosed," or "laid bare" when Christ returns in judgment of the living and the dead.[500]

---

[495] This follows the reading of the NA27, based upon ℵ B P 1175. 1448. 1739[txt]. 1852 sy[ph mss txt] sy[hmg], rather than the reading of οὐχ εὑρεθήσεται in the NA28 on the basis of sy[ph mss] sa cv[vid].

[496] (a) after ἔργα the word ἄργα has fallen out (Bradshaw), 'the earth and the things in it will be found *useless*'; (b) εὑρεθήσεται is a scribal corruption of ῥυήσεται or ῥεύσεται (Hort), 'the earth and the things in it *will flow*'; (c) συρρυήσεται (Naber), '... will flow together'; (d) ἐκπυρωθήσεται (Olivier), '... will be burnt to ashes'; (e) ἀρθήσεται (J. B. Mayor), '... will be taken away'; (f) κριθήσεται (Eb. Nestle), '... will be judged'; (g) ἰαθήσεται (or ἐξιαθήσεται) (Chase), '... will be healed (thoroughly)'; (h) πυρωθήσεται (Vansittart), '... will be burned' (Metzger, *A Textual Commentary on the Greek New Testament*, 636-37).

[497] Metzger, *A Textual Commentary on the Greek New Testament*, 636. See also Al Wolters, "Worldview and Textual Criticism in 2 Peter 3:10," *Westminster Theological Journal* 49.2 (1987): 405-13.

[498] See David Wenham, "Being 'Found' on the Last Day: New Light on 2 Peter 3.10 and 2 Corinthians 5.3," *NTS* 33 (1987): 477-79.

[499] Neyrey, *2 Peter, Jude*, 244.

[500] Contra Middleton who sees "disclosed" here as a statement of God's saving activity (Middleton, *A New Heaven and a New Earth*, 161).

3:11 – Peter now draws his first implication of his eschatological exploration, stating, "since all these things are going to be destroyed in this way" (τούτων οὕτως[501] πάντων λυομένων). The "all these things" could be taken as a reference to the heavens and the στοιχεῖα, or to the heavens, στοιχεῖα, and earth, though the latter is not specified as an object of destruction in the previous verses. Even if the earth is included in that destruction, as noted above, this need not be seen as an entire annihilation of the earth but rather that the "way things are" currently on the earth will be destroyed (cf. 2 Pet. 3:6). In that the phrase here is framed around a participial construction, translating it as "since" indicates the participle is being read as causal.[502]

The result of the knowledge of this coming destruction is a reflection on "what kind of people should you be" (ποταποὺς δεῖ ὑπάρχειν ὑμᾶς).[503] Eschatology is regularly deployed in the New Testament in service of ethics.[504] As Bauckham observes, "Eschatological paraenesis is not uncommon in the concluding sections of NT letters (cf. 1 Cor 15:58; Gal 5:7-10; Eph 5:10-16; Phil 4:5; Col 4:5; 1 Tim 6:14; 2 Tim 4:15; 1 Pet 5:1-10)."[505] Similar to the connections made here, Eph. 5:11-13 acknowledges that all things will be exposed by the light, and thus Christ's followers must attend to how they live until he returns. Assurance about the coming of the Lord served in the New Testament both as a source of boldness in the midst of trials and suffering (1 Cor 15:58; Col. 4:5; 2 Tim. 4:1-2, 15; Jas. 5:8-9; 1 Pet. 5:8-9; 1 John 2:28), peace in the midst of fear (Mark 13:32-37; 1 Thess. 5:1-11), and holiness in the midst of temptations (Rom. 13:12; Eph. 5:10-16; Phil. 4:5; 1 Pet. 1:13-17; 4:7). Though constructed as a statement (i.e., indicative verb), Green suggests rightly that this sentence carries an imperatival force.[506]

---

[501] There are a handful of variants here primarily involving the substitution of various conjunctions (δέ or οὖν in place of οὕτως or alongside of it) or the omittance or alteration of πάντων.

[502] See Davids, *II Peter and Jude*, 105.

[503] The NA27 brackets ὑμᾶς on the basis of 630 241 209 104 *א *al* reading ἡμᾶς instead and no pronoun being present in $\mathfrak{P}^{72*,\ vid}$ B 1175 *al*. The NA28 removes the brackets and retains ὑμᾶς though noting the variants.

[504] Cf. Green, *Jude and 2 Peter*, 332.

[505] Bauckham, *Jude-2 Peter*, 323. See also Mark 13:32-37; Rom. 13:12; 1 Thess. 5:1-11; Jas. 5:8-9; 1 Pet. 1:13-17; 4:7; 1 John 2:28.

[506] Cf. Green, *Jude and 2 Peter*, 333.

How this assurance of the coming judgment should influence their living is made explicit with the prepositional phrase "in holy behaviors and godly actions" (ἐν ἁγίαις ἀναστροφαῖς καὶ εὐσεβείαις). Both nouns here are in the plural, though they are often translated as conceptual singulars ("holiness and godliness"). As Davids indicates, the use of the plural here likely reinforces the behaviors expected to flow from one whose character is formed by an eager anticipation of the return of the Lord.[507] The language here has several connection points with previous sections of the letter. The "holy behaviors" here stand in contrast to the "lawless behaviors" (τῆς τῶν ἀθέσμων ... ἀναστροφῆς; cf. 2:7) of the citizens of Sodom and Gomorrah and the false teachers who are "living in error" (ἐν πλάνῃ ἀναστρεφομένους; cf. 2:18). The "godly actions" (εὐσεβείαις) that are expected of the audience reinforce material from 2 Pet. 1:3, 6, 7; 2:9. This term appeared in the "theosis" section of the letter ("all things necessary for life and devotion to God (εὐσέβειαν) have been presented to us"; cf. 1:3), as well as in the virtue list ("with perseverance devotion to God (τὴν εὐσέβειαν), with devotion to God (ἐν δὲ τῇ εὐσεβείᾳ) sibling affection"; cf. 1:6-7), and in the conclusion of examples of judgment and deliverance ("the Lord knows how to rescue the devout (εὐσεβεῖς) from trials"; cf. 2:9). Those actions that demonstrate devotion to God are now connected to the expectation of the return of Christ. As in the opening section of the letter (1:3-11), it is transformative communion with God that aligns the desires and behaviors of the believer with those of God himself. This alignment is reinforced by those who eagerly await the coming of the Son and his "making all things right." Davids' reflection here is insightful:

> Given the massive investment of contemporary Christians in the nationalism, materialism, and pleasure orientation of Western culture, this passage should serve as a wake-up call. When the Day comes, one's retirement fund will not be important, but rather what one has invested in the kingdom of our Sovereign Lord.[508]

It is this type of alignment with kingdom values and priorities that Peter has in mind for his audience, understanding that nothing in this life or world is of greater importance than one's commitment to loving service of God for the good of others.

---

[507] Davids, *II Peter and Jude*, 105.
[508] Davids, *The Letters of 2 Peter and Jude*, 289.

3:12 – The thought of 3:11 is extended here by a cluster of two participial phrases (προσδοκῶντας καὶ σπεύδοντας . . .) and a relative pronoun clause (δι' ἥν . . .). The participial phrases come first: "while looking for and hastening the coming day of God" (προσδοκῶντας καὶ σπεύδοντας τὴν παρουσίαν τῆς τοῦ θεοῦ ἡμέρας). The language of "day of judgment" (cf. 3:7) and "day of the Lord" (cf. 3:10) is replaced here with "day of God,"[509] but it is reasonable to assume that this alteration has the same previous references in mind (compare Rev. 16:14). All three phrases refer to the same event.[510] It is the audience that is expected to be "waiting for" (προσδοκῶντας) and "hastening" (σπεύδοντας) the coming of this day. Green notes that the "waiting for" here "does not mean simply 'hope for,' as if the coming of the day were some unsure future event, but rather suggests a firm expectation . . . (cf. Matt. 11:3; Luke 1:21; 8:40; Acts 3:5; 10:24; 28:6; and in an eschatological context, Matt. 24:50; Luke 12:46)."[511] In what way might a believer be said to "hasten" the day of the Lord? The gloss that BDAG attaches to the verb here is to "cause something to happen by exercising special effort."[512] On this text, Bauckham asks, "Does the author mean that lack of repentance on humanity's part can defer the Parousia (3:9), while repentance and good works can hasten its coming (3:12), so that it is really not God, but humanity, that determines the date of the Parousia?"[513]

Answering such a question must be contextualized within the realm of Jewish literature and biblical texts from which our author may be drawing. As previously noted, biblical prophecy often functions not to give direct predictions of events but to offer divine warnings, so that, should a prophet succeed, the people will repent and the predicted judgment might be averted.[514] There is thus a conditional element to prophetic activity

---

[509] Some mss., cf. the NA28, read κυριου instead of θεοῦ (C P 442. 642. 1175. 1243. 1739. 1852 t vg^cl sy^ph ms * sy; Spec).
[510] Cf. Davids, *The Letters of 2 Peter and Jude*, 289.
[511] Cf. Green, *Jude and 2 Peter*, 333.
[512] Arndt et al., *A Greek-English Lexicon*, 938.
[513] Bauckham, *Jude–2 Peter*, 313.
[514] See Brent Sandy, *Plowshares and Pruning Hooks: Rethinking the Language of Biblical Prophecy and Apocalyptic* (Downers Grove: IVP Academic, 2002); C. A. Strine, "Reconceiving Prophecy: Activation, Not Prognostication," in *When the Son of Man Didn't Come: A Constructive Proposal on the Delay of the Parousia*, ed. Christopher M. Hays (Minneapolis: Fortress Press, 2016), 39–58.

apparent in many Old Testament texts. Strine suggests we must recognize "predictive prophecy as conditioned by human response while also accepting that a genuinely pious turn might not preclude a prophetic prediction from coming to pass,"[515] and so, "prophecy is an invitation to affect divine action."[516] God always maintains the prerogative to exercise his will (e.g., Isa. 60:22) but does not do so apart from consideration of human response and activity. Second Esdras 4 illustrates this tension where, on the one hand, it is said that the world is "rushing to its end" (2 Esd. 4:26), and yet eschatological fulfillment will not come until "the number of those like you is complete" and "the prescribed measure is fulfilled" (2 Esd. 4:36–37). This prompts the prophet to inquire in 4:39, "Is it perhaps because of us, and because of the sins of those who live on earth, that the harvest of the just is delayed?" Such eschatological contingencies can be observed in the New Testament as well. In Matt. 24:14, Jesus is said to state, "his gospel of the kingdom will be preached in the whole world as a testimony to all nations, and then the end will come." Here Keener, for example, recognizes that Jesus' followers "must complete the commission of discipling all nations before this age will come to a close (28:19–20; cf. Rom 11:25–26; 2 Pet 3:9–15; Acts 1:6–11)."[517] Similarly, Acts 3:19–20 indicates that the return of Christ and eschatological renewal is dependent upon the response of repentance from the people. Here Marshall comments, "the coming of the 'messianic age' or the future kingdom of God, for which the Jews longed, was dependent upon their acceptance of Jesus as the Messiah."[518]

To return to our text, Peter here indicates that the divine timeline is within God's hands alone, yet God seeks to delay the day of judgment for the sake of repentance while the Church ought to be hastening its coming through their personal piety, and likely, as Matthew and Acts indicate, through their spreading the message of the kingdom to the world. Such a perspective can also be found both in the rabbinic writings and in the early church fathers. Bauckham notes the tradition of disagreement between R. Eliezer and R. Joshua, recounting:

---

[515] Strine, "Reconceiving Prophecy," 55.
[516] Strine, "Reconceiving Prophecy," 57.
[517] Craig S. Keener, *The Gospel of Matthew: A Socio-Rhetorical Commentary* (Grand Rapids: Eerdmans, 2009), 572.
[518] I. Howard Marshall, *Acts: An Introduction and Commentary*, Tyndale New Testament Commentaries (Downers Grove: InterVarsity Press, 1980), 100.

R. Eliezer says, "If Israel repents, they will be redeemed."

R. Joshua says, "Whether or not they repent, when the end comes, they will forthwith be redeemed, as it is said, 'I the Lord in its time will hasten it' (Is. 60:22)."[519]

Their discussion evidences a debate within Jewish traditions of the relevance of human contingencies, chiefly repentance, for the timing of eschatological events. In the early Church, several texts also display such a tension (e.g., Herm. *Sim.* 8.11.1; 10.4.4; Justin, *1 Apol.* 28; 2 Clem. 12.6). Justin writes in his *First Apology*, for example, that God has delayed the time of divine punishment for the sake of human repentance, and 2 Clem. 12.6 perceives that the piety of the Church is the contingency of the coming of the fullness of the kingdom of God.

Hays notes three major theological tensions to be considered in this discussion: (1) Jesus' depiction of the immediacy of his return and the apparent delay in his return,[520] (2) the tension in prophecy between prediction-fulfillment and God's right to alter prophetic proclamations in response to human repentance, and (3) the paradox between divine sovereignty and human freedom.[521] Such tensions create a complex context for engaging this question on a theological level, and avoidance of polarity in these tensions is necessary based on the nature of the biblical texts. In light of these tensions, Gallaher and Konstantinovsky suggest:

God remains free to determine the ways and means of his coming again, albeit within the bounds of a determinate number of possibilities that cohere with what has already been accomplished in the life, death, resurrection, and ascension of Christ. God will not take back his word that Jesus will come again, but God can adapt the times and means of that coming because the prophecies that speak of an imminent second coming are correctly understood as ways of motivating his creation so that the day of the Lord might come soon.[522]

---

[519] Bauckham, "The Delay of the *Parousia*," 12.
[520] On this tension, See Bauckham, "The Delay of the *Parousia*," 3–36.
[521] Christopher M. Hays, "The Delay of the Parousia: A Traditional and Historical-Critical Reading of Scripture: Part 2," in *When the Son of Man Didn't Come: A Constructive Proposal on the Delay of the Parousia* (Minneapolis: Fortress Press, 2016), 104–5.
[522] Brandon Gallaher and Julia S. Konstantinovsky, "Divine Action in Christ: The Christocentric and Trinitarian Nature of Human Cooperation with God," in Christopher M. Hays, *When the Son of Man Didn't Come: A Constructive Proposal on the Delay of the Parousia* (Minneapolis: Fortress Press, 2016), 176.

Such a dynamic necessitates not only careful theological reflection and biblical interpretation but also a renewed sense of urgency for the Church to take seriously its own personal holiness and its mission of discipleship among all people groups. Throughout the New Testament, mission and transformation go hand in hand.[523]

Our author now indicates two results ("because of which"; δι' ἥν) of the coming of the day of God. The first result is "the heavens will be destroyed by being burned up" (δι' ἥν οὐρανοὶ πυρούμενοι λυθήσονται). As noted above, "heavens" here could have a range of references, dealing only with the material heavens ("sky," "atmosphere," or the place where the stars and planets exist) with the identification of dwelling place of spiritual beings, or some combination thereof. As also noted earlier, the use of fire or melting/dissolving as an image of eschatological judgment, specifically against the heavens, occurs elsewhere in biblical literature (e.g., Isa. 34:4; Mal. 4:1).

The second result ("because of which"; δι' ἥν) of the day of God we find is "the celestial bodies are being dissolved by burning" (καὶ στοιχεῖα καυσούμενα τήκεται). As also noted above, στοιχεῖα here could refer to (1) the elements of nature, (2) heavenly beings/fallen angels, or (3) heavenly objects (sun, moon, stars, etc.), or some combination thereof. We again ought not to see here the complete annihilation of the existing heavens and earth in view and ought to imagine that the present universe in its material construction will have, as Witherington suggests, "some continuity with the new heaven and the new earth."[524] Our author's language here is apocalyptic[525] and contextually does not demand such a reading of total annihilation, though the present order of the world, with the influence of the wicked (both human and angelic) and the presence of sin, injustice, and other corrupting forces, will be fundamentally ended and transformed. Our author would no doubt respond at the prospect at such a transformation of the cosmos through the coming of the kingdom of God in a way similar to Rev. 22:21: "Amen, come Lord Jesus!"

---

[523] See, for example, Gorman, *Becoming the Gospel*.
[524] Witherington, *Letters for Hellenized Christians*, 380.
[525] So, Witherington, again, suggests: "It is difficult to say how much of this our author intends to be taken literally and how much is simply eschatological and metaphorical language used to describe the very real and coming event of the Parousia, which will involve real redemption and judgment" (Witherington, *Letters for Hellenized Christians*, 381).

3:13 – Though δέ can be used to mark new sections, here it introduces new information and a transitional summary of sorts between this unit and the beginning of the new unit, which is clearly identified in 3:14. "Now, according to His promise" (δὲ ... κατὰ τὸ ἐπάγγελμα[526] αὐτοῦ) reintroduces a word-group ("promise"; ἐπαγγελία, ἐπάγγελμα, ἐπαγγέλλομαι) found elsewhere in 2 Peter (1:4; 2:19; 3:4, 9). Whereas most recently it referred to the deceptive promise of "freedom" from the false teachers (cf. 2:19) and the promise of the coming of Christ (3:4, 9), here the sense seems to broaden, similar to 1:4, where it referred to his "great and precious promises" (τίμια καὶ μέγιστα ... ἐπαγγέλματα). While the second coming of Christ will certainly have bearing on the renewal of the heavens and earth in the "new creation," the promise in mind here would likely relate to the proclamations of Isaiah or to God's promises in a more generic sense (e.g., *Ps. Sol.* 12:6; 17:5).

The details of the promise are specified in stating, "we are waiting for new heavens and a new earth" (καινοὺς ... οὐρανοὺς καὶ γῆν καινὴν ... προσδοκῶμεν). The ordering of this verse begins with the object phrase καινοὺς δὲ οὐρανοὺς καὶ γῆν καινὴν ("Now the new heavens and new earth"), a reference to Isa. 65:17 and 66:22, which is frontloaded here in the Greek text to make it prominent. The idea of eschatological renewal develops in the Old Testament prophets and is expanded in unique ways by the New Testament and other Second Temple Jewish texts. As Middleton observes, the concept of renewal carries with it several major features in the Old Testament prophets, though all are not always present together. As he enumerates, these are (1) Israel's return to the land; (2) the restoration and healing of God's people in society; (3) the flourishing of the natural world; (4) new relationships with the nations, centered in Zion; (5) renewal from sin and enabling of obedience to Torah; (6) restoration of righteous leadership in Israel; and (7) God's presence renewed in the land.[527] These themes are prominent especially in Isaiah, where our primary texts that describe the coming of a new heaven and new earth reside.[528]

---

[526] Several variants of the prepositional phrase κατὰ τὸ ἐπάγγελμα exist, which render "promise" in the plural, though not significantly impacting the meaning of the verse.
[527] Middleton, *A New Heaven and a New Earth*, 105-7.
[528] For example, see Isa. 9:7; 11:4-5; 16:5; 32:16-19; 60:21; 65:17-25; 66:15-24 alongside Matt. 5:6; 19:28; Rom. 8:19-21; 14:17; Rev. 21.

A number of Second Temple texts expand on these ideas (e.g., *1 En.* 45:4–5; 72:1; 91:16–17; *2 Bar.* 32:6; 44:12; 57:2; 4 Ezra 7:75; *Jub.* 1:29; *Ps. Sol.* 17:40; *Sib. Or.* 5.211–12). First Enoch 45:4–5 foresees the transformation of the heaven and earth to a state of blessedness, absent of sin and evil. Fourth Ezra 7:75 is similar, noting "we shall be kept in rest until those times come when you will renew the creation." A common theme throughout these traditions is that the nature of the earth, and society in particular, will be transformed. Blessing, mercy, peace, and righteousness are common themes evoked in these texts of eschatological renewal. This cluster of associated ideas is likely in the mind of our author as well, as he describes the new heaven and new earth as a place "in which righteousness resides" (ἐν οἷς δικαιοσύνη κατοικεῖ). These characteristics of the age to come are associated with the reign of the Messiah in the Old Testament (e.g., Ps. 72:1–7; Isa. 2:2–4; 9:7; 11:4–5; 16:5; 32:16–19; Jer. 23:5–6; Mic. 4:1–4; Zech. 9:9–10) and likely informs our author here. This also affirms that it is the transformation of the world about which our author is most concerned, reinforcing the symbiotic nature of ethics and eschatology in the New Testament.[529]

2 PETER 3:14–18: CLOSING REMARKS

[14] Therefore, loved ones, while waiting for these things, make every effort to be found at peace, pure and blameless in Him,

[15] and regard the patience of our Lord as salvation, just as also our beloved brother Paul wrote to you, in accordance with the wisdom which was given to him,

[16] as he does also in all his letters, speaking in them about these things, in which some things are hard to understand, which the ignorant and unstable will distort to their own ruin, as they do with the rest of the Scriptures.

[17] Therefore, loved ones, knowing this beforehand, keep guarding yourselves in order that you might not lose your own steadfastness through being led astray by the error of unruly people.

[18] But keep growing in the grace and knowledge of our Lord and Savior Jesus Christ. To him be the glory, both now and into the day of the age. [Amen.]"

---

[529] So Bauckham comments, "Such passages emphasize the radical discontinuity between the old and the new, but it is nevertheless clear that they intend to describe a renewal, not an abolition, of creation (cf. *1 Enoch* 54:4–5; Rom. 8:21)" (Bauckham, *Jude–2 Peter*, 326. See also Witherington, *Letters for Hellenized Christians*, 382).

3:14 – The start of a distinct textual unit is marked here by three indicators: (1) the preposition διό ("Therefore"), which draws logical inference from the previous unit, and to some extent the entire discourse; (2) the reorientation to the audience via the vocative ἀγαπητοί ("loved ones"); and (3) the transition to imperatival material in the hortatory unit that follows (here σπουδάσατε). As Neyrey details, NT letters frequently contain a greeting, postscript, and doxology in their closing sections, though not all letters contain each of these elements.

Greetings	Postscripts	Doxologies
Rom 16:3–16, 21–23	—	Rom 16:25–27
1 Cor 16:19–20	1 Cor 16:21–22	1 Cor 16:23–24
2 Cor 13:12–13	—	2 Cor 13:14
—	Gal 6:18	Gal 6:16, 18
—	Eph 6:21–22	Eph 6:23–24
Phil 4:21–22	Phil 4:14–19	Phil 4:20, 23
1 Thess 5:26	1 Thess 5:27	1 Thess 5:24
—	2 Thess 3:17	2 Thess 3:16, 18
2 Tim 4:19	2 Tim 4:20–21	2 Tim 4:22
Titus 3:15a	—	Titus 3:15b
Philemon 23–24	—	Philemon 25
1 Peter 5:13–14	1 Peter 5:12	1 Peter 5:11, 14b[530]

Second Peter, by comparison, contains no personal greetings or personal remarks but concludes with ethical exhortations and a brief doxology. The concluding *peroratio* of the letter follows the customary rhetorical convention of offering a concluding recap to the argument. Both Watson and Witherington identify the *peroratio* of the letter within 3:14–18a.[531] In this section, the author summarizes the major argument of the letter and/or makes a final appeal in order to complete the act of persuasion.[532] As Witherington summarizes, "In any rhetorical discourse the *peroratio* was of great importance as it brought the discourse to its rational and emotional conclusion. It was expected to include some repetition of previous main points, an appeal to the deeper emotions, and perhaps some amplification on a particular sticking point as well (Aristotle, *Rhet.*,

---

[530] Adapted from Neyrey, *2 Peter, Jude*, 246.
[531] Watson, *Invention, Arrangement, and Style*, 141–42; Witherington, *Letters for Hellenized Christians*, 274–75.
[532] Witherington and Myers, *New Testament Rhetoric*, 21.

3.19.1419b.1; Cicero, *Part. Or.*, 15.52–17.58; Quintilian, *Inst.*, 6.1)."[533] Michael Frye has argued that 2 Peter's *peroratio* offers an inverse recapitulation of the letter which can be identified through lexical ties with the previous sections.

Lexeme	Location in 3:14–18a	Reference earlier in 2 Peter
ἀγαπητοί	3:14	3:1, 3:8, 3:17
προσδοκῶντες	3:14	3:12, 13
σπουδάσατε	3:14	1:5, 1:10, 1:15, 3:12
ἄσπιλοι καί ἀμώμητοι	3:14	2:13 (positive forms)
εὑρεθῆναι	3:14	3:10
εἰρήνῃ	3:14	1:2
μακροθυμίαν	3:15	3:9
σοφίαν	3:15b	1:16
ἔγραψεν/ γραφὰς	3:15b, 3:16	1:20, 3:1
ἀστήρικτοι	3:16	2:14
ἀπώλειαν	3:16	2:1 (twice), 2:3, 3:7
φυλάσσεσθε	3:17	2:5
ἀθεσμων	3:17	2:7
πλάνῃ	3:17	2:18
στηριγμοῦ	3:17	1:12
χάριτι	3:18	1:2
γνώσει	3:18	1:5, 1:6, 1:16, 1:22; negative forms in 2:12, 3:3; ἐπι- forms in 1:2, 1:3, 1:8, 2:20, 2:21 (twice)[534]

While 2 Peter is sometimes thought to be a disjointed letter, such analyses reveal that it is quite carefully crafted and contains a number of elements of cohesion which tie the major units together.

After marking his conclusion and reorientating his address to his audience ("Therefore loved ones"; Διό ἀγαπητοί), our author ties the eschatological events described in the previous section ("while waiting for these things" [ταῦτα προσδοκῶντες]) with the first of a string of imperatives in 3:14–18 (σπουδάσατε [also 1:10], ἡγεῖσθε, φυλάσσεσθε, αὐξάνετε). Such a

---

[533] Witherington, *Letters for Hellenized Christians*, 382–83.
[534] Cited from Michael Frye, "Identifying a Summarizing Structure in 2 Peter 3:14–18a through Discourse Analysis," Unpublished paper submitted to PhD Seminar, Liberty University, Lynchburg, VA, May 10, 2024.

clustering of commands, which by nature carry prominence, creates a crescendo for our author's conclusion.[535] The command states: "make every effort to be found at peace" (σπουδάσατε ... εὑρεθῆναι ἐν εἰρήνῃ). The imperative here is completed by the infinitive εὑρεθῆναι ("to be found") and reinforces a cluster of ideas connected to this word group from chapter 1 ("contributing all **eagerness**," σπουδὴν πᾶσαν παρεισενέγκαντες, cf. 1:5; "**be** all the more **eager**," μᾶλλον ... **σπουδάσατε**, cf. 1:10; "I will make every effort," **σπουδάσω**, cf. 1:15). He reactivates those ideas here while contextualizing them in the eschatological scenario described in chapter 3. They are now to direct their efforts at being found "at peace" (ἐν εἰρήνῃ), a term used elsewhere in the letter only in the opening greeting ("may grace and **peace** be multiplied to you"). While the "peace" envisioned here would no doubt carry over into their communal relationships,[536] the focus appears to be placed upon peace before Christ,[537] relating particularly to the coming judgment, as the activity is qualified with the attached modifiers "pure and blameless in Him" (ἄσπιλοι καὶ ἀμώμητοι[538] αὐτῷ). "Pure" and "blameless" are terms that occur several times in Paul's letters (Eph. 1:4; 5:27; Phil. 2:15; Col. 1:22; 1 Tim. 6:14) and contrast directly with how the false teachers were described as "blots and blemishes" (σπίλοι καὶ μῶμοι; cf. 2:13). It is clear from Peter's urgent language that the moral transformation that comes through communion with God (cf. 2 Pet. 1:3-4) requires intentionality. Davids is insightful: "The appropriate lifestyle of a follower of Jesus does not just happen; it requires effort, especially since the forces of the surrounding culture will attempt to make apprentices of Jesus adjust their behavior back to that of the majority culture."[539]

3:15 – The thought from the previous verse is continued (καὶ; "and") in 3:15, where our author adds a second imperative: "regard the patience of our Lord as salvation" (καὶ τὴν τοῦ κυρίου ἡμῶν μακροθυμίαν σωτηρίαν ἡγεῖσθε). The "patience" (μακροθυμίαν) in mind here connects back to Peter's discussion of the apparent delay of the παρουσία (cf. 2 Pet. 3:4),

---

[535] See Fresch, "2 Peter," 624.
[536] See Davids, *The Letters of 2 Peter and Jude*, 296.
[537] See Bauckham, *Jude–2 Peter*, 327.
[538] Some mss. read αμωμοι (A 5. 33. 442. 642. 1243. 1448. 1611. 1852. 2344cf. NA28), though the better witnesses have ἀμώμητοι, which is to be preferred.
[539] Davids, *The Letters of 2 Peter and Jude*, 294.

which Peter answered, in part, by explaining God was "being patient" (μακροθυμεῖ) for the sake of human repentance (cf. 3:9). This is further connected in that the patience referenced is to be understood as "salvation" (σωτηρίαν), meaning eschatological deliverance.

Peter invokes a new source of support for his argument, commenting: "just as also our beloved brother Paul wrote to you" (καθὼς καὶ ὁ ἀγαπητὸς ἡμῶν ἀδελφὸς Παῦλος . . . ἔγραψεν ὑμῖν). The immediate context would seem to indicate that Paul also wrote about God's patience as grounds for the delay in the return of Christ and coming judgment, though it's possible the previous statement of "being found at peace" could be included as well. The concept of divine forbearance as related to judgment can be found in Paul's letter to the Romans (2:4; 9:22), which contains the same lemma used for "patience" (μακροθυμία) here. If we broaden the reference to also include the main clause of 3:14, which discusses being found at peace and being spotless and blameless, the list of relevant Pauline texts would expand significantly.[540]

In referring to Paul as "our beloved brother," our author does not follow the more common convention of the fathers of referring to Paul as apostle but uses familial language that may even seem to lessen Paul's authority, though contextually that is not the author's intent, since he appeals to Paul in support of his own argument. Davids here suggests, "What is noticeable in 2 Peter is that our author does not refer to Paul as an apostle, which virtually all passages in the apostolic fathers do, but uses the normal term for a fellow worker in the fictive family of the Jesus movement."[541] Whether this is evidence of a discerning pseudepigrapher or a mark of authenticity is debated, but the convention certainly stands out and resonates more with the depiction of Christian workers in the book of Acts than the works of the second-century fathers (cf. Acts 16:40; 21:7, 17–20; 28:15, though it is also used of non-Christian Jewish addressees as well, cf. Acts 23:1, 5–6; 28:17; see also Philem. 1).

It is worth considering why our author felt the need to invoke Paul's name. Frey's suggestion seems likely: "The reference to Paul is necessitated

---

[540] See Introduction: Authorship and Date – Reference to Paul's Letters for discussion. Neyrey, for example, suggests at least five Pauline letters which have significant overlap with 2 Peter.

[541] Davids, *The Letters of 2 Peter and Jude*, 298.

by the situation. The author cannot ignore Paul, probably because others – the opponents, or perhaps other 'unstable' people in the communities – referred to him in justifying their positions."[542] This may mean that the confusion that existed in Peter's audience concerning the parousia paralleled similar kinds of confusion that Paul's teachings sometimes created, such as over the day of the Lord in 2 Thessa. 2:1–17, or Paul's teachings on Law and grace as in Rom. 6:1–14. It is possible Paul's teachings were being misused by the false teachers to support their perspective, and Peter must thus address this part of their argumentation.

While it is sometimes doubted that the historical Peter would reference Paul in support of his argument given the criticisms that Paul brought against Peter in Galatians 2, Gregory the Great saw this instead as a mark of Peter's humility:

Look how Peter says that there is much to be admired in Paul's writings. Yet in his letters, Paul criticized Peter. Peter could have hardly said what he did if he had not read Paul, but when he read him he would have discovered criticism of himself in them. Thus, the friend of truth was able to praise even the fact that he had been criticized, and he was happy to do so because he realized that he had been wrong.[543]

Bauckham agrees that this supposed apostolic tension is often overstated, arguing that "it is naïve to suppose that their disagreement at Antioch need have prevented Peter from writing of Paul in the terms used here. It was only one incident in a long relationship of which we otherwise know next to nothing."[544] Since Peter and Paul also shared common associates (e.g., Barnabas [cf. Acts 9:27], John Mark [cf. Acts 12:12; 1 Pet. 5:13], Silas/Silvanus [cf. Acts 15:40; 1 Pet. 5:12]), it is hard to imagine this disagreement caused a lifelong separation or antagonism.

While we learn that Peter's audience was also written to by Paul,[545] this does not help much to narrow the audience's location or situation, since

---

[542] Frey, *The Letter of Jude and the Second Letter of Peter*, 428. See also Green, *Jude and 2 Peter*, 338.
[543] Gregory the Great, "Lessons in Job," 2.6.9, in *Patrologia Latina*, ed. J. P. Migne (Paris: Migne, 1844–64), 79: 1, 100.
[544] Bauckham, *Jude–2 Peter*, 328.
[545] Though some commentators believe this to be fictive, it is hard to imagine the reference would make sense if the recipients of this text were not also recipients of a Pauline letter. If they had not received such a letter, the appeal would be unconvincing, and if they had,

Paul's footprint of extant writings is significant, and there are likely other letters sent and possibly even circulated that were not preserved in the final Pauline collection (cf. Col. 4:16).[546] If the Asiatic style of the letter would aid in identification of the audience, the "letters" in mind could be narrowed to Colossians, Ephesians, and possibly Galatians.[547] Discussions of this passage often conclude that Peter's statement here is evidence of the late and pseudepigraphal nature of the text, since a formal collection of Paul's letters would not be circulating until the second century.[548] As Laird, among others, has recently argued,[549] based on ancient literary conventions, it is not unthinkable that a collection of Paul's letters was prepared by Paul and/or his associates during or shortly after Paul's lifetime, with direction from Paul himself, which was possibly expanded later over time.[550] It is also likely that partial collections of Paul's letters were circulated among churches during his lifetime as well (cf. Col. 4:16). This statement can provide neither definitive evidence for or against the authenticity of the letter. At minimum it would illustrate the familiarity shared by the intended audience with some of Paul's teachings and at least a few of Paul's letters.

Paul's letter writing is said to have been produced "in accordance with the wisdom which was given to him" (κατὰ τὴν δοθεῖσαν αὐτῷ σοφίαν). Wisdom as a divine gift occurs with some commonality in the New Testament (e.g., 1 Cor. 12:8; Eph. 1:17; Col. 1:19; Jas. 1:5). James 1:5, for example, reads "if any among you is lacking wisdom, ask God, who gives

---

the author clearly knows the recipients or at least knows of them. It seems unlikely to me that 2 Peter was sent to "nowhere." Reese agrees, adding, "The reference to Paul at this point most likely indicates that the church or churches that are addressed in this letter are familiar with Paul. They may be churches that were founded by Paul or the Pauline mission, and they are churches that have received a letter or letters from Paul" (Reese, *2 Peter & Jude*, 174).

[546] Some scholars believe this to refer to the letter to the Ephesians (e.g., see Douglas A. Campbell, *Framing Paul: An Epistolary Biography* [Grand Rapids: Eerdmans, 2014], 267–96).

[547] See Bauckham, *Jude-2 Peter*, 330.

[548] E.g., Kelly, *The Epistles of Peter and Jude*, 370–71.

[549] E.g., Richards, *Paul and First-Century Letter Writing*, 218–23.

[550] Laird, *The Pauline Corpus in Early Christianity*, 17–39. Bauckham agrees, stating, "Pauline letters may have begun to circulate to churches other than those to which they were written even before Paul's death, and small local collections probably preceded the formation of the corpus of ten letters" (Bauckham, *Jude-2 Peter*, 331). Contra Witherington, *Letters for Hellenized Christians*, 386.

generously to all without reproaching, and it will be given to you." In other places in the New Testament, wisdom is specifically construed as a gift of the Spirit (e.g., Acts 6:3–10; 1 Cor. 2:1–16; 12:7–8; Eph. 1:17; Col. 1:9), so that being given divine wisdom may be akin in some sense to texts in the New Testament that speak of "divine inspiration" (e.g., 2 Tim. 3:16; 2 Pet. 1:21). Peter's language here depicts Paul in a similar way as his discussion of prophetic inspiration in 1:16–21, where the Holy Spirit carried along the prophets to bring about a true "word from the Lord." Like the prophets, Paul may also be considered a trusted voice because his message is of divine, not human origin. Associating divine inspiration with Paul's writings is sometimes seen as a product of late Christianity, again pushing our text into the late first or early second century, but it is clear from the texts cited above that Paul and other apostles understood their teaching to already carry divine inspiration and authority, derived from their commission by and proclamation of Jesus Christ. If they believed their verbal proclamations about Christ to have such authority, it is reasonable to assume their written proclamations would have been understood to have carried the same weight.

3:16 – Peter's appeal to Paul continues here, expanding from recognizing the wisdom in Paul's writings to this audience to "as he does also in all his letters" (ὡς καὶ ἐν πάσαις ἐπιστολαῖς). As noted above, our text here need not require a full accounting of Paul's complete collection of letters to have existed when this letter was written. It requires knowledge of Paul's ministry of letter writing and knowledge that Paul produced multiple letters. As discussed previously, these letters were likely shared between churches during Paul's lifetime. If Paul followed the ancient literary practice of keeping personal copies of his letters, either himself or among his associates, it is reasonable to assume an initial collection of Paul's letters to be collated near the end of his life or shortly after his death. For the purposes of 2 Peter, this text requires merely the knowledge of multiple letters of Paul being in existence (πάσαις ["all"] would imply at least three or more) and that some circulation of those letters has occurred. To demand anything beyond this is an overdetermination of the text.

Our author gives further reference to his reason for invoking Paul in stating: "speaking in them about these things" (λαλῶν ἐν αὐταῖς περὶ τούτων). The "these things" (τούτων) that our text alludes to would likely, again, be the return of Christ, the notion of divine forbearance related to eschatological judgment, and possibly the concepts of peace with Christ and moral purity (cf. 3:14–15, via 3:8–10). Particularly with the themes of divine forbearance and the return of Christ, the conceptual overlap here would loom largest with Romans, 1 and/or 2 Thessalonians, and possibly 1 Corinthians, though if the concepts of peace with Christ and moral purity are included, this would expand to a much larger list of possible Pauline texts that our author has in mind.

A clarifying prepositional phrase follows: "in which some things are hard to understand" (ἐν αἷς ἐστιν δυσνόητά τινα). "In which" (ἐν αἷς) here references "all his letters" (πάσαις ταῖς ἐπιστολαῖς) in the previous participial phrase, and Peter here recognizes that Paul's letters can be difficult to interpret. It is possible that our author admits here their personal difficulty with interpreting Paul's letters, though he may also be speaking generally of how Paul's letters have been misunderstood and misused. This issue can be seen in the Pauline corpus in the comparison of 1 and 2 Corinthians or 1 and 2 Thessalonians, where Paul seeks to reinforce and correct misperceptions of his first letter.[551] Our word for "hard to understand" (δυσνόητά) is another biblical *hapax*, found only here, and also sparingly in other early Christian literature (e.g., *Herm. Sim.* 9.14.4).

Our author indicates that the difficulty of interpreting Paul's letters has created an opportunity for the false teachers to spread misunderstanding: "which the ignorant and unstable will distort to their own ruin" (ἃ οἱ ἀμαθεῖς καὶ ἀστήρικτοι στρεβλώσουσιν[552] ... πρὸς τὴν ἰδίαν αὐτῶν ἀπώλειαν). The false teachers are "ignorant" (ἀμαθεῖς; "without learning"), though this likely does not mean that they have not been taught, since they have some knowledge of foundational Christian teachings and were apparently considered genuine followers at one point (see discussions on 2 Pet. 2:20–22). Rather, they have chosen ignorance and "deliberately suppressed" (cf. 2 Pet. 3:5) the knowledge they had received. They are also "unstable"

---

[551] There is debate among scholars on whether 2 Thessalonians should be regarded as authentic, often based on the argument that the letters do not cohere. For a recent examination, see Sydney Tooth, *Suddenness and Signs: The Eschatologies of 1 and 2 Thessalonians* (Tübingen: Mohr Siebeck, 2024).

[552] Some mss. read στρεβλουσιν (ℵ A B C² Ψ 5. 33. 81. 307. 436. 1448. 1611ᶜ. 1735. 2492 Byz co; cf. NA28), which is followed in the NA27, while the NA28 reads στρεβλώσουσιν, following 𝔓⁷² C*ᵛⁱᵈ P 442. 642. 1175. 1243. 1611*. 1739. 1852. The change of reading here follows the future tense reading rather than the present.

(ἀστήρικτοι), a term used in 2:14 for the targets of the false teachers (δελεάζοντες ψυχὰς ἀστηρίκτους; "enticing weak souls") and a positive form of which Peter used to describe his goal of ensuring these believers are "confirmed ('stabilized') in the truth you possess" (ἐστηριγμένους ἐν τῇ παρούσῃ ἀληθείᾳ). The work of the false teachers is thus depicted as an "undoing" of the ministry of the apostles. The two groups are moving in precisely opposite directions.

The false teachers "will distort" (στρεβλώσουσιν) these teachings "to their own ruin" (πρὸς τὴν ἰδίαν αὐτῶν ἀπώλειαν). The "destruction" (ἀπώλειαν) of the false teachers is a prevalent theme in 2 Peter. Their "destructive beliefs" (αἱρέσεις ἀπωλείας; cf. 2:1) bring confusion and corruption to the community, and their rejection of Christ brings "swift destruction" (ταχινὴν ἀπώλειαν; cf. 2:1) upon them, and destruction that is "not asleep" (οὐ νυστάζει). Just as the world at the time of Noah was "destroyed" (ἀπώλετο; cf. 3:6) by flood, so too the ungodly of this age will face judgment and "destruction" (ἀπωλείας; 3:7) on the day of the Lord.

The distortion of the false teachers of Paul's teachings is being done "as they do with the rest of the Scriptures" (ὡς καὶ τὰς λοιπὰς γραφὰς). The theological and ethical agenda of the false teachers thus finds itself in opposition to the trajectory of the Scriptures in their denial of holy living and their denial of the authority of God to judge and the imminence of the day of judgment. It is frequently noted here that our author appears to include Paul's letters as a part of "the Scriptures." Reese states forthright, "Peter places Paul's letters on the same footing as the Old Testament."[553] The New Testament portrays a clear regard for the Jewish Scriptures as authoritative and a true "word from God." Though one might debate what texts were included in that list of Jewish Scriptures,[554] the bulk of what we would call the "Old Testament" is referenced and quoted as authoritative texts in the NT. Jesus' teachings formed the core of the teachings of the apostles and were clearly regarded by the NT authors with that same sense of being an authoritative and true "word from God."

When we ask the question of when, how, and where the New Testament took on that same level of authoritative status, we enter slightly foggier territory. As mentioned previously, the teachings of the apostles as those

---

[553] Reese, *2 Peter & Jude*, 174–75.
[554] Texts like Esther and Song of Solomon, for example, are not referenced by NT authors.

taught and commissioned by Jesus were clearly viewed as authoritative by the churches in the first century, though even there, some struggles existed.[555] Following the trajectory from Jesus, to the apostles, to their writings, to the canon has a certain coherence about it, but the historical details of the development of this trajectory are sometimes more vague than one might desire.[556] Davids' assessment here is helpful:

> The truth is that we will likely never pin down when the psychological barrier between "the Scriptures" and the newly produced writings of the Jesus movement (including the writings of Paul) was crossed; it was probably crossed at different times in different communities and even in different individuals within the various communities. If a community had been founded by Paul, they certainly believed they had heard "the word of the Lord" from him as he preached; he had been their source of truth and enlightenment, including their source of how to interpret the Jewish Scriptures.[557]

An emerging authoritative sense can be found within the New Testament itself, though how one arrives from there to the complete NT canon of twenty-seven texts, particularly with texts like 2 Peter, contains some points of ambiguity and controversy that cannot fully be avoided.

3:17 – Our author signals he is drawing the letter to a close with οὖν ("Therefore"). Two imperatival sentences will follow along with a closing benediction.[558] Our author also, for a fifth time (see 3:1, 8, 14, 15), addresses his audience as "loved ones" (ἀγαπητοί), reinforcing the familial vision that he has for this faith community and continuing to build rapport and connection with his audience. The first imperative is attached to several phrases and a subordinate clause, beginning with the participial phrase "knowing *this* beforehand" (προγινώσκοντες). What is known before is not clear from the grammatical structure of the sentence, though from the context it seems likely the "reminders" (cf. 1:12, 13; 3:1-2) that Peter has offered throughout the letter form the content of this prior knowledge.

The imperfective (present tense) command is issued to "keep guarding yourselves" (Ὑμεῖς ... φυλάσσεσθε). Though some debate exists among

---

[555] Note Paul's relationship with the Corinthian church, for example.
[556] For a recent study, see Benjamin P. Laird, *Creating the Canon: Composition, Controversy, and the Authority of the New Testament* (Downers Grove: IVP Academic, 2023).
[557] Davids, *The Letters of 2 Peter and Jude*, 308.
[558] On comparison with other NT letter closings, see Davids, *The Letters of 2 Peter and Jude*, 313-14.

grammarians as to the impact of verbal aspect on the imperative mood, it is likely here that the choice of tense is either to encourage this activity as a matter of ongoing importance or to highlight the urgency or prominence of this command.[559] The clustering of ethical commands at the end of the letter represent the climax of our author's intended response for his audience to the teaching they have received. Whereas the false teachers have strayed from their allegiance to Christ and rejected the apostles' teachings about his lordship and coming judgment, these believers are to be on guard against such teachings and behaviors that would likewise pull them astray.

The purpose of the command is "in order that you might not lose your own steadfastness" (ἵνα μὴ ... ἐκπέσητε τοῦ ἰδίου στηριγμοῦ). As Witherington states, "The pathos of this appeal is apparent: our author is genuinely concerned about the possibility of apostasy, and he believes there is a real danger that the audience might not continue on the good path they have already been following."[560] Here again our author uses lexical ties to reinforce the rhetorical force of his discourse, with his audience being "confirmed in the truth" (ἐστηριγμένους ἐν τῇ ... ἀληθείᾳ; cf. 1:12), the false teachers "enticing weak souls" (δελεάζοντες ψυχὰς ἀστηρίκτους; cf. 2:14), and themselves being "unstable" (ἀστήρικτοι; cf. 3:16) people. The discourse has been shaped to demonstrate that those who follow apostolic teaching stand on a firm foundation, while those who stray from or resist it are unsteady and insecure.

The means by which they might lose their own steadfastness is "through being led astray" (συναπαχθέντες), obviously by the false teachers. The language of journeying has occurred with some consistency throughout the

---

[559] For some of the key sources in the emergence of the debate, see Stanley E. Porter, *Verbal Aspect in the Greek of the New Testament, with Reference to Tense and Mood* (New York: Peter Lang, 1989); Buist M. Fanning, *Verbal Aspect in New Testament Greek* (Oxford: Clarendon Press, 1990); Constantine R. Campbell, *Verbal Aspect, the Indicative Mood, and Narrative: Soundings in the Greek of the New Testament* (New York: Peter Lang, 2007); Steven E. Runge, *Discourse Grammar of the Greek New Testament: A Practical Introduction for Teaching and Exegesis* (Peabody: Hendrickson, 2010); Steve E. Runge and Christopher J. Fresch, eds., *The Greek Verb Revisited: A Fresh Approach for Biblical Exegesis* (Bellingham: Lexham Press, 2016); David L. Mathewson "Verbal Aspect in Imperatival Constructions in Pauline Ethical Injunctions," *Filología Neotestamentaria* 9.17 (1996): 21–35; Stanley E. Porter, "Aspect and Imperatives Once More," *BAGL* 7 (2018): 141–72.

[560] Witherington, *Letters and Homilies for Hellenized Christians*, 383.

discourse and is reinforced again here (e.g., 2 Pet. 1:4, 10–11; 2:2, 15, 20–21; 3:9).[561] Peter envisions his audience as partaking in the journey of faith, with the "eternal kingdom" (cf. 1:11) as their ultimate destination, one that he himself hoped to soon reach (cf. 1:15). Along the way are many dangers, and the chief danger now is those who would cast aside the way of faith and hope in Christ for pursuit of greed, ambition, sexual desire, and detachment from the divine life (cf. 2:10–22, via 1:3–4).

The means of being led astray is further narrowed in stating: "by the error of unruly people" (τῇ τῶν ἀθέσμων πλάνῃ). Additional lexical ties here create cohesion with earlier portions of the discourse. Just as Lot was worn down "by lawless persons" (τῶν **ἀθέσμων**; cf. 2:7), so too Peter's audience is in danger of following the wrong path of the "unruly" (τῶν ἀθέσμων). The false teachers have gone "astray" (ἐπλανήθησαν; cf. 2:15) and live "in error" (ἐν **πλάνῃ**; cf. 2:18), and it is this "error" (τῇ ... πλάνῃ) that Peter's audience must avoid.

3:18 – The final imperative of the discourse is given here at the close of the letter: "But keep growing in the grace and knowledge" (αὐξάνετε δὲ ἐν χάριτι καὶ γνώσει). Our letter opened with a prayer for "grace and peace" (χάρις ... καὶ εἰρήνη) to be "multiplied" among the recipients through their "knowledge of God and of Jesus our Lord" (ἐν ἐπιγνώσει τοῦ θεοῦ καὶ Ἰησοῦ τοῦ κυρίου ἡμῶν). The repetition here of "grace" (χάρις) and "knowledge" (γνώσει / ἐπιγνώσει) again creates cohesion through lexical ties between the opening of the letter and its introductory themes and its closing. Further cohesion is obtained with the direction of this knowledge being specified as "of our Lord and Savior Jesus Christ" (τοῦ κυρίου ἡμῶν καὶ σωτῆρος Ἰησοῦ Χριστοῦ), also paralleling the knowledge of God and "Jesus our Lord" in 1:2. The Christology of our letter sees Jesus as the ascended king, ruling the kingdom as Lord on high, and one to whom is owed great allegiance.

The greatness of Jesus is further established with the prayer: "To him be the glory" (αὐτῷ ἡ δόξα). The glory of God/Christ has been established elsewhere in the letter (cf. 1:3, 17) and is reinforced again here in the closing benediction. Since dishonor and denial of the lordship and authority of Jesus, particularly related to the coming judgment, were the central points

---

[561] See also Sylva, "A Unified Field Picture of Second Peter 1.3–15," 91–118.

of emphasis in our discourse, it is fitting here for a closing recognition of honor to conclude the letter. This glory is described as existing "both now and into the day of the age" (καὶ νῦν καὶ εἰς ἡμέραν αἰῶνος),[562] echoing the establishment of Christ's transfiguration, authority and rule, and future return earlier in the letter. As Neyrey describes:

> The letter's doxology, moreover, speaks of Jesus' glory both now and on the day of eternity; the mention of that future day seems to summarize the recent discussion about the day of his coming. These are not bland formulas, for the letter was concerned with acknowledging the debt of honor due Jesus, both as benefactor and as judge at the parousia. And part of his benefaction was the very promises and prophecies of his coming.[563]

Our author has provided a potent defense of the reliability of the apostolic witness concerning the reign and rule of the glorified Christ who is promised to come again from heaven to bring about the fulness of the kingdom, his eschatological reign, and the judgment of the living and the dead. Though this is a text often neglected in the church today, the vigor of 2 Peter's rhetoric urgently reminds the Church to take seriously their calling to live life in union with the Triune God in anticipation of the return of our Lord Jesus Christ. Such a reminder calls his church to holiness, to mission, to worship, and to love.

---

[562] The bracketed "Amen" (αμην) included in the NA27 text as possibly authentic is removed here on the basis of witnesses B 1175. 1243. 1739. vg^{mss}. Metzger had noted here: "If the word were present originally, it is difficult to account for its absence in such notable Eastern and Western witnesses" (Metzger, *A Textual Commentary on the Greek New Testament*, 638).

[563] Neyrey, *2 Peter, Jude*, 247.

A Theology of 2 Peter

Having examined the background and context of the letter and its various parts, a reflection upon the major themes of 2 Peter would be an appropriate conclusion to the task of analysis and reflection. While the letter of 2 Peter is mostly focused on the issues of the denial of the return of Christ and the promotion of moral libertinism, several other themes emerge in the analysis of the letter. While other less prevalent themes may be present in the letter, the major themes addressed below are 2 Peter's portrayal of (1) God the Father and Jesus Christ; (2) revelation, prophecy, and inspiration, (3) judgment and salvation, and (4) "theosis."

GOD THE FATHER AND JESUS CHRIST

The relationship between God and Jesus does not find clear definition in 2 Peter. From the beginning of the letter, the two are mentioned as sharing in divine activities, such that at times it is unclear if it is God "the Father" (cf. 1:17) or Jesus, "the Son" (1:17) in view. In 1:1, Peter writes concerning τοῦ θεοῦ ἡμῶν καὶ σωτῆρος Ἰησοῦ Χριστοῦ ("our God and Savior Jesus Christ"), a construction that has a similar repetition in 1:2, which states τοῦ θεοῦ καὶ Ἰησοῦ τοῦ κυρίου ἡμῶν ("God and Jesus Christ our Lord"). Commentators debate the application of the "Granville Sharp Rule" in this section. As Merkle summarizes the rule, the construction obtains "when a single article governs two nouns (substantives) of the same case that are connected by καί, the refer to the same person. This rule applies only to nouns that are (1) singular, (2) personal, (3) nonproper, and (4) in the same case."[1] In the first construction,

---

[1] Benjamin L. Merkle, *Exegetical Gems from Biblical Greek: A Refreshing Guide to Grammar and Interpretation* (Grand Rapids: Baker Academic, 2019), 39.

all four conditions of the rule obtain (τοῦ θεοῦ . . . καὶ σωτῆρος), while in the second, only three of the four obtain, since Ἰησοῦ is a personal noun. It would seem then that Peter here both references Jesus as God and references Jesus and God as distinct persons, language that will appear again in 1:17.

A similar intertwining of terms appears in relation to 2 Peter's use of the noun κύριος. Davids notes that of the fourteen uses of "Lord" (κύριος) in 2 Peter, eight are clearly references to Christ, while six are ambiguous, meaning they could refer to God the Father or to Jesus, though he concludes they are all likely references to Jesus.[2] Peter's Christology thus imagines Jesus' identity as being intertwined with that of God the Father, manifesting divine attributes and activities throughout the letter, while also being distinguishable from God "the Father" (cf. 1:3, 17).

Second Peter speaks less often of "God" (θεός) by name or title than he does of Jesus the Lord. In the opening section, God is one who possesses or bestows righteousness (1:1), provides grace and peace (1:2), provides all things for life and godliness (1:3), issues "great and precious promises" (1:4), and shares the divine nature (1:4). We learn later in the letter that God also bestows honor and glory on the Son (1:17); speaks from heaven (1:17); inspires prophetic utterances through the power of the Holy Spirit (1:21); did not spare the rebellious angels, the ancient world, or Sodom and Gomorrah (2:4–6); spared Noah and Lot (2:5–7); forms and sustains creation (3:5–6); and will judge the earth in the "day of God" (3:12). Such descriptions and activities are fitting both of Jewish and Christian understandings of the activity and nature of God, finding parallels throughout the Old Testament as well.

Second Peter describes Jesus through numerous titles and activities throughout the letter. As noted above, Peter begins with the statement that Jesus is God (cf. 2 Pet. 1:1) and that Peter is an emissary or ambassador (ἀπόστολος) who represents the Lord Jesus to the world. In the opening verses (1:1–2), Jesus is also referred to as "Christ" (Χριστοῦ), "Savior" (σωτῆρος), and "Lord" (κυρίου). As Christ, Jesus is the anointed Davidic heir who now occupies the eternal throne of the promised kingdom (cf. 2 Sam. 7:13, 16; 1 Chr. 17:14; 22:10; 28:7; Isa. 9:7; Dan. 4:3, 34; Luke 1:33; 2 Pet. 1:11), a position he occupies in the New Testament because of his

---

[2] Peter H. Davids, *A Theology of James, Peter, and Jude*, Biblical Theology of the New Testament (Grand Rapids: Zondervan, 2014), 234.

descent from David (cf. Matt. 1:1, 6; Luke 3:31; Rom. 1:4; 2 Tim. 2:8) and his anointing for this role (cf. Matt. 3:13-17; 26:6-13; Mark 1:9-11; 14:1-11; Luke 3:21-22; 4:18; 7:36-50; John 12:1-11; Acts 4:26-27; 10:38). As Savior, Jesus brings not only salvation from sins (cf. Matt. 1:21) but also from the eschatological judgment that is coming, the latter of which is the focal point of salvation for 2 Peter. The title "Savior" was also attributed at times to the Roman emperor, as well as to Israel's God (e.g., Isa. 40-55). As "Lord," Jesus is described both as one who has dominion and authority but also as one intimately connected to the divine identity of Israel's God. Κυρίος was a favorite way for the LXX translators to render the divine name, and a connection likely exists, particularly in certain "charged" contexts, with Jesus' presentation through this shared title.[3] Christ thus holds a place of supreme honor and authority. As Davids notes, Christ here supplants all other lords. There is no indication of other lords to whom this community is to bow the knee. Jesus is Lord over all. Jesus, as Lord, is ruler of the heavenly kingdom, and this kingdom is above all others.[4] Davids suggests, "The accent in 2 Peter is on Jesus as at least world ruler and, to the extent that his exercise of rule appears to have cosmic effects (at least in his parousia), as cosmic ruler."[5]

The relationship between God and Jesus is also framed in 2 Peter in terms of the dynamic of "Father" and "Son," as it is elsewhere in the New Testament, though particularly in the Gospel of John (e.g., Matt. 3:17; 17:5; 6:9; Mark 9:7; Luke 9:35; John 3:16; 5:19-20; 10:30; 14:6-10; Rom. 8:15, 29). While Peter's conception of God is not framed explicitly in the metaphysic of later Christian Trinitarian theism, it does, similar to Paul's conception,[6]

---

[3] For discussions, see Richard J. Bauckham, *Jesus and the God of Israel: God Crucified and Other Studies on the New Testament's Christology of Divine Identity* (Grand Rapids: Eerdmans, 2008); Simon J. Gathercole, *The Preexistent Son: Recovering the Christologies of Matthew, Mark, and Luke* (Grand Rapids: Eerdmans, 2006); Larry W. Hurtado, *Lord Jesus Christ: Devotion to Jesus in Earliest Christianity* (Grand Rapids: Eerdmans, 2003); C. Kavin Rowe, *Early Narrative Christology: The Lord in the Gospel of Luke* (Berlin: de Gruyter, 2006); N. T. Wright, *Jesus and the Victory of God* (Minneapolis: Fortress Press, 1996).
[4] As Davids notes (*The Letters of 2 Peter and Jude*, 152), citing Wright, *Jesus and the Victory of God*.
[5] Davids, *A Theology of James, Peter, and Jude*, 236.
[6] See Chris Tilling, *Paul's Divine Christology* (Grand Rapids: Eerdmans, 2015).

seem to beg the articulation of such a metaphysic. Jesus bears both categories of "human" identity (e.g., Christ), as well as close identification with Israel's God (God and Lord), with a relational dynamic being recognized between God as Father and Jesus as Son. Such conceptions certainly contain the necessary ingredients for what would be articulated later at Nicaea and Chalcedon concerning the nature(s) of God and Jesus.

The relationship of Jesus as "Son" and God as "Father" is specifically laid out in 2 Peter's recollection of the Transfiguration, an event recounted elsewhere in each of the Synoptic Gospels (Matt. 17:1–13; Mark 9:2–13; Luke 9:28–36). The Gospels portray that event as a significant moment of the affirmation and revelation of the identity of Jesus, confirming his close familial relation with Israel's God and his Messianic identity. Second Peter, playing off of those descriptions, directs the significance of the event primarily to the assurance of Christ's return. Just as a glimpse of the glory of Jesus was given at the Transfiguration, the full "unveiling" of the glory of Christ will be shown to the world in his return and the judgment that follows.[7] Such glory, derived from the Father, further affirms the exalted status that Jesus possesses as Lord, Savior, and Christ.

As "Lord," "Savior," and "Christ," Jesus also reigns over the "eternal kingdom" (cf. 1:11). The nature of this kingdom is not precisely defined in the letter, though certain elements can be drawn out from its details. Christ is the one who rules over this kingdom and is closely associated with Israel's God. This kingdom is also open to new inhabitants, as Peter himself is about to enter into it (cf. 1:15) and admonishes his audience to enter into it themselves (1:11). Entrance into this kingdom requires moral transformation (cf. 1:5–11), but the necessary qualifications are provided for those who seek entrance (i.e., "richly supplied," cf. 1:11; "all things necessary for life and devotion to God have been presented to us," cf. 1:3). The kingdom thus contains at least a King, Rule, People, and Law, and given that it has a spatial component to enter into, also a "Land" or Place.[8]

---

[7] See Bauckham, *2 Peter–Jude*, 81.

[8] See Scot McKnight, *Kingdom Conspiracy: Returning to the Radical Mission of the Local Church* (Grand Rapids: Brazos Press, 2016), where he develops and discusses these dimensions of the kingdom.

Entrance is obtained by those who submit to the King, his authority ("Rule"), and his "Law," which 2 Peter defines primarily in terms of the cultivation of those virtues that are derived from the very character and nature of God (cf. 1:5-7).

It is frequently noted by scholars that 2 Peter seems to omit several core elements of the gospel from its theological conceptions, and especially the cross and resurrection. Käsemann, for example, famously noted, "The Cross has disappeared from the Christian message; the *gloria Christi* dominates all else."[9] Käsemann's judgment may be overly harsh for several reasons. First, 2 Peter mentions itself as the "second letter" written to this audience (3:1), which thereby creates natural connections between itself and 1 Peter. This would mean, at least implicitly, a tacit agreement of the author with the content of that letter, which does discuss the cross and resurrection in more detail. Second, 2 Peter also speaks of Christ as the "Master who bought them" (2:1), and implicit here are connections to various "atonement theories" scattered across the New Testament. As Marshall recognizes, the redemptive language in 2:1 presents a case for an implicit recognition of the death of Jesus and its saving significance. This, coupled with Peter's emphasis on the future return of Jesus as Lord to judge the earth, then also implies acceptance of his resurrection, for it is the heavenly kingdom that he rules and not the underworld.[10] Second Peter's explicit attention is upon the glory of Christ, as Käsemann rightly recognizes, but this is because of his concern with the false teachers' denial of the reality of that event, not because he entirely supplants the cross and resurrection in his theology.

REVELATION, PROPHECY, AND INSPIRATION

Second Peter has become a central text in discussions on the inspiration of the text of Scripture, centered particularly around 1:16-21. Indeed, it

---

[9] Käsemann, "An Apologia for Primitive Christian Eschatology," 183.
[10] Marshall, *New Testament Theology*, 664-65. Bauckham here agrees, adding, "Christ is the Master of his Christian slaves because he has bought them (at the cost of his death). The image is the rather common New Testament one of redemption as the transferal of slaves by purchase from one owner to another (cf., Acts 20:28; Rom. 6:17-18; 1 Cor. 6:20; 7:23; 1 Pet. 1:18-19; Rev. 5:9; 14:3-4)" (Bauckham, *2 Peter-Jude*, WBT, 73).

would be surprising to find a theological source discussing this topic that did not make mention of this text, typically alongside of 2 Tim. 3:16–17. While implications for canonicity, inerrancy, and other such topics derived from this text are not, of course, 2 Peter's focus, the letter's discussion of these topics are unavoidable in such discussion. While this material is found primarily in chapter 1, chapters 2 and 3 add relevant material as well, all centered on the defense of the reliability of divine revelation over and against the denials of the false teachers, who likely have portrayed these traditions about Christ and his return as "cleverly created myths" (1:16).

For 2 Peter, there is a connection between the revelation of God's past action through the prophets (cf. 1:19–21; 3:4–6) and the reliability of prophetic teachings concerning the future return of Christ and final judgment (cf. 1:16–18; 3:7–13). The fact that God has acted justly and the prophets spoken truly in the past ensures the reliability that such prophetic pronouncements concerning the future, now sourced in the testimony of the apostles, can be trusted (cf. 1:16–18; 3:2, 15). Indeed, such speaking is reliable not on the basis of the authority of the prophets or apostles themselves but because their speaking is an act in which they are "brought along by the Holy Spirit" and thus "spoke from God" (1:21). Here is contained the only explicit reference to the Holy Spirit in 2 Peter in 1:21, where the Spirit is the means of prophetic inspiration and thus the assurance of its reliability. Such divine speaking provides humanity with the only reliable message concerning God, his desires for human lives, and the future consummation of his plans. As Bauckham summarizes, "The darkness of the present world is its ignorance of God. Prophecy is a lamp in this darkness because it is a provisional, partial revelation of God. It points forward in hope to the full revelation of God which will be possible for the first time at the Parousia and will characterize the age to come."[11]

While 2 Peter draws both from various OT and Jewish sources (Genesis, Exodus, Numbers, Psalms, Proverbs, Isaiah, Ezekiel, Daniel, Habakkuk, Malachi, 1 Enoch, Testament of the Twelve Patriarchs, Assumption of Moses, Sibylline Oracles, etc.), he also assigns a place of authority to Paul and his writings. For 2 Peter, Paul writes and teaches "with wisdom" (3:15),

---

[11] Bauckham, *2 Peter–Jude*, 98.

a sign of belief in his own divine leading, and appears to assign a status to Paul's writings that places them on the same level with "the rest of the Scriptures" (3:16).

As argued above, the teachings of the apostles as persons themselves taught and commissioned by Jesus were clearly viewed as authoritative by the churches in the first century, even when tensions concerning their authority might have existed. Given that the apostles understood themselves as agents of Jesus, commissioned to spread the message of his teachings by his authority, it ought not be controversial that the authority with which they taught, which was viewed as extending from Jesus himself, would also apply to their writings, even when the complete historical picture may be lacking in certain respects. This sense of authority and reliability carries over into the early church as well, as the church fathers took up both the Old Testament (primarily in the form of the LXX) and the writings of the apostles, twenty-seven of which were eventually deemed as canonical and authoritative for the universal church. It is this core "canon" that the church continues, with some derivations present in various traditions around the globe, to affirm as representing a divine "word from the Lord," inspired, trustworthy, and true, and able to guide the Church into truth and faithful practice of the teachings and commissioning that Jesus bestowed upon His Church.

JUDGMENT AND SALVATION

The major focus of the letter of 2 Peter is upon eschatological judgment (specifically related to the return of Christ) and the ethical living necessitated by such a reality. While eschatology is often seen as a topic of embarrassment by the late-modern church, it is engrained as a central element of the apostolic teachings in the New Testament. Indeed, so central was this to the core teaching of the early Church that it can be found in the NT definition of the gospel itself.[12] As such, the teachings on the return of Christ were distilled in the early creeds of the Church, being found in the Apostles' Creed ("he will come to judge the living and the dead"), the Nicene Creed ("He will come again in glory to judge the living

---

[12] See Bates, *Salvation by Allegiance Alone*, 50–51, who draws from C. H. Dodd, *The Apostolic Preaching and Its Developments* (New York: Harper & Row, 1964), 17.

and the dead and his kingdom will have no end"), and the Athanasian Creed ("He will come to judge the living and the dead, at whose coming all people will arise bodily and give an accounting of their own deeds. Those who have done good will enter eternal life and those who have done evil will enter eternal fire").

The two sides of the coin of the return of Christ, closely tied by 2 Peter to the "day of the Lord" teaching from the Old Testament (e.g., Isa. 13:6, 9; Ezek. 7:19; 13:5; 30:3; Joel 1:15; 2:1, 11, 31; 3:14; Amos 5:18, 20; Obad. 15; Zeph. 1:7–8, 14, 18; 2:2–3; Zech. 14:1; Mal. 4:5), are the judgment of the ungodly and the deliverance of the righteous. For 2 Peter, the focus of judgment, though extending to all the ungodly, is the false teachers. He assures his readers that their deceptive, reckless, and shameful lifestyle will be judged by God to their destruction. Because they have denied the Master who "bought" them (2:1), and embraced the vices of greed, lust, and deception, their deeds will result in their judgment and punishment, along with the examples of God's past judgment recalled by the author. Just as the rebellious angels, the world at the time of Noah, the inhabitants of Sodom and Gomorrah, and the prophet Balaam did not escape divine judgment for their ungodly living, so too the false teachers face a similar fate. Their destructive influence has the potential to lead, or possibly already has led, others from the Christian community astray. Their rejection of Jesus as Lord manifests primarily in their rejection of his Second Coming and authority to judge, perhaps influenced by Epicurean or Sophist teachings, and such a rejection now positions them as outsiders to the faith.[13]

The other side of the coin of the return of Christ is salvation. As Davids notes, "judgment in the ancient world always had a positive side, namely, rewarding the faithful."[14] This salvation in 2 Peter is described as characterized by grace, peace, and knowledge. It may be viewed both as a gift that God provides,[15] as well as a responsibility entrusted to its recipients. Here again, past examples of salvation, such as Noah and his family and

---

[13] Davids, among others, notes the close relationship between ethics and eschatology throughout the New Testament (Davids, *A Theology of James, Peter, and Jude*, 241).
[14] Davids, *A Theology of James, Peter, and Jude*, 241.
[15] For a discussion of the concept in Paul, which has helpful implications for other parts of the NT, see Barclay, *Paul and the Gift*.

"righteous" Lot, assure the faithful that they have not been abandoned by the Lord and will be delivered through eschatological salvation. For 2 Peter, this salvation is chiefly administered through "knowledge," particularly of Christ, which the author seems to view not just in terms of mental assent but of a personal and transformative commitment. Davids suggests, "Commitment [πιστίς] appears to mean the same as coming to epignosis [knowledge], at least a positive epignosis, for 2 Peter never gives a content object of *pistis*, but a personal object, and with a personal object *pistis* means commitment or allegiance."[16] The result of such knowledge is a hope of "entering the kingdom" and the culmination of their "sharing in the divine nature," which has begun in the present through the virtuous transformation of those belonging to Christ. Such transformation anticipates a point of future consummation as well. The responsibility required of the recipients of this divine gift is their ongoing commitment to Christ and cultivation of the virtues that flow from the very character and nature of God. Those who neglect or reject this transformative participation are in danger, like the false teachers, of being objects of judgment instead of salvation.

The return of Christ will bring with it not only the salvation of those committed to him and the completion of their moral transformation but also the transformation of the entire universe. A "new heavens and a new earth" will come about as a part of the coming day of the Lord, and the judgment of the heavenly powers will take place along with the judgment of humans. As a result, an eschatological renewal will take place, where the kingdom reaches its culmination and righteousness will be found throughout the earth. As Bauckham notes of these emphases, "Here he stands within the mainstream of Jewish and Christian eschatology, at the heart of which is the theocentric hope for the eventual triumph of God's will over all evil, the vindication and establishment of God's righteousness in his world."[17] The natural outflow of the eschatological focus of the letter is not just a look toward the future renewal of the universe and its inhabits but a refocusing toward the present renewal that must take place for those who belong to God in Christ.

---

[16] Davids, *A Theology of James, Peter, and Jude*, 239.
[17] Bauckham, *2 Peter–Jude*, 61.

THEOSIS

The opening theme, which is threaded through the entirety of 2 Peter, is that of transformative participation in the life of God. For 2 Peter, the ethical life is a gift from God who provides believers all that is needed for godly living. The pursuit of godly living culminates for the faithful who endure in their transformative entrance into the eternal kingdom. Second Peter envisions this transformative participation in the life of God as a fulfillment of the divine promises, resulting in "knowers of God" becoming "sharers in the divine nature" (1:3–4). In the orthodox tradition, this is often described as *theosis* or *deification*, a term and concept that has found more influence in Protestant theology in recent decades.

The virtues that flow from this transformative participation are outlined in 1:5–7 (faith, virtue, knowledge, self-control, perseverance, devotion to God, sibling affection, and love) and in many ways serve as the positive contrast to the false teachers who are discussed directly in chapters 2–3. Those who share in the life of God through true knowledge of Christ diligently pursue the alignment of their character and behavior with that of God. The false teachers, in contrast, embrace vices that place them on the path to judgment and destruction rather than salvation and deliverance. Their lives are typified by greed, lust, and pursuing sinful desires, lacking the virtue, self-control, devotion to God, and love that comes to those who share in the life of God.

This concept of *theosis*, or transformative participation in the life of God,[18] finds its focus in 2 Peter concerning ethical transformation and eternal life. Second Peter does not envision believers becoming like God in all ways that God is God. They are not, for example, the eschatological judge or source of the power and promises necessary for such transformation.[19] Rather, they will share in the eternal life that is found in the divine

---

[18] While 2 Peter is sometimes thought to be the major text that presents this idea, other NT texts articulate something similar. As Marshall notes, "Something similar is implied by Pauline statements that give believers a share in divine glory and Johannine statements that envisage believers being joined to God or Christ in a way that is similar to that in which God and Christ are joined to each other" (Marshall, *New Testament Theology*, 666–67).

[19] Skaggs suggests also the possibility of viewing the Spirit as the agent in mind in 1:3–4, stating, "It is tempting to equate the phrase 'divine power' (θεία δυνάμεως) in 1:3–4 with the Holy Spirit (πνεύματος ἁγίου) (1:21). If the two are the same, the role of the Spirit in 2 Peter would mirror that of 1 Peter, namely, that the Holy Spirit is the agent for

nature and will be transformed to align with the character of God. This transformation process begins, however, in the present, as knowledge of Christ has led them into sharing already in the divine nature. The present age is marked by the need of perseverance in the face of temptations and trials. For those who stray, repentance is necessary. Those, like the false teachers, who stray to the point of rejection of the Lordship of Jesus (cf. 2:1) will find themselves as recipients of divine judgment and punishment when the "day of God" comes (cf. 3:12).

Second Peter frames this transformative participation as a gift, bestowed upon believers through God's power and in keeping with his promises. Though participation and cultivation of this life is required, it is not merited. As Bauckham reminds, "We do not have to add to God's grace from our human resources. What we have to do is live a godly life out of the resources of divine grace which have been given to us,"[20] and so, "The Christian's response to God's grace in *faith* is the root from which the whole of their ethical obedience to God must grow. Within this context, however, it lays great stress on the necessity for faith to bear fruit in ethical behavior, because without it final salvation cannot be attained."[21] Salvation is thus viewed as a participatory and transformative enterprise.

Such a transformation represents an "escape from the corruption in the world." Similar to Paul's articulation in Romans 6 in which he sees humans as enslaved either to the forces of Sin and Death or to God, 2 Peter understand the human situation as one either entrapped within the corrupting influences of the world or liberated from such forces through knowledge of Christ. Bauckham again notes here, "Once the desire for absolute autonomy is recognized as illusory and unobtainable, we can see that the real choice is between these: alienating subjection to forces destruction of human reality and liberating obedience to the truth of human existence."[22] The culmination of this rescue, which has happened already through knowledge of Christ, but will be fully realized in the future, is the return of Christ. This moment of eschatological fulfillment, described by 2 Peter as the *parousia*, the "promise of his coming" (3:4), the day of the

bringing transformation of the believer in God" (Rebecca Skaggs, "The Spirit in 1 Peter, 2 Peter, and Jude: Transformation and Transcendence," *Pneuma* 43 [2021]: 540).
[20] Bauckham, *2 Peter-Jude*, 55.
[21] Bauckham, *2 Peter-Jude*, 59.
[22] Bauckham, *2 Peter-Jude*, 72.

Lord (3:10), and the day of God (3:12), is envisioned as the moment of culmination for the deliverance of those who belong to God in Christ. While waiting for this day, patience is necessary for God's people, as well as a commitment to holiness and obedience as they prepare for the return of their King. Their present life must be marked by a growth in Christ-like, or God-like, virtue, awaiting the glory to be revealed in full on that triumphal day (3:18).

Appendix A: A Structural Diagram of 2 Peter (Phrases and Clauses)

1:1 Συμεὼν Πέτρος (*Simeon Peter*)
   δοῦλος καὶ ἀπόστολος Ἰησοῦ Χριστοῦ (*a slave of and apostle of Jesus Christ*)
τοῖς ἰσότιμον ἡμῖν λαχοῦσιν πίστιν (*to those who obtained a faith equal to us*)
   ἐν δικαιοσύνῃ τοῦ θεοῦ ἡμῶν καὶ σωτῆρος Ἰησοῦ Χριστοῦ, (*in the justice of our God and Savior Jesus Christ*)
2 χάρις ὑμῖν καὶ εἰρήνη πληθυνθείη (*May grace and peace be multiplied to you*)
   ἐν ἐπιγνώσει τοῦ θεοῦ καὶ Ἰησοῦ τοῦ κυρίου ἡμῶν. (*in the knowledge of God and of Jesus our Lord*)
3 Ὡς πάντα ἡμῖν τῆς θείας δυνάμεως αὐτοῦ τὰ (*as all things necessary to us through his divine power*)
   πρὸς ζωὴν καὶ εὐσέβειαν (*for life and devotion to God*)
δεδωρημένης (*have been presented*)
   διὰ τῆς ἐπιγνώσεως τοῦ καλέσαντος ἡμᾶς ἰδίᾳ δόξῃ καὶ ἀρετῇ, (*through the knowledge of the one who called us by his own glory and virtue*)
     4 δι' ὧν τὰ τίμια καὶ μέγιστα ἡμῖν ἐπαγγέλματα δεδώρηται, (*through which he has presented to us precious and great promises*)
        ἵνα (*in order that*)
           διὰ τούτων (*through these things*)
        γένησθε θείας κοινωνοὶ φύσεως (*you may become sharers in the divine nature*)
           ἀποφυγόντες τῆς (*escaping from*)

ἐν τῷ κόσμῳ (*in the world*)
ἐν ἐπιθυμίᾳ (*because of distorted desires*)
φθορᾶς. (*the corruption*)
5 καὶ αὐτὸ τοῦτο δὲ (*and now for this same reason*)
σπουδὴν πᾶσαν παρεισενέγκαντες (*by contributing all eagerness*)
ἐπιχορηγήσατε (*supply*)
ἐν τῇ πίστει ὑμῶν (*with your faith*)
τὴν ἀρετήν, (*virtue*)
ἐν δὲ τῇ ἀρετῇ (*and with virtue*)
τὴν γνῶσιν, (*knowledge*)
6 ἐν δὲ τῇ γνώσει (*and with knowledge*)
τὴν ἐγκράτειαν, (*self-control*)
ἐν δὲ τῇ ἐγκρατείᾳ (*and with self-control*)
τὴν ὑπομονήν, (*perseverance*)
ἐν δὲ τῇ ὑπομονῇ (*and with perseverance*)
τὴν εὐσέβειαν, (*devotion to God*)
7 ἐν δὲ τῇ εὐσεβείᾳ (and with devotion to God)
τὴν φιλαδελφίαν, (*sibling affection*)
ἐν δὲ τῇ φιλαδελφίᾳ (*and with sibling affection*)
τὴν ἀγάπην. (*love*)
8 ταῦτα γὰρ ὑμῖν ὑπάρχοντα καὶ πλεονάζοντα (*for if these things are yours and increasing*)
οὐκ ἀργοὺς οὐδὲ ἀκάρπους καθίστησιν (*they will not make you useless or unfruitful*)
εἰς τὴν τοῦ κυρίου ἡμῶν Ἰησοῦ Χριστοῦ ἐπίγνωσιν· (*in the knowledge of our Lord Jesus Christ*)
9 ᾧ γὰρ μὴ πάρεστιν ταῦτα, (*For to the one for whom these things are not present*)
τυφλός ἐστιν (*they are blind*)
μυωπάζων, (*being nearsighted*)
λήθην λαβὼν τοῦ καθαρισμοῦ τῶν πάλαι αὐτοῦ ἁμαρτιῶν. (*choosing to forget the cleansing of their former sins*).
10 διὸ μᾶλλον, ἀδελφοί, σπουδάσατε (*Therefore, siblings, be even more eager*)
Βεβαίαν ὑμῶν τὴν κλῆσιν καὶ ἐκλογὴν ποιεῖσθαι· (*to make certain your calling and election*)
ταῦτα γὰρ ποιοῦντες (*for in doing these things*)

οὐ μὴ πταίσητέ ποτε. (*you will never ever stumble*)
11 οὕτως γὰρ πλουσίως ἐπιχορηγηθήσεται ὑμῖν ἡ εἴσοδος (*For in this way entrance will be richly supplied to you*)
    εἰς τὴν αἰώνιον βασιλείαν τοῦ κυρίου ἡμῶν καὶ σωτῆρος Ἰησοῦ Χριστοῦ. (*into the eternal kingdom of our Lord and Savior Jesus Christ*)
12 Διὸ μελλήσω ἀεὶ ὑμᾶς ὑπομιμνῄσκειν (*Therefore, I will continue to remind you*)
    περὶ τούτων (*about these things*)
    καίπερ εἰδότας καὶ ἐστηριγμένους (*although you know them and are confirmed*)
    ἐν τῇ παρούσῃ ἀληθείᾳ. (*in the truth you possess*)
13 δίκαιον δὲ ἡγοῦμαι, (*Now, I consider it right*)
    ἐφ' ὅσον εἰμὶ (*as long as I*)
        ἐν τούτῳ τῷ σκηνώματι, (*inhabit this body*)
    διεγείρειν ὑμᾶς (*to awaken you*)
        ἐν ὑπομνήσει, (*by reminder*)
14 εἰδὼς (*knowing*)
    ὅτι ταχινή ἐστιν ἡ ἀπόθεσις τοῦ σκηνώματός μου (*that the laying aside of this habitation is coming soon*)
        καθὼς καὶ ὁ κύριτολμος ἡμῶν Ἰησοῦς Χριστὸς ἐδήλωσέν μοι, (*just as our Lord Jesus Christ revealed to me*)
15 σπουδάσω δὲ καὶ ἑκάστοτε (*so I will make every effort*)
    ἔχειν ὑμᾶς (*to have you*)
        μετὰ τὴν ἐμὴν ἔξοδον (*after my departure*)
    τὴν τούτων μνήμην ποιεῖσθαι. (*make recollection of these things*)
16 Οὐ γὰρ σεσοφισμένοις μύθοις ἐξακολουθήσαντες (*For we did not by following cleverly created myths*)
ἐγνωρίσαμεν ὑμῖν τὴν τοῦ κυρίου ἡμῶν Ἰησοῦ Χριστοῦ δύναμιν καὶ παρουσίαν (*make known to you the power and presence of our Lord Jesus Christ*)
    ἀλλ' ἐπόπται γενηθέντες τῆς ἐκείνου μεγαλειότητος. (*but by becoming eyewitnesses of that man's majesty*)
17 λαβὼν γὰρ παρὰ θεοῦ πατρὸς τιμὴν καὶ δόξαν (*For when he received honor and glory from God*)
φωνῆς ἐνεχθείσης αὐτῷ τοιᾶσδε (*a voice such as this was brought to him*)

ὑπὸ τῆς μεγαλοπρεποῦς δόξης· (*by the Majestic Glory*)
Ὁ υἱός μου ὁ ἀγαπητός μου οὗτός ἐστιν εἰς ὃν ἐγὼ
εὐδόκησα, (*This is my son, my beloved, this is one with
whom I take delight*)
18 καὶ ταύτην τὴν φωνὴν ἡμεῖς ἠκούσαμεν (*and we heard this voice*)
ἐξ οὐρανοῦ ἐνεχθεῖσαν (*brought from heaven*)
σὺν αὐτῷ ὄντες (*when we were with him*)
ἐν τῷ ἁγίῳ ὄρει. (*on the holy mountain*)
19 καὶ ἔχομεν βεβαιότερον τὸν προφητικὸν λόγον, (*and we have the
utmost reliable prophetic word*)
ᾧ καλῶς ποιεῖτε (*to which you do well*)
προσέχοντες (*to pay attention*)
ὡς λύχνῳ φαίνοντι (*as to a lamp shining*)
ἐν αὐχμηρῷ τόπῳ, (*in a dark place*)
ἕως οὗ ἡμέρα διαυγάσῃ (*until the day dawns*)
καὶ φωσφόρος ἀνατείλῃ (*and the morning
star rises*)
ἐν ταῖς καρδίαις ὑμῶν, (*in your hearts*)
20 τοῦτο πρῶτον γινώσκοντες (*knowing this first*)
ὅτι πᾶσα προφητεία γραφῆς ἰδίας ἐπιλύσεως οὐ
γίνεται· (*that every prophecy of Scripture does not
come from one's own interpretation*)
21 οὐ γὰρ (*for it was not*)
θελήματι ἀνθρώπου (*by the will of a human*)
ἠνέχθη προφητεία ποτέ, (*that a prophecy was every produced*)
ἀλλὰ (*but*)
ὑπὸ πνεύματος ἁγίου (*by the Holy Spirit*)
φερόμενοι (*brought along*)
ἐλάλησαν (*spoke*)
ἀπὸ θεοῦ (*from God*)
ἄνθρωποι. (*people*)
2:1 Ἐγένοντο δὲ καὶ ψευδοπροφῆται (*Now false prophets came*)
ἐν τῷ λαῷ, (*among the people*)
ὡς καὶ (*just as*)
ἐν ὑμῖν (*among you*)
ἔσονται ψευδοδιδάσκαλοι, (*there will also be false
teachers*)

οἵτινες παρεισάξουσιν αἱρέσεις ἀπωλείας (who
will introduce destructive beliefs)
καὶ τὸν ἀγοράσαντα αὐτοὺς δεσπότην
ἀρνούμενοι. (even denying the Master who
bought them)
ἐπάγοντες ἑαυτοῖς ταχινὴν ἀπώλειαν,
(bringing upon themselves swift
destruction)
2 καὶ πολλοὶ ἐξακολουθήσουσιν αὐτῶν ταῖς ἀσελγείαις (and many will
follow their immoral ways)
δι' οὓς ἡ ὁδὸς τῆς ἀληθείας βλασφημηθήσεται, (because of
whom they way of truth will be slandered)
3 καὶ (and)
ἐν πλεονεξίᾳ (in greed)
πλαστοῖς λόγοις ὑμᾶς ἐμπορεύσονται, (they will buy you with fake words)
οἷς τὸ κρίμα ἔκπαλαι οὐκ ἀργεῖ (for whom condemnation is
not idle)
καὶ ἡ ἀπώλεια αὐτῶν οὐ νυστάζει. (and their destruction is
not asleep)
4 Εἰ γὰρ ὁ θεὸς ἀγγέλων ἁμαρτησάντων οὐκ ἐφείσατο (For if
God did not spare the angels who sinned)
ἀλλὰ σειραῖς ζόφου ταρταρώσας παρέδωκεν (held them captive
in Tartarus in chains of darkness [and] handed over)
εἰς κρίσιν τηρουμένους, (those being kept for judgment)
5 καὶ ἀρχαίου κόσμου οὐκ ἐφείσατο (and [if he] did not spare the
ancient world)
ἀλλὰ ὄγδοον Νῶε δικαιοσύνης κήρυκα ἐφύλαξεν (but preserved
eight, including Noah, a herald of righteousness)
κατακλυσμὸν κόσμῳ ἀσεβῶν ἐπάξας, (when he brought a
great flood upon the world of the ungodly)
6 καὶ πόλεις Σοδόμων καὶ Γομόρρας. . . [καταστροφῇ]
κατέκρινεν (and [if he] condemned the cities of Sodom and
Gomorrah [to destruction],)
Τεφρώσας (reducing them to ashes)
ὑπόδειγμα μελλόντων ἀσεβέ[σ]ιν τεθεικώς, (having
appointed them as an example for those who were going
to be ungodly)

7 καὶ δίκαιον Λὼτ (*and if righteous Lot*)
    Καταπονούμενον (*who was worn down*)
        ὑπὸ τῆς τῶν ἀθέσμων... ἀναστροφῆς (*by the behavior of lawless persons*)
        ἐν ἀσελγείᾳ (*in immorality*)
ἐρρύσατο· (*he rescued*)
    8 βλέμματι γὰρ καὶ ἀκοῇ ὁ δίκαιος ἐγκατοικῶν (*for that righteous man living... by seeing and hearing*)
        ἐν αὐτοῖς (*among them*)
        ἡμέραν ἐξ ἡμέρας (*day after day*)
        ψυχὴν δικαίαν ἀνόμοις ἔργοις ἐβασάνιζεν· (*their lawless deeds... was torturing his righteous soul*)
9 οἶδεν κύριος εὐσεβεῖς (*[so] the Lord knows... the devout*)
    ἐκ πειρασμοῦ (*from trials*)
ῥύεσθαι, (*how to rescue*)
ἀδίκους δὲ (*and the unrighteous*)
    εἰς ἡμέραν κρίσεως (*for the day of judgment*)
    κολαζομένους τηρεῖν, (*who are going to be punished... to keep*)
        10 μάλιστα δὲ τοὺς ὀπίσω σαρκὸς (*and especially those who... after the flesh*)
            ἐν ἐπιθυμίᾳ μιασμοῦ πορευομένους (*in defiling desires... are following*)
            καὶ κυριότητος καταφρονοῦντας. (*and who are despising the One Who Rules*)
Τολμηταὶ αὐθάδεις, ... οὐ τρέμουσιν, (*Bold, arrogant... they are not trembling*)
    ... δόξας... βλασφημοῦντες (*while defaming glorious beings*)
11 ὅπου ἄγγελοι (*whereas angels,*)
    ἰσχύϊ καὶ δυνάμει μείζονες ὄντες (*being greater in strength and power*)
οὐ φέρουσιν (*are not bringing*)
    κατ' αὐτῶν (*against them*)
    παρὰ κυρίου (*from the Lord*)
    βλάσφημον κρίσιν. (*a judgment of defamation*)
12 οὗτοι δὲ ὡς ἄλογα ζῷα (*But these people are like irrational animals*)

> γεγεννημένα φυσικὰ (*born by nature*)
>> εἰς ἅλωσιν καὶ φθορὰν (*for capturing and killing*)
>> ἐν οἷς... βλασφημοῦντες (*concerning things which they are defaming*)
> ἀγνοοῦσιν (*are ignorant*)
>> ἐν τῇ φθορᾷ αὐτῶν καὶ φθαρήσονται (*in their destruction, they will be destroyed*)
>> 13 ἀδικούμενοι μισθὸν ἀδικίας, (*suffering harm for the wages of their harmful ways*)
>> ἡδονὴν ἡγούμενοι τὴν... τρυφήν, (*considering self-indulgence... a pleasure*)
>>> ἐν ἡμέρᾳ (*during the daytime*)
> σπίλοι καὶ μῶμοι (*they are stains and blemishes*)
>> ἐντρυφῶντες (*delighting*)
>>> ἐν ταῖς ἀπάταις αὐτῶν (*in their deception*)
>>> συνευωχούμενοι ὑμῖν, (*while feasting together with you*)
>> 14 ὀφθαλμοὺς ἔχοντες μεστοὺς μοιχαλίδος καὶ ἀκαταπαύστους ἁμαρτίας, (*having eyes full of adultery and unceasing sin*)
>> δελεάζοντες ψυχὰς ἀστηρίκτους, (*enticing weak souls*)
>> καρδίαν γεγυμνασμένην πλεονεξίας ἔχοντες, (*having a heart which has been trained for greediness*)
> κατάρας τέκνα· (*they are accursed children*)
>> 15 καταλείποντες εὐθεῖαν ὁδὸν (*having forsaken the proper way*)
> ἐπλανήθησαν, (*they went astray*)
>> ἐξακολουθήσαντες τῇ ὁδῷ τοῦ Βαλαὰμ τοῦ Βοσόρ, (*having followed the way of Balaam of Bosor*)
>>> ὃς μισθὸν ἀδικίας ἠγάπησεν (*who loved the wages of his harmful ways*)
16 ἔλεγξιν δὲ ἔσχεν ἰδίας παρανομίας· (*but he received a rebuke for his own lawlessness*)
> ὑποζύγιον ἄφωνον (*a speechless donkey*)
>> ἐν ἀνθρώπου φωνῇ φθεγξάμενον (*speaking with a human voice*)
> ἐκώλυσεν τὴν τοῦ προφήτου παραφρονίαν. (*restrained the prophet's madness*)

17 Οὗτοί εἰσιν πηγαὶ ἄνυδροι καὶ ὁμίχλαι (*These people are dry fountains and mists driven*)
    ὑπὸ λαίλαπος (*by a hurricane*)
    ἐλαυνόμεναι, (*being driven*)
    οἷς ὁ ζόφος τοῦ σκότους τετήρηται. (*for whom the gloom of darkness has been reserved*)
    18 ὑπέρογκα γὰρ ματαιότητος (*For bombastic [words] of emptiness*)
    Φθεγγόμενοι (*by speaking*)
Δελεάζουσιν (*they are enticing*)
    ἐν ἐπιθυμίαις σαρκὸς ἀσελγείαις (*with the desires of the flesh and immoralities*)
τοὺς ὀλίγως ἀποφεύγοντας (*those who are barely escaping*)
τοὺς... ἀναστρεφομένους. (*those ones who are living*)
    ἐν πλάνῃ (*in error*)
    19 ἐλευθερίαν αὐτοῖς ἐπαγγελλόμενοι, (*promising them freedom*)
    αὐτοὶ δοῦλοι ὑπάρχοντες τῆς φθορᾶς· (*though themselves being slaves of depravity*)
        ᾧ γάρ τις ἥττηται, (*for to whatever one succumbs*)
        τούτῳ δεδούλωται. (*by this they are enslaved*)
    20 εἰ γὰρ (*For, if*)
        ἀποφυγόντες τὰ μιάσματα τοῦ κόσμου (*after escaping the corruption of the world*)
        ἐν ἐπιγνώσει τοῦ κυρίου [ἡμῶν] καὶ σωτῆρος Ἰησοῦ Χριστοῦ, (*through the knowledge of [our] Lord and Savior Jesus Christ*)
        τούτοις δὲ πάλιν ἐμπλακέντες ἡττῶνται, (*but having again become entangled in these things*)
γέγονεν αὐτοῖς τὰ ἔσχατα χείρονα τῶν πρώτων. (*the last things have become worse than the first ones*)
21 κρεῖττον γὰρ ἦν αὐτοῖς μὴ ἐπεγνωκέναι τὴν ὁδὸν τῆς δικαιοσύνης (*For it would have been better for them to have not know the way of righteousness*)
ἢ ἐπιγνοῦσιν (*than, having known it*)
ὑποστρέψαι (*to turn back*)
    ἐκ τῆς παραδοθείσης αὐτοῖς ἁγίας ἐντολῆς. (*from the holy commandment which had been delivered to them*)

A Structural Diagram of 2 Peter (Phrases and Clauses)   227

22 συμβέβηκεν αὐτοῖς τὸ τῆς ἀληθοῦς παροιμίας· (*What the true proverb says has happened to them*)
    Κύων ἐπιστρέψας (*A dog returns*)
        ἐπὶ τὸ ἴδιον ἐξέραμα, (*to its own vomit*)
    καί· Ὗς (*and, A sow*)
        λουσαμένη (*having washed*)
        εἰς κυλισμὸν βορβόρου. (*returns to wallowing in the mud*)
3:1 Ταύτην ἤδη, (*This already*)
    ἀγαπητοί, (*Loved ones*)
δευτέραν ὑμῖν γράφω ἐπιστολήν, (*is the second letter I am writing to you*)
    ἐν αἷς διεγείρω ὑμῶν (*through which I am stirring up*)
        ἐν ὑπομνήσει (*through remembrance*)
    τὴν εἰλικρινῆ διάνοιαν (*your sincere thinking*)
        2 μνησθῆναι τῶν προειρημένων ῥημάτων (*to remember the words spoken beforehand*)
            ὑπὸ τῶν ἁγίων προφητῶν (*by the holy prophets*)
            καὶ τῆς τῶν ἀποστόλων ὑμῶν ἐντολῆς τοῦ κυρίου καὶ σωτῆρος, (*and the commandment of the Lord and Savior through your apostles*)
        3 τοῦτο πρῶτον γινώσκοντες (*knowing this especially*)
            ὅτι ἐλεύσονται (*that they will come*)
                ἐπ' ἐσχάτων τῶν ἡμερῶν (*in the last days*)
                [ἐν] ἐμπαιγμονῇ (*with ridicule*)
            ἐμπαῖκται (*mockers*)
            κατὰ τὰς ἰδίας ἐπιθυμίας αὐτῶν (*according to their own desires*)
            πορευόμενοι (*following*)
        4 καὶ λέγοντες· (*and saying*)
            Ποῦ ἐστιν ἡ ἐπαγγελία τῆς παρουσίας αὐτοῦ; (*Where is the promise of his coming*)
ἀφ' ἧς γὰρ οἱ πατέρες ἐκοιμήθησαν, (*For from the time since our fathers died*)
πάντα οὕτως διαμένει (*all things are continuing on as they have*)
    ἀπ' ἀρχῆς κτίσεως. (*from the beginning of creation*)
5 λανθάνει γὰρ αὐτοὺς (*For it is deliberately suppressed by those*)

τοῦτο θέλοντας (*who maintain this*)
    ὅτι οὐρανοὶ ἦσαν ἔκπαλαι (*that the heavens existed a long time ago*)
    καὶ γῆ (*and the earth*)
        ἐξ ὕδατος (*by water*)
        καὶ δι' ὕδατος (*and through water*)
    συνεστῶσα τῷ τοῦ θεοῦ λόγῳ, (*has been established by the word of God*)
        6 δι' ὧν ὁ τότε κόσμος ... ἀπώλετο· (*through which the world at that time was itself then destroyed*)
            ὕδατι κατακλυσθεὶς (*being flooded by water*)
7 οἱ δὲ νῦν οὐρανοὶ καὶ ἡ γῆ τῷ αὐτῷ λόγῳ τεθησαυρισμένοι εἰσὶν πυρὶ (*now by the same word the heavens and the earth are being reserved for fire*)
    Τηρούμενοι (*being kept*)
        εἰς ἡμέραν κρίσεως καὶ ἀπωλείας τῶν ἀσεβῶν ἀνθρώπων. (*for the day of the judgment and destruction of ungodly people*)
8 Ἓν δὲ τοῦτο μὴ λανθανέτω ὑμᾶς, (*Now do not let this one thing escape your notice*)
    ἀγαπητοί, (*loved ones*)
    ὅτι μία ἡμέρα (*that one day*)
        παρὰ κυρίῳ (*with the Lord*)
    ὡς χίλια ἔτη (*is like one thousand years*)
    καὶ χίλια ἔτη ὡς ἡμέρα μία. (*and one thousand years like one day*)
9 οὐ βραδύνει κύριος τῆς ἐπαγγελίας, (*The Lord of the promise is not slow*)
    ὥς τινες βραδύτητα ἡγοῦνται, (*as some regard slowness*)
ἀλλὰ μακροθυμεῖ εἰς ὑμᾶς, (*but is being patient for you*)
    μὴ βουλόμενός τινας ἀπολέσθαι (*not wanting any to lose out*)
    ἀλλὰ πάντας εἰς μετάνοιαν χωρῆσαι. (*but all to come to repentance*)
10 Ἥξει δὲ ἡμέρα κυρίου ὡς κλέπτης, (*Now the day of the Lord will come as a thief*)

> ἐν ᾗ οἱ οὐρανοὶ ῥοιζηδὸν παρελεύσονται (*in which the heavens will pass away with a rushing noise*)
> στοιχεῖα δὲ (*and the celestial bodies*)
> > καυσούμενα (*by burning away*)
> λυθήσεται (*will be destroyed*)
> καὶ γῆ καὶ τὰ (*and the earth and*)
> > ἐν αὐτῇ (*upon it*)
> ἔργα εὑρεθήσεται. (*the deeds done... will be disclosed*)
> **11** τούτων οὕτως πάντων λυομένων (*since all these things are going to be destroyed in this way*)

ποταποὺς δεῖ ὑπάρχειν [ὑμᾶς] (*what kind of people should you be*)
> ἐν ἁγίαις ἀναστροφαῖς καὶ εὐσεβείαις, (*in holy behaviors and godly actions*)
> **12** προσδοκῶντας καὶ σπεύδοντας τὴν παρουσίαν τῆς τοῦ θεοῦ ἡμέρας (*while looking for and hastening the coming day of God*)
> > δι' ἣν οὐρανοὶ πυρούμενοι λυθήσονται (*because of which the heavens will be destroyed by being burned up*)
> > καὶ στοιχεῖα καυσούμενα τήκεται. (*and the celestial bodies are being dissolved by burning*)

13 *καινοὺς δὲ οὐρανοὺς καὶ γῆν καινὴν* (*Now... new heavens and a new earth*)
> κατὰ τὸ ἐπάγγελμα αὐτοῦ (*according to His promise*)

προσδοκῶμεν, (*we are waiting for*)
> ἐν οἷς δικαιοσύνη κατοικεῖ. (*in which righteousness resides*)

14 Διό, (*Therefore*)
> ἀγαπητοί, (*loved ones*)
> ταῦτα προσδοκῶντες (*while waiting for these things*)

σπουδάσατε ἄσπιλοι καὶ ἀμώμητοι αὐτῷ (*make every effort pure and blameless in Him*)
> εὑρεθῆναι (*to be found*)
> > ἐν εἰρήνῃ (*at peace*)

15 καὶ τὴν τοῦ κυρίου ἡμῶν μακροθυμίαν σωτηρίαν ἡγεῖσθε, (*and regard the patience of our Lord as salvation*)

καθὼς καὶ ὁ ἀγαπητὸς ἡμῶν ἀδελφὸς Παῦλος (*just as also our beloved brother Paul*)
> κατὰ τὴν δοθεῖσαν αὐτῷ σοφίαν (*in accordance with the wisdom which was given to him*)

ἔγραψεν ὑμῖν, (*wrote to you*)
16 ὡς καὶ (*as also*)
    ἐν πάσαις ἐπιστολαῖς (*in all his letters*)
    λαλῶν (*speaking*)
        ἐν αὐταῖς (*in them*)
        περὶ τούτων, (*about these things*)
        ἐν αἷς ἐστιν δυσνόητά τινα, (*in which some things are hard to understand*)
            ἃ οἱ ἀμαθεῖς καὶ ἀστήρικτοι στρεβλοῦσιν (*which the ignorant and unstable will distort*)
                ὡς καὶ τὰς λοιπὰς γραφὰς (*as they do with the rest of the Scriptures*)
                πρὸς τὴν ἰδίαν αὐτῶν ἀπώλειαν. (*to their own ruin*)
17 Ὑμεῖς οὖν, (*Therefore, you*)
    ἀγαπητοί, (*loved ones*)
    προγινώσκοντες (*knowing this beforehand*)
φυλάσσεσθε, (*keep guarding yourselves*)
    ἵνα μὴ τῇ τῶν ἀθέσμων πλάνῃ (*in order that you might not by the error of unruly people*)
        συναπαχθέντες (*through being led astray*)
    ἐκπέσητε (*lose*)
        τοῦ ἰδίου στηριγμοῦ, (*your own steadfastness*)
18 αὐξάνετε δὲ (*But keep growing*)
    ἐν χάριτι καὶ γνώσει τοῦ κυρίου ἡμῶν καὶ σωτῆρος Ἰησοῦ Χριστοῦ. (*in the grace and knowledge of our Lord and Savior Jesus Christ*)
    αὐτῷ ἡ δόξα καὶ νῦν καὶ εἰς ἡμέραν αἰῶνος. [ἀμήν.] (*To him be the glory, both now and into the day of the age. [Amen.]*)

Appendix B: Hapaxes in 2 Peter

Lexical form	2 Peter location	Other select literary uses	TLG occurence statistics (between 8 BC and AD 4)	Earliest textual attestation (TLG)	Note
ἄθεσμος ἀκατάπαστος	2:17; 3:17 2:14	3 Macc. 5:16; 6:26 (LXX) Only occurs in 2 Pet. 2:14, but may be a misspelling of ἀκατάπαυστος, which occurs in the works of Plutarch, Josephus, Polybius, Diodorus Siculus, Apollonius of Rhodes, and Heliodorus.	ἀκατάπαυστος occurs 132 times.	N/A. ἀκατάπαυστος first occurs in the third century BC	No other biblical occurrences
ἅλωσις ἀμαθής	2:12 3:16	Jer. 27:46 (LXX) Occurs in the works of Plato, Plutarch, Philo, Josephus, Epictetus, Dionysius of of Halicarnassus, Euripides, Aristophanes, Appian, Lucian, Athenaeus, Pausanias, Strabo, Herodotus, Callimachus, Diodorus Siculus, Diogenes Laertius, Xenophon, Aelius Aristides, Dio Chrysostom, Andocides, Lysias, and Demosthenes.	1,284 times	fifth century BC	No other biblical occurrences

ἀμώμητος	3:14	Occurs in *Let. Aris.* 93, and also in the works of Plutarch, Philo, Pausanias, Quintus Smyrnaeus, Strabo, Herodotus, Pindar, Aelius Aristides, Aristophanes, and Hesiod.	371 times	eighth century BC
ἀποφεύγω	1:4; 2:18, 20	Sir. 22:22 (LXX)		
ἀργεῖν	2:3	Eccl. 12:3; 1 Esd. 2:26; 2 Esd. 4:24 (x2); 2 Macc. 5:25; Sir. 33:28 (LXX)		
ἀστήρικτος	2:14; 3:16	Occurs in the works of Nonnus of Panopolis.	111 times	second century BC	No other biblical occurrences
αὐχμηρός	1:19	Occurs in *Sib. Or.* 8.203; 14:235; *Apoc. Pet.* A 21, and in the works of Plato, Plutarch, Philo, Diodorus Siculus, Dionysius of Halicarnassus, Pausanias, Aretaeus, Strabo, Hippocrates, Pseudo-Apollodorus, Xenophor, Aelius Aristides, Euripides, and Lucian.	399 times	fifth century BC	No other biblical occurrences

Note: "No other biblical occurrences" applies to ἀμώμητος, ἀστήρικτος, and αὐχμηρός.

βλέμμα	2:8	Occurs in 4 Ezra 8:23; T. Reu. 5:3; T. Ab. 12:1; T. Sol. 5:2–3; His. Jos. B (Recto) 2; Herm. Sim. 6.2.5, and in the works of Plutarch, Philo, Josephus, Lucian, Appian, Athenaeus, Euripides, Aelius Aristides, Dio Chrysostom, Demosthenes, and Epictetus.	642 times	fourth century BC	No other biblical occurrences
βραδύτης	3:9	Occurs in the works of Plato, Aristotle, Plutarch, Philo, Josephus, Sophocles, Dionysius of Halicarnassus, Diodorus Siculus, Lucian, Theophrastus, Appian, Oppion, Xenophon, Polybius, Aelius Aristides, and Demosthenes.	604 times	sixth century BC	No other biblical occurrences
διαυγάζω	1:19	Occurs in the works of Plutarch, Josephus, Lucian, and Dionysius of Halicarnassus.	103 times	fourth century BC	No other biblical occurrences
δυσνόητος	3:16	Occurs in Herm. Sim. 9.14.4	49 times	first century AD	No other biblical occurrences

ἐγκατοικέω	2:8	Occurs in *Barn. 1:4* and in the works of Plato, Josephus, Herodotus, Lycophron, and Dio Chrysostom.	38 times	fifth century BC	No other biblical occurrences
ἑκάστοτε	1:15	Occurs in the works of Plato, Aristotle, Plutarch, Philo, JOsephus, Xenophon, Dionysius of Halicarnassus, Aelius Aristides, Appian, Aristophanes, Athenaeus, Pausanias, Hippocrates, Herodotus, Polybius, Diogenes Laertius, Aelius Aristides, Dio Chrysostom, Lysias, Demosthenes, and Epictetus.	1,071 times	fifth century BC	No other biblical occurrences
ἔκπαλαι	2:3; 3:5	Occurs in the works of Plutarch, Philo, and Josephus.	105 times	fourth century BC	No other biblical occurrences
ἐμπαιγμονή	3:3	Only occurs in 2 Pet. 3:3; but may be a variation of ἐμπαίζω, which occurs roughly 40 times in the NT and LXX.	2 times	first century AD	No other biblical occurrences
ἐξέραμα	2:22	Occurs in the medical writings of Dioscurides and Philumenus.	19 times	first century AD	No other biblical occurrences

ἐπάγγελμα	1:4; 3:13	Occurs Apocr. Ezek 5 and in the works of Plato, Philo, Appian, Dionysius of Halicarnassus, Apollodorus, Aeschines, Demosthenes, and Epictetus.	248 times	fifth century BC
ἐπίλυσις	1:20	Occurs in Jub. 11:8; Herm. Sim. 5–9 and in the works Aeschylus.	149 times	fifth century BC
ἐπόπτης	1:16	Esth. 5:1; 2 Macc. 3:39; 7:35; 3 Macc. 2:21 (LXX)		No other biblical occurrences
ἰσότιμος	1:1	Occurs in the works of Plutarch, Philo, Josephus, Dionysius of Halicarnassus, Lucian, Strabo, and Dio Chrysostom.	253 times	fifth/fourth century BC
κατακλύζω	3:5	Ps. 77:20; Job 14:19; Wis. 10:4, 19; Jer. 29:2; Ezek. 13:11, 13; 38:22 (LXX)		No other biblical occurrences
καυσόω	3:10, 12	Occurs in the medical writings of Dioscurides and Philumenus.	96 times	first century AD
κυλισμός	2:22	Occurs in Prov. 2:18 (Theodotion)	4 times	first century AD
λήθη	1:9	Lev. 5:15; Num. 5:27; Deut. 8:19; 3 Macc. 5:28; 6:20; 4 Macc. 1:5; 2:24; Job 7:21; Wis. 16:11; 17:3; Sir. 14:7 (LXX)		

236

μεγαλοπρεπής	1:17	Deut. 33:26; 2 Macc. 8:15; 15:13; 3 Macc. 2:9 (LXX)		
μέγιστος	1:4	Job 26:3; 31:28; Esth. 8:12; 2 Macc. 2:19; 3:35 (LXX)		
μίασμα	2:20	Lev. 7:18; Jdt. 9:2, 4; 13:16; 1 Macc. 13:50; Jer. 39:34; Ezek. 33:31 (LXX)		
μιασμός	2:10	Wis. 14:26; 1 Macc. 4:43 (LXX)		
μνήμη	1:15	2 Macc. 2:25; 7:20; Ps. 29:5; 96:12; 144:7; Prov. 1:12; 10:7; Eccl. 1:11; 2:16; 9:5; Wis. 4:1, 19; 8:13; 11:12; (LXX) Ps. Sol. 16:6, 9 (OT Pseud.)		
μυωπάζω	1:9	Occurs in the works of Aristotle, Apollonius Rhodius, Nonnus of Panopolis, Polybius, Diogenes Laertius, Lucian, and Aeschylus.	20 times	first century BC	No other biblical occurrences
μῶμος	2:13	Lev. 21:17, 18, 21, 23; 22:20–21, 25; 24:19–20; Num. 19:2; Deut. 15:21; 17:1; 2 Kgdms. 14:25; Song. 4:7; Sir. 11:31, 33; 18:15; 20:24; 33:23; 47:20 (LXX)		
ὀλίγος	2:18	Occurs in Isa. 10:7 (Aquila)	27 times	fifth century BC

237

ὀμίχλη	2:17	Ps. 147:5; Job 24:20; 38:9; Wis. 2:4; Sir. 24:3; 43:22; Amos 4:13; Joel 2:2; Zeph. 1:15; Isa. 29:18 (LXX)		
παρανομία	2:16	4 Macc. 2:11; 4:19; 5:13; 9:3; Ps. 36:7; Prov. 5:22; 10:26; Ps. Sol. 4:1, 12; 8:9; 17:20 (LXX)		
παραφρονία	2:16	Only occurs in 2 Pet. 2:16, but may be a variation of παραφροσύνη/παραφρονήσις, which occurs in Zech. 12:4.	3 times (παραφροσύνη/παραφρονήσις occur 570 times, beginning in the 5th century B.C.)	first century AD
παρεισάγω	2:1	Occurs in the works of Plutarch, Philo, Diodorus Siculus, Herodotus, Polybius, and Dio Chrysostom.	492 times	sixth century BC	No other biblical occurrences
παρεισφέρω	1:5	Occurs in the works of Athenaeus and Demosthenes.	115 times	sixth century BC	No other biblical occurrences
πλαστός	2:3	Occurs in the works of Plato, Plutarch, Philo, Josephus, Aelius Aristides, Euripides, Dionysius of Halicarnassus, Lucian, Pausanias, Strabo, Herodotus, Xenophon, and Dio Chrysostom.	189 times	eighth century BC	No other biblical occurrences

ῥοιζηδόν	3:10	Occurs in the works of Lycophron, Nicander, and Polyaenus.	118 times	sixth century BC	No other biblical occurrences
σειρός/ σειρά	2:4	Occurs in the LXX (Jdg. 16:13–14; Prov. 5:22) and in Greek literature, though in the variant σειρά and not σειρός			
στηριγμός	3:17	Occurs in the works of Plutarch, Diodorus Siculus, and Dionysius of Halicarnassus.	264 times	fourth century BC	No other biblical occurrences
στρεβλόω	3:16	2 Kgdms. 22:27; 3 Macc. 4:14; 9:17; 12:3, 11; 15:14 (LXX)			
ταρταρόω	2:4	Occurs in the works of Plato, Plutarch, Dionysius of Halicarnassus, Euripides, Apollodorus, Sophocles, Lucian, Aeschylus, and Hesiod.	44 times	fifth century BC	No other biblical occurrences
ταχινός	1:14; 2:1	Prov. 1:16; Wis. 13:2; Sir. 11:22; 18:26; Hab. 1:6; Isa. 59:7 (LXX)			
τεφρόω	2:6	Occurs in *Sib. Or.*, 5.124, 315 and in the works of Philo.	83 times	fourth century BC	No other biblical occurrences
τήκω	3:12	50 occurrences in the LXX			
τοιόσδε	1:17	2 Macc. 11:27; 15:12 (LXX)			

239

τολμητής	2:10	Occurs in the works of Plutarch, Philo, Josephus, Livy, Dionysius of Halicarnassus, and Sophocles.	59 times	fifth century BC	No other biblical occurrences
ὗς	2:22	Lev. 11:7; Deut. 14:8; 2 Kgdms. 17:8; 3 Kgdms. 20:19; 22:38; Prov. 11:22 (LXX)			
φωσφόρος	1:19	Occurs in the works of Plato, Plutarch, Philo, Athenaeus, Nonnus, Aristophanes, Euripides, and Diogenes Laertius.	219 times	fifth century BC	No other biblical occurrences
ψευδοδιδάσκαλος	2:1	Earliest attested use outside of 2 Peter occurs in Justin Martyr's *Diolague with Trypho* 82.1.5 (c. 150 AD).	Occurs 126 times across 44 texts.	first century AD	No other biblical occurrences

Appendix C: Common Vocabulary between 1 and 2 Peter, including Cognate Terms

ἀγαπάω	ἀναστρέφω	δέ	ἔντιμος	καλέω	μετάνοια	ποιέω	ὑπακούω
ἀγάπη	ἀναστροφή	δεῖ	ἐξαγγέλλω	καλός	μή	πολύς	ὑπό
ἀγαπητός	ἀναφέρω	δεσπότης	ἐξουσία	καρδία	νῦν	πορεύομαι	ὑπόκρισις
ἄγγελος	ἄνθρωπος	δηλόω	ἐπαγγελία	κατά	Νῶε	ποτέ	ὑπομένω
ἁγιάζω	ἄνθρωπος	διά	ἐπαγγέλλομαι	κατακρίνω	ὁ	πού	ὑποφέρω
ἁγιασμός	ἀντίδικος	διαμένω	ἐπάγγελμα	κατακυριεύω	οἶδα	προγινώσκω	φαίνω
ἅγιος	ἀπέχω	διάνοια	ἐπί	καταλαλέω	ὀλίγος	πρόγνωσις	φέρω
ἀγνοέω	ἀπιστέω	διασώζω	ἐπιγινώσκω	καταλαλιά	ὀλίγως	προεῖπον	φιλαδελφία
ἄγνοια	ἀπό	δίδωμι	ἐπίγνωσις	κατεργάζομαι	ὅς	πρός	φιλάδελφος
ἀδελφός	ἀπογίνομαι	διεγείρω	ἐπιθυμέω	κῆρυξ	ὅστις	προφητεία	φυλακή
ἀδελφότης	ἀποδίδωμι	δίκαιος	ἐπιθυμία	κηρύσσω	ὅτι	προφητεύω	φυλάσσω
ἀδικέω	ἀπόθεσις	δικαιοσύνη	ἐπικαλέω	κλέπτης	οὐ	προφήτης	φῶς
ἀδικία	ἀπόλλυμι	δικαίως	ἐπίλοιπος	κλῆσις	οὐδέ	προφητικός	φωσφόρος
ἄδικος	ἀπολογία	διό	ἐπίλοιπος	κοινωνέω	οὖν	πρῶτος	χαίρω
ἀδίκως	ἀπόστολος	δόξα	ἐπιστρέφω	κοινωνός	οὐρανός	πῦρ	χαρά
ἀεί	ἀποτίθημι	δοξάζω	ἐποπτεύω	κοσμέω	οὗτος	πυρόω	χάρις
ἀθέμιτος	ἀρετή	δοῦλος	ἐπόπτης	κόσμος	οὕτως	πύρωσις	χάρισμα
ἄθεσμος	ἀρχαῖος	δουλόω	ἔργον	κρείττων	ὀφθαλμός	ῥῆμα	Χριστός
αἷμα	ἀρχή	δύναμις	ἔρχομαι	κρίμα	παρά	σαρκικός	ψυχή
αἵρεσις	ἄρχω	ἑαυτοῦ	ἔσχατος	κρίνω	παραδίδωμι	σάρξ	ὡς
αἰών	ἀσεβής	ἐγείρω	εὑρίσκω	κρίσις	παρακαλέω	σκότος	
αἰώνιος	ἀσέλγεια	ἐγώ	ἔχω	κτίσις	παρατίθημι	στηρίζω	
ἀκοή	ἄσπιλος	εἰ	ζάω	κτίστης	πάρειμι	σύ	
ἀκούω	αὐξάνω	εἰμί	ζωή	κυλισμός	παρεισφέρω	συμβαίνω	
			ζῷον				

ἀλήθεια	αὐτός	εἰρήνη	ζωοποιέω	κύριος	παρέρχομαι	συνάγω
ἀληθής	βασιλεία	εἰς	ἤ	λαλέω	πᾶς	συνίστημι
ἀλλά	βασίλειος	εἴτε	ἡμέρα	λαμβάνω	πατήρ	σῴζω
ἄλογος	βασιλεύς	ἐκ	θεῖος	λαός	πειρασμός	σωτήρ
ἀμαράντινος	βλασφημέω	ἕκαστος	θέλημα	λογίζομαι	περί	σωτηρία
ἀμάραντος	βλάσφημος	ἑκάστοτε	θέλω	λογικός	περιέχω	τέκνον
ἁμαρτάνω	βούλημα	ἐκλεκτός	θεός	λόγιον	περιποίησις	τηρέω
ἁμάρτημα	βούλομαι	ἐκλογή	ἴδιος	λόγος	Πέτρος	τίθημι
ἁμαρτία	γάρ	ἐκπίπτω	Ἰησοῦς	λοιπός	πιστεύω	τιμάω
ἁμαρτωλός	γεννάω	ἐλευθερία	ἵνα	μακροθυμέω	πίστις	τιμή
ἀμήν	γίνομαι	ἐλεύθερος	ἰσότιμος	μακροθυμία	πιστός	τίμιος
ἀμνός	γινώσκω	ἐμπλέκω	ἰσχύς	μάταιος	πλανάω	τίς
ἀμώμητος	γνωρίζω	ἐμπλοκή	καθαρισμός	ματαιότης	πλῆθος	τις
ἄμωμος	γνῶσις	ἐμπορεύομαι	καθαρός	μέλλω	πληθύνω	ὕδωρ
ἀναγγέλλω	γραφή	ἐν	καθώς	μένω	πνεῦμα	υἱός
ἀναγεννάω	γράφω	ἔννοια	καί	μετά	πνευματικός	ὑπακοή

Bibliography

Achtemeier, Paul. *1 Peter*, Hermeneia. Minneapolis: Fortress Press, 1996.
Achtemeier, Paul J., Joel B. Green, and Marianne Meye Thompson. *Introducing the New Testament: Its Literature and Theology*. Grand Rapids: Eerdmans, 2001.
Anatolios, Khaled. *Deification through the Cross: An Eastern Christian Theology of Salvation*. Grand Rapids: Eerdmans, 2020.
Arndt, William, et al. *A Greek-English Lexicon of the New Testament and Other Early Christian Literature*. Chicago: University of Chicago Press, 2000.
Auksi, Peter. *Christian Plain Style: The Evolution of a Spiritual Ideal*. Montreal and Kingston: McGill-Queen's University Press, 1995.
Aune, David E. *Rereading Paul Together: Protestant and Catholic Perspectives on Justification*. Grand Rapids: Baker, 2006.
Barclay, John M. G. *Paul and the Gift*. Grand Rapids: Eerdmans, 2017.
Barclay, Katie. "Love and Violence in the Music of Late Modernity." *Popular Music and Society* 41.5 (2018): 539–55.
Bartholomew, Craig G., and Michael W. Goheen. "Story and Biblical Theology." In *Out of Egypt: Biblical Theology and Biblical Interpretation*. Edited by Craig Bartholomew, Mary Healy, Karl Moller, and Robin Parry, 144–71. Grand Rapids: Zondervan, 2004.
Bateman, Herbert W., IV. "'Memories' about the Old Testament in Jewish and Christian Tradition Inform 2 Peter and Jude, Part 1." *JETS* 67.1 (2024): 103–12.
Bates, Matthew. *Salvation by Allegiance Alone: Rethinking Faith, Works, and the Gospel of Jesus the King*. Grand Rapids: Baker Academic, 2017.
Bauckham, Richard J. "The Apocalypse of Peter: A Jewish Christian Apocalypse from the Time of Bar Kokhba." *Apocrypha* 5 (1994): 7–111.
Bauckham, Richard J. "The Delay of the *Parousia*." *TB* 31.1 (1980): 3–36.
Bauckham, Richard J. *Jesus and the Eyewitnesses: The Gospels as Eyewitness Testimony*. Grand Rapids: Eerdmans, 2008.
Bauckham, Richard J. *Jesus and the God of Israel: God Crucified and Other Studies on the New Testament's Christology of Divine Identity*. Grand Rapids: Eerdmans, 2008.
Bauckham, Richard J. *Jude–2 Peter*, WBC. Nashville: Word, 1983.
Bauckham, Richard J. "Pseudo-Apostolic Letters." *JBL* 107.3 (1988): 469–94.
Bauckham, Richard J. "2 Peter and the Apocalypse of Peter Revisited: A Response to Jörg Frey." In *2 Peter and the Apocalypse of Peter: Towards a New Perspective*. Edited by Jörg Frey, Matthijs Dulk, and Jan van der Watt, 261–81. Leiden: Brill, 2019.
Baum, Armin D. "Content and Form: Authorship Attribution and Pseudonymity in Ancient Speeches, Letters, Lectures, and Translations – A Rejoinder to Bart Ehrman." *JBL* 136.2 (2017): 381–403.
Bavinck, Herman. *Reformed Dogmatics*. Vol. 1. Grand Rapids: Baker, 2003.
Beilby, James K., and Paul Rhodes Eddy. *Justification: Five Views*. Downers Grove: IVP Academic, 2011.

Bernier, Jonathan. *Rethinking the Dates of the New Testament: The Evidence for Early Composition*. Grand Rapids: Baker, 2022.
Bigg, Charles. *A Critical and Exegetical Commentary on the Epistles of St. Peter and St. Jude*, ICC. Edinburgh: T&T Clark, 1910.
Bird, Michael F. *The Gospel of the Lord: How the Early Church Wrote the Story of Jesus*. Grand Rapids: Eerdmans, 2014.
Bloesch, Donald. *Holy Scripture: Revelation, Inspiration, & Interpretation*. Downers Grove: IVP Academic, 2005.
Boda, Mark J. *The Heartbeat of Old Testament Theology: Three Creedal Expressions*, Acadia Studies in Bible and Theology. Grand Rapids: Baker Academic, 2017.
Bonhoeffer, Dietrich. *Dietrich Bonhoeffer's Christmas Sermons*. Translated and edited by Edwin H. Robertson. Grand Rapids: Zondervan, 2011.
Bonhoeffer, Dietrich. *Discipleship*. Minneapolis: Fortress Press, 2015.
Boobyer, G. H. "The Indebtedness of 2 Peter to 1 Peter." In *New Testament Essays: Studies in Memory of T. W. Manson*. Edited by A. J. B. Higgins, 34–53. Manchester: University of Manchester Press, 1959.
Boring, Eugene M. *An Introduction to the New Testament: History, Literature, Theology*. Louisville: Westminster John Knox Press, 2012.
Bowersock, G. W. *Greek Sophists in the Roman Empire*. Oxford: Clarendon Press, 1969.
Brueggemann, Walter. *The Psalms and the Life of Faith*. Minneapolis: Fortress Press, 1995.
Burge, David K. "A Sub-Christian Epistle? Appreciating 2 Peter as an Anti-Sophistic Polemic." *JSNT* 44.2 (2021), 310–32.
Callan, Terrance. "A Note on 2 Peter 1:19–20." *JBL* 125.1 (2006): 143–50.
Callan, Terrance. "Reading the Earliest Copies of 2 Peter." *Biblica* 93.3 (2012): 427–50.
Callan, Terrence. "The Second Letter of Peter, Josephus and Gnosticism." In *2 Peter and the Apocalypse of Peter: Towards a New Perspective*. Edited by Jörg Frey, Matthijs Dulk, and Jan van der Watt, 128–44. Leiden: Brill, 2019.
Callan, Terrence. "The Style of the Second Letter of Peter." *Biblica* 84 (2003): 202–24.
Calvin, John. *Commentaries on the Catholic Epistles*. Edinburgh: The Calvin Translation Society, 1855.
Campbell, Constantine R. *Paul and Union with Christ: An Exegetical and Theological Study*. Grand Rapids: Zondervan, 2012.
Campbell, Constantine R. *Verbal Aspect, the Indicative Mood, and Narrative: Soundings in the Greek of the New Testament*. New York: Peter Lang, 2007.
Campbell, Douglas A. *Framing Paul: An Epistolary Biography*. Grand Rapids: Eerdmans, 2014.
Campbell, Douglas A. *The Deliverance of God: An Apocalyptic Rereading of Justification in Paul*. Grand Rapids: Eerdmans, 2009.
Campbell, Douglas A. *The Quest for Paul's Gospel: A Suggested Strategy*. New York: T&T Clark, 2005.
Chapman, Stephen B. "Reclaiming Inspiration for the Bible." In *Canon and Biblical Interpretation*. Edited by Craig Bartholomew et al., 167–206. Grand Rapids: Zondervan, 2006.
Charles, J. Daryl. "The Language and Logic of Virtue in 2 Peter 1:5–7." *BBR* 8 (1998): 55–73.
Charles, J. Daryl. *Virtue Amidst Vice: The Catalog of Virtues in 2 Peter 1*, JSNTSup, 150. Sheffield: Sheffield Academic Press, 1997.
Chang, Andrew D. "Second Peter 2:1 and the Extent of the Atonement." *BibSac* 142 (1985): 52–63.
Chatraw, Joshua D., and Jack Carson. *Surprised by Doubt: How Disillusionment Can Invite Us into Deeper Faith*. Grand Rapids: Brazos Press, 2023.
Cokayne, Karen. *Experiencing Old Age in Ancient Rome*. Abingdon: Taylor & Francis, 2013.
Crisp, Oliver D. *Participation and Atonement: An Analytic and Constructive Account*. Grand Rapids: Baker Academic, 2022.
Crisp, Oliver D., James M. Arcadi, and Jordan Wessling, eds. *Love, Divine and Human: Contemporary Essays in Systematic and Philosophical Theology*. New York: Bloomsbury, 2019.
Crump, David. *Feeling Like God: A Spiritual Journey to Emotional Wholeness*. Toronto: Clements, 2005.
Danker, Frederick W. "2 Peter 1: A Solemn Decree." *CBQ*, 40.1 (1978): 64–82.

Davids, Peter H. *The Letters of 2 Peter and Jude*. Grand Rapids: Eerdmans, 2006.
Davids, Peter H. *II Peter and Jude: A Handbook on the Greek Text*. Waco: Baylor University Press, 2011.
Davids, Peter H. *A Theology of James, Peter, and Jude*, Biblical Theology of the New Testament. Grand Rapids: Zondervan, 2014.
Davids, Peter H. "What Glasses Are You Wearing? Reading Hebrew Narratives through Second Temple Lenses." *JETS* 55.4 (2012): 763–71.
deSilva, David A. *An Introduction to the New Testament: Contexts, Methods, and Ministry Formation*. Downers Grove: IVP Academic, 2004.
deSilva, David A. "Testament of Moses." In *Dictionary of New Testament Background*. Edited by Craig A. Evans and Stanley E. Porter, 1192–99. Downers Grove: InterVarsity Press, 2000.
Dockery, David. *Christian Scripture: An Evangelical Perspective on Inspiration, Authority, and Interpretation*. Nashville: Broadman & Holman, 1995.
Dodd, C. H. *The Apostolic Preaching and Its Developments*. New York: Harper & Row, 1964.
Doering, Lutz. *Ancient Jewish Letters and the Beginnings of Christian Epistolography*. Tübingen: Mohr Siebeck, 2012.
Donelson, Lewis R. *I & II Peter and Jude*, New Testament Library. Louisville: Westminster John Knox Press, 2010.
Dunn, James D. G. *The Partings of the Ways: Between Christianity and Judaism and Their Significance for the Character of Christianity*. Norwich: SCM Press, 2006.
Dunn, James D. G. *The Theology of Paul the Apostle*. Grand Rapids: Eerdmans, 1998.
Emerson, Matthew Y. "Does God Own a Death Star? The Destruction of the Cosmos in 2 Peter 3:1–13." *SWJT* 57.2 (2015): 281–93.
Estelle, Bryan D. *Echoes of Exodus: Tracing a Biblical Motif*. Downers Grove: InterVarsity Press, 2018.
Estrada III, Rodolfo Gavan. "Blaspheming Angels: The Presence of Magicians in Jude 8–10." *JETS* 63.4 (2020): 739–58.
Evans, C. Stephen. "Canonicity, Apostolicity, and Biblical Authority." In *Canon and Biblical Interpretation*. Edited by Craig Bartholomew et al., 146–66. Grand Rapids: Zondervan, 2006.
Fanning, Buist M. *Verbal Aspect in New Testament Greek*. Oxford: Clarendon Press, 1990.
Farkasfalvy, Denis. *Inspiration & Interpretation: A Theological Introduction to Sacred Scripture* Washington DC: Catholic University of America Press, 2010.
Feinberg, Paul D. "The Meaning of Inerrancy." In *Inerrancy*. Edited by Norman L. Geisler, 267–304. Grand Rapids: Zondervan, 1980.
Feldmeier, Reinhard. *The First Letter of Peter: A Commentary on the Greek Text*. Waco: Baylor University Press, 2008.
Ferda, Tucker S. *Jesus and His Promised Second Coming: Jewish Eschatology and Christian Origins*. Grand Rapids: Eerdmans, 2024.
Fitzgerald, John T. "Virtue/Vice Lists." In *The Anchor Bible Dictionary*. Edited by David Noel Freedman, 857–59. New Haven: Yale University Press, 1992.
Foster, Paul. "Does the Apocalypse of Peter Help to Determine the Date of 2 Peter?" In *2 Peter and the Apocalypse of Peter: Towards a New Perspective*. Edited by Jörg Frey, Matthijs Dulk, and Jan van der Watt, 217–60. Leiden: Brill, 2019.
Frame, John M. *The Doctrine of the Word of God*, A Theology of Lordship. Vol. 4. Philipsburg: P&R, 2010.
Fredericksen, Paula. *When Christians Were Jews: The First Generation*. New Haven: Yale University Press, 2018.
Fresch, Christopher J. "2 Peter." In *Discourse Analysis of the New Testament Writings*. Edited by Todd A. Scacewater, 621–50. Minneapolis: Fortress Press, 2020.
Frey, Jörg. *The Letter of Jude and the Second Letter of Peter: A Theological Commentary*. Waco: Baylor University Press, 2018.
Frey, Jörg, Matthijs den Dulk, and Jan G. van der Watt, eds. *2 Peter and the Apocalypse of Peter: Towards a New Perspective*. Leiden: Brill, 2019.
Frey, Jörg. "Second Peter in New Perspective." In *2 Peter and the Apocalypse of Peter: Towards a New Perspective*. Edited by Jörg Frey, Matthijs Dulk, and Jan van der Watt, 7–74. Leiden: Brill, 2019.

Frye, Michael. "Identifying a Summarizing Structure in 2 Peter 3:14–18a through Discourse Analysis." Unpublished paper submitted to PhD Seminar. Liberty University, Lynchburg, VA, May 10, 2024.
Fuhr, Richard Alan, Jr., and Gary E. Yates. *The Message of the Twelve: Hearing the Voice of the Minor Prophets*. Nashville: B&H, 2016.
Galek, Kathleen, et al. "Religious Doubt and Mental Health Across the Lifespan." *Journal of Adult Development* 14.1–2 (June 2007): 16–25.
Gallaher, Brandon, and Julia S. Konstantinovsky. "Divine Action in Christ: The Christocentric and Trinitarian Nature of Human Cooperation with God." In *When the Son of Man Didn't Come: A Constructive Proposal on the Delay of the Parousia*. Edited by Christopher M. Hays, 147–74. Minneapolis: Fortress Press, 2016.
Gathercole, Simon J. *The Preexistent Son: Recovering the Christologies of Matthew, Mark, and Luke*. Grand Rapids: Eerdmans, 2006.
Gempf, Conrad. "Pseudonymity and the New Testament." *Themelios*, 17.2 (1992): 8–10.
Gilmour, Michael J. "Reflections on the Authorship of 2 Peter." *EQ* 73.4 (2001): 291–309.
Gilmour, Michael J. *The Significance of Parallels Between 2 Peter and Other Early Christian Literature*, Academia Biblica 10. Atlanta; Leiden: SBL; Brill, 2002.
Gladd, Benjamin L., and Matthew S. Harmon. *Making All Things New: Inaugurated Eschatology for the Life of the Church*. Grand Rapids: Baker, 2016.
Goldstein, Jonah, and Jeremy Rayner. "The Politics of Identity in Late Modern Society." *Theory and Society* 23.3 (1994): 367–84.
Gordley, Matthew. *New Testament Christological Hymns: Exploring Texts, Contexts, and Significance*. Downers Grove: InterVarsity Press, 2018.
Gorman, Michael J. *Becoming the Gospel: Paul, Participation, and Mission*. Grand Rapids: Eerdmans, 2015.
Gorman, Michael J. *Inhabiting the Cruciform God: Kenosis, Justification, and Theosis in Paul's Narrative Soteriology*. Grand Rapids: Eerdmans, 2009.
Gorman, Michael J. *Participating in Christ: Explorations in Paul's Theology and Spirituality*. Grand Rapids: Baker Academic, 2019.
Graves, Michael. *The Inspiration and Interpretation of Scripture: What the Early Church Can Teach Us*. Grand Rapids: Eerdmans, 2014.
Green, Gene L. *Jude and 2 Peter*, BECNT. Grand Rapids: Baker Academic, 2008.
Green, Joel B. "Narrating the Gospel in 1 and 2 Peter." *Interpretation* 60.3 (2006): 262–77.
Green, Joel B., and Stuart L. Palmer. *In Search of The Soul: Four Views of The Mind-body Problem*. Downers Grove: IVP Academic, 2005.
Green, Michael. *2 Peter & Jude*, TNTC. Downers Grove: IVP Academic, 1987.
Gruber, Mayer I. *Hosea: A Textual Commentary*. New York: Bloomsbury T&T Clark, 2017.
Grünstäudl, Wolfgang. "'On Slavery' A Possible *Herrenwort* in 2 Pet. 2:19." *Novum Testam* 57 (2015): 57–71.
Grünstäudl, Wolfgang. *Petrus Alexandrinus: Studien zum historischen und theologischen Ort des Zweiten Petrusbriefes*, WUNT 2.315. Tübingen: Mohr Siebeck, 2013.
Gupta, Nijay K. *Paul and the Language of Faith*. Grand Rapid: Eerdmans, 2020.
Guinness, Os. *God in the Dark: The Assurance of Faith Beyond a Shadow of Doubt*. Wheaton: Crossway Books, 1996.
Guthrie, Donald. *New Testament Introduction*. 4th ed. Downers Grove: IVP Academic, 1990.
Hafemann, Scott. "'Noah, the Preacher of (God's) Righteousness': The Argument from Scripture in 2 Peter 2:5 and 9." *CBQ* 76 (2014): 306–20.
Hagner, Donald A. *The New Testament: A Historical and Theological Introduction*. Grand Rapids: Baker Academic, 2012.
Harink, Douglas. *1 & 2 Peter*, BTCB. Grand Rapids: Brazos Press, 2009.
Harrill, J. Albert. "Slavery." In *Dictionary of New Testament Background*. Edited by Craig A. Evans and Stanley E. Porter, 1124–27. Downers Grove: IVP Academic, 2000.
Harrington, Hannah K. "Sin." In *Eerdmans Dictionary of Early Judaism*. Edited by John J. Collins and Daniel C. Harlow, 1230–31. Grand Rapids: Eerdmans, 2010.
Hart, David J. H. *Christianity: A New Look at Ancient Wisdom*. Kelowna, BC: Wood Lake, 2005.

Hays, Christopher M. "The Delay of the Parousia: A Traditional and Historical-Critical Reading of Scripture: Part 2." In *When the Son of Man Didn't Come: A Constructive Proposal on the Delay of the Parousia*. Edited by Christopher M. Hays, 79–108. Minneapolis: Fortress Press, 2016.

Hays, Christopher M., ed. *When the Son of Man Didn't Come: A Constructive Proposal on the Delay of the Parousia*. Minneapolis: Fortress Press, 2016.

Hays, Richard B. *The Faith of Jesus Christ: The Narrative Substructure of Gal. 3:1–4:11*. Grand Rapids: Eerdmans, 2002.

Heide, Gale Z. "What Is New about the New Heaven and the New Earth? A Theology of Creation from Revelation 21 and 2 Peter 3." *JETS* 40.1 (1997): 37–56.

Heiser, Michael S. *The Unseen Realm: Recovering the Supernatural Worldview of the Bible*. Bellingham: Lexham Press, 2015.

Hellerman, Joseph H. *The Ancient Church as Family*. Minneapolis: Fortress Press, 2001.

Hellerman, Joseph H. *Jesus and the People of God: Reconfiguring Ethnic Identity*, New Testament Monographs. Sheffield: Sheffield Phoenix Press, 2007.

Hellerman, Joseph H. *When the Church Was a Family: Recapturing Jesus' Vision for Authentic Christian Community*. Nashville: B&H, 2009.

Henry, Carl H. F. "Canonical Theology: An Evangelical Appraisal." *Scottish Bulletin of Evangelical Theology* 8 (1990): 76–108.

Hoag, Gary G. *Wealth in Ancient Ephesus and the First Letter to Timothy: Fresh Insights from Ephesiaca by Xenophon of Ephesus*. University Park: Penn State University Press, 2015.

Horton, Michael. *Justification*. Grand Rapids: Zondervan, 2018.

Hunsberger, Bruce, and Susan Alisat, S. Mark Pancer, and Michael W. Pratt. "Religious Fundamentalism and Religious Doubts: Content, Connections and Complexity of Thinking." *International Journal for the Psychology of Religion* 6:3 (July 1996): 201–20.

Hurtado, Larry W. *Lord Jesus Christ: Devotion to Jesus in Earliest Christianity*. Grand Rapids: Eerdmans, 2003.

Jensen, Matthew D. "Noah, the Eighth Proclaimer of Righteousness: Understanding 2 Peter 2.5 in Light of Genesis 4.26." *JSNT* 37.4 (2015): 458–69.

Jobes, Karen H. *1 Peter*, BECNT. Grand Rapids: Baker Academic, 2005.

Johnson, Luke T. "The New Testament's Anti-Jewish Slander and the Conventions of Ancient Polemic." *SBL* 108.3 (1989): 419–41.

Judd, Andrew. *Modern Genre Theory: An Introduction for Biblical Studies*, HarperCollins Christian, 2024.

Kärkkäinen, Veli-Matti. *Trinity and Revelation*, A Constructive Christian Theology for the Pluralist World. Vol. 2. Grand Rapids: Eerdmans, 2014.

Käsemann, Ernst. "An Apologia for Primitive Christian Eschatology." In *Essays on New Testament Themes*. Translated by W. J. Montague, 169–95. SBT 41. London: SCM, 1964.

Keating, James, and Thomas Joseph White. *Divine Impassibility and the Mystery of Human Suffering*. Grand Rapids: Eerdmans, 2009.

Keener, Craig S. "Adultery, Divorce." In *Dictionary of New Testament Background*. Edited by Craig A. Evans and Stanley E. Porter, 6–8. Downers Grove: IVP Academic, 2000.

Keener, Craig S. *The Gospel of Matthew: A Socio-Rhetorical Commentary*. Grand Rapids: Eerdmans, 2009.

Keener, Craig S. *1 Peter: A Commentary*. Grand Rapids: Baker Academic, 2021.

Kelly, J. N. D. *The Epistles of Peter and of Jude*, BNTC. London, Adam and Charles Black Limited, 1969.

Knopf, Rudolf. *Die Briefe Petri und Juda*, Kritisch-exegetischer Kommentar über das Neue Testament 12. Göttingen: Vandenhoeck & Ruprecht, 1912.

Koester, Craig R. "The Savior of the World (John 4:42)." *Journal of Biblical Literature*, 109 (1990): 665–80.

Krause, Neal, Berit Ingersoll-Dayton, Christopher G. Ellison, and Keith M. Wulff. "Aging, Religious Doubt, and Psychological Well-Being." *Gerontologist* 39.5 (1999): 525–33.

Kruger, Michael J. "The Authenticity of 2 Peter." *JETS* 42 (1999): 645–71.

Kruger, Michael J. "2 Peter 3:2, the Apostolate, and a Bi-Covenantal Canon." *JETS* 63.1 (2020): 5–24.

Kugler, Robert A. "Testaments." In *The Eerdman's Dictionary of Early Judaism*. Edited by John J. Collins and Daniel C. Harlow, 1295–97. Grand Rapids: Eerdmans, 2010.
Kuhn, Karl. "2 Peter 3:1–13." *Interpretation: A Journal of Bible and Theology* 60.3 (2006): 310–12.
Kümmel, Werner George. *Introduction to the New Testament*. Rev. ed. Nashville: Abingdon Press, 1975.
Ladd, George Eldon. *The Presence of the Future: The Eschatology of Biblical Realism*. Grand Rapids: Eerdmans, 1974.
Laird, Benjamin P. *Creating the Canon: Composition, Controversy, and the Authority of the New Testament*. Downers Grove: IVP Academic, 2023.
Laird, Benjamin P. *The Pauline Corpus in Early Christianity: Its Formation, Publication, and Circulation*. Peabody: Hendrickson Academic, 2022.
Levenson, Jon D. *The Love of God: Divine Gift, Human Gratitude, and Mutual Faithfulness in Judaism*. Princeton: Princeton University Press, 2015.
Liddell, Henry George and Robert Scott. *A Greek-English Lexicon*. Oxford: Clarendon Press, 1940.
Lövestam, Evald. "Eschatologie und Tradition im 2 Petrusbrief." In *The New Testament Age: Essays in Honor of Bo Reicke*. Vol. 2. Edited by William C. Weinrich, 287–300. Macon: Mercer University Press, 1984.
Louw, Johannes P., and Eugene Albert Nida. *Greek-English Lexicon of the New Testament: Based on Semantic Domains*. New York: United Bible Societies, 1996.
Lyons, Kelly. "Spotify Wrapped 2023: Top Songs, Artists, Podcasts and Listening Trends." www.newsweek.com/spotify-wrapped-2023-listening-trends-1848048.
Lyons, William John. *Canon and Exegesis: Canonical Praxis and the Sodom Narrative*. Sheffield: Sheffield Academic Press, 2002.
Machiela, Daniel A. "Flood." In *Eerdman's Dictionary of Early Judaism*. Edited by John. C. Collins and Daniel C. Harlow, 645–46. Grand Rapids: Eerdmans, 2010.
Makujina, John. "The 'Trouble' with Lot in 2 Peter: Locating Peter's Source for Lot's Torment." *Westminster Theological Journal* 60.2 (1998): 255–69.
Malina, Bruce J. "Christ and Time: Swiss or Mediterranean?" *CBQ* 51.1 (1989): 1–31.
Malina, Bruce J. *The New Testament World: Insights from Cultural Anthropology*. Louisville: Westminster John Knox Press, 2001.
Marshall, I. Howard. *New Testament Theology: Many Witnesses, One Gospel*. Downers Grove: IVP Academic, 2004.
Mathews, Mark D. "The Genre of 2 Peter: A Comparison with Jewish and Early Christian Testaments." *Bulletin of Biblical Research* 21.1 (2011): 51–64.
Mathewson, David L., and Elodi Ballantine Emig. *Intermediate Greek Grammar: Syntax of Students of the New Testament*. Grand Rapids: Baker, 2016.
Mathewson, David L. "Verbal Aspect in Imperative Constructions in Pauline Ethical Injunctions." *Filología Neotestamentaria* 9.17 (1996): 21–35.
Matz, Robert J., and A. Chadwick Thornhill. *Divine Impassibility: Four Views of God's Emotions and Suffering*. Downers Grove: IVP Academic, 2019.
Mayor, Joseph B. *The Epistle of St. Jude and the Second Epistle of St. Peter: Greek Text with Introductions, Notes and Comments*. Minneapolis: Klock and Klock, 1978.
McCormack, Bruce L. *Justification in Perspective: Historical Developments and Contemporary Challenges*. Grand Rapids: Baker Academic, 2006.
McDowell, Sean. *The Fate of the Apostles: Examining the Martyrdom Accounts of the Closest Followers of Jesus*. New York: Routledge, 2015.
McKnight, Scot. *Kingdom Conspiracy: Returning to the Radical Mission of the Local Church*. Grand Rapids: Brazos Press, 2016.
McKnight, Scot. *The King Jesus Gospel: The Original Good News Revisited*. Grand Rapids: Zondervan, 2016.
McKnight, Scot, and Joseph B. Modica. *Jesus is Lord, Caesar is Not: Evaluation Empire in New Testament Studies*. Downers Grove: InterVarsity Press, 2013.
McIntyre, Hugh. "Americans Are Spending More Time Listening to Music Than Ever Before." Forbes. www.forbes.com/sites/hughmcintyre/2017/11/09/americans-are-spending-more-time-listening-to-music-than-ever-before/?sh = 471de9c92f7f.

Meier, John P. "Forming the Canon on the Edge of the Canon: 2 Peter 3:8–18." *Mid-Stream*, 38 (1999): 65–70.
Merkle, Benjamin L. *Exegetical Gems from Biblical Greek: A Refreshing Guide to Grammar and Interpretation*. Grand Rapids: Baker Academic, 2019.
Metzger, Bruce M. "Literary Forgeries and Canonical Pseudepigrapha." *JBL* 92 (1972): 5–12.
Metzger, Bruce M. *A Textual Commentary on the Greek New Testament*. 2nd ed. London: United Bible Societies, 1994.
Middleton, J. Richard *A New Heaven and a New Earth: Reclaiming Biblical Eschatology*. Grand Rapids: Baker Academic, 2014.
Miller, James C. "The Sociological Category of 'Collective Identity' and Its Implications for Understanding Second Peter." In *Reading Second Peter with New Eyes: Methodological Reassessments of the Letter of Second Peter*. Edited by Robert L. Webb and Duane F. Watson, 147–78. Bloomsbury, 2010.
Miszczyński, Damian. "Justice for Animals According to Plutarch." *Mare Nostrom* 10.1 (2019): 54–76.
Moltmann, Jürgen. *The Crucified God: The Cross of Christ as the Foundation and Criticism of Christian Theology*. Minneapolis: Fortress, 1993.
Morrison, John Douglas. *Has God Said? Scripture, the Word of God, and the Crisis of Theological Authority*. Eugene: Pickwick, 2006.
Morrison, John D. "Scripture as Word of God: Evangelical Assumption or Evangelical Question?" *Trinity Journal* 20:2 (1999): 165–90.
Moses, A. D. A. *Matthew's Transfiguration Story and Jewish-Christian Controversy*, JSNT Supp 122. Sheffield: Sheffield Academic Press, 1996.
Muck, Johannes. "Discours d'Adieu dans le Nouveau Testament et dans la Literature Biblique." In *Aux Sources de la Tradition Chrétienne Mélanges Offerts a M. Maurice Goguel a l'Occasion de Son Soixante-Dixième Anniversaire*. Paris: Neuchâtel Delachaux & Niestlé, 1950.
Nellas, Panayiotis. *Deification in Christ: Orthodox Perspectives on the Nature of the Human Person*. Yonkers: St. Vladimir's Seminary Press, 1987.
Neyrey, Jerome H. "The Apologetic Use of the Transfiguration in 2 Peter 1:16–21." *CBQ* 42.4 (1980): 504–19.
Neyrey, Jerome H. "The Form and Background of the Polemic in 2 Peter." *JBL* 99.3 (1980): 407–31.
Neyrey, Jerome. *2 Peter, Jude*, ABC. New Haven: Yale University Press, 2004.
Nickelsburg, George W. E. "Apocalyptic and Myth in 1 Enoch 6–11." *JBL* 96.3 (1977): 399–404.
Noble, Alan. *Disruptive Witness: Speaking Truth in a Distracted Age*. Downers Grove: IVP, 2018.
Noort, Ed, and Eibert Tigchelaar, eds. *Sodom's Sin: Genesis 18–19 and Its Interpretations*. Leiden: Brill, 2021.
Nouwen, Henri J. M. *Finding My Way Home: Pathways to Life and the Spirit*. New York: Crossroad, 2001.
O'Mathúna, D. P. "Divination, Magic." In *Dictionary of the Old Testament: Pentateuch*. Edited by T. Desmond Alexander and David W. Baker, 457–68. Downers Grove: IVP Academic, 2002.
Oropeza, B. J. *Churches under Siege of Persecution and Assimilation: Apostasy in the New Testament Communities, Volume 3: The General Epistles and Revelation*. Eugene: Wipf & Stock, 2012.
Orr, James. *Revelation and Inspiration*. New York: Scribner's, 1910.
Packer, J. I. *"Fundamentalism" and the Word of God*. Grand Rapids: Eerdmans, 1958.
Peckham, John C. *The Love of God: A Canonical Model*. Downers Grove: IVP, 2015.
Perkins, Pheme. *First and Second Peter, James, and Jude*, Interpretation: A Bible Commentary for Teaching and Preaching. Louisville: Westminster John Knox Press, 1995.
Picirilli, Robert E. "Allusions to 2 Peter in the Apostolic Fathers." *Journal for the Study of the New Testament* 33 (1988): 57–83.
Porter, Stanley E. "Aspect and Imperatives Once More." *BAGL* 7 (2018): 141–72.
Porter, Stanley E. *Verbal Aspect in the Greek of the New Testament, with Reference to Tense and Mood*. New York: Peter Lang, 1989.
Porter, Stanley E., and Andrew W. Pitts. "τοῦτο πρῶτον γινώσκοντες ὅτι in 2 Peter 1:20 and Hellenistic Epistolary Convention." *JBL* 127.1 (2008): 165–71.

Ramsay, Sir William Mitchell. *The Cities of St. Paul: Their Influence on His Life and Thought.* New York: A. C. Armstrong, 1908.

Reed, Annette Yoshiko. *Fallen Angels and the History of Judaism and Christianity: The Reception of Enochic Literature.* Cambridge: Cambridge University Press, 2005.

Reed, Annette Yoshiko, ed. *Jewish-Christianity and the History of Judaism: Collected Essays.* Tübingen: Mohr Siebeck, 2018.

Reese, Ruth Anne. "Narrative Method and the Letter of Second Peter." In *Reading Second Peter with New Eyes: Methodological Reassessments of the Letter of Second Peter.* Edited by Robert L. Webb and Duane F. Watson, 119–46. Bloomsbury, 2010.

Reese, Ruth Anne. *2 Peter & Jude*, The Two Horizons New Testament Commentary. Grand Rapids: Eerdmans, 2007.

Reuschling, Wyndy Corbin. "The Means and End in 2 Peter 1:3–11: The Theological and Moral Significance of Theosis." *Journal of Theological Interpretation* 8.2 (2014): 275–86.

Richard, Earl J. *Reading 1 Peter, Jude, and 2 Peter: A Literary and Theological Commentary.* Macon: Smyth and Helwys Publishing, 2013.

Richards, E. Randolph. *Paul and First-Century Letter Writing: Secretaries, Composition and Collection.* Downers Grove: IVP Academic, 2004.

Richards, E. Randolph, and Kevin J. Boyle. "Did the Ancients Know the Testaments Were Pseudepigraphic? Implications for 2 Peter." *Bulletin for Biblical Research* 30.3 (2020): 403–23.

Rodogno, Raffaele. "Shame, Guilt, and Punishment." *Law and Philosophy* 28 (2009): 429–64.

Rösel, Martin. "The Reading and Translation of the Divine Name in the Masoretic Tradition and the Greek Pentateuch." *JSOT* 31 (2007): 411–28.

Rothwell, Jonathan. "Teens Spend Average of 4.8 Hours on Social Media Per Day." https://news.gallup.com/poll/512576/teens-spend-average-hours-social-media-per-day.aspx.

Rowe, C. Kavin. *Early Narrative Christology: The Lord in the Gospel of Luke.* Berlin: de Gruyter, 2006.

Rowling, J. K. *Harry Potter and the Goblet of Fire.* New York: Scholastic Press, 2000.

Runge, Steven E. *Discourse Grammar of the Greek New Testament: A Practical Introduction for Teaching and Exegesis.* Peabody, MA: Hendrickson, 2010.

Runge, Steve E., and Christopher J. Fresch, eds. *The Greek Verb Revisited: A Fresh Approach for Biblical Exegesis.* Bellingham: Lexham Press, 2016.

Russell, Norman. *The Doctrine of Deification in the Greek Patristic Tradition.* Oxford: Oxford University Press, 2006.

Sandy, Brent. *Plowshares and Pruning Hooks: Rethinking the Language of Biblical Prophecy and Apocalyptic.* Downers Grove: IVP Academic, 2002.

Schreiner, Patrick. *The Kingdom of God and the Glory of the Cross*, Short Studies in Biblical Theology. Wheaton: Crossway, 2018.

Schreiner, Patrick. *The Transfiguration of Christ: An Exegetical and Theological Reading.* Grand Rapids: Baker Academic, 2024.

Schreiner, Thomas R. *1 & 2 Peter and Jude*, Christian Standard Commentary. Nashville: Holman, 2020.

Schreiner, Thomas R. *Faith Alone: The Doctrine of Justification and Why It Still Matters.* Grand Rapids: Zondervan, 2015.

Schooping, Joshua. *A Manual of Theosis: Orthodox Christian Instruction on the Theory and Practice of Stillness, Watchfulness, and Ceaseless Prayer.* Olyphant: St. Theophan the Recluse Press, 2020.

Schumacher, Leonhard. *Sklaverei in der Antike: Alltag und Schicksal der Unfreien.* Munich: C. H. Beck, 2001.

Seely, Kelly Adair. *A Study of Petrine Christology from Key Texts in 2 Peter.* Eugene: Wipf & Stock 2021.

Skaggs, Rebecca. "The Spirit in 1 Peter, 2 Peter, and Jude: Transformation and Transcendence." *Pneuma* 43 (2021): 538–42.

Sidebottom, E. M. *James, Jude, 2 Peter.* Grand Rapids: Eerdmans, 1982.

Silva, Moisés, ed. *New International Dictionary of New Testament Theology and Exegesis.* Vol. 2. Grand Rapids: Zondervan, 2014.

Skarsaune, Oskar, and Reidar Hvalvik, eds., *Jewish Believers in Jesus: The Early Centuries*. Grand Rapids: Baker Academic, 2017.
Smith, Terence V. *Petrine Controversies in Early Christian: Attitudes Toward Peter in Christian Writings of the First Two Centuries*, WUNT 2.15. Tübingen: Mohr Siebeck, 1985.
Starr, J. M. *Sharers in the Divine Nature: 2 Peter 1:4 in Its Hellenistic Context, Coniectanea biblica*: New Testament Series. Stockholm: Almquist & Wiksell, 2000.
Steinmann, Andrew E. *Genesis: An Introduction and Commentary*, TOTC. Downers Grove: IVP Academic, 2019.
Streett, R. Alan. *Subversive Meals: An Analysis of the Lord's Supper Under Roman Domination During the First Century*. Eugene: Wipf & Stock, 2013.
Strine, C. A. "Reconceiving Prophecy: Activation, Not Prognostication." In *When the Son of Man Didn't Come: A Constructive Proposal on the Delay of the Parousia*. Edited by Christopher M. Hays, 39–58. Minneapolis: Fortress Press, 2016.
Sylva, Dennis D. "A Unified Field Picture of Second Peter 1.3–15: Making Rhetorical Sense Out of Individual Images." In *Reading Second Peter with New Eyes: Methodological Reassessments of the Letter of Second Peter*. Edited by Robert L. Webb and Duane F. Watson, 91–118. New York: Bloomsbury Publishing, 2010.
Taylor, Charles. *The Malaise of Modernity*. Toronto: House of Anansi Press, 1991.
Teslina, Margaryta. "'Apostles' in 2 Peter 3.2: Literal Predecessors in Faith or Literary Records of their Witness?" *JSNT* 44.1 (2021): 170–93.
Thiede, Carsten Peter. "A Pagan Reader of 2 Peter: Cosmic Conflagration in 2 Peter 3 and the *Octavius* of Minucius Feux." *JSNT* 26 (1986): 79–96.
Thiselton, Anthony C. *The Two Horizons: New Testament Hermeneutics and Philosophical Description with Special Reference to Heidegger, Bultmann, Gadamer, and Wittgenstein*. Grand Rapids: Eerdmans, 1980.
Thomson, Christopher J. "What Is Aspect? Contrasting Definitions in General Linguistics and New Testament Studies." In *The Greek Verb Revisited: A Fresh Approach for Biblical Exegesis*. Edited by Steven E. Runge and Christopher J. Fresch, 13–80. Bellingham: Lexham Press, 2016.
Thornhill, A. Chadwick. *The Chosen People: Election, Paul, and Second Temple Judaism*. Downers Grove: IVP Academic, 2013.
Thornhill, A. Chadwick. "Does the Spirit Have a Story? A Narrative Theology of the Holy Spirit." *Journal of Theological Interpretation* 14.2 (2020): 246–66.
Thornhill, A. Chadwick. "Election and Predestination." In *The Dictionary of Paul and His Letters: A Compendium of Contemporary Biblical Scholarship*. Edited by Lynn Cohick, Nijay Gupta, and Scot McKnight. Downers Grove: IVP Academic, 2022.
Thornhill, A. Chadwick. "Emotional Doubt and Divine Hiddenness." *Eleutheria* 1.2 (2014): 1–18.
Thornhill, A. Chadwick. "A Theology of Psalm 88." *EQ* 87.1 (2015): 45–57.
Thurén, Lauri. "Style Never Goes out of Fashion: 2 Peter Re-evaluated." In *Rhetoric, Scripture and Theology: Essays from the 1994 Pretoria Conference*. Edited by S. E. Porter and T. H. Olbricht, 329–47. Sheffield: Sheffield Academic Press, 1996.
Tilling, Chris. *Paul's Divine Christology*. Grand Rapids: Eerdmans, 2015.
Tooth, Sydney. *Suddenness and Signs: The Eschatologies of 1 and 2 Thessalonians*. Tübingen: Mohr Siebeck, 2024.
Trapp, Michael, ed. *Greek and Latin Letters: An Anthology with Translation*. Cambridge: Cambridge University Press, 2003.
van der Kold, Bessel. *The Body Keeps the Score: Brain, Mind, and Body in the Healing of Trauma*. London: Penguin Books, 2015.
Vanhoozer, Kevin J. *The Drama of Doctrine: A Canonical Linguistic Approach to Christian Doctrine*. Philadelphia: Westminster John Knox Press, 2005.
Vasaly, Ann. "Cicero's Early Speeches." In *Brill's Companion to Cicero*. Edited by James M. May, 71–111. Leiden: Brill, 2002.
Wall, Robert W. "The Canonical Function of 2 Peter." *Biblical Interpretation* 9.1 (2001): 64–81.
Walton, John H. *The Lost World of Genesis One: Ancient Cosmology and the Origins Debate*. Downers Grove: InterVarsity Press, 2010.

Walton, John H. *The Lost World of Scripture: Ancient Literary Culture and Biblical Authority*. Downers Grove: IVP Academic, 2013.
Wand, J. W. C. *The General Epistles of St. Peter and St. Jude*. London: Methuen, 1934.
Watson, Duane F., and Terrance D. Callan. *First and Second Peter*, PCNT. Grand Rapids: Baker, 2012.
Watson, Duane Frederick. *Invention, Arrangement, and Style: Rhetorical Criticism of Jude and 2 Peter*, SBL Dissertation Series, 104. Atlanta: Scholars Press, 1988.
Weima, Jeffrey A. D. *Paul the Ancient Letter Writer: An Introduction to Epistolary Analysis*. Grand Rapids: Baker Academic, 2016.
Wenham, David. "Being 'Found' on the Last Day: New Light on 2 Peter 3.10 and 2 Corinthians 5.3." *NTS* 33 (1987): 477–79.
Werse, Nicholas R. "Second Temple Jewish Literary Traditions in 2 Peter." *CBQ* 78 (2016): 111–30.
Wessling, Jordan. *Love Divine: A Systematic Account of God's Love for Humanity*. Oxford: Oxford University Press, 2020.
West, Thomas H. *Jesus and the Quest for Meaning: Entering Theology*. Minneapolis: Fortress Press, 2001.
Westerholm, Stephen. *Justification Reconsidered: Rethinking a Pauline Theme*. Grand Rapids: Eerdmans, 2013.
White, Carolinne. *The Correspondence (394–419) between Jerome and Augustine of Hippo*. Lewiston: Mellen, 1990.
White, John. "The Greek Documentary Letter Tradition Third Century BCE to Third Century CE." *Semeia* 22 (1981): 89–106.
Wilder, Jim. *Renovated; God, Dallas Willard, and the Church That Transforms*. Colorado Springs: NavPress, 2020.
Wilder, Terry L. *Pseudonymity, the New Testament, and Deception: An Inquiry into Intention and Reception*. Lanham: University Press of America, 2004.
Wilder, Terry L. "Revisiting Pseudonymity, the New Testament, and the Noble Lie." *JBTM* 19.2 (2022): 367–80.
Willard, Dallas. *Life Without Lack: Living in the Fullness of Psalm 23*. Nashville: Thomas Nelson, 2018.
Williams, Travis B. "The Amanuensis Hypothesis in New Testament Scholarship: Its Origin, Evidential Basis, and Application." *CBR* 22.1 (2023): 7–82.
Williams, Travis B. "Confirming Scripture through Eyewitness Testimony (2 Peter 1.19a): Resolving a *Crux Interpretum*." *JSNT* 43.4 (2021): 605–24.
Windisch, Hans. *Die Katholischen Briefe*. 3rd ed., Handbuch zum Neuen Testament 15. Tübingen: J.C.B. Mohr (Paul Siebeck), 1951.
Winter, Bruce W. "Is Paul among the Sophists?" *RTR* 53.1 (1994): 28–38.
Winter, Bruce W. *Philo and Paul among the Sophists*. Grand Rapids: Eerdmans, 2002.
Winters, Clifford D. "A Strange Death: Cosmic Conflagration as Conceptual Metaphor in 2 Peter 3:6–13." *Conversations with the Biblical World* 33 (2013): 147–62.
Witherington, Ben, III. *Letters for Hellenized Christians*. Vol. II. Downers Grove: IVP Academic, 2007.
Witherington, Ben, III. *The Letters to Philemon, the Colossians, and the Ephesians: A Socio-Rhetorical Commentary on the Captivity Epistles*. Grand Rapids: Eerdmans, 2007.
Witherington, Ben, III, and Jason A. Myers. *New Testament Rhetoric*. 2nd ed. Eugene: Cascade Books, 2022.
Wolters, Al. "Worldview and Textual Criticism in 2 Peter 3:10." *Westminster Theological Journal* 49.2 (1987): 405–13.
Wolterstorff, Nicholas. *Divine Discourse: Philosophical Reflections on the Claim that God Speaks*. Cambridge: Cambridge University Press, 1995.
Wright, N. T. *How God Became King: Getting to the Heart of the Gospels*. New York: HarperOne, 2012.
Wright, N. T. *Jesus and the Victory of God*. Minneapolis: Fortress Press, 1996.
Wright, N. T. *Justification: God's Plan and Paul's Vision*. Downers Grove: IVP Academic, 2009.

Wright, N. T. *The New Testament and the People of God*, Christian Origins and the Question of God. Vol. 1. Minneapolis: Fortress Press, 1992.
Wright, N. T. *Surprised by Hope: Rethinking Heaven, the Resurrection, and the Mission of the Church*. New York: HarperOne, 2008.
Wright, N. T., and Michael Bird, *The New Testament in Its World: An Introduction to the History, Literature, and Theology of the First Christians*. Grand Rapids: Zondervan, 2019.
Zerwick Max, and Mary Grosvenor. *Grammatical Analysis of the Greek New Testament*. Vol. 2, *Epistles-Apocalypse*. Rome: Biblical Institute Press, 1979.

Ancient Sources Index

Old Testament

Genesis

1:1, 44
1:3–30, 171
1–2, 170
4:20, 92
6:1–4, 117, 123, 172
6:5, 118
6:9, 121
6:17, 44, 121
6–8, 121
7:1, 121
7:11, 171
9:11, 173
11:1–9, 172
11:10–32, 172
12:8, 92
13:1–14, 126
13:3, 92
13:5, 92
13:10–14, 124
13:12, 92
13:13, 126
14:1–12, 126
14:16, 126
15:11, 177
18:1, 92
18:19, 114
19:8, 124
19:9, 126
19:12–29, 122
19:13, 124
19:14, 124
19:16, 124
19:24–25, 184
19:29, 44
19:33, 124
49, 181
50:20, 78

Exodus

15:11, 131
18:18, 70
19:1, 87
20:14, 125
20:17, 125
22:8, 185
22:31, 155
24:27, 47
28:2, 98
28:40, 98
34:6–7, 180

Leviticus

10:1–2, 184
11:7, 155
18:24–30, 126
18–20, 125
19:2, 126
19:9–10, 125
19:26, 145
21:17–23, 139
22:20–25, 139
24:19–20, 139
26:18–19, 125

Numbers

8:6, 82
11:25–26, 107
11:29, 196
14:18, 180
19:2, 139
22:5, 143–44
22:7, 145
22:21–35, 44
22:28, 144
22:30, 143–44
22–24, 143, 145
23:7, 144
23:23, 145
24:1, 145
24:6, 92
24:17, 44, 103–4
25, 143–44
31:8, 143
31:16, 143–44

Deuteronomy

4:3, 129
5:21, 125
6:4, 78
6:14, 129
8:11–18, 125
11:26–28, 141
14:8, 155
15:7–11, 125
15:21, 139
16:16, 92
17:1, 139
18:10–14, 145
18:20, 106, 110
22:22, 185
22:22–30, 125
22:28, 185
23:4–5, 142–43
23:6, 141
24:14–15, 125
28:14, 129
28:15, 141
28:45, 141
29:18–21, 126
29:23, 122
30:1, 141
30:15–20, 126
30:19, 141
31:10, 92
31–33, 181
32:8, 118
33:18, 92
32:22, 174
32:32, 122
33:26, 100

Joshua

3:14, 92
13:22, 143
24:1–28, 90
24:9–10, 142–43

Judges

2:22, 114
5:17, 92
19:9, 122

1 Samuel

2:10, 183
7:10, 183
10:1, 104
10:6, 107
19:20, 104
19:23, 107

2 Samuel

7:8–17, 58
7:12–16, 86
7:13, 208
7:16, 208
7:23, 122
22:29, 103
23:2, 107

1 Kingdoms

12:23, 142

2 Kingdoms

14:25, 139

2 Kings

1:10, 184
9:10, 155
18:28, 116

3 Kingdoms

11:10, 129

1 Chronicles

17:14, 208
22:10, 208
28:7, 208

2 Chronicles

15:8, 102

Ezra

10:18, 185

Nehemiah

9:17, 180
9:30, 107
13:2, 142–43

Esther

5:1a, 97

Job

1:6, 118
2:1, 118
7:21, 83, 236
29:3, 103
38:4–7, 170
38:6–7, 184
38:7, 118
38:9, 146
40:9, 183
40:20, 119

Psalms

1:6, 115
2:6, 98
2:6–7, 44
2:7, 103
3:5, 98
8:5, 44
14:1, 98
18:13–15, 183
18:28, 103
24:2, 170
29:1, 118
33:6, 171
35:23, 168
42:3, 98
42:10, 165
44:23, 116
44:23–24, 168
47:2, 98
72:1–7, 193
77:18, 183
79:10, 165
86:1, 98
86:15, 180
88, 169
88:6–9, 169
88:15, 169
89:6, 118
90:2, 177
90:4, 44, 177
90:9–10, 177
90:15, 177
98:9, 98
102:4, 70
103:8, 180
104:7, 183
106:7, 142
113:1, 87
118:30, 114
119:33, 115
119:105, 103
120:4, 116
121:4, 116
136:6, 170
145:8, 180
148:2–5, 170
148:5, 171

Proverbs

2:13, 142
2:16, 142

4:11, 115
5:6, 115
6:23, 103
8:20, 115
10:29, 114
12:28, 115
13:14, 146
16:31, 115
26:11, 44, 155

Ecclesiastes

10:16, 138

Song of Solomon

4:7, 139

Isaiah

1:9–10, 122
2:2, 164
2:2–4, 193
3:9, 122
5:11, 138
5:18–20, 164
5:28, 116
9:7, 193, 208
11:4–5, 193
11:9, 98
11:32, 100
13:6, 92, 182, 214
13:9, 92, 182, 214
13:10, 182
13:19, 122
13:22, 179
16:5, 193
24:3, 70
26:7, 115
27:6, 164
27:13, 98
29:6, 174, 183
29:18, 147
30:27–33, 174
30:8, 164
32:16–19, 193
32:27, 174
33:14, 174
33:15, 142
33:3, 183
34:4, 44, 182, 191
37:28, 87
38:12, 92
40–55, 209
42:1, 100
42:8, 73
42:12, 73
42:18–19, 82
42:21, 73
43:8, 82
45:12, 170
51:6, 182
51:14, 179
52:5, 44
54:9, 121
56:7, 98
56:10, 82
56:13, 98
59:8, 115
59:10, 82
60:1, 104
60:22, 44, 189
61:1, 107
63:7, 73
65, 174
65:2, 129
65:11, 98
65:17, 44, 192
65:25, 98
66:15–16, 184
66:15–24, 174
66:22, 192

Jeremiah

5:4–5, 114
5:12–24, 164
6:13, 110
8:4–7, 135
14:14, 106, 110
14:3, 146
17:15, 165
20:9, 106
21:8, 115
23:14, 122
23:16, 106, 110
23:20, 164
23:5–6, 193
25:30, 183

30:24, 166
36:4, 47
36:32, 47
38:23, 98
48:47, 164
49:18, 122
49:39, 164
50:24, 185
50:40, 122

Lamentations

4:6, 122
4:14, 82

Ezekiel

7:19, 92, 182, 214
13:3, 106, 110
13:5, 104, 182, 214
14:14, 121
14:20, 121
16:46–56, 122
16:47, 122
16:49, 123
18:23, 180
18:23–32, 181
18:25, 114
18:29, 114
20:40, 98
28:14, 98
30:3, 104, 182, 214
32:7–8, 182
32:27, 118
33:11, 180–81
33:17, 114
33:20, 114
38:16, 164

Daniel

2:28, 164
2:37, 98
3:92, 70
4:3, 208
4:30, 98
4:34, 208
7:13–14, 103
7:14, 44, 86
7:27, 44
9:16–17, 98
9:20, 98
10:8, 70
11:45, 98

Hosea

2:4, 187
3:5, 164
11:10, 129
14:10, 142

Joel

1:15, 104, 182, 214
2, 58
2:1, 98, 104, 165, 182, 214
2:2, 107, 146, 238
2:8, 107
2:10, 182
2:11, 104, 182, 214
2:12–13, 180
2:13, 180
2:17, 165
2:30, 174
2:31, 104, 182, 214
3:14, 104, 182, 214
3:15, 182
3:16, 183
4:16, 183
4:17, 98

Amos

1:2, 183
2:11, 82
4:11, 122
4:13, 147, 238
5:18, 104, 182, 214
5:20, 104, 182, 214
9:10, 164

Obadiah

15, 104, 182, 214
16–17, 98

Jonah

2:7, 70
4:2, 180

Micah

2:10, 70
4:1, 164
4:1-4, 193
6:5, 143

Nahum

1:3, 55
1:6, 174

Habakkuk

2:3, 44, 179
3:3, 73, 98

Zephaniah

1:7-8, 104, 182, 214
1:12, 164
1:14, 104, 182, 214
1:15, 147
1:17, 82
1:18, 104, 174, 182, 184, 214
2:2-3, 104, 182, 214
2:9, 112
3:8, 174
3:11, 98
8:3, 98

Zechariah

4:6, 107
6:13, 73
7:12, 107
9:9-10, 193
13:2, 110
14:1, 104, 182, 214
14:16, 122
14:18-19, 122

Malachi

2:17, 164-65
3:2, 184

3:19, 184
3:20, 104
4:1, 174, 191
4:5, 104, 182, 214

New Testament

Matthew

1:1, 58, 209
1:6, 209
1:21, 209
3:11-12, 184
3:13-17, 209
3:17, 79, 100, 209
4:17, 164
4:18-19, 9
5:9, 79, 142
5:15, 103
5:18, 182
5:20, 87
5:25, 113
5:28, 140
5:43-44, 76
5:45, 79, 142
6:9, 209
6:13, 20
7:15-21, 110
8:18, 79
10:1-15, 58
10:15, 122
10:23, 166
10:24, 57
10:33, 112
10:42, 146
11:3, 188
11:23-24, 122
12:45, 20, 152
13:22, 80
13:38, 79
13:39, 132
13:41, 86, 132
13:49, 132
15:3, 154
15:14, 82
15:19, 110
16:17-18, 57
16:27, 66, 98, 132

Ancient Sources Index

16:27–28, 96
16:28, 86, 166
17:1, 97
17:1–13, 210
17:5, 79, 97, 209
18:3, 87
20:21, 86
21:9–15, 58
21:32, 115
22:16, 114
22:3–14, 84
22:40, 80
22:44, 164
23:16, 82
23:24, 82
24:11, 110
24:11–13, 79
24:14, 189
24:24, 110
24:29, 182
24:29–34, 166
24:30–51, 2
24:31, 132
24:35, 182
24:36, 183
24:37–38, 121
24:43, 20
24:44, 182
24:46, 185
24:50, 188
25:1–13, 2
25:1–46, 166
25:31, 132
25:31–46, 2
26:6–13, 209
26:59, 110
26:60, 70
26:69–75, 9
26:70, 112
26:72, 112
28:7, 113
28:19–20, 189

Mark

1:9–11, 209
1:11, 79, 100
1:15, 164
1:16, 9
1:20, 174
1:44, 83
2:17, 174
3:13–18, 9
4:19, 80
4:21, 103
4:38, 91, 160
7:13, 155
8:38–9:1, 96
9:1, 20, 166
9:2, 97
9:2–13, 210
9:7, 79, 209
9:41, 146
9:42–47, 153
10:23, 87
10:44, 58
10:45, 112
12:24, 114
12:30–31, 76
12:36, 107
13:20, 84
13:20–37, 2
13:22, 110
13:22–23, 165
13:24–25, 182
13:30, 166
13;31, 182
13:32, 186
13:32–37, 186
13:36, 185
14:1–11, 209
14:21, 153
14:62, 58
14:66–72, 9
14:68, 112
15:43, 131

Luke

1:21, 188
1:32, 58
1:33, 208
1:67, 107
1:70, 161
1:78, 104
2:22, 83
3:21–22, 209
3:22, 79, 100

3:31, 209
4:18, 209
5:32, 178
6:13, 58, 84
6:26, 110
6:35, 79, 142
6:39, 82
7:36–50, 209
8:16, 103
8:24, 91, 160
9:1, 58
9:26–27, 96
9:28, 97
9:28–36, 210
9:31, 94
9:31–32, 98
9:32, 66
9:35, 79, 84, 209
10:11, 164
10:12, 122
10:42, 84
11:26, 152
11:33, 103
11:42, 79
12:9, 112
12:35–59, 2
12:37–38, 185
12:40, 182
12:43, 185
12:45, 166
12:46, 188
12:47–48, 154
13:15, 146
14:7, 84
14:15–24, 84
15:22, 113
16:17, 182
16:23, 128
16:24, 146
17:20–21, 164
17:20–37, 2
17:29, 122
18:17, 87
20:21, 115
20:36, 79
20:37, 93
21:5–38, 2
21:25–26, 182
21:33, 182

22:14–36, 90
22:54–62, 9
22:57, 112
22:69, 58
23:4, 185

John

1:1, 132, 142
1:1–3, 171
1:12, 79, 142
1:14, 47, 141
1:16, 47
2:6, 83
3:5, 87
3:16, 76, 78–79, 209
3:25, 83
4:13–15, 146
4:42, 61
5:19–20, 209
5:42, 79
6:18, 160
6:70, 84
7:22, 167
7:38, 146
8:32, 151
8:34, 150
9:40–41, 82
10:30, 209
10:34–36, 69
11:29, 113
11:52, 79, 142
12:1–11, 209
12:36, 79
12:40, 82
13:16, 57
13:18, 84
13:36, 93
13:36–38, 93
13:38, 112
13–17, 90
14:6–10, 209
15:15, 96
15:16, 84
15:19, 84
17:3, 62
17:26, 96
18:15–18, 9
18:25, 112

18:25–27, 9
18:27, 112
18:36, 86
18:38, 185
19:4, 185
21:15, 112
21:18, 20
21:18–19, 93
21:19, 112
21:22–23, 166
21:24, 47

Acts

1:10–11, 2
1:16, 107
1:18, 137
1:2, 84
1:23, 58
1:24, 84
1:6–11, 189
2:17, 70, 164
2:17–18, 107
2:18, 58
2:19, 79, 184
2:20, 70, 182
2:28, 96
2:33, 164
3:5, 188
3:19–20, 189
3:21, 161
4:13, 10, 13
4:24, 112
4:26–27, 209
5:17, 111
5:31, 58
6:3–10, 200
6:5, 84
7:46, 146
7:55–56, 58
9:15, 84
9:27, 198
10:24, 188
10:38, 209
12:12, 198
13:6, 110
13:10, 142
13:17, 84
13:23, 67

13:28, 185
13:32, 167
14:14, 58, 162
15:5, 111
15:7, 84
15:9, 83
15:14, 57
15:22, 84
15:25, 157
15:40, 198
16:4, 155
16:17, 58
16:40, 197
17:18, 37
17:29, 64
17:30–31, 181
19:6, 107
20:17–35, 90
20:28, 211
21:7, 197
21:17–20, 197
22:1, 66, 83
22:16, 83
23:1, 197
23:5–6, 197
23:9, 185
24:14, 111
26:5, 111
26:6, 67
28:15, 197
28:17, 197
28:25, 107
28:6, 188

Romans

1:1, 57
1:1–4, 58
1:4, 209
1:7, 62, 157
1:28, 22, 62
2:4, 22, 180
2:5, 22
2:19, 82
3:3, 72
3:20, 62
5:1–5, 70
5:3–4, 74
5:3–5, 76

5:5, 79
5:8, 76, 78–79
6, 150
6:4, 66
6:13, 60
6:17, 155, 211
6:17–18, 112
6:17–19, 58
6:20, 150
7:7, 70
7:12, 154
8:14, 142
8:14–19, 79
8:15, 209
8:19, 142
8:21, 70, 79, 142
8:23, 79
8:28, 78
8:29, 209
8:30, 84
8:34, 58
9:5, 61, 167
9:7, 84
9:11, 84
9:12, 84
9:22–23, 96
9:24–26, 84
9:26, 142
9:29, 122
10:2, 62
11:5, 84
11:7, 84
11:25–26, 189
11:28, 84
11:29, 70, 84
11:32, 181
12:10, 22
13:10, 76
13:12, 186
13:14, 148
14:17, 86
15:5, 74
15:15, 131
15:30, 79
16:3–16, 194
16:7, 58, 162
16:21–23, 194
16:22, 13, 47
16:25–27, 194
16:26, 96

1 Corinthians

1:3, 62
1:9, 84
1:12, 21
1:26, 70, 84
1:27–28, 84
2:1–16, 200
2:5, 72
3:10, 22
3:13, 93
3:22, 21
4:2, 22
4:6–13, 58
4:9, 162
4:17, 157
4:20, 86
5:5, 70, 182
6:9, 22
6:9–10, 86
6:20, 22, 112, 211
7:15–24, 84
7:20, 84
7:23, 22, 112, 211
8:7, 75
9:5, 21, 162
11:2, 155
11:17–34, 139
11:19, 111
11:23, 155
12:3, 96
12:7–8, 199
12:8, 199
12:28–29, 162
13:13, 76
14:14, 22, 80
14:37, 154
15:1, 96
15:3, 155
15:5, 21, 162
15:7, 162
15:9, 162
15:10, 22
15:15, 110
15:24, 86
15:35–58, 2
15:38, 97
15:42, 70
15:50, 70
15:58, 186

16:19-20, 194
16:21, 13
16:21-22, 194
16:23-24, 194

2 Corinthians

1:14, 70, 182
1:2, 62
4:14, 82
5:1-4, 22
5:3, 185
5:4, 153
6:6-7, 70, 73
7:1, 83
8:1, 96
8:7, 70, 72-73
8:23, 58, 162
11:13, 110
11:26, 107
12:2-4, 183
13:11, 79
13:12-13, 194
13:14, 79, 194

Galatians

1:3, 62
1:6, 84
1:11, 96
1:11-17, 180
1:15, 84
1:17, 162
1:19, 58, 162
2:4, 110
2:11-14, 21
2:20, 168
3:26, 79, 142
4:1-6, 154
4:3, 184
5:7-10, 186
5:8, 84
5:13, 92
5:16, 85, 148
5:20, 111
5:21, 86
5:22, 76
5:22-23, 70, 72, 74
5:24, 70
6:8, 70

6:11, 13
6:16, 194
6:18, 194

Ephesians

1:2, 62
1:3-14, 137
1:4, 84, 139, 196
1:5, 161
1:9, 96
1:17, 62, 199
1:18, 84, 92
1:20, 58
1:21, 131
2:3, 142, 148
2:4, 180
2:20, 162
3:3, 96
3:5, 70, 96, 162
3:6, 67
3:10, 96
3:19, 90
4:1, 84, 92
4:4, 84, 169
4:11, 70, 162
4:13, 62
5:1, 70, 157
5:2, 79
5:5, 86
5:8, 142
5:10-16, 186
5:11, 80
5:11-13, 186
5:26, 83
5:27, 138, 196
6:14-17, 70, 72
6:19, 96
6:21-22, 194
6:23-24, 194

Philippians

1:1, 47
1:9, 62
2:15, 22, 139, 142, 196
2:25, 58, 162
3:14, 84, 184
3:20, 2, 87
4:5, 186

4:8, 70, 73
4:14-19, 194
4:21-22, 194

Colossians

1:1, 47
1:2, 62
1:9-10, 62
1:11, 74
1:13, 86
1:16, 131
1:19, 199
1:22, 139, 196
1:27, 96
2:2, 62
2:8, 184
2:20, 184
2:22, 70
3:1, 58
3:4, 2
3:5, 70
3:10, 62
3:12-14, 70, 168
3:14, 76
3:15, 70
4:5, 186
4:11, 86
4:16, 22, 199
4:18, 13

1 Thessalonians

1:1, 47, 58, 62, 162
1:3, 22
1:3-4, 74
1:4, 84
1:9, 22
1:9-10, 2
2:1, 22
2:6, 162
2:7, 162
2:9, 92
2:12, 86, 186
2:14, 70
3:4, 92
3:13, 22
4:1, 92
4:5, 70
4:7, 107
4:9, 22
4:15, 22
4:16-17, 2
5:1-2, 92
5:1-11, 186
5:2, 22, 79, 182-83
5:2-4, 2
5:5, 162
5:8, 22
5:24, 79, 194
5:26, 194
5:27, 194

2 Thessalonians

1:1, 47
1:2, 62
1:5, 86
1:7, 132
1:7-10, 2
1:7-9, 185
1:8, 174
1:11, 84, 107
1:12, 61
2:1, 198
2:1-8, 2
2:2, 182
2:3, 70
3:5, 74, 79, 92
3:10, 92
3:16, 194
3:17, 194
3:18, 194

1 Timothy

1:17, 98
1:2, 62
1:3, 110
2:4, 62, 180-81
2:4-6, 181
3:2-3, 70
4:1, 112
4:7-8, 141
4:10, 181
6:1, 115
6:9, 70
6:11, 70, 72, 74
6:12, 70

6:14, 154, 186, 196
6:14-15, 2

2 Timothy

1:1, 67
1:2, 62
1:9, 84, 122
2:8, 209
2:22, 70
2:25, 62
3:1, 164
3:7, 62
3:10, 74
3:16, 45, 107, 200
3:16-17, 212
4:1, 86
4:1-2, 186
4:15, 186
4:18, 86
4:19, 194
4:20-21, 194
4:22, 194

Titus

1:1, 57, 62, 80
1:2-3, 67
1:4, 62
1:7-8, 70
1:12, 80
2:2, 74
2:5, 115
2:11, 181
2:13, 2, 61
2:14, 83
3:4, 79
3:5, 83
3:14, 80
3:15a, 194
3:15b, 194

Philemon

1, 197
3, 62
6, 62
19, 13
23-24, 194
25, 194

Hebrews

1:1, 167
1:2, 164
1:3, 58, 83, 100
1:8, 86
2:7, 66
2:10, 164
3:1, 84, 122
3:7, 107
3:14, 69
4:1, 67
5:1, 82
5:14, 141
6:4, 152
6:4-8, 154, 181
6:6, 152
6:8, 184
6:12, 67
8:1, 58
8:6, 67
9:8, 93
9:14, 83, 139
9:15, 67, 122
9:19, 154
9:28, 2
10:15-16, 70
10:22, 83
10:26, 154
10:36, 67
10:36-37, 166
11:3, 171
11:7, 121
11:8, 70
11:13, 67
11:39, 67
12:2, 58
12:5-8, 79
12:11, 141
12:28, 86
12:29, 174

James

1:3-4, 74
1:5, 199
1:12, 67
1:14, 70, 140
1:17, 62
1:19, 113

2:5, 67, 84, 86
2:8–13, 76
2:14–26, 72
2:20, 80
3:17–18, 70
4:8, 83
5:3, 164
5:7–8, 2, 166
5:8–9, 186

1 Peter

1:1, 160
1:2, 16, 62, 158
1:7, 2
1:10–12, 16, 91, 158, 161
1:11, 107, 121
1:13–17, 186
1:14, 142
1:15, 129
1:17, 121
1:18–19, 112, 211
1:19, 16, 139, 158
2:9, 142
2:12, 97
2:21, 149
2:24, 60
3:1, 121
3:2, 2, 97
3:4, 121
3:8, 75
3:9, 162
3:12, 60
3:12–13, 60
3:14, 60
3:16, 115
3:18, 60
3:19, 16, 158
3:19–20, 123
3:20, 16, 120–21, 158
3:22, 58
4:3, 70
4:4, 121
4:7, 186
4:14, 121
4:18, 60
5:1, 186
5:8–9, 186
5:10, 164
5:11, 194
5:12, 194, 198
5:12–14, 55
5:13, 198
5:13–14, 194
5:14b, 194

1 John

1:7, 83
2:5, 76
2:7–8, 155
2:16, 140
2:25, 67
2:28, 2, 186
3:1–2, 142
3:2, 164
3:10, 142, 167
3:11–17, 76
3:23, 76
4:1, 110
4:7, 76
4:9–11, 92
4:19, 185
5:2, 79, 142
5:4, 76
5:20, 61
11:37, 98

2 John

1:3, 62

Jude

2, 62
3, 155
4, 112
4–18, 18
6, 123
7, 122–23
11, 143
12, 80, 139
17, 162
18, 164
24, 139

Revelation

1:4, 62
1:6, 86

1:7, 2
1:9, 86
2:14, 143–44
2:16, 113
2:19, 70, 72
3:3, 183
3:11, 2, 113
3:21, 164
4:11, 66
5:9, 112, 211
5:10, 86
5:12, 66
5:12–13, 98
7:2, 132
7:17, 146
8:2, 132
8:6, 132
8:13, 132
9:15, 132
9:17–18, 174
9:18, 185
11:8, 122
11:14, 113
11:15, 86
12:10, 86
13:6, 162
14:3–4, 112, 211
14:5, 139, 185
16:8, 174
16:13, 110
16:14, 188
16:15, 2, 183
18:8, 185
19:9, 174
19:20, 110
20:9, 174
20:9–10, 185
20:10, 110
20:11, 182
21:1, 182
21:3, 164
21:23, 103
22:5, 103
22:7, 113
22:7–20, 2
22:12, 113
22:16, 104
22:20, 113
22:21, 191

Apocrypha

2 Esdras

2:8–9, 122
16:12, 102

4 Ezra

3:30, 180
4:26, 189
4:36–37, 189
5:1–13, 112
6:38, 171
6:42, 170
7:32–34, 112
7:75, 193
7:79, 128
14:28–36, 4

2 Maccabees

2:16, 83
3:39, 97
6:31, 73
7:35, 97
8:15, 100
8:33, 137
10:6, 130
10:28, 73
15:12, 73
15:13, 100
15:17, 73

3 Maccabees

2:4–5, 123
2:21, 97
6:1, 73

4 Maccabees

1:2, 73
1:10, 73
1:30, 73
1:8, 73
2:10, 73
7:22, 73
9:8, 73
9:18, 73

10:10, 73
11:2, 73
12:14, 73
13:24, 73
13:27, 73
17:12, 73
17:23, 73

Sirach

5:4-7, 180
16:7, 118
16:7-8, 73
16:8, 123
18:9-11, 177-78
20:24, 139
24:3, 146
32:22, 179
33:23, 139
35:22, 179
38:23, 87
41:9, 142
43:22, 146
47:20, 139
48:1, 103

Tobit

14:3-11, 4

Wisdom of Solomon

2:4, 146
2:21, 82
2:22, 137
3:2, 87
4:1, 73
4:25, 70
5:6, 114
5:13, 73
7:6, 94
8:7, 73
9:1, 171
9:8, 98
9:15, 129
10:6, 123-24
10:9, 124
10:17, 137
11:15, 135
11:23, 180
14:12, 70

15:1, 180
18:4, 103
19:17, 124

Old Testament Pseudepigrapha

2 Baruch

12:4, 180
32:6, 193
41:3, 112
42:4, 112
44:12, 193
48:12-13, 177
48:13, 177
57:2, 193
57-86, 4
77:13-15, 103

1 Enoch

1:6-7, 174
6:12, 117
6-16, 123
10:4-12, 120
10:4-6, 118
18:11, 120
20:2, 119
21:7, 120
22:10-11, 128
45:4-5, 193
52:6, 174
72:1, 193
88:1-3, 120
90, 185
90:26, 112
91:16, 182
91:16-17, 193
91-104, 4
93:4, 121
93:9, 112
102:3, 100
108, 185

2 Enoch

3-22, 183
33:1, 177
47:5, 170

Ancient Sources Index

Jubilees

1:29, 193
2:2–7, 170
4:4, 118
4:30, 177
5:10, 120
7:20–21, 110
7:21–24, 118
16:5, 123
20:5, 123
21–22, 4
35:1–36:8, 4

L.A.B.

9:8, 103
15:6, 103
18:13, 144
19:1–5, 4
19:5, 103
19:13a, 177
24:1–5, 4
28:33, 4
28:3–4, 4
28:5–10, 4

Letter of Aristeas

141–166, 130

Life of Adam and Eve

25–29, 4

Odes of Solomon

4:3, 73
6:7, 70

Psalms of Solomon

4:6, 70
12:6, 192
15:4, 112
17:5, 192
17:40, 193

Sibylline Oracles

1:155, 121
1:195–270, 121
1:215–244, 121
2:196–213, 121, 174
2:303, 119
3:80–93, 174
4:171–82, 174
4:175b, 183
5:155–61, 174
5:206–13, 70
5:211–12, 193

Testament of Benjamin

8:2–3, 130

Testament of Dan

2:4, 82

Testament of Judah

13:2, 129
18:3, 82
18:6, 82
19:4, 82
24:1, 104
25:2, 131

Testament of Levi

2–5, 183
3:4, 100
17:8, 130
18:3, 104

Testament of Moses

7:4, 138

Testament of Naphtali

1:26–27, 123
3:4–5, 112

Testament of Simeon

2:7, 82

Philo

Allegorical Interpretation
1:64, 70
3:43, 102
3:9:30, 135

Decalogue
104, 68

On Agriculture
32, 144, 155

On the Embassy to Gaius
7:49, 119
14:103, 119

On the Life of Abraham
144, 68

On the Life of Joseph
5:26, 141

On the Life of Moses
1:45, 295–304, 143
1:48, 266–68, 143
1:48, 268, 143
1:281–83, 106
1:283, 107
1:295–300, 144
2:53–65, 123
2:58, 123, 125
I:154, 74
I:161, 74
I:303, 74
II:185, 74

On the Sacrifices of Cain and Abel
27, 70

On the Special Laws
1:29, 148,155
1:65, 106–7
4:49, 106
I:149–150, 74
I:173–175, 74
I:186, 74
I:193, 74
II:195, 74
III:22, 74

On the Virtues
127, 74
180, 74

Questions and Answers on Genesis
3:10, 106

Who Is the Heir?
259, 106

Josephus

Jewish Antiquities
1:2:3, 174
1:22, 174
1:70–71, 121
1:73, 118
4:119, 107
4:121, 106
4:126–30, 144
4:189, 94
4:309–19, 4
8:107, 68
10:11:6, 135

Jewish War
4:5:2, 130

Against Apion
1:31§282, 83
1:232, 68
2:29–31, 135
2:33:240, 119
2:256, 174

Index

ancient letter, 3, 7, 15
angels, 35, 96, 108, 117–19, 123, 126–27, 131–32, 147, 183–84, 208, 214, 221, 223
Apocalypse of Peter, 20, 24, 26–28, 35, 98, 164, 180–81
apocalyptic, 4, 6, 35, 99, 101, 166, 173, 178, 184, 191
apostolic, 2, 8–9, 23, 25–26, 28, 31, 33, 37–38, 46, 50–52, 62, 91, 95–96, 101, 111, 147, 155, 162, 164, 170, 175, 197–98, 204, 206, 213
Asiatic, 11–16, 32, 34, 64, 67, 70–71, 91, 108, 137, 145, 147–48, 160, 199
Attic, 11
authenticity, 2, 9, 11, 13–15, 17–20, 23–24, 27, 29, 45, 55, 77, 197, 199

canon, 1, 25, 27–28, 31, 43, 46, 49, 91, 163, 203, 213

day of the Lord, 20, 22, 61, 103, 128, 164, 176, 182–83, 188, 190, 198, 202, 214–15, 218, 228
digressio, 18, 55

early Christianity, 9, 166
election, 63, 83, 178, 220
Epicurean, 36, 167, 214
eschatology, 36, 67, 69, 114, 127, 164, 166, 193, 213–15

faith, 2, 22–23, 42–43, 56, 59–60, 63, 66, 71–72, 77, 81, 85, 112–13, 115, 168–69, 178, 203, 205, 214, 216–17, 219–20
farewell speech, 5–7, 90
final judgment, 36, 120, 130, 132–33, 171, 212
freedom, 19, 36–37, 112, 116, 132–33, 149–50, 165, 167, 190, 192, 226

genre, 3–7, 90
Gnosticism, 34–35, 149, 152
gospel, 32–33, 45, 65, 101, 189, 211, 213

hapax legomena, 11, 129
Hellenistic style, 9, 14, 33, 40
holiness, 2, 15, 69, 137, 186–87, 191, 206, 218
Holy Spirit, 46, 52, 90, 100, 107, 189, 200, 208, 212, 216, 222

inerrancy, 31, 45–46, 49–52, 212
inspiration, 45–48, 50, 52–53, 106–7, 161, 164, 200, 207, 211–12

Judaism, 3–4, 6, 40, 45, 64, 78, 84, 118, 121, 162, 164, 173–74
justice, 36, 56, 59–60, 72, 116, 135, 219

kingdom, 22–23, 38, 42, 58, 61, 63, 86–87, 94, 143, 150, 153–54, 187, 189–91, 205–6, 208, 210–11, 214–16, 221

narratio, 18

παρουσία, 2, 38, 96, 113
peroratio, 18, 56, 194
probatio, 18, 56, 117
pseudepigraphy, 9, 30
pseudonymous, 5, 9–10, 14, 31–33, 46, 50–52

revelation, 48, 50–51, 93, 96, 101, 103, 105, 107, 110, 147, 169, 179, 207, 210, 212
rhetoric, 12, 14, 16, 42, 54, 59, 63, 71, 89, 130–31, 137, 144, 147, 206

righteousness, 58, 60, 87, 98, 104, 108, 115, 120–21, 133, 150, 153–54, 156–57, 193, 208, 215, 223, 226, 229

salvation, 2, 35, 41, 49, 61, 66–67, 79, 84–85, 87, 91, 99, 101, 112, 120–21, 124, 152–53, 178, 182, 193, 196, 207, 209, 214–17, 229
secretary, 13–15, 17, 19, 32–33
Sophist, 214
Stoic, 71, 73, 174–75
suffering, 15, 128, 133, 136–37, 168–69, 186, 225

testament, 3–7, 20, 28, 52, 63, 90, 170
theosis, 2, 68, 187, 207, 216

Transfiguration, 1, 19–20, 24, 29, 44, 59, 96–97, 99–105, 107, 165, 181, 210
truth, 25, 32, 48, 52, 60, 63, 79, 82, 89, 99, 103, 107–8, 114–15, 124, 126, 139, 149, 151, 153–54, 198, 202–4, 213, 217, 221, 223

vice, 72, 95, 114, 130, 138, 145, 150
virtue, 6, 37, 42, 59, 63–64, 70–75, 80–82, 84, 87, 92, 94–95, 141, 157, 178, 187, 216, 218–20

wisdom, 2, 21–22, 72, 115, 123–24, 193, 199–200, 212, 229

For EU product safety concerns, contact us at Calle de José Abascal, 56–1°,
28003 Madrid, Spain or eugpsr@cambridge.org.

www.ingramcontent.com/pod-product-compliance
Lightning Source LLC
LaVergne TN
LVHW011805060526
838200LV00053B/3674